HISTORY

OF

RATIONALISM

EMBRACING

A SURVEY OF THE PRESENT STATE OF PROTESTANT THEOLOGY.

By JOHN F. HURST, D.D.

With Appendix of Literature.

THIRD EDITION, REVISED.

New York:
PUBLISHED BY CARLTON & PORTER,
200 MULBERRY-STREET.
1867.

The Rationalists are like the spiders, they spin all out of their own bowels. But give me a philosopher who, like the bee, hath a middle faculty, gathering from abroad, but digesting that which is gathered by its own virtue.—LORD BACON.

The Bible, I say the Bible only, is the religion of Protestants. . . . There is no safe certaintie but of Scripture only, for any considering man to build upon. This therefore, and this only I have reason to beleeve; this I will professe; according to this I will live, and for this I will not only willingly, but even gladly loose my life, though I should be sorry that Christians should take it from me. Propose me anything out of this book, and require whether I believe it or no, and secure it never so incomprehensible to humane reason, I will subscribe it hand and heart, as knowing no demonstration can be stronger than this, God hath said so, therefore it is true. In other things I will take no man's libertie of judgment from him; neither shall any man take mine from me. I will think no man the worse man nor the worse Christian. I will love no man the lesse for differing in opinion with me. And what measure I meet to others I expect from them againe. I am fully assured that God does not, and therefore that men out not to require any more of any man, than this: to believe the Scripture to be God's word, to endeavor to finde the true sense of it, and to live according to it.—CHILLINGWORTH.

Are those enthusiasts who profess to follow reason? Yes, undoubtedly, if by reason they mean only conceits. Therefore such persons are now commonly called *Reasonists* or *Rationalists* to distinguish them from true reasoners or rational inquirers.—WATERLAND.

PREFACE.

THERE were no prefatory remarks to the first and second editions of the following work. It was thought, when the printer made his final call for copy, that a preface might be written with more propriety if the public should indicate sufficient interest in the book to make its improvement and enlargement necessary. That interest, owing to the theme rather than the treatment, has not been withheld. The investigation of the subject was pursued in the midst of varied and pressing pastoral duties, with a pleasure which no reader of the result of the labor can enjoy; for, first, the author felt that Rationalism was soon to be the chief topic of theological inquiry in the Anglo-Saxon lands; and, second, he regarded the doubt, not less than the faith, of his fellow men as entitled to far more respect and patient investigation than it had usually received at the hands of orthodox inquirers.

The author would probably never have studied the genetic development of Rationalism in Germany, and its varied forms in other countries, if he had not been a personal witness to the ruin it had wrought in the land of Luther, Spener, and Zinzendorf. In compliance with the instruction of a trusted medical adviser, he sailed for Germany in the summer of 1856, as a final resort for relief from serious pulmonary disease. But, through the mercy of God, he regained health so rapidly that he was enabled to matriculate in the University of Halle in the following autumn, and to be a daily attendant upon the lectures of such men as Tholuck, Julius Müller, Jacobi, and Roediger. From some theologians he heard Rationalism defended with an energy worthy of Wolff and Semler; from others with a devotion worthy of the beloved Neander. In the railroad car, the stage, the counting-room, the workshop, the parlor, and the peasant-hut, Rationalism was found still lingering with a strong, though relaxing grasp. The evangelical churches were attended by only a few listless hearers. His prayer to God was, "May the American Church never be reduced to this sad fate." The history of that movement, resulting in such actual disaster to some lands and threatened ruin to others, took a deep hold upon his mind; and if he has failed in any respect to trace it with an impartial pen, his hope is that his failure will not cause any bright color of the truth to be obscured for a moment. For no man and no cause can ultimately triumph by giving an undue prominence to favorite party or principles; it is only by justice to all that the truth can win its unfading laurels.

Criticism was to have been expected, from the very nature of the topic of investigation. But the author has endeavored, as a student at the feet of his judges, to derive the largest possible benefit from criticism. No word of censure, however wide of the mark, has been unwelcome to him, whether from the sceptical or orthodox press. To all questioned passages he has given a careful re-examination, in some instances finding cause for alteration, but in others seeing his ground more strongly sustained than was at first imagined. He has, for example, been informed by many esteemed persons that his representation of Coleridge was hardly just; and, in obedience to that suggestion, he has given that author's works a more careful study than ever, having previously resolved to completely reverse his judgment of that profound thinker's faith, if he found his own utterances would justify him in that course. The result was, as far as he can now recall, that he could alter but one adjective in the entire section relating to Coleridge. Of course, the author finds no fault with those who differ from him on Coleridge, or on any other writer who has come under treatment; but he must be granted by others what he concedes to them. For the criticism, as a whole, which he has received both through the press and private sources, he owes a debt of gratitude which he cannot hope to pay. It gives him profound pleasure to know, that the highest theological journals in the United States which wage open war against orthodoxy, have conceded, with marked unanimity, the general correctness of his statements, though they naturally take issue with his conclusions.

Every effort has been bestowed on the present edition to make it as free from blemishes as possible. The appendix of literature has been slightly enlarged, many typographical errors—occurring in consequence of the too rapid passage of the work through the press, and the abundance of words of different languages with which the printer was not always well acquainted—have disappeared; and, in many cases, the narrative has been brought down to the present time. In the prosecution of revision, a large number of the stereotype plates have been cancelled; and no labor has been wanting to make this edition worthy of the goodwill expressed toward the two editions which have preceded it.

Through a strange providence the author is now about to commence a term of theological instruction in Germany, where Rationalism first excited his attention, and where his apprehensions were first raised that Great Britain and the United States might be seriously invaded by it. His presence at its old hearthstone leads him to indulge the hope that, in some future though distant day, if life be spared, he may be able to enlarge this history greatly, and thus to render it better adapted to its purpose, more approximative to his first ideal, and more commensurate with the present universal interest in religious and theological themes.

BREMEN, GERMANY, *November* 5, 1866.

CONTENTS.

INTRODUCTION.

CHAPTER I.

CONTROVERSIAL PERIOD SUCCEEDING THE REFORMATION.

CHAPTER II.

RELIGIOUS CONDITION OF THE PROTESTANT CHURCH AT THE PEACE OF WESTPHALIA.

CHAPTER III.

PIETISM AND ITS MISSION.

CHAPTER IV.

THE POPULAR PHILOSOPHY OF WOLFF.—SKEPTICAL TENDENCIES FROM ABROAD.

CHAPTER V.

SEMLER AND THE DESTRUCTIVE SCHOOL.—1750–1810.

CHAPTER VI.

CONTRIBUTIONS OF LITERATURE AND PHILOSOPHY.

CHAPTER VII.

THE REIGN OF THE WEIMAR CIRCLE.—REVOLUTION IN EDUCATION AND HYMNOLOGY.

CHAPTER VIII.

DOCTRINES OF RATIONALISM IN THE DAY OF ITS STRENGTH.

CHAPTER IX.

RENOVATION INAUGURATED BY SCHLEIERMACHER.

CHAPTER X.

RELATIONS OF RATIONALISM AND SUPERNATURALISM.—1810–1835.

CHAPTER XI.

THE REACTION PRODUCED BY STRAUSS' LIFE OF JESUS.—1835–1848.

CHAPTER XII.

THE EVANGELICAL SCHOOL: ITS OPINIONS AND PRESENT PROSPECTS.

CHAPTER XVII.

FRANCE CONTINUED: EVANGELICAL THEOLOGY OPPOSING RATIONALISM.

CHAPTER XVIII.

SWITZERLAND: ORTHODOXY IN GENEVA, AND THE NEW SPECULATIVE RATIONALISM IN ZÜRICH.

CHAPTER XIX.

ENGLAND: THE SOIL PREPARED FOR THE INTRODUCTION OF RATIONALISM.

CHAPTER XVI.

FRANCE: RATIONALISM IN THE PROTESTANT CHURCH—THE CRITICAL SCHOOL.

CHAPTER XIII.

PRACTICAL MOVEMENTS INDICATING NEW LIFE.

CHAPTER XIV.

HOLLAND: THEOLOGY AND RELIGION FROM THE SYNOD OF DORT TO THE COMMENCEMENT OF THE PRESENT CENTURY.

CHAPTER XV.

HOLLAND CONTINUED: THE NEW THEOLOGICAL SCHOOLS, AND THE GREAT CONTROVERSY NOW PENDING BETWEEN ORTHODOXY AND RATIONALISM.

CHAPTER XX.

ENGLAND CONTINUED: PHILOSOPHICAL AND LITERARY RATIONALISM.—COLERIDGE AND CARLYLE.

CHAPTER XXI.

ENGLAND CONTINUED: CRITICAL RATIONALISM—JOWETT, THE ESSAYS AND REVIEWS, AND COLENSO.

CHAPTER XXII.

ENGLAND CONTINUED: SURVEY OF CHURCH PARTIES.

CHAPTER XXIV.

THE UNITED STATES CONTINUED: THEODORE PARKER AND HIS SCHOOL.

CHAPTER XXV.

INDIRECT SERVICE OF SKEPTICISM—PRESENT OUTLOOK.

APPENDIX.

HISTORY OF RATIONALISM.

INTRODUCTION.

RATIONALISM DEFINED—ITS CHARACTER AS A SKEPTICAL DEVELOPMENT.

Rationalism is the most recent, but not the least violent and insidious, of all the developments of skepticism. We purpose to show its historical position, and to present, as faithfully as possible, its antagonism to evangelical Christianity. The guardians of the interests of the church cannot excuse themselves from effort toward the eradication of this error by saying that it is one which will soon decay by the force of its natural autumn. Posterity will not hesitate to charge us with gross negligence if we fail to appreciate the magnitude of Rationalism, and only deal with it as the growth of a day. We have half conquered an enemy when we have gained a full knowledge of his strength.

There was a time when Rationalism was a theme of interest to the Protestant church of Germany alone. But that day is now past. Having well nigh run its race in the land of Luther, it has crossed the Rhine into France and the Netherlands, invaded England, and now threatens the integrity of the domain of Anglo-Saxon theology. Thus it has assumed an importance which should not be overlooked by British and American thinkers who love those dearly-bought treasures of truth that they have received as a sacred legacy from the martyrs and reformers of the English church. The recent writings of the exegetical Rationalists of England are sufficient to induce us to gather up our armor and adjust it for immediate defence. Delay will entail evil. The reason why skepticism has wrought such fearful ravages at various stages during the career of the church has been the tardiness of the church in watching the sure and steady approach, and then in underrating the real strength of her adversary. The present History will be written for the specific purpose of awakening an interest in the danger that now threatens us. We have no ambition to deal with the past, further than to enable it to minister to the immediate demands of the present. We all belong to this generation; it calls for our energies; it has its great wants; and we shall be held justly responsible if we neglect to contribute our share toward the progress of our contemporaries.

The three principles which have influenced us to undertake a discussion of the present theme—and of the truth of which we are profoundly convinced—are the following:

I. That Infidelity presents a systematic and harmonious History. Our customary view of error is, that its history is disjointed, rendered so by the ardent, but unsteady, labors of the doubters of all periods since the origin of Christianity. We have ignored the historical movement of skepticism. Even the storms have their mysterious laws. The work of Satan is never planless. He adapts his measures to the new dangers that arise to threaten his dominion. The analogy between the Rationalism of to-day and the infidelity of past ages is so striking that we can with difficulty recognize the interval of centuries. We see the new faces, but the foes are old. Rationalism has repeatedly varied its method of attack; but if we follow the marches of its whole campaign we shall find that the enemy which stands at our fortress-gate with the *Essays and Reviews* and *Notes on Pentateuch and Joshua* in hand, is the same one that assailed Protestant Germany with the Accommodation-theory and the *Wolfenbüttel Fragments.*

II. A History of a mischievous Tendency is the very best Method for its Refutation and Extirpation. We can learn the full character of the good or evil of any abstract principle only by seeing its practical workings. The tree is known by its fruits. Rationalism may be of evil character, but we must see the results it has produced,—the great overthrow of faith it has effected, and its influence upon the pulpit and press of the countries invaded by it, before we can comprehend the vastness of our danger. An enumeration of the evil doings of a public enemy is the best plan to forestall his future misdeeds. We are not to judge Rationalism by its professions. The question is not, What does it wish? At what does it aim? or, What is its creed? But the true way to measure, understand, and judge it, is by answering the inquiry, *What has it done?* Its work must determine its character. This work has been most injurious to the faith and life of the church, and its deeds must therefore be its condemnation. There are those who say, "Tell us nothing about skepticism; we know too much about it already." Would it be a prudent request, if, before penetrating the jungles of Asia, we should say, "Tell us nothing of the habits of the lion"; or, before visiting a malarious region of Africa, we should beg of the physician not to inform us of the prevalent fever and its appropriate remedy? Forewarned is forearmed. We are surrounded by Rationalism in many phases; it comes to us in the periodical and the closely-printed volume. Even children are reading it in some shape or other. Shall we know its danger; then we must know its deeds.

III. Of Rationalism it may be affirmed, as of all the Phases of Infidelity, that it is not in its Results an unmixed Evil, since God overrules its Work for the Purification and Progress of his Church. A nation is never so pure as when emerging from the sevenfold-heated furnace. It was not before Manasseh was caught among thorns, bound with fetters, and carried to Babylon, that he "besought the Lord his God, and humbled himself greatly before the God of his fathers;" nor was it before this humiliation that the Lord "brought him again to Jerusalem into his kingdom." The whole history of religious error shows that the church is cold, formal, and controversial before the visitation of skepticism. When every power is in full exercise, infidelity stands aloof. God has so provided for his people that he has even caused the delusion by which they have suffered to contribute great benefits but little anticipated by the deluded or the deluders themselves. The intellectual labors of the German Rationalists have already shed an incalculable degree of light on the sacred books, and upon almost every branch of theology. But thus has God ever caused the wrath of man to praise him.

Taking this view of the indirect benefits resulting

from skepticism, we cannot lament, without an admixture of solace, that the path of Truth has always been rough. The Master, who declared himself "The Truth," premonished us by his own life that his doctrines were not destined to pervade the mind and heart of our race without encountering violent blows, and passing through whole winters of frost and storm. Many things attending the origin and planting of Christianity gave omen of antagonism to its claims in coming generations. Nor could it be expected that the unsanctified reason of man would accept as the only worthy guide of faith and life what Judaism, Paganism, and Philosophy had long since decidedly rejected. But the spirit of Christianity is so totally at variance with that of the world that it is vain to expect harmony between them. Truth, however, will not suffer on that account; and when the issues appear it will shine all the brighter for the fires through which it has passed. The country where Rationalism has exerted its first and chief influence is Germany, than which no nation of modern times has been more prospered or passed through deeper affliction. At one time she was the leader of religious liberty and truth, not only in Europe, but throughout the world. She was thirty years fighting the battles of Protestantism, but the end of the long conflict found her victorious. Since that day, however, she has lost her prestige of adherence to evangelical Christianity; and her representative theologians and thinkers have distorted the Bible which she was the very first to unseal. We rejoice that her condition is more hopeful to-day than it was twenty-five years ago; but recovery is not easy from a century-night of cold, repulsive Rationalism. As a large number of those stupendous battles that have decided the political and territorial condition of Europe have been fought on the narrow soil of Belgium, so has Germany been for ages the contested field on which were determined the great doctrinal and ecclesiastical questions of the European continent and of the world. Happily, the result has generally been favorable; and let no friend of evangelical truth fear that Rationalism will not meet its merited fate.

We must not imagine that, because the term Rationalism has been frequently employed within the last few years, it is of very recent origin either as a word or skeptical type. The Aristotelian Humanists of Helmstedt were called *Rationalists* in the beginning of the seventeenth century, and Comenius applied the same epithet to the Socinians in 1688.[1] It was a common word in England two hundred years ago. Nor was it imported into the English language from the German, either in a theological or a philosophical sense. There was a sect of Rationalists, in the time of the Commonwealth, who called themselves such exactly on the same grounds as their successors have done in recent years. Some one writing the news from London under date of October 14, 1646, says: "There is a new sect sprung up among them [the Presbyterians and Independents], and these are the *Rationalists, and what their reason dictates them in church or state stands for good until they be convinced with better.*"[2] But Rationalists, in fact if not in name, existed on the Continent long anterior to this date. The Anti-Trinitarians, and Bodin, and Pucci were rigid disciples of Reason; and their tenets harmonize with those of a later day.[3]

[1] Tholuck, Herzog's *Real-Encyclopædie.* Art. *Rationalismus.*

[2] Trench, *Study of Words*, p. 147.

[3] As a fair specimen of the extent to which philological criticism is often

In order to arrive at a proper definition of Rationalism we should consult those authors who have given no little attention to this department of theological inquiry. Nor would we be impartial if we adduced the language of one class to the exclusion of the other. We shall hear alike from the friends and adversaries of the whole movement, and endeavor to draw a proper conclusion from their united testimony. It was Selden's advice to the students of ecclesiastical history, "to study the exaggerated statements of Baronius on the one side, and of the Magdeburg Centuriators on the other, and be their own judges." Fortunately enough for a proper understanding of Rationalism, there is no such diversity of statement presented by our authori-

carried by some of our German friends, when advocating a doubtful cause, we quote a paragraph in point from Dr. Rückert's work, *Der Rationalismus*, one of the latest and feeblest apologies for neological thought:

"What is Rationalism? We must try to get the meaning from the term itself. And what sort of a term is it? Barbarous enough! Its root is *ratio*, but it is directly from *rationalis* that the word in question is derived. Now this word is good enough in itself, for it signifies *what is conformable to reason, that which possesses the attributes and methods of reason.* Man is a *rational* animal, and it is his rationality that distinguishes him from all other animals. So much for this part of the word Rationalism. Now for the barbarous part of it, the -ism. This termination belongs to another language, the Greek -ισμός, and is derived from a verbal ending which cannot be expressed in Latin, namely—ίζειν. Now if we examine certain intransitive verbs, such as μηδίζειν, λακωνίζειν, ῥωμαΐζειν, ἀττικίζειν, we shall find their common peculiarity is that the persons meant are not the real persons which the words seem to signify, but only act in their capacity. Not a real Mede μηδίζει; no true Spartan λακωνίζει; and so of all the rest. But those Greeks who would rather belong to the Medes than be freemen, *act like Medes, would prefer to be under Median rule*—μηδίζουσιν. This -ισμός is a termination from this class of verbs, and is employed in reproach and not in praise. Hence *Rationalist* is a term of contempt, and means *not one who is really reasonable, but would like to pass for such.*" Of course the Doctor concludes that the word is a most flagrant and unrighteous misnomer; but we accept his philology and return him our thanks for his etymological *study*.

ties. On the contrary, we shall perceive an unexpected and gratifying harmony.

In Wegscheider's *Institutiones Dogmaticæ*, a work which for nearly half a century has stood as an acknowledged and highly respected authority on the systematic theology of the Rationalists, we read language to this effect: "Since that doctrine (of supernaturalism) is encumbered with various difficulties, every day made more manifest by the advances of learning, especially historical, physical, and philosophical, there have been amongst more recent theologians and philosophers not a few who, in various ways, departing from it, thought it right to admit, even in the investigation and explanation of divine things, not only that formal use of human reason which regards only the method of expounding dogmas, but also the material use, by which the subject-matter of the particular doctrines is submitted to inquiry.

"Thus arose that of which the generic name is Rationalism, or that law or rule of thinking, intimately united with the cultivation of talent and mind, by which we think that as well in examining and judging of all things presented to us in life and the range of universal learning, as in those matters of most grave importance which relate to religion and morals, we must follow strenuously the norm of reason rightly applied, as of the highest faculty of the mind; which law of thinking and perceiving, if it be applied to prove any positive religion (theological Rationalism) lays it down as an axiom that religion is revealed to men in no other manner than that which is agreeable both to the nature of things and to reason, as the witness and interpreter of divine providence; and teaches that the subject-matter of every supposed supernatural revelation, is to be examined and judged according to the ideas regard ing religion and morality, which we have formed in the mind by the help of reason. . . . Whosoever, therefore, despising that supremacy of human reason, maintains that the authority of a revelation, said to have been communicated to certain men in a supernatural manner, is such that it must be obeyed by all means, without any doubt,—that man takes away and overturns from the foundation the true nature and dignity of man, at the same time cherishes the most pernicious laziness and sloth, or stirs up the depraved errors of fanaticism. . . . As to that which is said to be above reason, the truth of which can by no means be understood, there is no possible way open to the human mind to demonstrate or affirm it; wherefore to acknowledge or affirm that which is thought to be above reason is rightly said to be against reason and contrary to it.

"The persuasion concerning the supernatural and miraculous, and at the same time immediate, revelation of God, cannot be reconciled with the idea of God eternal, always consistent with himself, omnipotent, omniscient, and most wise, by whose power, operative through all eternity and exerted in perfect harmony with the highest wisdom, we rightly teach that the whole nature of things exists and is preserved. . . . This being so, it seems that the natural revelation or manifestation of God, made by the works of nature, is the only one which can be rightly defended, and this may be divided into universal or common, and particular or singular. The universal indeed is affected by the natural faculties of the mind, and other helps of the universal nature of things, by which man is led to conceive and cultivate the knowledge of divine things. That we call *particular* and *mediate*, in a sense different from the elder writers, which is contained in the compass of things happening according to nature, by which, God being the author, some men are excited above others to attain the principles of true religion, and to impart with signal success those things, accommodated indeed to the desires of their countrymen, and sanctioned by some particular form of religious instruction. A revelation of this kind consists as well in singular gifts of genius and mind, with which the messenger, and, as it were, its interpreter, is perceived to be furnished, as in illustrious proofs of divine providence, conspicuous in his external life. But the more agreeably to the will of that same God he uses these helps to be ascribed to God, and full of a certain divine fervor, and excelling in zeal for virtue and piety, the more he scatters the seeds of a doctrine truly divine, *i. e.*, true in itself, and worthy of God, and to be propagated by suitable institutions, the more truly will he flourish amongst other men with the authority of a divine teacher or ambassador. For as our mind partakes of the divine nature and disposition (2 Peter i. 4), so without the favor and help of the Deity it is not carried out to a more true species of religion.

"But whatever narrations especially accommodated to a certain age, and relating miracles and mysteries, are united with the history and subject-matter of revelation of this kind, these ought to be referred to the natural sources and true nature of human knowledge. By how much the more clearly the author of the Christian religion, not without the help of Deity, exhibited to men the idea of reason imbued with true religion, so as to represent as it were an *apaugasma* of the divine reason, or the divine spirit, by so much the more diligently ought man to strive to approach as nearly as possible to form that archetype in the mind, and to study to imitate it in life and manners to the utmost of his ability. Behold here the intimate and eternal union and agreement of Christianity with Rationalism."

Stäudlin, at first a Rationalist, but in later life more inclined to supernaturalism, says: "I do not now look to the various meanings in which the word Rationalism has been used. I understand by it here only generally the opinion that mankind are led by their reason and especially by the natural powers of their mind and soul, and by the observation of nature which surrounds them, to a true knowledge of divine and sensible things, and that reason has the highest authority and right of decision in matters of faith and morality, so that an edifice of faith and morals built on this foundation shall be called Rationalism. It still remains undecided whether this system declares that a supernatural revelation is impossible and ought to be rejected. That notion rather lies in the word Naturalism, which however is sometimes used as synonymous with Rationalism. It has been well said that Naturalism is distinguished from Rationalism by rejecting all and every revelation of God, especially any extraordinary one through certain men. This, however, is not the case with many persons called Naturalists both by themselves and others. Supernaturalism consists in general in the conviction that God has revealed himself supernaturally and immediately. What is revealed might perhaps be discovered by natural methods, but either not at all or very late by those to whom it is revealed. It may also be something which man could never have known by natural methods; and then arises the question, whether man is capable of such a revelation. The notion of a miracle cannot well be separated from such a revelation, whether it happens out of, on, or in men. What is revealed may belong to the order of nature, but an order higher and unknown to us, which we could never have known without miracles, and cannot bring under the law of nature."[1]

Professor Hahn, in speaking of the work just referred to, and of the subject in general, makes the following remarks: "In very recent times, during which Rationalism has excited so much attention, two persons especially, Bretschneider and Stäudlin, have endeavored to point out the historical use of the word, but both have failed. It is therefore worth while to examine the matter afresh. With respect to the Rationalists, they give out Rationalism as a very different matter from Naturalism. Röhr, the author of the *Letters on Rationalism*, chooses to understand by Naturalism only Materialism; and Wegscheider, only Pantheism. In this way those persons who have been usually reckoned the heads of the Naturalists; namely, Herbert, Tindal, and others; will be entirely separated from them, for they were far removed from Pantheism or Materialism. Bretschneider, who has set on foot the best inquiry on this point, says that the word Rationalism has been confused with the word Naturalism since the appearance of the Kantian philosophy, and that it was introduced into theology by Reinhard and Gabler. An accurate examination respecting these words gives the following results: The word Naturalism arose first in the sixteenth century, and was spread in the seventeenth. It was understood to include those who allowed no other knowledge of religion except the natural, which man could shape out of his own strength, and consequently excluded all supernatural revelation. As to

[1] *Geschichte des Rationalismus und Supernaturalismus*, pp. 3–4.

the different forms of Naturalism, theologians say there are three; the first, which they call Pelagianism, and which considers human dispositions and notions as perfectly pure and clear by themselves, and the religious knowledge derived from them as sufficiently explicit. A grosser kind denies all particular revelation; and the grossest of all considers the world as God. As to Rationalism, this word was used in the seventeenth and eighteenth centuries by those who considered reason as the source and norm of faith. Amos Comenius seems first to have used this word in 1661, and it never had a good sense. In the eighteenth century it was applied to those who were in earlier times called by the name of Naturalist."[1]

Of all writers on the subject of Rationalism we give the palm of excellence to the devout and learned Hugh James Rose, of Cambridge University. As far as we know he was the first to expose to the English-speaking world the sad state to which this form of skepticism had reduced Germany. Having visited that country in 1824, he delivered four discourses on the subject before the university, which were afterward published under the title of *The State of Protestantism in Germany.* Thus far, in spite of the new works which may have appeared, this account of Rationalism has not been superseded. We shall have occasion more than once to refer to its interesting pages. Of Rationalism he says:

"The word has been used in Germany in various senses, and has been made to embrace alike those who positively reject all revelation and those who profess to receive it. I am inclined, however, to believe that the distinction between Naturalists and Rationalists is not quite so wide, either, as it would appear to be at first

[1] *De Rationalismi*: A Disputation at Leipzig.

sight, or as one of them assuredly wishes it to appear. For if I receive a system, be it of religion, of morals, or of politics, only so far as it approve itself to my reason, whatever be the authority that presents it to me, it is idle to say that I receive the system out of any respect to that authority. I receive it *only* because my reason approves it, and I should of course do so if an authority of far inferior value were to present the system to me. This is what that division of Rationalists, which professes to receive Christianity and at the same time to make reason the supreme arbiter in matters of faith, has done. *Their* system, in a word, is this: they assume certain general principles, which they 'maintain to be the necessary deductions of reason from an extended and unprejudiced contemplation of the natural and moral order of things, and to be in themselves immutable and universal. Consequently anything which, on however good authority, may be advanced in apparent opposition to them must either be rejected as unworthy of rational belief, or at least explained away, till it is made to accord with the assumed principles,—and the truth or falsehood of all doctrines proposed is to be decided according to their agreement or disagreement with those principles.' When Christianity, then, is presented to them, they inquire what there is in it which agrees with their assumed principles, and whatsoever does so agree, they receive as *true*. But whatever is *true* comes from God, and consequently all of Christianity which they admit to be true, they hold to be *divine*.

"'Those who are generally termed Rationalists, says Dr. Bretschneider, 'admit universally, in Christianity, a divine, benevolent, and positive appointment for the good of mankind, and Jesus as a Messenger of divine Providence, believing that the true and everlasting word of God is contained in the Holy Scripture, and that by the same the welfare of mankind will be obtained and extended. But they deny therein a supernatural and miraculous working of God, and consider the object of Christianity to be that of introducing into the world such a religion as reason can comprehend; and they distinguish the essential from the unessential, and what is local and temporary from that which is universal and permanent in Christianity.' There is, however, a third class of divines, which in fact differs very little from this, though very widely in profession. They affect to allow 'a revealing operation of God,' but establish on internal proofs rather than on miracles the divine nature of Christianity. They allow that revelation *may* contain much out of the power of reason to explain, but say that it should assert nothing contrary to reason, but rather what may be proved by it. This sounds better, but they who are acquainted with the writings of the persons thus described, know that by establishing Christianity on internal proofs, they only mean the accepting those doctrines which they like, and which seem to them *reasonable*, and that though they allow in theory that revelation may contain what are technically called much above reason, yet in practice they reject the positive doctrines of Christianity (I mean especially the doctrines of the Trinity, the Atonement, the Mediation and Intercession of our Lord, Original Sin, and Justification by Faith), because they allege that those doctrines are contrary to reason. The difference between them and the others is therefore simply this, that while the others set no limits at all to the powers of reason in matters of faith, they set such a limit in theory but not in practice, and consequently cannot justly demand to be separated from the others."[1]

One of the ablest advocates of Supernaturalism among English divines is the late Dr. A. McCaul, of London. He joins issue successfully with the Rationalists. We quote a specimen of his method of argument. His definition of Rationalism is beautifully lucid and logical. He says:

"This doctrine then plainly denies the existence and the possibility of a supernatural and immediate revelation from the Almighty, and maintains that to claim supreme authority for any supposed supernatural religion is degrading to the dignity and the nature of man. It enters into direct conflict with the statements of the Old Testament writers, who clearly and unmistakably assert the existence of a divine communication which is called 'The law of the Lord,' 'The law of his mouth,' 'The testimony of God,' 'The saying of God,' 'The word of the Lord,' 'The word that goeth forth out of his mouth,' 'The judgment of the Lord,' 'The command ment of the Lord.'

"Now it is not intended to strain the allusion to the mouth or lips of the Lord beyond that which the figure may fairly bear. But the expression does certainly mean that there is some direct, immediate, and therefore supernatural communication from the great Creator of all things. The writers who used these expressions did not mean that as reason is given by God, so whatever reason may excogitate is the word of God. They would not have used these expressions concerning Truth that may be found in heathen writers. They believed and recorded that God had manifested himself audibly to the ears, and visibly to the eyes of men.

[1] *State of Protestantism in Germany.* pp. XXII–XXVI.

They did not therefore hold the doctrine that supernatural revelation is impossible, or derogatory to reason or inconsistent with the nature and attributes of Him who is eternal.

"It is almost needless to refer to instances. God spake with Adam, with Cain, with Noah. In the latter case the communication led to such actions, and was followed by such results, that without rejecting the history altogether, there can be no doubt of a miraculous communication. Noah knew of the coming flood—built an ark for himself and a multitude of animals—prepared food—was saved with his family, while the world perished—floated for months on the waters, and when he came out, had again a manifestation of the Deity. So Abraham, so Moses, not now to recount any more. Indeed the writer referred to does not deny this. He admits that in Scripture the knowledge of divine things is referred immediately to the Revelation of God, and that though the modes of this Revelation are various, they appear often to overstep the laws and course of nature. He enumerates as modes of revelation, Epiphanies of God himself, of angels—heavenly voices—dreams—afflatus, or the Holy Spirit.

"How then does he reconcile this with his denial of all supernatural revelation, or show that these Epiphanies of God and angels, were mere developments of reason? He does not try to reconcile them at all. He simply rejects them as false. He comes directly into collision with the credibility and veracity of the Scripture narratives, and therefore leaves us no alternative but to disbelieve the Bible as fabulous, or to reject Rationalism as inconsistent with our rule of faith. This system not only generally denies the possibility of supernatural revelation, but asserts that all the particular narratives of all such communications from God are incredible; nothing better than ghost stories or fairy tales; equally unworthy of God and man, the offspring of an ignorant and unenlightened age and nation, and therefore rejected by these men of reason and science. How this differs from the doctrine of Deists and open opposers of Christianity, it is difficult to conceive, except that it seems to be rather worse. Even Bolingbroke admits supernatural Revelation to be possible. Tom Paine himself says, 'Revelation when applied to religion means something immediately communicated from God to man. No one will deny or dispute the power of the Almighty to make such a communication if he pleases.' Spinoza asserts that the "Israelites heard a true voice at the delivery of the ten commandments; that God spoke face to face with Moses; and generally, that God can communicate immediately with men, and that though natural science is divine, yet its propagators cannot be called prophets.' That the Rationalist view of revelation is contrary to the popular belief of Christians generally, and of Christian churches and divines particularly, there can be no doubt. It is intended so to be. . . .

"The Rationalist professes to believe that all the knowledge of truth at which man arrives is owing to the original wisdom, will, and power of the Almighty in giving man a certain intellectual constitution, to be unfolded by the circumstances of human history and necessities—that therefore moral and religious truth, such as the Rationalists acknowledge, is still to be ascribed to the purposes and power and efficacy of the Great Spirit, acting upon that which is material and compound.

"Why, then, should it be impossible for the Creator

to shorten the process, to help man in his painful and often unsuccessful search after truth, and to make known that which exists in the Divine mind and purpose? To say that he cannot, is in fact to depose him from the throne of omnipotence, and to bring us back either to two eternal independent principles, incapable of all communication, or to drive us to Pantheism. If there ever was a period in duration in which God could act upon matter, or endue infinite intelligences with the means and capability of knowledge, he can do so still."[1]

M. Saintes, who has investigated the history of this subject more thoroughly than any other writer, says of the significations and limits of Rationalism:

"I myself at first imagined that it signified the wise and constant exercise of reason on religious subjects, but in studying the matter historically I soon found that it is the same with this word as with many others which, having lost their original meaning, now express an idea directly contrary to that which their etymology seems to indicate. It is indisputably true that God, in granting reason to man, has not forbidden its exercise. As religion, the queen of all minds, possesses indestructible rights over them, so has human reason also rights which cannot be disputed. Kant has justly said, The faith which should oppose itself to reason could not longer exist. With this view we form an idea of Rationalism similar to that conceived by the great Leibnitz, which, with our present ideas of truth, we cannot regard as unreasonable. But this right of human reason to examine and discuss differs widely from its self-constitution as supreme judge on religious matters, and from the wish to submit God and conscience to its own tribunal, which it declares to be infallible. This,

[1] *Thoughts on Rationalism.* pp. 23–32.

however, has been the case in modern times when Philosophy has openly avowed itself the enemy of Christianity, and when those who were terrified by its rash demands have sought to confound them by the devices of Rationalism—thus hastening to ruin the edifice which they aspired to restore. . . . . Rationalism must not, therefore, be understood to signify the use which theologians have made of reason in matters of faith. Did the reader thus interpret it he would mistake our aim. He would be deceived as to the character of the labors which it is our wish to describe. He would attribute to the author of this history intentions which he could not entertain, and religious opinions which his respect for human reason would compel him to disavow. The apostles of the gospel continually appeal to the reason of their hearers, and Christ himself argues the increasing exercise of the *eye of the soul*, as he calls conscience, in judging of the truth which he announces—Matt. vi. 23. For a good conscience is always better disposed to rise to the knowledge of the truth; while one heavy laden and harassed is exceedingly prone to receive dogmas without properly understanding their import, because it feels their truth through the consolations which they offer. In no age of Christianity has there arisen a serious discussion on this subject, though the extravagant pretensions of Rationalism have provoked some exaggerations which can never prevail over the ancient Christian system. That system by no means forbade the exercise of human intelligence in religious matters, though it employed a superior and only infallible reason—the divine reason, the doctrinal expression of which is found in the books which all Christians have hitherto considered divine, and whose authenticity and truth cannot be disputed without overturning that

Christianity, which has been professed during eighteen centuries. But modern Rationalism has done more than assert the right of exercising reason; it has pretended that to this faculty alone belongs the privilege of deciding on man's religious belief and his moral duty; and that if, from long custom, any respect is still due to revelation, it should only receive it when it is not opposed to the judgments of reason. But if this reason were sufficient for mankind, why should divine revelation be in any case opposed to it?

"Rationalism is not a systematic incredulity as to religious truths. Far from being so, it makes pretensions of developing the religious feelings to the highest degree; and there is in the writings of its most distinguished disciples something which arouses even the most lethargic minds. But it is far from attaining its end; for although it constitutes itself the supreme judge of Christianity, it does not really adopt one of the leading doctrines of that religion which alone has power over the moral nature of man. Its influence, if we observe it closely, extends only over his feelings; it fails to penetrate into the depths of his being; and can we forget that one of its essential characteristics is to wage deadly war against the supernatural element which abounds in the Bible, and which Rationalism would wholly eradicate? An enlightened Supernaturalist will then very willingly confess that Naturalism may be professed with a semblance of reason and in good faith, and he can even consider it as a system of philosophy wherein are to be found fewer philosophical elements than in any other. But simple good sense forbids him to imagine it possible to profess Rationalism and at the same time to retain the name of Christian."[1]

[1] *Histoire du Rationalisme.* pp. 1–6.

The most recent defence of Rationalism is by Mr. Lecky.[1] He has written in great calmness, taken great pains to generalize his investigations, and followed closely in the steps of the late Mr. Buckle, in his fragment of the *History of Civilization*. But his argument is false. According to Mr. Lecky, human reason is the only factor of history. The agency of the Holy Spirit is ignored. Elaborate creeds and liturgical services are a barrier to the mind's progress, because they shackle the intellect by impure traditions. Rationalism is the only relief of these later times. "Its central conception," says our author, "is the elevation of conscience into a position of supreme authority as the religious organ, a verifying faculty discriminating between truth and error. It regards Christianity as designed to preside over the moral development of mankind, as a conception which was to become more and more sublimated and spiritualized as the human mind passed into new phases, and was able to bear the splendor of a more unclouded light. Religion it believes to be no exception to the general law of progress, but rather the highest form of its manifestation, and its earlier systems but the necessary steps of an imperfect development. In its eyes the moral element of Christianity is as the sun in heaven, and dogmatic systems are as the clouds that intercept and temper the exceeding brightness of its rays. The insect, whose existence is but for a moment, might well imagine that these were indeed eternal, that their majestic columns could never fail, and that their luminous folds were the very source and centre of light. And yet they shift and vary with each changing breeze; they blend and separate; they assume new forms and

[1] *History of the Rise and Influence of the Spirit of Rationalism in Europe.* By W. E. H. Lecky, M. A. 2 vols. Longmans, London, 1865.

exhibit new dimensions; as the sun that is above them waxes more glorious in its power, they are permeated and at last absorbed by its increasing splendor; they recede, and wither, and disappear, and the eye ranges far beyond the sphere they had occupied into the infinity of glory that is before them. . . . Rationalism is a system which would unite in one sublime synthesis all the past forms of human belief, which accepts with triumphant alacrity each new development of science, having no stereotyped standard to defend, and which represents the human mind as pursuing on the highest subjects a path of continual progress toward the fullest and most transcendent knowledge of the Deity. . . . It clusters around a series of essentially Christian conceptions—equality, fraternity, the suppression of war, the elevation of the poor, the love of truth, and the diffusion of liberty. *It revolves around the ideal of Christianity, and represents its spirit without its dogmatic system and its supernatural narratives. From both of these it unhesitatingly recoils, while deriving all its strength and nourishment from Christian ethics.*"[1]

The present age, if we hearken to Mr. Lecky, is purely Rationalistic, because purely progressive. The world has emerged from its blindness and ignorance by the innate force of the mind. Reason, the great magician, has uplifted its wand; and lo, the creatures of night disappear! It has dispelled the foolish old notions of magic, witchcraft, and miracles. It has overcome the spirit of persecution, the childish conception of original sin, and the doctrine of eternal punishment. It has put an end to bull-baiting, cock-fighting, and all the lower forms of vicious pleasure. It has secularized

[1] *History of the Rise and Spirit of Rationalism in Europe*, vol. I., pp. 183–185.

politics, overthrown the notion of the divine right of kings, and now creates and fosters all the industrial developments of the age. Protestantism is excellent when allied to Rationalism; but when opposed to it, it is no better than any other conglomeration of creeds and liturgies. There is no such thing as a fixed notion of God and Providence. The conceptions of man on these subjects will change with the progress of the race. Human reason, therefore, and not revelation, is the sole arbiter of truth.

Thus Mr. Lecky places himself beside his predecessors in ignoring the agency of the Holy Spirit, either in giving inspired truth to the world, or in educating the church.

From the foregoing authorities it is very apparent that the Rationalists do not deny the special features of skepticism with which their opponents charge them. They admit frankly that they give the precedence to Reason, when the alternative is Reason or Revelation, instead of adopting a positive creed from the principle, that, if we would ascertain the character of Revelation, we must begin our inquiry by examining the doctrines it contains, and then by comparing them with our notions of what a Revelation ought to be. Thus the capricious dictates of reason are made to decide the quality of revealed truth. Besides, wherever a mysterious account is contained in a book which in the main is accepted, such mystery is cast out as altogether unlikely, probably the poetic version of some early legend. A miracle is recounted; one of the best attested of all. "It could never have happened," the Rationalists say, "for Nature has made it impossible."

There have been several classes of Rationalists. Some were men of very worthy character; and, save in their opinions, were entitled to the high respect of their generation. Semler lived a beautiful life; and his glowing utterance on his daughter's death exhibited not only a father's love, but a Christian's faith. Bretschneider, himself a Rationalist, gives the following classification of his confreres:

The *first* class consider Revelation a superstition, and Jesus either an enthusiast or a deceiver. To this class belong Wünsch and Paalzow, but no divine. The second class do not allow that there was any divine operation in Christianity in any way, and refer the origin of Christianity to mere natural causes. They make the life of Christ a mere romance, and himself a member of secret associations; and consider the Scriptures as only human writings in which the word of God is not to be found. To this class belong Bahrdt, Reimarus, and Venturini (the last two not divines), and Brennecke. The third class comprise the persons usually called Rationalists. They acknowledge in Christianity an institution divine, beneficent, and for the good of the world; and Jesus as a messenger of God; and they think that in Scripture is found a true and eternal word of God,—only they deny *any supernatural and miraculous* working of God, and make the object of Christianity to be the introduction of religion into the world, its preservation, and extension. They distinguish between what is essential and non-essential in Christianity, between what is local and temporal, and what is universal. That is to say, they allow that there is good in Christianity—that all that is good comes from God; but miracles, inspiration, everything *immediately* coming from God, they wholly disbelieve. Among this class are Kant, Steinbart, Krug, as philosophers; and, as divines, W. A. Teller, Löffler, Thiess, Henke, J. E. C.

Schmidt, De Wette, Paulus, Wegscheider, and Röhr. The *fourth* class go a little higher. They consider the Bible and Christianity as a divine revelation in a higher sense than the Rationalists. They assume a revealing operation of God distinguishable from his common providence; carefully distinguish the periods of this divine direction; found the divinity of Christianity more on its internal evidence than on miracles; but especially separate church belief from the doctrines of Scripture; reform it according to the sentiments of the Divine Word; and require that Reason should try Revelation, and that Revelation should contain nothing against, though it may well have much above, Reason. Döderlein, Morus, Reinhard, Ammon, Schott, Niemeyer, Bretschneider, and others, belong to this class.

The only objection to this classification is the one urged by Rose; namely, that only a few of the theological writers would appear to have been violent Rationalists, while the larger class would seem to have held the moderate opinions which Bretschneider himself professes to adopt. The contrary is the fact, as any one at all acquainted with the number of theological writers of the period in question can determine. The spirit of the Rationalistic literature of the time was decidedly violent and destructive.

In glancing at some of the general causes which have made Rationalism so successful in its hold upon the popular mind, we find that it has possessed many advantages over almost any other form of skepticism that has appeared during the history of the church.

Prominent among these causes were its multiplied affiliations with the church. It had thus a fine vantage-ground on which to wage deadly war against the text and doctrines of the Bible. The first antagonists of Christianity came from without; and they dealt their heaviest blows with a deep and thorough conviction that the whole system they were combating was absolutely false, absurd, and base. And, in fact, many later enemies of Revelation have come from without the pale of Christianity. But the great Coryphæi of Rationalism have sprung from the very bosom of the church, were educated under her maternal care; and, at the same time that they were endeavoring to demolish the superstructure of divine inspiration, they were, in the eyes of the people, its strongest pillars, the accredited spiritual guides of the land, teaching in the most famed universities of the Continent, and preaching in churches which had been hallowed by the struggles and triumphs of the Reformation.

German Protestantism cannot complain that Rationalism was the work of acknowledged foes; but is bound to confess, with confusion of face, that it has been produced by her own sons; and that English Deism and French Atheism were welcomed, and transmuted into far more insidious and destructive agencies than they had ever been at home. The Rationalists did not discard the Bible, but professed the strongest attachment to it. They ever boasted that their sole object was the defence and elevation of it. "Because we love it," they said, "we are putting ourselves to all this trouble of elucidating it. It grieves us beyond measure to see how it has been suffering from the vagaries of weak minds. We are going to place it in the hands of impartial Reason; so that, for once at least, it may become plain to the masses. We will call in all the languages and sciences to aid us in exhuming its long-buried treasures, in order that the wayfaring man, though a fool, may appropriate them. And as to the church, who would say aught against our venerable mother? We love her dearly. We confess, indeed, that we love the green fields and gray mountain-rocks better than her Sabbath services; nor do we have much respect for her Sabbath at all. But we cherish her memories, and are proud of her glory. Yet the people do not understand her mysteries well enough. They do not love her as much as we do. Therefore we will stir them up to the performance of long-neglected duties. They ignorantly cling too proudly to her forms and confessions. But we will aid them to behold her in a better light. We know the true path of her prosperity, for do you not see that we have been born and bred within her dear fold? Let everybody follow us. We will bring you into light." Had outspoken enemies of the church and inspiration, though doubly gifted and multiplied in number, set themselves to the same destructive work that engaged the labors of these so-called friends, they could not have inflicted half the injury. They had razed to the ground tower after tower of the popular faith before their designs were discovered. And yet we must do them the credit to say that they did not intend to do the harm that they eventually accomplished. But human agencies achieve their legitimate results without regard to the motives that give them impulse. No doubt, many a Rationalist, as he looked back from his death-bed on the ruin to which he had contributed, trembled with astonishment at the poisonous fruit of his labors. Christ beheld a broader field than we can see, when he said, "A man's foes shall be they of his own household."

This religious exterior has been a powerful auxiliary to the growth of Rationalism. In the earlier stages of its history, every utterance regarding the authenticity of any books of Scripture was carefully guarded. The boldest stroke that this species of skepticism has made has been a recent one, Strauss' *Life of Jesus*; but that work was only the outgrowth of long doubt, and the honest, frank expression of what a certain class of Rationalists had been burning to say for a century. Parents who sent their sons to the university to listen to such men as Semler, Thomasius, and Paulus, had not the remotest idea that institutions of such renown for learning and religion were at that very time the hotbeds of rank infidelity. Even the State cabinets that controlled the professorial chairs could not believe for a long time that men who had been chosen to teach theology were spending all their power in corrupting the religious sentiment of the land. Large congregations were sometimes startled with strange announcements from their pastors, to the effect that the supposed miraculous dividing of the Red Sea was only occasioned by certain natural forces of wind and tide; that all the rest of the Old Testament miracles were pure myths; and that many parts of the New Testament were written at a later time and by other authors than those whose names are usually associated with them. "Heterodoxy," was whispered. But the reply was, "Better have heterodoxy than these miserable disputes on Election and the Lord's Supper, to which we have been compelled to listen almost ever since Luther laid his body down to die." Fledgling theologians would come home from the university, and read aloud to the family-group the notes of lectures which they had heard during the last semester. The aged pair, looking up in wonder, would say, "The good and great doctors of our Reformation never taught such things as these." But their sons would answer, "Oh, the world has grown much wiser since their day. New discoveries in philosophy and science have opened new avenues of truth, and our eyes are blessed that we see, and our ears that we hear. Just wait until we get into the pulpit, and we will set the people to thinking in a new way." Thus the enemy was sowing tares while the church was dreaming of a plenteous harvest.

Rationalism was very adroit in its initial steps. Its method of betrayal was, Judas-like, to sit in friendly intercourse beside its victim, and afterwards, when the fulness of malevolent inspiration had come, to give the fatal kiss in the presence of enemies. The people did not know the ills they were about to suffer until deliverance was well-nigh hopeless. Had Rationalism begun by laying down its platform and planning the work of proof, the forces of the opposition might have been organized. But it commenced without a platform, and worked long without one. The systematic theology of Bretschneider would by no means be accepted by the entire class of Rationalistic divines. To get a fair conception of what has been the aggregate sentiment of the whole class, one must wander through hundreds of volumes of exegesis, history, philosophy, and romance; and these covering a space of many years. Even when you hold up your treasure, and cry "Eureka!" your shrewd opponent will coolly say that you have given a false interpretation, and have drawn wrong conclusions,—that his masters never claimed such an absurdity. Rationalism looked upon Revelation as a tottering edifice, and set itself busily at work to destroy the entire superstructure. But sometimes it is the surrounding vines and trees that shake in the autumn storm, and not the building itself; and often beneath the worm-eaten bark there is a great oaken heart, which no arm is strong enough and no axe sufficiently keen to cleave.

Rationalism has been striving to destroy a house which was built upon a rock; and if it fell not, the fault lay not in the absence of ingenuity and strength of attack, but in the undecayed material and deeply-grounded solidity of the structure.

We are not blind to the extenuating circumstances that are adduced for Rationalism. The motives of its founders seemed pure enough, for these men held their life-task to be the purification of faith from the misconceptions of inspiration, and the deliverance of the church from the thraldom of stiff formularies. Some of their successors held that their labors were only philosophical, and hence could not affect theology. They all claimed relationship with the Reformers, and with the good and great of all ages. Bretschneider says that Luther talked of miracles as only fit for the ignorant and vulgar, as apples and pears are for children.

Paulus tries to prove the great Saxon a Rationalist by the following circumstance. The Elector of Brandenburg having asked Luther if it were true that he had said he should not stop unless convinced from Scripture, received this reply: "Yes, my lord, unless I am convinced by clear and evident reasons!" It was a favorite view of the Rationalists that the Reformation had been produced by Reason asserting her rights; and it was then an easy step to take, when they claimed as much right to use Reason within the domain of Protestantism as their fathers possessed when within the pale of Catholicism.

But there were wide points of difference between the Reformers and Rationalists. The former would return to the spirit and letter of the Word of God, while the latter did not hesitate to depart from both. The former accepted the Bible as it is, making Faith its interpreter; the latter would only construe its utterances as Reason would dictate.

With the Reformers there was a conflict between the Bible and the Roman church, but harmony between Reason and the Bible; hence these two homogeneous elements should be united and the rebellious one forever discarded. But with the Rationalists there was an irreconcilable difference between Reason and Revelation, and the latter must be moulded into whatever shape the former chose to mark out. The Reformers celebrated the reunion of both; but the Rationalists never rested as long as there was any hope of putting asunder those whom they believed God had never joined together. But the later Rationalists, least of all, could claim consanguinity with the Reformers. How could they who banished miracles from the Scriptures and reduced Christ to a much lower personality than even the Ebionites declared him to be, dare to range themselves in the circle of the honored ones who had unsealed the long-locked treasures of inspiration, and declared that Christ, instead of being an inferior Socrates, was divine, and the only worthy mediator between God and man? After we accept every reasonable apology for this destructive skepticism there will still be found a large balance against it. There are four considerations which must always be borne in mind when we would decide on the character of any development of religious doubt and innovation. 1. *The necessity for its origin and development;* 2. *Its point of attack;* 3. *The spirit with which it conducts its warfare;* and 4. *The success which it achieves.*

Let us see how Rationalism stands the test of these

criteria. It must be confessed that the German Protestant church, both the Lutheran and Reformed, called loudly for reinvigoration. But it was Faith, not Reason, that could furnish the remedy. The Pietistic influence was gaining ground and fast achieving a good work; but it was reprobated by the idolaters of Reason, and the tender plant was touched by the fatal frost. Had Pietism, with all its extravagances, been fostered by the intellect of the pulpits and universities it would have accomplished the same work for Germany in the seventeenth that the Wesleys and Whitefield wrought in England in the eighteenth century. There was no call for Rationalism, though its literary contributions to the church and the times will eventually be highly useful; but they were ill-timed in that season of remarkable religious doubt. It was the warmth of the heart, and not the cold logic of the intellect that could rejuvenate the church.

Nor do we find the position of Rationalism to be any better when we call to mind that it really acknowledges no hallowed ground. It attacked the most endeared doctrines of our faith, and applied its enginery to those very parts of our citadel which we would be most likely to defend the longest. Had it contented itself with the mere discussion of minor points, with here and there a quibble about a miracle or a prophecy, we could excuse many of its vagaries on the score of enthusiasm. But its premiss was, "We will accept nothing between the two lids of this Book if our Reason cannot fathom it." Hence, all truth, every book of the Bible, even the sacraments of the church, came in for their share of discussion and pruning. In this respect Rationalism takes rank as one of the most corrupt tendencies of infidelity which appears anywhere upon the page of ecclesiastical history. But do we find its spirit mild and amiable? Some of the Rationalists were naturally men of admirable temperament, but this was no effect of their faith. The most lamentable feature of this whole system was the ruthless character of its warfare. The professions of love for the Scriptures and the church, which we so often meet with in the writings of the early Rationalistic divines, were soon laid aside. The demon of destruction presided over the storm. And the work of ruin was rapid, by forced marches and through devious paths,—in the true military style. When the hour of fight came there was no swerving. Men full of the spirit of a bad cause will sometimes fight as valiantly as others for a good one; but it is then that God determines the victor. The evangelical Christians of Protestant Germany saw their banner captured by their foes. And it was their foes who gave the first fire; but they will not be so fortunate in the last encounter. We challenge Deism and even Atheism itself, to furnish proof of a more malignant antipathy to some of the cardinal doctrines of the common faith of Christendom than Rationalism has produced in certain ones of its exponents, and which we shall strive to expose in future pages of this work. Some of the Rationalists were John-like in all they did, save when they discussed the holy truths of inspiration. Then they were possessed by the evil spirit. Nowhere can we find a more deplorable example of the disastrous effects of a false creed on the human character. It is an infallible law of our nature that the mind, not less than the body, becomes depraved by an impure diet. Many persons have been permanently injured by reading the *Briefe über den Rationalismus*, and other works which Rationalism has published against the doctrines of Revelation.

As far as the completeness and speed of the work of Rationalism are concerned we shall find that it ranks with the most rapid and destructive errors that have ever risen in conflict with the church. Instead of striving to build up a land that had so long been cursed with the blight of Papacy, and had not yet been redeemed a full century, this evil brought its quota of poison into the university, the pulpit, and the household circle. Nor did it cease, as we shall see, until it corrupted nearly all the land for several generations. To-day the humblest peasant who steps on our shore at Castle Garden will stare in wonder as you speak of the final judgment, the immortality of the soul, and the authenticity of the Scriptures. Naturalism could not live thus long in Italy, nor Deism in England, nor the blind Atheism of the Encyclopædists in France; neither in either land was the work of destruction so complete.

But the church has proved herself able to depose many *corruptions of her faith;* yet this *attack upon her faith* she has still to vanquish thoroughly. It is not works on the evidences of Christianity that she needs for the consummation of her great aim; and we trust that, by the divine blessing, the inquiry into the vagaries of Reason upon which we are now entering will not be without its effect upon the young mind of America. Our task is simply to lift the finger of warning against the increasing influx of Rationalistic tendencies from France and England; which lands had first received them from Germany. One of our great dangers lies in permitting Reason to take our premises and build her own conclusions upon them. There is an intimate union between theology and philosophy; and anything less than the pursuit and cultivation of a sound philosophy will endanger our theology. Tenny-son gives a beautiful word of advice when he says:

> "Hold thou the good: define it well:
> For fear divine Philosophy
> Should push beyond her mark, and be
> Procuress to the Lords of Hell."

CHAPTER I.

CONTROVERSIAL PERIOD SUCCEEDING THE REFORMATION.

A WORK of such magnitude as the Reformation could not easily be consummated in one generation. The real severance from the Roman Catholic church was effected by Luther and Melanchthon; but these men did not live long enough to give the symmetry and polish to their work which it really needed. Unfortunately, their successors failed to perform the necessary task. But lofty as our ideas of the Reformation should be, we must not be blind to the fact that German Protestantism bears sad evidences of early mismanagement. To-day, the Sabbath in Prussia, Baden, and all the Protestant nationalities is hardly distinguishable from that of Bavaria, Austria, Belgium, or France. But a few bold words from Martin Luther on the sanctity of that day, as the Scriptures declare it, would have made it as holy in Germany as it now is in England and the United States. Another error, not so great in itself as in the evils it induced, was the concessions which Protestantism granted to the civil magistrate. The friendly and heroic part which the Elector of Saxony took in the labors of the Reformers, made it a matter of deference to vest much ecclesiastical authority in the civil head. But when, in later years, this confidence was abused, it was not so easy to alter the conditions of power. We see in this very fact one of the underlying causes of the great Rationalistic defection. The individual conscience was allowed almost no freedom at certain periods. The slightest deviation from the mere expression of doctrine was visited with severe penalty. Strigel was imprisoned; Hardenberg was deposed and banished; Peucer doomed to ten years' imprisonment; Cracau put to death on the slightest pretences; and Huber was deposed and expatriated for a mere variation in stating the Lutheran doctrine that none are excluded from salvation.[1]

There were several causes which contributed to the intemperate controversies that sprang up immediately after the Reformation. The Reformers were involved in serious disputes among themselves. Had Luther and Zwinglius never uttered the word *Consubstantiation* they would have gained multitudes to the cause they both loved so dearly. Many other questions, which unfortunately occupied so much public attention, caused minute divisions among those who should have stood firm and united in that plastic period of the great movement. But it is to the numerous confessions of faith that we must attribute most of these controversies. Perhaps the grave character of the master-points at issue with Romanism demanded these closely-succeeding expressions of doctrinal opinion; but we question if the advantage was not much less than the outlay. First of all came Melanchthon's celebrated *Augsburg Confession*, in 1530. The Roman Catholics replied by their *Confutation*, which, in turn, was answered by Melanchthon in the *Apology of the Confession*. Luther followed in 1536–'37 with his *Articles of Smalcald*, and still later by his two *Catechisms*. In

[1] Pusey, *Historical Inquiry*, pp. 16, 17.

1577 came the *Formula Concordiæ*, and in 1580 the symbolical canon entitled *Liber Concordiæ*.

Amid this mass of doctrinal opinion in which many conflicting points were easy enough to find, it was no small task to know what to accept. The air was filled with the sounds of strife. Those who had fought so steadfastly against Papacy were now turning their weapons in deadly strife against each other.

The very names by which Church History has recorded the memory of these strifes indicate the real littleness of many of the points in question. The *Antinomian Controversy* originated with John Agricola during Luther's life-time. Agricola, in many severe expressions, contended against the utility of the Law; though Mosheim thinks he intended to say nothing more than that the ten laws of Moses were intended chiefly for the Jews, and that Christians are warranted in laying them aside. The *Adiaphoristic Controversy* was caused by the difference between the moderate views of Melanchthon and the more rigid doctrines of the orthodox Lutherans. We have next the controversy between George Major and Nicolas Amsdorf, as to whether good works are necessary to salvation, or whether they possess a dangerous tendency. The *Synergistic Controversy* considered the relations of divine grace and human liberty. The dispute between Victorin Strigel and Matthias Flacius was on the nature of Original Sin. Then we have the *Osiandric Controversy*, on the relation of justification to sanctification; and the *Crypto-Calvinistic Controversy*, concerning the Lord's Supper, which extended through the Palatinate to Bremen and through Saxony. The *Formula Concordiæ* thus sums up the Lutheran controversies: 1. Against the Antinomians insisting on the preaching of the law. 2. Justification as a declarative act, against Osiander; good works are its fruits. 3. Synergism is disavowed, but the difficulty left indefinite. 4. Adiaphora are admitted, but in times of trial declared to be important. 5. Consubstantiation, and ubiquity of Christ's body.

The Reformed or Calvinistic church was likewise engaged in doctrinal disputation, but there was more internal unity. Hence, while Calvinism was rooting itself in England, Scotland, and Holland, Lutheranism was spending itself in internal strife.

The *Syncretistic Controversy* was remarkable on account of the great men who engaged in it and the noble purpose which caused it. It arose from an attempt to reconcile all the disputants under the Apostles' Creed.

George Calixtus was the chief actor in the movement. He was a most cultivated theologian. But, like so many of his fellow countrymen, whose merits have not yet been appreciated by the English-speaking people, he is little known to our readers of ecclesiastical history. He applied himself first to the study of the Church Fathers, poring over their voluminous productions with all the zeal of an enthusiast. He was eager to gain an insight into contemporaneous theology as it was believed and practised by all the sects. He concluded that he could gain his object only by travel and personal observation. Consequently, he commenced a tour through Belgium, England, France, and various parts of Germany. Nor did he hasten from one place to another, but continued a length of time, in order to become imbued with the local spirit, make the acquaintance of the most illustrious men, hold conversations with them, and commit his thoughts to writing.

On his return he commenced the labors of a professor of theology at Helmstedt. Thus, few men ever brought to their aid more extensive acquirements than Calixtus. Besides the advantages he derived from his travels, he was possessed of strong and brilliant natural talents. He was bold and striking in his style; had great originality of conception, and remarkable logical acuteness. Yet he received but little justice from his generation; for almost everything he wrote was made the theme of mad disputes and violent abuse.

The controversies of the period made a profound impression on the mind of Calixtus. The anger and personality with which they were conducted were sufficient proof to him of the little service they were able to contribute to either the improvement of theology or the religious growth of the people. To reconcile the various sects was the dream of his whole life. Referring to his early desires in this direction, he thus wrote in later years: "I was cogitating methods, even at that early age, for mitigating the feuds and dissensions of Christians. . . . One thing, however, is clear, that if men's minds were not bound by prejudices, they would remit a great deal of rigor."[1] Those were sincere words, too, which he said on beholding the rancor of sectarianism: "If I may but help towards the healing of our schisms, I will shrink from no cares and no night-watchings; no effort and no dangers; . . . nay, I will never spare either my life or my blood, if so be I may purchase the peace of the church. For nothing can ever be laid upon me so heavy but that I would undertake it, not only with readiness, but also with gladness." The abuses of preaching, then prevalent, were also a theme of intense sorrow to him.

[1] *Responsum Moguntinis Theologis*, p. 129.

What some of them were may be easily gathered from a passage in his course of lectures on the Four Evangelists to the students of Helmstedt. "It is evident," he says, "that in every interpretation the chief heed is to be given to the *literal sense.* In every address to the people this must be made the principal point—so to explain the text of Scripture that men may understand what the Holy Spirit chiefly and primarily intends to teach by it. Inasmuch, too, as the language is addressed to the people, it is the part of prudence to decide what words may suit their capacity. We should strive to state the fact on the doctrine itself in words as fitting and simple as possible, and (omitting all controversial subtleties) to prove the truth as far as it is necessary for salvation to be known, by a few words of Scripture:—few, that they may not escape the memory of the hearers; evident and convincing, lest the proofs seem doubtful, and the minds of the more intelligent be left in suspense and be disturbed to their very exceeding harm. The words of the Fathers (if used by way of evidence) should be used sparingly and with caution; lest the ignorant should confound the Apostles and Prophets with the Fathers, and persuade themselves that all have equal authority. For it is to be borne in mind that sermons are preached not so much for the benefit of the learned as for the sake of the people generally; that they may be rightly instructed in the doctrine of salvation and of Christian morals. In the meantime we must do our best to satisfy *all;* that the simple be not left without needful teaching; the more acute find no want of force and argument; nor the learned charge the preacher with a pride of knowledge foreign to the occasion and not always thorough."[1]

[1] *Conc. Evang.*, in Henke, vol. I. p. 274, note.

In his first controversial work, *Chief Points of the Christian Religion*, Calixtus gave expression to many solid thoughts, which subsequently produced an abundant harvest. His *Theological Apparatus* was written for young ministers, and designed to meet the immediate necessities of the times. But it is to his great work, the *Desire and Effort for Ecclesiastical Concord*, that we must turn to find the true man spending his greatest power toward the unification of Christians. In terms of communion, he contends, we must distinguish between what is, and what is not, essential to salvation. In all that relates to the Christian mysteries we must content ourselves with the *quod* and not dispute about the *quo modo*. In stating these mysteries we should use the simplest language. There is a natural brotherhood of men, and this should bind them together in matters of religion. We must love all men, even idolaters, in order to save them. The Jews and Mohammedans stand nearer to us than they, and we should cherish affection also for them. Those who are most closely united to us are all who believe that they can be saved only by the merits of Christ. All who thus recognize the saving power of Christ are members of his body, brothers and sisters with him. We should live, therefore, as members of one family, though adhering to different sects.

But we must not be neutral. Every one should join the church to which his own conscientious convictions would lead him. Yet when we do this, we must love all who think differently. Those who have been martyrs for the Christian faith were in the right path; we cannot do better than to follow them in love and doctrine. The outpouring of the Spirit would be meagre indeed if the church existed for the stringent Lutherans alone.[1]

But the intense desire of Calixtus to unite the various Christian bodies was poorly rewarded by the sympathy of his contemporaries. He was charged with religious indifference because he looked with mildness on those who differed from him. Though a strict Lutheran, he was accused of secretly favoring the Reformed church; and Arianism and Judaism were imputed to him, because he thought that the doctrine of the Trinity was not revealed with equal clearness in the Old and New Testaments! When he affirmed that the epithets Lutheran, Reformed, and Romanist should not destroy the idea of Christian in each, he was foully vilified for opening the gate of heaven to the abandoned of all the earth. A friendly man said that he was "a good and venerable theologian," and for this utterance the offender was subjected to a heavy fine. The friends of Calixtus were termed by one individual "blood-hounds and perjurers." Another declared that "he tuned his lyre to Judaizers and Arianizers and Romanizers and Calvinizers, and that he showed a spirit so coarse and shameless that never the like had been before." Still another compared him to Julian the Apostate.

But previous controversies and the ever-increasing points of divergence had so estranged the different churches that the labors of Calixtus to unite them proved unavailing. His influence was lessened because of the disputes into which his bold undertaking led him. But he quickened national thought, turned theologians to looking deeper into the Scriptures than had been the practice since the Reformation, and estab-

[1] Dowding, *Life and Correspondence of Calixtus*, pp. 313–315.

lished the difference between the essential and non-essential in matters of faith. The cause of his failure to unite the discordant church was his fearless attack on popular error. But his disappointment detracts nothing from the grandeur of his work; and his name is one which will not be denied its meed of praise when theological peace is once more restored to Germany. No generation can duly value a character whose life is not in consonance with the prevailing spirit of that generation. As the military hero must not expect his greenest laurels in time of peace, and as the sage must not dream of praise in an uncultivated period, so must such men as George Calixtus wait for a coming day whose untainted atmosphere will be in harmony with their own pure life and thoughts.

The spirituality of the German church having suffered materially from the controversies of which we have spoken, the beneficial results of the Reformation were greatly endangered by them. The German version of the Bible had been an incalculable blessing to the masses; and the commentaries written by the Reformers and their immediate successors gave promise of a wide-spread Scriptural knowledge. But the religious disputes distracted the mind from this necessary department of thought, and neutralized much of the good which would otherwise have been lasting. The danger in which the Protestant church now stood was great. Sectarian strife, formalism, neglect of the high functions of the pastorate, and other flagrant evils of the day, made the devout and far-seeing tremble for the cause which had engaged the great minds of the Reformation era. What could be done? A steady and gigantic effort was necessary to be made or the great Reformation would die by its own hand. Happily there were men, though somewhat removed at first from public observation, whom God was intending to employ as conservative agents. Often in the history of the church, when there has been no prospect of success and progress, and when the votaries of error seemed everywhere triumphant, God was secretly preparing the instrumentality which, Joseph-like, would in due time perform the work of preservation and restoration. There have been pessimists who were ever ready to cry: "Lord, they have killed thy prophets, and digged down thine altars; and I am left alone, and they seek my life." But when the hour of crisis came, God's answer was heard: "I have reserved to myself seven thousand men who have not bowed the knee to Baal." This was true at the present period, for there were a few men whose services were destined to be of great value to the Protestantism of Europe.

We mention first of all the prince of mystics, Jacob Boehme, shoemaker of Gorlitz. Gieseler chooses to stigmatize him with "contempt of all Christianity of the letter and of all scientific theology;" but men can only be measured by the standard of their age. Did they serve their generation well? If so, we grant them all honor for their work. Let Boehme be tested by this method, and we do not fear the result. We are not unmindful of many of his absurd notions, of the fanaticism of his followers—for which he is not in the least chargeable—and of the many extravagances scattered through his twenty-eight treatises. But that he intended well, served his church and his Master, led thousands to self-examination, taught his nation that controversy was not the path to success or immortality, his whole career proves beyond confutation.

His life, from beginning to end, is a marvel. He

was born of poor peasant parentage in 1575; and, after being taught to read and write, was apprenticed to a shoemaker. His time was divided between reading his Bible, going to church, making shoes, and taking care of the cow. But in that boy's heart there were as deep a conscientiousness, imperturbable patience, purity of soul, and love of God as can be found in a like period of spiritual dearth. Having reproved his master one day, he was dispatched on his apprentice-pilgrimage somewhat sooner than he had anticipated. It has been truthfully said of him that his characteristic lay in his pneumatic realism. His was ecstacy of the loftiest type; but with him it was something almost tangible, real, and akin to actual life. A late author, the lamented Vaughan, thus fancies him: "Behold him early in his study, with bolted door. The boy must see to the shop to-day, no sublunary care of awl or leather, customers and groschen, must check the rushing flood of thought. The sunshine streams in emblem, to his high-raised phantasy, of a more glorious light. As he writes, the thin cheeks are flushed, the gray eye kindles, the whole frame is damp, and trembling with excitement. Sheet after sheet is covered. The headlong pen, too precipitate for caligraphy, for punctuation, for spelling, for syntax, dashes on. The lines which darken down the waiting page are, to the writer, furrows, into which heaven is raining a driven shower of celestial seed. On the chapters thus fiercely written the eye of the modern student rests, cool and critical, wearily scanning paragraphs, digressive as Juliet's nurse, and protesting, with contracting eyebrow, that this easy writing is abominably hard to read." [1]

He was four times in ecstacy. He writes of him-

[1] *Hours with the Mystics*, vol. 2, p. 67.

self: "I have never desired to know anything of divine mystery; much less have I wished to seek or find it. I sought only the heart of Jesus Christ, that there I might hide myself from the anger of God and the grasp of the devil. And I have besought God to grant me his grace and Holy Spirit, that he would lead me and take from me everything that would tend to alienate me from him; that I might lose my own will in his, and that I might be his child in his son Jesus Christ. While in this earnest seeking and longing, the door has opened before me, so that I have seen and learned more in a quarter of an hour than I could have gained in many years at great schools. . . . When I think why it is that I write as I do, I learn that my spirit is set on fire of this spirit about which I write. If I would set down other things, I cannot do it: a living fire seems to be kindled up within me. I have prayed God many hundreds of times, weeping, that if my knowledge did not contribute to his honor and the improvement of my brethren, he would take it away from me, and hold me only in his love. But I found that my weeping only made the inner fire burn all the more; and it has been in such ecstacy and knowledge that I have composed my works."

The *Aurora* was his greatest production. His extreme modesty forbade the publication of it; and it was first discovered accidentally in manuscript by a nobleman who was visiting him. Of the literary character of his works Schlegel says: "If we consider him merely as a poet, and in comparison with other Christian poets who have attempted the same supernatural themes—such as Klopstock, Milton, or even Dante,—we shall find that in fulness of emotion and depth of imagination he almost surpasses them. And in poetic expression and single beauties he does not stand a whit behind them. The great intellectual wealth of the German language has rarely been revealed to such an extent in any age as in this writer. His power of imagery flowed from an inexhaustible fountain." His last words declared the inward life of the man, "O Lord of Sabaoth save me according to thy pleasure! O thou crucified Lord Jesus Christ, have mercy on me, and take me to thy kingdom! Now I am going into Paradise!"

John Arndt was not the subtle mystic that Boehme was, and his writings are subjected to fewer misapprehensions. The service he rendered the church and the cause of truth was important; and his influence is still felt upon the practical life of the German people. While yet young he no sooner became awakened to his spiritual condition then he saw the great religious defects of his day. He first yielded to the prevalent passion for the study of chemistry and medicine; but, through a severe illness, he was subsequently led to give himself to the service of God. But few works have obtained the celebrity which his *True Christianity* has enjoyed, not only while its author lived, but at every period since that time. He was induced to write it on account of the controversial and formal spirit which petrified the church. In a letter to Duke Augustus, in 1621, he thus explained his motives: "I have first endeavored to withdraw the minds of students and preachers from this disputation and contentious theology which threatens to bring upon us once more the evil of a scholastic theology. Another reason that has impelled me to this course is my strong desire to incline dead Christians to become fruitful. A third one is to lead people from the study of human theory and science to the real exercise of faith and devotion. A fourth reason is to show what that true Christian life is which harmonizes with vital faith—and what that is which Paul meant when he said, 'I live; yet not I, but Christ liveth in me.'"

Immediately after the publication of the *True Christianity* it found a hearty welcome. The learned and ignorant took equal pleasure in its living thoughts. Next to the Bible and Kempis' *Imitation of Christ*, it has been circulated more widely on the Continent than any other book. It was translated into all the European languages, and missionaries rendered it into heathen tongues. The Roman Catholics received it, and claimed it as one of their treasures. When Professor Anton visited the Jesuit Library at Madrid, in 1687, he inquired for the best ascetical writer. The librarian produced a copy of Arndt's *True Christianity*, which, though without preface or introduction, had this simple expression on the first page: "*This book is more edifying than all others.*"

The spirit with which Arndt wrote all his works was calm and heavenly. He possessed that beautiful Moravian type of character which defied persecution by its submission, love, tenderness, and energy. In referring to his many enemies he wrote on one occasion, "I am delighted to suffer, and I would endure a thousand times more, sooner than bury my talent." He was somewhat ascetical in temperament, but he differed from all that class of thinkers by the clearness of his appreciation of the wants of his time and his unwearied efforts to meet them successfully. He did not escape the censure of mysticism; for that was more than any devout spirit in that age could expect. Some of the most learned took umbrage at his ardent sentiments and bitter complaint at the impiety of his times. The opposition to him was well organized, and continued long after his death. Even at the end of the seventeenth century we find various writers replying to his celebrated work. But all the blows of his adversaries have only tended to deepen the love of the people for his name and writings. It is not an unfrequent occurrence for minds in Germany, even at the present day, to be led to accept the truths of the Gospel by the reading of the *True Christianity.* What Thomas à Kempis was to the pre-Reformation age, Fenelon to France, and Jeremy Taylor to England, John Arndt has been to the Protestant countries of the Continent for the last three centuries. Superintendent Wagner only gave expression to the world's real conviction when he wrote of him: "*Vir placidus, candidus, pius et doctus.*"

A personal friend and spiritual son of Arndt, John Gerhard, followed closely in his footsteps. He was possessed of the same general characteristics which we have traced in connection with the two preceding names. His love was boundless, his spirit unruffled, his piety deep and lasting. He was more serviceable in some respects to the interests of the orthodox church than any other theologian of that time. Like Arndt he had been inclined to the study of medicine, but a dangerous sickness turned his mind to religious contemplation and to the study of theology. His mental capacities had been cast in a great mould. He grasped whatever he undertook with gigantic comprehension. His attainments were so rapid that at the age of twenty-four he received the degree of doctor of divinity; and, somewhat later, was the most famous and admired of all the professors of the university of

Jena. His influence was such that princes placed themselves before him for his counsel, and the highest ecclesiastical tribunals deemed themselves honored in receiving a share of his attention. His works embrace the departments of exegesis, doctrine, and practical religion.

But it was chiefly the two former branches of theology that engaged his attention. In his *Exegetical Explication of Particular Passages* he accomplished an important service for the church. He introduced all the leading doctrines of inspiration into this work, and discussed the merits of contemporary controversy in connection with them. He explained those almost indefinable terms which had been so variously employed by the schoolmen, and summed up the literature on the points in question. His style was prolix but his conclusions carried great weight with them. As a specimen of his tedious method, he begins his discussion of original sin with the questions, "Is there such a thing as original sin? Then, what is it? What is its subject? How is it continued?" Many other inquiries are made in the same manner, but it is only after a hundred pages have been passed over that he gives his own definition of it. But we should not smile at such latitude of style when we remember the literary standard of those times. The German language was then in its plastic state; and by far the greater portion of writers had been much more interested in gaining points than rounding periods. It is almost a hopeless task to wade through the ridiculously lengthy terms of the seventeenth century. But it may be said, in their defence, that the method of verbose composition was not without some appearance of utility. The intelligence of the reader could not be relied upon to such an extent as now, and the eager eyes of so many opponents made it necessary to guard every word of importance with a wall of sentences.

We have now to mention a fourth actor in the great drama of these dangerous times, John Valentine Andreä. His mind was not of the serious tone that marked the other writers of whom we have spoken. That he looked deeply, calmly, and wisely into the surrounding evils no one can doubt. Every work he wrote established this fact. But the method which he adopted to cure them was of a totally different order from that employed by others. His personal history bears all the evidences of romance. He was the son of a poor widow, who, having spent all her property to give him an education, found her boy at the conclusion of his studies desirous of making the usual academic tour. She has but a pittance left, so she puts into his hand twelve kreutzer, and a rusty old coin, as a pocketpiece. Her eyes follow him until they are blinded in a flood of tears. Years pass on and Valentine comes home, having travelled, by dint of self-denial and perseverance, over the most interesting portions of the Continent. He returns to the fatherland and settles quietly down as an orthodox Lutheran pastor.

It is now that the evils of his generation loom up before him in terrible blackness. He attacks them by satire. He sits down and writes a little book, dedicated to all the great men of Europe, and entitled, *The Discovery of the Brotherhood of the Honorable Order of the Holy Cross.* This work aims to show that there had once lived a certain Christian Rosenkranz. He was a man of remarkable learning, and communicated his knowledge to eight disciples, who lived with him, in a house called the Temple of the Holy Ghost.

This building has come to light, and behold the uncorrupted body of Rosenkranz, who has been dead a hundred and twenty years! The various disciples whom he left, and who are scattered throughout Germany, claim to be true Protestants, and call upon all men to help them in their efforts to promote learning and religion. They possess great secrets and the world ought to know them. They are perfectly at home in bottling the elixir of life, and have been in possession of the philosopher's stone a long time. Their great object is to benefit their fellow creatures. Who will follow them?

Such was the burden of Andreä's little book. The consequence was, it set all Germany on fire. People never dreamed for a moment that it was a burlesque on the times. Thousands left their labor to follow the advice of the earnest disciples of Rosenkranz. On seeing that he had caused some mischief, Andreä wrote book after book affirming that his previous one on Christian Rosenkranz was a pure fiction intended to teach a useful lesson. But nobody believed him; the people were sure that they could not be so sadly deceived. His first work was the only one that was heartily received; and multitudes ran mad after the fabulous knowledge of the famous master and his imaginary disciples. But when the land awoke to the real idea of Andreä, the reaction was tremendous. Perhaps no satire, not even the *Laus Stultitiœ* of Erasmus, created such a fury of excitement as this; seldom has one been followed with more astounding and beneficial results. We say *beneficial* from purpose; for *Andreä succeeded in attracting the popular mind from its old habits of controversy.* This was his great service. As a man he was of unexceptionable life and ardent sympathies. He passed peacefully to his rest after uttering the words, "It is our joy that our names are written in the Book of Life."

Thus were these devoted men performing their great mission of improving the life of the Church. We shall soon see how low the current of that life was, and how great the burden placed upon them. Each one had his special endowment, and was eminently qualified to contribute to a more healthy religious tone throughout the Protestant lands. But, after all, their work was only preparative. The culmination of their labors was, in later years, the great Pietistic Reform; and they marked out the path along which Spener subsequently passed. Theirs was a great part in the drama of providence; but their achievements would have accomplished no permanent advantage had they not been succeeded by the triumphs of the Father of Pietism. It has sometimes been a noticeable part of the divine plan in our great struggles with the powers of darkness, that, when the heroes of truth fall at their post, the contest does not need to rage long before others, with hearts of equal fervor and weapons more brightly polished, take their places in the advancing lines. What wonder, then, that, by and by, the mountains echo back the shouts of victory!

CHAPTER II.

RELIGIOUS CONDITION OF THE PROTESTANT CHURCH AT THE PEACE OF WESTPHALIA—1648.

THEOLOGICAL STRIFE was the precursor of the all-devastating Thirty Years' War. The forces had been long at work before the fearful carnage began. The principles involved were of such moment that, whatever power took part in the struggle, did so with all the energy with which it was endowed. The Emperor Rudolph II. had, in 1609, guaranteed to Bohemia the liberty of Protestantism, but his successor, Matthias, violated the pledge by preventing the erection of a Protestant church edifice. The imperial councillors were cast out of the window; the priests driven off; and the Elector Frederick V. of the Palatinate, chosen King of Bohemia. But the Protestants were overcome. Ferdinand II. tore up the imperial pledge; led back the priests into authority, and expelled the Protestant clergy. Certain concessions having been previously made to the Protestants, Ferdinand II. issued in 1629 his infamous *Edict of Restitution*, by which the Protestants were to deliver up all the monasteries confiscated after the Treaty of Passau. Calvinists were excluded from the Peace; and the Catholic States were granted unconditional liberty to suppress Protestantism in their hereditary countries.[1] The fearful carnage commenced in bit-

[1] Kurtz, *Church History*, vol. 11, p. 177.

ter earnestness. No war was ever carried on with more desperation; none can be found more repulsive in brutality, or more beautiful in fortitude and sublime in bravery. Great sanguinary contests often receive their appellation from the influences that produce them, or the nations conducting them; but this one, extending from 1618 to 1648, combined all these elements to such an extent that the historian finds it most convenient to denominate it by the period of its duration. It was the bloody mould in which the continent of Europe received its modern shape. It extended, with but slight exceptions, over the entire extent of Germany. Some portions of that singularly picturesque country were permitted to hope for immunity from its devastations; but, by and by, they too were visited; and all that remained were a decimated population and smoking ruins.

Pastoral work was necessarily neglected. Large sections of the country were deprived of all spiritual cultivation and oversight. The children were deprived of both their natural protectors and those guardians whom the church had provided for them. Out of ten hundred and forty-six pastors in Würtemberg, for example, only three hundred and thirty were left by the ravages of war. Food could hardly be provided for the Seminary students, few as these were; for nearly all the young men had been compelled to yield to the repeated conscriptions. The princes themselves were in many cases driven from their jurisdiction; and when the prince was gone the church was usually disorganized. Duke Eberhard of Würtemberg and many of the Rhenish rulers were compelled to seek an asylum in Strasburg. The Margrave of Baden-Durlach was a refugee to Switzerland; Dukes Adolph Frederic I. and John II. of Mecklenburg fled to Lübeck.[1]

The desolation caused by this protracted war baffles all description. No writer has been competent for it. Schiller found it a task to which even his fervid imagination and glowing diction could not measure. Wherever it went it left destruction in its path. The population of Bohemia was reduced from three millions to seven hundred and eighty thousand. Only a fiftieth part of the inhabitants of the Rhine-lands were left alive. Saxony lost nine hundred thousand of her citizens within the brief space of two years. The city of Augsburg could number only eighteen thousand out of her enterprising population of eighty thousand. In 1646 alone, Bavaria saw more than one hundred of her thriving towns laid in ashes; while little Hesse lost seventeen cities, forty-seven castles, and four hundred towns.

The cruelty which characterized some of the participants in this war may be conceived from the awful scene of the siege of Magdeburg; a picture for which, says Schiller, "History has no speech, and Poetry no pencil." "Neither childhood, nor age," another author affirms, "nor sex, nor rank, nor beauty were able to disarm the conqueror's wrath. Wives were mishandled in the arms of their husbands, daughters at the feet of their fathers. Women were found beheaded in a church, whilst the troopers amused themselves by throwing infants into the flames, or by spearing sucklings at their mothers' breasts. 'Come again in an hour,' was Tilly's only reply when some of his officers (utterly horrified at what

[1] Tholuck, *Das Kirchliche Leben des Siebzehnten Jahrhunderts. Erste Abtheilung.* For much information in the present chapter we are greatly indebted to this valuable repository.

they saw) besought him to put a hand upon this bath of blood:—'Come again in an hour and I will see what I can do. The soldier must have something for his labor and risk.' With unchecked fury did these horrors go forward, till smoke and flame set bounds to plunder. The city had been fired in several places; and a gale spread the flames with rampant speed. In less than twelve hours the town lay in ashes; two churches, and some few huts excepted. Scarcely had the rage of the fire slackened, when the troops returned again to grope for plunder. Horrible was the scene which now presented itself. Living men crept out from under corpses; lost children, shrieking, sought their parents; infants were sucking the dead breasts of their mothers. More than six thousand bodies were thrown into the Elbe, before the streets could be made passable; whilst an infinitely larger number were consumed by the fire. Thirty thousand persons are supposed to have perished." [1]

At the outset of the war, and at many times during its continuance, the Protestants fought with but little apparent prospect of success. But their heroic zeal continued unabated until it was crowned with triumph. The peace of Westphalia, which concluded the protracted struggle, secured the abolition of the oppressive Decree of 1635; granted legal rights to the Protestant churches; established Lutheranism in Central Germany, Norway, Denmark, Sweden, and Livonia; recognized the Swiss and Dutch Republics; and, under certain conditions, allowed future changes of religion by princes and people.[2]

The religious effect of the first few years of this san-

[1] Dowding, *Life and Correspondence of Calixtus*, pp. 153–154.

[2] *H. B. Smith, D. D.*, *History of Church of Christ in Chronological Tables*, pp. 56-61.

guinary period was beneficial. There were indications of more seriousness in common life, and a deeper love of truth among the thinking circles. The people manifested a disposition to trust in the Divine arm for deliverance from their sorrows; and this new confidence developed itself particularly in benefactions for the impoverished and young. But as the war progressed and peace seemed farther off with every new year, the heart of the people relaxed into coldness, distrust, and desperation. Thus, dark as was the picture of religious life before the outbreak of hostilities, it was darker still during their progress and at their close. So literally was this the case that Kahnis declares its termination to have been the beginning of the reign of secularism. He says: "Up to the period of the Thirty Years' War religion was the chief moving power of the time. The question regarding the confession prevailed over everything, and even secular questions, that they might excite interest and be carried, were compelled to clothe themselves in the garb of religion. But the result of the Thirty Years' War was indifference, not only to the confession, but to religion in general. Ever since that period secular interests decidedly occupy the foreground, and the leading power of Europe is France."[1]

It shall now be our business to inquire into that dwarfed vitality which Kahnis elevates so high as to denominate "religion." We believe that, in all the course of ecclesiastical history on the Continent, no period of equal intelligence is marked by the same degree of religious coldness and petrifaction. Theology was a special sufferer. The most useful departments were neglected, while the least essential were raised to superlative importance. Andreä places the following language

[1] *History of German Protestantism*, p. 21.

on the neglect of the study of church history, in the mouth of Truth: "History, since she is exiled with me, readily consents to be silent and laughs at the experience of those who, because they can but relate their exploits from the A. B. C. school to the Professor's chair, that is, from the rod to the sceptre, dream that they are in possession of a compendium of the whole world. Hence their city is to them a compendium of the world, their class book a library, their school a monarchy, their doctor's cap a diadem, their rod of office a lictor's staff, each scholastic rule an anathema: in short everything appears to them exaggerated. Oh! the hapless human learning that is shut up in these scholastic Athens, that whatever offences may everywhere besides be committed by ignorance, all the severest punishments are in store for these alone to overwhelm it."

Again, in his *Christianopolis*, or ideal Christian state, he says: "Since the inhabitants of Christianopolis value the church above everything else in this world, they are occupied in her history more than in any other. For since this is the ark which contains those who are to be saved, they prefer to busy themselves about it more than about all the waters of the deluge. They relate then by what immense mercy of God this soul flock was brought together, received into covenant, formed by laws enforced by his word; by what weak instruments it was extended, by what mighty engines attacked, by what manifest aid defended; what blood and prayers its safety had cost; amid what anger of Satan the standard of the Cross triumphed; how easily the tares spring up; how often its light is contracted to a narrow space; what great eclipses, and how very great and thick an one it suffered under Antichrist; how it has sometimes emerged from desperate circumstances, and especially in this our age under the mighty Luther; with what defilement and spots it is often stained; how much it is conversant with the flesh. Many other such things they have in store; as also its periodical changes, and the harmonious vicissitudes of its seasons. They diligently impress them on the youth that they may learn to trust in God, to mistrust the flesh, to despise the threats of the world, to endure the darkness of this age. And this is right, however others may not even dissemble their neglect of ecclesiastical history; for how little any knowledge of it is now required even from ecclesiastics, or how, where it is found, it is sold cheap in comparison with a syllogism or two—it does not belong to this place to discuss more at length."

The existing state of impiety may be inferred from the low estimate of childhood. The Roman Catholic Church of that day was not so careful of the indoctrination of the young as she is at the present time. Mathesius says that in the twenty-five years he spent within her fold he had seen no case in which the catechism had been elucidated, and that he had not once heard it explained from the pulpit. Luther took great pains to have children and the lowest classes trained in the elements of religious knowledge. His express language, in reference to the catechetical instruction of the young and ignorant was, "It is not merely enough that they should be taught and counselled, but care must be taken that, in the answers returned, every sentence must be evidently understood." But like so many other lessons of the great Reformer, this was not remembered by his successors; and in course of time all that the youth and laboring classes could boast in favor of their doctrinal training was a smattering of contemporary controversy. There were sermons and expository lectures intended for children ; but they were often at unseasonable hours, and of such insufferable dryness as to tax the mind and patience of maturity. A certain author, in a catalogue of this class of literature, enumerates *fifteen hundred and ninety catechetical sermons for the young that were directed solely against the Calvinists !*

No one is better able to inform us, however, of the low state of religious training than he who labored most for its improvement. Spener's language, though written in reference to the melancholy prostration which his own eyes beheld, applies equally well to the very time of which we speak :

"If one were to say that catechizing and the Christian instruction of youth is one of the principal, most important, and most necessary of our duties, and not of less value than preaching, would he not be contradicted or even laughed at by many uninstructed preachers, or by others ignorant of their duty, who seek only their own honor ; as if such care were too small and contemptible for an office instituted for more important employment? Yet such is but the real truth. Meantime this duty is by many considered so ridiculous that there are preachers who think it degrading to their dignity to undertake it, or even see that it is diligently and faithfully performed by those appointed to it. It is no credit to our evangelical churches that catechetical instruction has been so little or not at all thought of in so many places ; though even Luther recommended it so strongly, and gave us so many admirable writings to promote it. But now it either does not exist at all, or is performed negligently, and thrown almost entirely upon schools and schoolmasters.

"These duties should not have been left to schoolmasters; for these are almost wholly unfit to discharge them on account of their own meagre attainments. But preachers should recollect that the souls of the *youth* are intrusted to them, and that they must give an account of them. They should therefore submit to this as well as to the other duties of their office. It is not indeed anywhere prescribed who among them should perform these duties. In places where there are several clergymen, and the pastors and superintendents are laden with so many other occupations that they cannot perform this duty, we cannot object to its being left for the deacons, or for others who may have more time for it. In large churches able catechists might be appointed. Superintendents, however, and theologians in high office would not do amiss if they would sometimes countenance this exercise by their presence, and even now and then perform it themselves in order to encourage others. If there were some who would voluntarily commence it themselves, *it would not be interpreted ill, or thought below their dignity.*

"I have become acquainted with the character of most instructors of youth, and I find that their real aim is not to lead the soul of youth to God, but their pay also, that they are chiefly not fit to impart a correct knowledge of God since they do not possess it themselves. And indeed there are very many who have not a knowledge even of the *letter* of that which is or is not to be believed; much less do they comprehend thoroughly and spiritually what is the will of God in faith and its fruits. Catechizing is as necessary to the church as any other religious agency can be."

We have also the important authority of Calixtus on the sad condition of the education of the young. "The chief cause and origin of the decay of learning," says he, "now tending to extinction, (which may God avert!) I hold for my own part, to be this:—that the younger children are not well grounded in the minor schools. Foundations ought to be laid there, which might afterwards support the whole weight of solid learning and true erudition. The children ought to learn from genuine authors the Greek and Latin languages; the Keys (as they are) of those treasures which preceding ages have laid up for our use. And they ought so to learn, as to be able to appreciate the thoughts of others (specially of the best authors), and to express their own in suitable and perspicuous words. . . . But now, in many places, we see the reverse of all this. Before they can speak (passing by preposterously, the matters essential to ultimate success), the boys are made to proceed, or rather leap, to higher subjects; 'real' subjects, as we have learned to call them. Pedagogues of this stamp seem to themselves learned, whilst they are teaching what they have never themselves mastered; and what their scholars neither understand, nor at their age *can* understand. In the meantime the writings of those good authors, who, by all past ages, have been recognized as masters of literature and style, are struck out of their hands, and they (the schoolmasters) substitute their own comments; disputing in a circle of children about Anti-Christ and the doctrine of predestination."[1]

The theological literature of these times was voluminous and confused. A work on an unimportant subject would occupy a dozen volumes, and then the writer would give his finishing touches with the apology that he had not done justice to his theme. No nation publishes to such an extent as Protestant Germany in the nineteenth century; but one cannot be adequately con-

[1] *Orationes Selectæ*, Henke, vol. 1, pp. 285–286.

vinced of the extent of the literary activity of her theologians of the former half of the seventeenth century without loitering among the alcoves of her antiquarian bookstores of the present day. The dusty tomes testify, by their multitude and care, to the character of the ecclesiastical age that gave them birth. The Germans do not sell their old books to the paper merchants because they are old. It is sacrilege to convert the printed sheet back again to pulp. The libraries of the universities are located in those portions of the city where land is cheap; the catalogue is a small library of itself. The Leipzig Fair keeps much of this long-printed literature before the world. It changes hands, migrates to Tübingen, Halle, or some other book-loving place; passes through a generation of owners, and turns up in some other spot, but little the worse for wear. The peasant is found at the book auction; the professor considers it a white day when a replenished purse and the sale of an old library are simultaneous facts. And when the hour arrives, the preparations are sometimes of the most comfortable and leisure-inviting character. We once attended an auction in picturesque old Brunswick which continued three days; and coffee, beer, sandwiches and other refreshments were freely enjoyed at frequent intervals by nearly all present. Every one had a long breathing spell when the auctioneer, or any one of his numerous secretaries, sipped his coffee and replenished his pipe.

We cannot affirm that there was as much a deficiency of talent or learning at the time of which we speak, as there was of an humble, subdued religious spirit, and of clearness of conception, all of which are equally necessary to give a high tone to theological writing and thinking. Dr. Pusey says of the theologians, that "they were highly learned but deficient in scientific spirit, freedom from prejudice, destitute of comprehensive and discriminating views, without which mere knowledge is useless." An illustration is furnished in Calov's mammoth production, entitled, *Systema locorum Theologicorum e sacra potissimum scriptura et antiquitate, nec non adversariorum confessione doctrinam, praxia et controversiarum fidei, cum veterum tum inprimis recentiorum pertractationem luculentam exhibens.* The author tried faithfully to redeem his pledge; and though he asserted that he had aimed at conciseness, his work only terminated with the twelfth quarto volume! The subject of the first part was the nature of Theology, Religion, Divine Inspiration, Holy Scriptures, and the articles of Faith. He defined Theology to be, that practical skill in the knowledge of true religion, as drawn from divine revelation, which is calculated to lead man after the fall through faith to eternal life. One of the important questions propounded is:

"Are the Calvinists to be considered heretics, and do they not teach very dangerous errors?" Of course an affirmative reply is returned with cogent reasons therefor. At the end of this part there is a prolix recital of the many errors of George Calixtus and his followers. Calov conformed to the *causal* method of composition. There were two systems of arrangement in vogue, the *causal* and *defining.* Under the former were grouped the *causæ principales, et minus principales, instrumentales, efficientes, materiales, formales, finales.* Under the latter, a definition was prefixed to each article, which comprised the whole doctrine of the church and all the opposed heresies. This was then redundantly illustrated until the subject was supposed to be exhausted. Schertzer, in his doctrinal work, begins with a definition of Christ, and occupies three quarto pages with one sentence. We venture only its commencement: "Christ is God-man; God and man, born of his heavenly Father and his virgin mother; and Christ is according to his humanity the natural son of God, constant in his unity to one person, his divine and human nature impeccable." The favorite class-book of those times was Koenig's *Theologia positiva acroamatica synoptice tractata;* and it does but partial justice to this work to say that in dryness and meagreness it almost defies a parallel.

There was a lamentable decrease of exegetical works and lectures toward the middle of the seventeenth century. The Reformation was the signal for Scriptural study; and the Reformers declared the word of God to be the origin of their gigantic movement. All the ordinances of the early Lutheran Church were in strict keeping with this principle. The Elector Augustus, in his church order of 1580, established professors *solely for the elucidation* of the Scriptures. He appointed two to lecture on the Old Testament, one on the Pentateuch and the other on the prophets; and two on the New Testament. His command was, that they should all read the Scriptures, as far as they could, in the same languages in which the prophets and apostles had written. Many of the universities had no other professors of theology than exegetical lecturers. The languages of the Bible were diligently studied, and great progress was made in their scientific understanding.

But after the rise of the long and exciting controversies of which we have spoken, the death-blow was given to Scriptural interpretation. The method of theological study was to spend the first year in learning what is orthodox. The second was occupied in obtaining a knowledge of controversies; the third was devoted to the Scriptures, a more intimate knowledge of controversial literature, and the scholastics. One day in the week was spent with the Fathers, Church Councils, and moral theology. The later years were chiefly consumed in controversial practice, as a preparation for the great arena. Francke as truthfully described these times as his own when he said: "Youths are sent to the universities with a moderate knowledge of Latin; but of Greek and especially of Hebrew they have next to none. And it would even then have been well, if what had been neglected before had been made up in the universities. There, however, most are borne, as by a torrent, with the multitude; they flock to logical, metaphysical, ethical, polemical, physical, pneumatical lectures and what not; treating least of all those things whose benefit is most permanent in their future office, especially deferring, and at last neglecting, the study of the sacred languages."

But while there were many evidences of religious torpor there were none more marked and unmistakable than the preaching of that time. The pulpit being an invariable index of the state of the national heart, it was not less the case during the present period. The preaching was of the most formal and methodical texture. It assumed a rhetorical and poetical appearance; the people calling it the *Italian style.* Petrarch had given shape to Italian thought, and through his influence Germany became sated with poetic imagery and overwrought fancy. Sagittarius founded a stipend for the preaching of a yearly sermon in the University Church "which should be more a practical illustration of Christian doctrine than of *lofty speech.*" Emblematical sermons were sometimes delivered in lengthy series.

Christopher Sunday descanted on the *Perpetual Heart-Calendar*, treating of genera and species, and dividing his themes into "Remarkable, Historical, and Annual events, Particular numbers, and the amounts of Roman currency, the Four Seasons, the Seven Planets, the Twelve Heavenly signs, and many aspects and useful directions." All these, this divine claimed, are to be found in the Gospel as in a perpetual calendar of the heart. Another preacher adopted as his theme for a funeral sermon, *The Secret of Roses and Flowers.* Daniel Keck preached a discourse in 1642 from Romans viii. 18, calling his subject "The Apostolic Syllogism," dividing it into *subject*, *predicate*, and *conclusion.* The subject, *suffering*, was again divided into *wicked*, *voluntary*, *stolid* and *righteous ;* and these further classed into *natural*, *civil* and *spiritual* suffering.

A sermon on Zaccheus from the words, *He was little of stature*, claims for its theme, "The stature and size of Zaccheus." The first division is, *he ;* the second, *was ;* third, *small stature.* Application *first*, The text teaches us the variety of God's works; *second*, it consoles the poor; *third*, it teaches us to make amends for our personal defects by virtue. Tholuck well asks, who would imagine that the author of this sermon was the minstrel of "When the early sun arises," "Oh Jesus, all thy bleeding wounds," and so many other deeply earnest Christian songs which have touched the hearts of many generations,—the immortal Hermann von Köben? A pastor of Wernigerode preached from Matthew x. 30. His divisions were, 1: Our hair—its origin, style, form and natural circumstances. 2: On the right use of the human hair. 3: The memories, admonition, warning and consolation that have come from the human hair. 4: How hair can be used in a

Christian way! A Brunswick pastor commenced his Sabbath discourse on one occasion with the words, "A preacher must have three things; a *good conscience*, a *good bite*, and a *good kiss;*" wherefore his transition was made to the theme under consideration: "*an increase of my salary*." But it is needless to continue illustrations of the almost universal dearth of preaching. One hardly knows whether to laugh at its absurdity or weep over its prostitution.

Andreä's caustic pen revelled in satire at the de preciation of this important agency of good. Some of his ideas are by no means ill-timed in the present century. In the Dialogue of the Pulpit Orator he thus speaks:[1]

A. Tell me earnestly, I pray you, what you find wanting in my present sermon.

B. One thing only, but that a main point.

A. It cannot be in the arrangement?

B. It was, I believe, according to all the rules of the methods.

A. Then the pronunciation was defective?

B. You must speak as God has made you; only you must not be an imitator.

A. Then the action was wrong?

B. About that I am indifferent, if it be only quiet and not gesticulatory.

A. My sermon must have been much too long?

B. *If a sermon be good it can't be too long: a bad one always is.*

A. Certainly I did not produce illustrations enough?

B. You could not have meant to empty a basket of quotations.

A. Then I spoke too slow?

[1] We use Dr. E. B. Pusey's version of Andreä's words.

B. Ha! In the pulpit we must teach, not talk too volubly.

A. I should have spoken louder too?

B. I like the voice of man, not the braying of an ass.

A. Should I not have used more subtle distinctions?

B. You were there to instruct the ignorant, not to dispute with heretics.

A. Do then explain yourself more fully.

B. Hear me: you said, "I think much, very much," which was good, but it only flowed through you as through a pipe.

A. Indeed!

B. Thus, much contracted the taste of the pipe and savored accordingly.

A. No good compliment, this.

B. It is the best I can make. For when you only cast forth good and wholesome doctrines, and show nothing of them expressed in your life and manners, are you not placed out of yourself to speak one thing and think another? You make us believe that your holy words are only practised solemn words, without any real feeling, just as poets make bridal songs and funeral dirges whenever called upon. You have many passages of Scripture in readiness; but they do not exhort, strengthen and instruct you, though others die with joy at hearing the divine word.

A. You are severe upon me.

B. It is not often the case that the worst men preach the best. I wish but one thing: that for the future you should say nothing but what you express in action by your example, or at least realize by serious endeavors after obedience to God.

A. This is harsh enough.

B. It is incomparably harsher, however, to openly contradict oneself before God both in words and works, and to convert the divine service into an empty clatter of words.

A. You speak truly.

B. And it is just as true, believe me, that a simple, plain sermon, exhibited and sealed by your life, is more valuable than a thousand clever declamations.

This want of consistency between the profession of the clergy and their daily life is indeed a dark picture. While we would not forget that there were noble exceptions to all the examples of declension that we have adduced, and that there were also exemplary illustrations of ministerial devotion amid all the deformity of these times, we must maintain that the ministerial spirit which characterized this period was not merely cold and indifferent, but wicked, and to a great extent abandoned.

The scenes of clerical immorality are enough to chill one's blood even at the distance of more than two centuries. The preachers were not licensed to preach until they had been graduated through a course of study extending from five to ten years. According to the judgment of the Lutheran Church, they must be fitted intellectually for exercising the functions of their office. But after settlement over the churches of the land, their conduct furnishes a sad proof that their intellectual qualifications were utterly barren without the more important adjunct of spiritual regeneration. They were not converted men, as the sequel will plainly show. The salary allowed them was usually small; and this is the apology pleaded for them by their friends; but scanty salaries are the outgrowth of scanty ministerial piety. The people, in no age of the world, have refused a proper and sufficient support to a zealous, God-fearing ministry.

A Church Order of 1600 reads thus: "Since we have received information that servants of the church (clergy) and schoolmasters, the parochial teachers, are guilty of whoredom and fornication, we command that if they are *notoriously* guilty they shall be suspended. We learn, too, that some of the village pastors do not possess the Bible. We command that they shall get a Bible and Concordance. Those whom we formerly suspended shall remain so until they give proof of a reformation." A pastor Pfeifer of Neukirchen and Lassau lived five unhappy years with his congregation; and from mere private prejudice refused the sacrament of the Lord's Supper to the sick and dying. On communion-day he overturned the baskets of the fish-venders; was wounded for his conduct; and then went into his church to the performance of his ministerial duties. He did not scruple to administer the elements with his bloody hands. Pastor Johansen of Detzböll wrote in his Church Record in 1647, the following: "The persons whom I will name have persecuted me in my office, but God delivered me miraculously out of their hands. J. Dirksen struck me down with a pitchfork: I was taken home as dead but recovered again; some years afterwards he was struck dead, and died in the street. J. Volkwartsen struck me with my own spade. Subsequently he was killed by his brother. Where his soul went, God only knows. P. Peusen was on the point of stabbing me through, but M. Payens saved me. A. Frese committed adultery with my wife, and followed me with a loaded rifle. D. Momsen broke two of my right ribs: he apologized afterwards for his offence. I forgave him. O Jesus, protect me and thy poor Christianity, that I may praise thee in eternity!" A church made the following charges against its pastor: I. He called certain people "scoundrels" from the pulpit; to which the offender pleaded "guilty." II. He had grown so angry in his sermon that he afterwards forgot the Lord's Prayer. He urged that "this had happened some time ago." III. When some women went out after the sermon, he called after them, and told them that if they would not stop to receive the blessing they would have his curse; "not guilty." IV. He had cohabited with a servant girl, and an illegitimate child was born; "others do the same thing." V. He forgot the cup at the communion; "that happened long ago." VI. He said to the officer, "All are devils who want me to go to Messing;" "that is true."

There were sad evidences of the same immorality in University life. Melanchthon's prophecy had proved too true: "We have seen already how religion has been put in peril by the irruption of barbarism, *and I am very much afraid that this will happen again.*" At a Disputation in the University of Wittenberg, the Chancellor addressed a disputant with such epithets as "Hear, thou hog! thou hound! thou fool! or whatever thou art, thou stolid ass!" Another prominent personage of Wittenberg, in a Disputation, became so enraged at hearing Melanchthon addressed as authority against him, that he pulled down the great Reformer's picture which hung near him, and trampled it under his feet. One Professor was so deeply in debt that he could not pay his creditors, "if every hair on his head were a ducat." Another was "in bed with seven wounds received in a fall when he was coming home drunk." Some read their newspapers at church-service. Nor did the wives and daughters of the Professors lead any better life. They were guilty of deeds of the grossest immorality, such indeed as would disgrace a less enlightened people than the Germans at that period.[1]

The great moral decline of the clergy was confined chiefly to the Lutheran church. The Reformed was earnest, pious, and aggressive. At this very time it was endeavoring to spread the leaven of the Gospel through other lands. It was, during the whole period, the conservative power of Protestantism. As might be expected, it suffered somewhat from the declension of Lutheranism; but it stood manfully up to the crisis, and met the issues with an heroic spirit. When the Roman Catholics saw these excesses of the Lutherans, and witnessed the return to their fold of many Protestants who had become disgusted with the vices of their brethren, they rejoiced greatly, and used every available means to bring back more of their erring friends.

We must remember, however, that it was the clergy and not the laity, who were the agents of the great declension. The theologians had submerged the land in fruitless controversy; they hesitated not to commit open sin when occasion demanded it; they neglected the youth of the whole country; the ignorant peasantry were not blessed with even the crumbs of truth; the pulpit was perverted to a cathedra for the declamation of the hyperbolical rhetoric that a corrupt taste had imported from Spain and Italy: the Apocrypha was the all-important part of the Bible; and the private

[1] 1602: Der Frau Gerlach (Prof. Theol.) Tochter ist in Geschrei, dass sie mit einem kinde gelie. 1613: Dr. Happrecht's Tochter hat ihre Jungfrauschaft verloren. 1622: Dr. Magirus klagt dass seine Frau die Dienstboten ihm nicht zur Disposition stelle, mit den *Alimentis* nicht zufrieden sei, immer Gäste einlade, und viel herum laufe. Frau Magirus klagt ihren Ehemann des Ehebruchs an. Tholuck, *Deutsche Universitäten.* Vol. 1, pp. 145–148. Also Dowding, *Life and Correspondence of Calixtus*, pp. 132–133.

life of the clergy was corrupt and odious to the Christian conscience. What wonder that the piety of the people suffered a similar decline? Let the ministry be steadfast, and the masses will never swerve. The result in the present case was, that the latter gradually became imbued with the same impiety that they had learned, to their sorrow, of the former.

Glancing first at the cultivated circles, we find a practical indifference well nigh akin to skepticism beginning to prevail among the noble and wealthy. The deference which the Reformers paid to the princes led the latter to a too free exercise of their power, and there are numberless instances of their despotic usurpations. They claimed supreme control over the religious interests of their jurisdiction, and came into frequent conflict with the ecclesiastical tribunals. They maintained a tolerable show of religion, however, considering it a matter of prime importance to have the services of chaplains, and to give due public prominence to doctrinal questions. Their courts were most generally irreligious, and sometimes notoriously corrupt.

Walther, the court chaplain of Ulrich II. of East Friesland, wrote in 1637 a letter from which we take the following words: "I would much rather be silent concerning my sore misfortune, which I am here undergoing than, by speaking, to make the wounds of my heart break out afresh. These infernal courtiers, among whom I am compelled to live against my will, doubt those truths which even the heathen have learned to believe." A writer of 1630 describes three classes of skeptics among the nobility of Hamburg; *first*, those who believe that religion is nothing but a mere fiction, invented to keep the masses within restraint; *second*, those who give preference to no faith, but think that all religions have a germ of truth; and *third*, those who, confessing that there must be one true religion, are unable to decide whether it is papal, Calvinist, or Lutheran; and consequently believe nothing at all.

This classification might be applied to the whole of Protestant Germany, as far as the higher classes are concerned. They exhibited a growing taste for antiquity; and, with them, there was but a slight difference between the sublime utterances of inspiration and the masterpieces of pagan genius. We find in a catechism of that time that the proverbs of Cato and the *Mimi Publiani* constitute an authorized appendix.

A practical infidelity, bearing the name of Epicureanism, prevailed even before the war; and it became more decided and injurious as the war progressed. The highest idea of religion was adherence to creed. Princes who even thought themselves devoted and earnest, had no experimental knowledge of regeneration; and in this, as we have shown, they were but little surpassed by the clergy themselves. Orthodoxy was the aim and pride of those religionists. Hear the dying testimony of John Christian Koenig, in 1664: "My dear Confessor, since I observe that the good Lord is about to take me out of this world, I want it understood that I remain unchanged and firm to the Augsburg Confession; I will live by it and die true to it. It is well known that I have directed my teaching according to its truths. *I die the avowed enemy of all innovation and Syncretistic error!*"

The licentiousness of life, not less than of faith, was deplorable in the German courts. Dancing was carried to great excess and indecorum; and though there were edicts issued against it during the Thirty Years' War, the custom seems to have undergone but little abatement. Drunkenness was very common, and even the highest dignitaries set but a sorry example in this respect. The Court of Ludwig of Würtemberg established six glasses of wine as the minimum evidence of good breeding; one to quench the thirst; the second for the King's health; the third for those present; the fourth for the feast-giver and his wife; the fifth for the permanence of the government, and the last for absent friends. The example of all nations proves that when the nobility thus indulge themselves, and become the devotees of passion and luxury, they do not need to wait long for imitators among the lower and poorer classes. The poor looked to the rich and their rulers as standards of fashion and religion. They esteemed it not less an honor than a privilege to follow in the footsteps of their acknowledged chiefs. The governing and the governed stood but a short distance from each other, both in faith and in morals.

There was great display and extravagance in the ordinary ceremonies of matrimony and baptism. It was quite common for the wedding festival to last three days, and the baptismal feast two days. The expenses were not at all justified by the means of the feast-makers; for the humblest mechanics indulged themselves to an excessive extent. Even funeral occasions were made to subserve the dissipating spirit of these times; they were the signal for hilarity and feasting. Distant friends were invited to be present; and the whole scene was at once repulsive to a healthy taste and pure religion. A writer from the very midst of the Thirty Years' War gives us the following item: "The number of courses served at funerals frequently amounted to as many as two hundred and thirty-four. The tables were furnished with expensive luxuries and costly wines, and the people gave themselves up to feasting and rioting until far into the night." The common people became more habituated to drinking strong liquors. New breweries arose in various localities, and drunkenness became a wide-spread evil. In 1600, the city of Zwickau numbered only ten thousand inhabitants; but it could claim thirty-four breweries to supply them with beer. During the war, in 1631, that number rose to seventy.

But it is needless to particularize the phases of popular immorality as they existed in the time of which we speak. It is enough to say that all classes betrayed a growing disgust at religion and a gradual decline in morals. The danger was imminent that the great work of the Reformation would be in vain, and that it would soon come to ruin.

Every department of ecclesiastical authority having become disarranged and weakened, there must now be a reäwakening, or the labors of Luther and his coadjutors will be swept away. The popular mind should be deflected from controversy, and become united, at least on some points of faith and theory. The pulpit needs a thorough regeneration, and the Gospel should reach the masses by a natural and earnest method. The university system calls for reorganization, and a rigid censorship exercised upon the teachings of the professors. Childhood must be no longer neglected, and the illiterate must become indoctrinated into the elements of Scriptural truth. The prevalent social evils should receive severe rebuke from the private Christian and the public teacher. Calixtus, Boehme, Arndt and Gerhard have done nobly, but they have pursued paths so totally divergent that their labors have not produced all the good effects of a *united* work. Their efforts were preparatory, but not homogeneous; and what is now needed to make their writings and example permanently effective, is a plan for infusing new life into the church. Then there must be inflexible system and heroic determination for the consummation of such a plan.

When the demand became most imperative, the great want was supplied. Let all the records of providential supply and guidance be studiously searched, and we believe that Pietism—the great movement which we are now about to trace—will take its place among them as one of the clearest, most decided, and most triumphant.

CHAPTER III.

PIETISM AND ITS MISSION.

If any apology can be offered in defence of the ecclesiastical evils already recounted, it will be, that the fearful devastations of the long warfare had wrought the public mind into a feverish and unnatural state. We must not, therefore, pass that cold criticism upon the Church and her representatives to which they would be justly entitled, had they been guilty of the same vices during a time of profound peace and material prosperity.

The philosophy of this whole period of ecclesiastical history may be summed up in a sentence: The numerous theological controversies, and the pastoral neglect of the people, before the war, had unfitted both the clergy and the masses for deriving from it that deep penitence and thorough reconsecration which a season of great national affliction should have engendered. The moral excesses apparent during this time had been produced by causes long anterior to it. Hence, when the protracted time of carnage and the destruction of property did come, there was no preparation of mind or heart to derive improvement from it. Had some provision been made, had theology not abounded in idle disputes, and had the moral education of the masses been faithfully cared for, instead of the evils which have been so reluctantly related, there would have been a lengthy succession of glowing instances of devout piety. And Protestantism, instead of emerging from the conflict with only equal rights before the law, would have possessed a sanctified heart, and a vigorous, truth-seeking mind.

Time was now needed to gather up the instruction taught by those pillaged towns, slain citizens, and broken social and ecclesiastical systems. A few years passed by, when the lessons began to be learned, and signs of rejuvenation appeared. After Spener had commenced his reformatory labors, he expressly and repeatedly declared that he did not originate, but only gave expression to, a spirit of religious earnestness that had already arisen in various quarters. To him belongs the honor of cultivating and guiding these reässured hearts who had derived most improvement from the Thirty Years' War. Pietism, the fruit of their union, became a triumph under the leadership of Spener.

But who were these persons who became aroused to a sense of the exigencies of the times, and saw that the danger which threatened the kingdom of God in Germany was now scarcely less than when Tilly was leading his maddened hordes through the fair fields and over the ruins of those once happy towns? Some of the clergy were the first to indicate new life. They preached with more unction, and addressed themselves to the immediate demands of the parish, especially to provide for the orphans and widows of those who had fallen in battle. Certain ministers who had spent their youth in vain theological wrangling, preached sermons which contained better matter than redundant metaphor and classical quotations. Müller and Scriver serve as fitting illustrations of the improvement. They avoided the extended analytical and rhetorical methods long in use, and adopted the more practical system of earnest appeal and exhortation.

The clergy needed not to wait long before beholding the fruit of their labors. For a better spirit manifested itself also among the lower classes. A singular interest arose in sacred music. Not only in those venerable Gothic Cathedrals, so long the glory of the Roman Catholic Church, but in the field and the workshop there could be heard the melodies of Luther, Sachs, and Paul Gerhard. Young men appeared in numbers, offering themselves as candidates for the ministry. But let it not be supposed that these encouraging signs were universal. While the eye of faith could read the most decided lessons of hope, the religious dearth was still wide-spread. Nor was it unlikely that in a short time it would triumph over all the efforts for new life. When Spener rose to a position of prominence and influence, he saw, as no one else was able to see, the real danger to the cause of truth; and those affecting descriptions which we find among his writings, revealing the real wants of the latter half of the seventeenth century, show how keenly his own heart had become impressed by them.

It was very evident that the Lutheran Church would require a long period for self-purification, if indeed she could achieve it at all. The shorter and more effectual way would be to operate *individually* upon the popular mind. And does not the entire history of the Church prove that reform has originated from no concerted action of the body needing reformation, but from the solemn conviction and persevering efforts of some single mind, which, working first alone, has afterward won to its assistance many others? Its work then reacted upon the parent organization in such way that the latter became animated with new power.

The enemies of Pietism made the same objection to it that all the opponents of reform have ever made: "This is very good in itself, but do you not see that it is not the Church that is working? We would love to see the cause of truth advanced and our torpid Church invigorated with the old Reformation-life; but we would rather see the whole matter done in a perfectly systematic and legitimate way. Now this Pietism has some good features about it, but it acts in its own name. We do not like this absurd fancy of *ecclesiolæ in ecclesia;* but we prefer the Church to act as the Church, and for its own purposes." Thus reasoned the enemies of Pietism, who claimed as heartily as any of their contemporaries that they were strict adherents of truth and warm supporters of spiritual life. But their reasoning, however baseless, found favor; and the Church gradually came to look upon Pietism not as a handmaid, but as an adversary.

But we must first learn what Pietism proposed to do before we can appreciate its historical importance. Dorner holds, with a large number of others, that this new tendency was a necessary stage in the development of Protestantism,—a supplement of the Reformation. Though laughed at for two centuries by the Churchists on the one hand, and by the Rationalists on the other, it has to-day a firmer hold upon the respect of those who know its history best than at any former period. What if Arnold, and Petersen and his wife, did indulge in great extravagances? Have not the same unpleasant things occurred in the Church at other times? Yet, because not classed under any sectarian name, there has been but a transient estimate placed upon them, and criticism has been merciless. Is not every good institution subject to perversion at any time? We believe Dorner to be correct, and that Spener was the veritable successor of Luther and Melanchthon. A recent author, who has shown a singular facility in grouping historical periods and discovering their great significance, says: "Pietism went back from the cold faith of the seventeenth century to the living faith of the Reformation. But just because this return was vital and produced by the agency of the Holy Spirit, it could not be termed a literal return. We must not forget that the orthodoxy of the seventeenth century was only the extreme elaboration of an error, the beginning of which we find as far back as Luther's time, and which became more and more a power in the Church through the influence of Melanchthon. It was this: Mistaking the faith by which we believe for the faith which is believed. The principle of the Reformation was justification by faith, not the doctrine of faith *and* justification. In reply to the Catholics it was deemed sufficient to show that this was the true doctrine which points out the way of salvation to man. And the great danger lay in mistaking faith itself for the doctrine of faith. Therefore, in the controversies concerning justifying faith, we find that faith gradually came to be considered in relation to its doctrinal aspects more than in connection with the personal, practical, and experimental knowledge of men. In this view Pietism is an *elaboration* of the faith of the sixteenth century. . . . . Without being heterodox, Spener even expressed himself in the most decided manner in favor of the doctrines of the Church. He would make faith consist less in the dogmatism of the head than in the motions of the heart; he would bring the doctrine away from the angry disputes of the schools and incorporate it into practical life. He was thoroughly united with the Reformers as to the real signification of justifying faith, but these contraries which were sought to be reëstablished he rejected. . . . . . From Spener's view a new phase of spiritual life began to pervade the heart. The orthodoxy of the State Church had been accustomed to consider all baptized persons as true believers if only they had been educated in wholesome doctrines. There was a general denial of that living, conscious, self-faith which was vital in Luther, and had transformed the world. The land, because it was furnished with the gospel and the sacraments, was considered an evangelical country. The contrast between mere worldly and spiritual life, between the living and dead members of the Church, was practically abolished, though there still remained a theoretical distinction between the visible and invisible Church. As to the world outside the pale of the Church, the Jews and Heathen, there was no thought whatever. Men believed they had done their whole duty when they had roundly combated the other Christian Churches. Thus lived the State Church in quiet confidence of its own safety and pure doctrine at the time when the nation was recovering from the devastations of the Thirty Years' War. 'In the times succeeding the Reformation,' says a Würtemberg pastor of the past century, 'the greater portion of the common people trusted that they would certainly be saved if they believed correct doctrines; if one is neither a Roman Catholic, nor a Calvinist, and confesses his opposition, he cannot possibly miss heaven; holiness is not so necessary after all.'"[1]

The enemies of Pietism have confounded it with Mysticism. There are undoubted points in common, but Pietism was aggressive instead of contemplative; it was practical rather than theoretical. Both systems made purity of life essential, but Mysticism could not guard against mental disease, while Pietism enjoyed a long season of healthful life. The latter was far too much engaged in relieving immediate and pressing wants to fall into the gross errors which mark almost the entire career of the former. Pietism was mystical in so far as it made purity of heart essential to salvation; but it was the very antipodes of Mysticism when organized and operating against a languid and torpid Church with such weapons as Spener and his coadjutors employed. Boehme and Spener were world-wide apart in many respects; but in purity of heart they were beautifully in unison.

Pietism commenced upon the principle that the Church was corrupt; that the ministry were generally guilty of gross neglect; and that the people were cursed with spiritual death. It proposed as a theological means of improvement: I. That the scholastic theology, which reigned in the academies, and was composed of the intricate and disputable doctrines and obscure and unusual forms of expression, should be totally abolished. II. That polemical divinity, which comprehended the controversies subsisting between Christians of different communions, should be less eagerly studied and less frequently treated, though not

[1] Auberlen: *Die Göttliche Offenbarung*, vol. I., pp. 278–281. The second volume of this important work has been completed, but the gifted author has just died. His book must therefore take its place in the catalogue of brilliant but hopeless fragments.

entirely neglected. III. That all mixture of philosophy and human science with divine wisdom was to be most carefully avoided; that is, that pagan philosophy and classical learning should be kept distinct from, and by no means supersede, Biblical theology. But, IV. That, on the contrary, all those students who were designed for the ministry should be kept accustomed from their early youth to the perusal and study of the Holy Scriptures, and be taught a plain system of theology drawn from these unerring sources of truth. V. That the whole course of their education should be so directed as to render them useful in life, by the practical power of their doctrine, and the commanding influence of their example.[1]

The founder of Pietism, Philip Jacob Spener, was in many respects the most remarkable man of his century. He was only thirteen years old at the close of the Thirty Years' War. His educational advantages were great; and after completing his theological studies at Strasburg, where he enjoyed the society and instruction of the younger Buxtorf, he made the customary tour of the universities. He visited Basle, Tübingen, Freiburg, Geneva, and Lyons; spending three years before his return home. From a child he was noted for his taciturn, peaceful, confiding disposition; and when he reached manhood these same qualities increased in strength and beauty. His studies had led him somewhat from the course of theology—at least certain branches of it—and he became greatly fascinated with heraldry. But gradually he identified himself with pastoral life, and into its wants and duties he entered with great enthusiasm. He was for a short time public preacher in Strasburg, but on removing from that city

[1] Watson, *Theolog. Dict.* Art. *Protestant Pietists.*

he assumed the same office in Frankfort-on-the-Main. Here the field opened fairly before him, and, confident of success, he began the work of reform.

The instruction of children in the doctrines of Christianity, as we have already said, had been sadly neglected, because the pastors of the church had committed the task to less competent hands. Spener determined that he would assume complete control of the matter himself, and, if possible, teach the children during the week without any coöperation. His labors proved a great success; and his reform in catechetical instruction, not only in Frankfort, but thence into many parts of Germany, eventuated in one of the chief triumphs of his life. But he had further noticed that the customary preaching was much above the capacity, and unsuited to the wants, of the masses. He resolved upon a simple and perspicuous style of discourse, such as the common mind could comprehend. But, seeing that this was not enough, he organized weekly meetings of his hearers, to which they were cordially invited. There he introduced the themes of the previous Sabbath, explained any difficult points that were not fully understood, and enlarged on the plain themes of the gospel. These meetings were the *Collegia Pietatis*, or *Schools of Devotion*, which gave the first occasion for the reproachful epithet of Pietism. They brought upon their founder much opposition and odium, but were destined to produce an abundant harvest throughout the land. Spener entertained young men at his own house, and prepared them, by careful instruction and his own godly example, for great ministerial usefulness. These, too, were nurtured in the *collegia*, and there they learned how to deal with the uneducated mind and to meet the great wants of the people. The meetings were, at the outset, scantily attended, but they increased so much in interest that, first his own dwelling, and then his church, became crowded to their utmost capacity.

In 1675 Spener published his great work, *Pia Desideria.* Here he laid down his platform: *That the word of God should be brought home to the popular heart; that laymen, when capable and pious, should act as preachers, thus becoming a valuable ally of the ministry; that deep love and practical piety are a necessity to every preacher; that kindness, moderation, and an effort to convince should be observed toward theological opponents; that great efforts should be made to have worthy and divinely-called young men properly instructed for the ministry; and that all preachers should urge upon the people the importance of faith and its fruits.* This book was the foundation of Spener's greatest influence and also of the strongest opposition with which he met. As long as he taught in private he escaped all general antagonism; but on the publication of his work he became the mark of envy, formalism, and high-churchism.

After he was invited to Dresden in 1686, the state church indicated a decided disapprobation of his measures. He incurred the displeasure of the Elector by his fearless preaching and novel course of educating the young. His teaching of the masses drew upon him the charge that "a court-preacher was invited to Dresden, but behold, nothing but a school teacher!" He deemed it his duty to accept the invitation of Frederic of Brandenburg to make Berlin his residence, where, in 1705, he ended his days, after a life of remarkable usefulness but of unusual strife.

It would be a pleasure to linger a while in the beautiful scenes which Spener's life affords us. Endowed with the most childlike nature, he was nevertheless a lion in contest. And yet who will find any bitterness in his words; where does he wax angry against his opponent? He did not shun controversy, because his mission demanded it; but no man loved peace more than Spener. His mind was always calm; and it was his lifelong aim to "do no sin." His enemies,—among whom we must not forget that he had a Schelwig, a Carpzov, an Alberti, and a whole Wittenberg Faculty,—never denied his amiable disposition; and it was one of his expressions in late life that "all the attacks of his enemies had never afflicted him with but one sleepless night." It was his personal character that went almost as far as his various writings to infuse practical piety into the church. He was respected by the great and good throughout the land. Crowned heads from distant parts of the Continent wrote to him, asking his advice on ecclesiastical questions. He was one of those men who, like Luther, Wesley, and others, was not blind to the great service of an extensive correspondence. He answered six hundred and twenty-two letters during one year, and at the end of that time there lay three hundred unanswered upon his table. His activity in composition knew no bounds. For many years of his life he was a member of the Consistory, and was engaged in its sessions from eight o'clock in the morning until seven in the evening. But still he found time, according to Canstein, to publish seven folio volumes, sixty-three quartos, seven octavos, and forty-six duodecimos; besides very many introductions and prefaces to the works of friends and admirers, and republications of practical books suited to the times and the cause he was serving. After his death his enemies did all in their power to cast reproach upon his name. They even maligned his moral character, which had hitherto stood above reproach. It was a grave question at the hostile universities whether the term *Beatus Spener* could be used of him. Professor Teck, of Rostock, published a work *On the Happiness of those who die in the Lord*, in which he decided that heaven will open its gates sometimes to the extremely impious who die without any external mark of repentance, and also to those who die in gross sin; but not to such a man as Spener.

The University of Halle was founded for the avowed purpose of promoting personal piety, Scriptural knowledge, and practical preaching throughout the land. It had already been a place of instruction, but not of theological training. The theological faculty was composed of Francke, Anton, and Breithaupt. These men were deeply imbued with the fervid zeal of Spener, and set themselves to work to improve and continue what he had inaugurated. The field was ample, but the task was arduous. While Spener lived at Dresden, Francke, who taught at Leipsic, enjoyed a brief personal intercourse with him, and became thoroughly animated with his spirit. On his return to Leipsic, he commenced exegetical lectures on various parts of the Bible, and instituted *Collegia Pietatis* for such students as felt disposed to attend them. So great was the increase of attendance, both at the lectures and also at the meetings, that Francke was suspended and Pietism forbidden. It was, therefore, with a wounded and injured spirit that he availed himself of the privilege afforded in the new seat of learning.

Francke was naturally an impulsive man, and his ardent temperament led him sometimes into unintended vagaries. An extravagance of his once caused Spener to remark, that "his friends gave him more trouble than all his enemies." But he was not more erroneous than most men of the same type of character; and there is not a real moral or intellectual blemish upon his reputation. His aim was fixed when he commenced to teach at Halle; and he prosecuted it with undivided assiduity until the close of his useful life. The story of his conversion is beautifully told in his own language. Like Chalmers, he was a minister to others before his own heart was changed. He was about to preach from the words, "But these are written, that ye might believe that Jesus is the Christ, the Son of God; and that believing ye might have life through his name." He says: "My whole former life came before my eyes just as one sees a whole city from a lofty spire. At first it seemed as if I could number all my sins; but soon there opened the great fountain of them—my own blind unbelief, which had so long deceived me; I was terrified with my lost condition, and wondered if God were merciful enough to bless me. I kneeled down and prayed. All doubt vanished; I was assured in my own heart of the grace of God in Christ. Now I know him, not alone as my God but as my Father. All melancholy and unrest vanished, and I was so overcome with joy, that from the fullness of my heart I could praise my Saviour. With great sorrow I had kneeled; but with wonderful ecstacy I had risen up. It seemed to me as if my whole previous life had been a deep sleep, as if I had only been dreaming, and now for the first time had waked up. I was convinced that the whole world, with all its temporal joy, could not kindle up such pleasure in my breast."

A few days afterwards he preached from the same text as before. The sermon was the first real one that he had preached. Henceforth his heart was in the work for which God had chosen him.

He preached in Halle statedly, for, in addition to the duties of the professor's chair, he was pastor of a church. His ministrations in the pulpit became extremely popular and attractive. Naturally eloquent, he won the masses to his ministry; and by his forcible presentation of truth he molded them into his own methods of faith and thought. Nor was he less zealous or successful in his theological lectures. He commenced them in 1698, by a course on the *Introduction to the Old Testament*, concluding with a second one on the New Testament.

In 1712, he published his *Hermeneutical Lectures*, containing his comments on sections and books of Scripture, particularly on the Psalms and the Gospel of John. In his early life he had observed the dearth of lectures on the Scriptures; and he accordingly applied himself to remedy the evil. His principles of instruction were, *first*, that the student be converted before he be trained for the ministry, otherwise his theology would be merely a sacred philosophy—*philosophia de rebus sacris; second*, that he be thoroughly taught in the Bible, for "a theologian is born in the Scriptures." His *Method of Theological Study* produced a profound impression, and was the means of regenerating the prevailing system of theological instruction at the universities.

But Francke is chiefly known to the present generation by his foundation of the Orphan House at Halle. This institution was the outgrowth of his truly practical and beneficent character; and from his day to the present, it has stood a monument of his strong faith and great humanity. Its origin was entirely providential. It was already a custom in Halle for the poor to convene every week at a stated time, and receive the alms which had been contributed for their support. Francke saw their weekly gatherings, and resolved to improve the occasion by religious teaching. But their children were also ignorant, and there was no hope that the parents would be able to educate them. So he resolved to do something also in this direction, and secured some money for this purpose. But yet the parents did not thus apply it; whereupon he placed a box in his own dwelling, that all who visited him might contribute. He knew that then he would have the personal distribution of such funds. During three months one person deposited four thalers and sixteen groschen; when Francke exclaimed, "That is a noble thing—something good must be established—with this money I will found a school." Two thalers were spent for twenty-seven books; but the children brought back only four out of the whole number that they had taken home. New books were bought, and henceforth it was required that they be left in the room. At first Francke's own study was the book depository and school-room; but in a short time his pupils so greatly increased that he hired adjacent accommodations. Voluntary contributions came in freely; new buildings were erected, and teachers provided; and before the death of the founder, the enterprise had grown into a mammoth institution, celebrated throughout Europe, and scattering the seeds of truth into all lands.[1] It became a living proof that Pietism was not only able to combat the religious errors

[1] Schmid, *Geschichte des Pietismus*, pp. 290–293. How greatly this movement was favored by Providence, may be seen from the Report presented to King Frederick William I, shortly after Francke's death:—1. The Normal School with 82 scholars and 70 teachers; 2. The Latin School of the Orphan House, with 3 Inspectors, 32 teachers, 400 scholars, and 10 servants; 3. The German Citizens' school, with 4 Inspectors, 102 Teachers, 1725 Boys and Girls; 4. Orphan Children, 134, and 10 overseers; 5. Number accommodated at the tables, 251 students, 3600 poor children; 6. Furniture, Apothecary, Bookstore, employing 53 persons; 7. Institution for women unable to work.

of the times but also to grapple with the grave wants of common life. Is not that a good and safe theology, which, in addition to teaching truth, can also clothe the naked and feed the hungry? Francke's prayer, so often offered in some secluded corner of the field or the woods, was answered even before his departure from labor to reward; "Lord, give me children as plenteous as the dew of the morning; as the sand upon the sea-shore; as the stars in the heavens; so numerous that I cannot number them!"

The theological instruction of Francke and his coadjutors in the University of Halle was very influential. During the first thirty years of its history six thousand and thirty-four theologians were trained within its walls, not to speak of the multitudes who received a thorough academic and religious instruction in the Orphan House. The Oriental Theological College, established in connection with the University, promoted the study of Biblical languages, and originated the first critical edition of the Hebrew Bible. Moreover, it founded missions to the Jews and Mohammedans. From Halle streams of the new life flowed out until there were traces of reawakening throughout Europe. First, the larger cities gave signs of returning faith; and the universities which were most bitter against Spener were influenced by the power of the teachings of his immediate successors. Switzerland was one of the first countries to adopt Pietism. Zürich, Basle, Berne, and all the larger towns received it with gladness. It penetrated as far east as the provinces bordering on the Baltic Sea, and as far North as Denmark, Norway, and Sweden. Many of the Continental courts welcomed it, and Orphan Houses, after the model of Francke's, became the fashion of the day. The Reformed church was influenced and impelled by it, and even England and the Netherlands indicated a strong sympathy for its practical and evangelical features. No higher tribute can be paid it than that of Tholuck, who avers, "*that the Protestant church of Germany has never possessed so many zealous Christian ministers and laymen as in the first forty years of the eighteenth century.*"

There are two names intimately connected with Pietism in its better days, which it would be improper to pass over. Arnold, the historian of Pietism, and Thomasius, the eminent jurist. They were both alike dangerous to the very cause they sought to befriend. The former, in his *History of Churches and Heretics*, took such decided ground against the existing church system that he was fairly charged with being a Separatist. He attached but little importance to dogmatics, despised orthodoxy, and inveighed against the church as if she were the veriest pest in the land. While a student at Wittenberg he applied himself to the study of Mysticism, and now claimed that its incorporation with Pietism was the only salvation of Christianity. He held that great sins had existed in the church ever since the days of the Apostles, the first century being the only period when it enjoyed comparative purity. Thomasius, very naturally, held Arnold in high esteem, and lauded his services in the following language: "He is the only man, or at least the first, who has avoided the follies into which others have fallen, and discovered and fully exposed the errors which have been especially committed by the Englishman Cave; he has maintained that the Church of Christ, with respect to life and conduct, had begun to fall into decay immediately after the ascension of our Saviour, and still more after the death of the Apostles, and that this degeneracy had enormously increased since the age of Constantine the Great."[1]

Thomasius, though not personally connected with Pietism, gave it all his influence. He was Director of the University of Halle, and defended the Pietists from the standpoint of statesmanship. He believed Pietism the only means of uprooting the long-existing corruptions of education, society, and religion. He opposed the custom of teaching and lecturing in Latin, warmly advocating the use of French, and subsequently of German. He wished to cultivate the German spirit, and spared no pains to accomplish his purpose. While yet a teacher at Leipzig he announced a course of lectures to be delivered in the German language. The outcry was great against him; but he persevered, and henceforth delivered all his lectures in his mother tongue. Since his time the use of Latin, as a colloquial, has gradually decreased, and at the present day the German is the chief language employed at the universities. Thomasius was also the first to combat the system of prosecutions for witchcraft, and the application of torture in criminal trials. He was a thorough and indefatigable reformer. His name was a tower of strength in his generation; and he left a vivid impress upon the German mind of the eighteenth century. He published many works, some of which were directed against the ministry because of their neglect of duty.

A new generation of professors arose in Halle. C. B. Michaelis, the younger Francke, Freilinghausen, the elder Knapp, Callenberg, and Baumgarten, took the place of their more vigorous predecessors. It is deplorable to see how Pietism now began to lose its first power and earnest spirit. The persistent inquiry into

[1] Schmid, *Geschichte des Pietismus*, pp. 475–486.

scriptural truth passed over into a tacit acquiescence of the understanding. Reliance was placed on the convictions, more than on the fruits of study. Spener had blended the emotions of the mind and heart, reason and faith, harmoniously; but the later Pietists cast off the former and blindly followed the latter. Hence they soon found themselves indulging in superstition, and repeating many of the errors of some of the most deluded Mystics. Science was frowned upon, because of its supposed conflict with the letter of Scripture. The language of Spener and Francke, which was full of practical earnestness, came into disuse. Definitions became loose and vague. The *Collegia*, which had done so much good, now grew formal, cold, and disputatious. The missions, which had begun very auspiciously, dwindled from want of means and men. External life became pharisaical. Great weight was attached to long prayers. A Duke of Coburg required the masters of schools to utter a long prayer in his presence, as a test of fitness for advancement. Pietism grew mystical, ascetic, and superstitious. Some of its advocates and votaries made great pretensions to holiness and unusual gifts. This had a tendency to bring the system into disrepute in certain quarters, though the good influences that it had exerted still existed and increased. It might disappear, but the good achieved by it would live after it. But a strong effort was made by Frederic William I. to maintain its prominence and weight. From 1729 to 1736, he continued his edict that no Lutheran theologian should be appointed in a Prussian pulpit who had not studied at least two years in Halle, and received from the faculty a testimonial of his state of grace. But when he was succeeded by Frederic II., commonly called Frederic the Great, that University no longer enjoyed the royal patronage, and Halle, instead of being the school of practical piety and scriptural study, degenerated into a seminary of Rationalism.

It was charged against the Pietists that they wrote but little. Writing was not their mission. It was theirs to act, to reform the practical life and faith of the people, not to waste all their strength in a war of books. They wrote what they needed to carry out their lofty aim; and this was, perhaps, sufficient. They did lack profundity of thought; but, let it be remembered that their work was restorative, not initial. Pietism, though it ceased its aggressive power after Francke and Thomasius, was destined to exert a reproductive power long afterwards. From their day to the present, whenever there has arisen a great religious want, the heart of the people has been directed towards this same agency as a ground of hope. Whatever be said against it, it cannot be denied that it has succeeded in finding a safe lodgment in the affections of the evangelical portion of the German church.

Witness Bengel, who was a Pietist of the Spener school. He was warmly devoted to the spread of practical truth and a correct understanding of the Bible. Kahnis says of him: "We might indeed call conscientiousness the fundamental virtue of Bengel. Whatever he utters, be it in science, or life, is more mature, more well-weighed, more pithy, more consecrated than most of what his verbose age has uttered. In the great he saw the little, in the little the great." In the present century the church has had recourse to Pietism as its only relief from a devastating Rationalism. Not the Pietism of Spener and Francke, we acknowledge, but the same general current belonging to both. Its organ was the *Evangelical Church Gazette*, in 1827, and among the celebrities who attached themselves to it we find the names of Heinroth, von Meyer, Schubert, von Raumer, Steffens, Schnorr, and Olivier.

Pietism lacked a homogeneous race of teachers. Here lay the secret of its overthrow. Had the founders been succeeded by men of much the same spirit, and equally strong intellect, its existence would have been guaranteed, as far as anything religious can be promised in a country where there is a state church to control the individual conscience. The great mistake of Lutheranism was in failing to adopt it as its child. The skeptical germ which soon afterwards took root, gave evidence that it could prove its overthrow for a time, at least; but the evils of Rationalism were partially anticipated by the practical teachings of the Pietists. Rationalism in Germany, without Pietism as its forerunner, would have been fatal for centuries. But the relation of these tendencies, so plainly seen in the ecclesiastical history of Germany, is one of long standing. From the days of Neo-Platonism to the present they have existed, the good to balance the evil, Faith to limit Reason. They have been called by different names; but Christianity could little afford to do without it or its equivalent, in the past; and the Church of the Future will still cling as tenaciously and fondly to it or to its representative.

CHAPTER IV.

THE POPULAR PHILOSOPHY OF WOLFF—SKEPTICAL TENDENCIES FROM ABROAD.

THE struggle between the Pietists and the Orthodox subsided on the appearance of Wolff's demonstrative philosophy. The church was glad enough to offer the friendly hand to Pietism when she saw her faith threatened by this ruthless foe; and if the followers of Spener had refused to accept it, their success would have been far more probable. Leibnitz was the father of Wolff's system. Descartes had protested against any external authority for the first principles of belief. Leibnitz and Spinoza followed him, though in different directions.[1] Leibnitz had no system in reality, and it is only from certain well-known views on particular points that we can infer his general direction of opinion. He sought to prove the conformity of reason with a belief in revelation on the principle that two truths cannot contradict each other. His doctrine of monads and preëstablished harmony was opposed to the scriptural and ecclesiastical doctrine of creation, inasmuch as by the assumption of the existence of atoms the Creator was thrown too much in the shade.[2] He wrote his *Théodicée* for the benefit of learned and theological circles, and both as a

[1] Farrar, *Critical History of Free Thought*, p. 214.
[2] Hagenbach, *History of Doctrines*, vol. 2, p. 340.

statesman and author he acquired great celebrity for his vast acquirements and discriminating mind.

But the philosophy of Leibnitz was confined to the learned; and had it been left solely to itself, it is probable that it would never have attracted great attention or possessed much importance in the history of thought. But Wolff, who studied all his works with the greatest care, deduced from them certain summaries of argument, which, with such others of his own as he felt disposed to incorporate with them, he published and taught. Whatever censure we may cast upon Wolff, we cannot ignore his good intentions. Even before his birth, he had been consecrated by his father to the service of God; and when he was old enough to manifest his own taste, he showed a strong predilection for theological study. He says of himself: "Having been devoted to the study of theology by a vow, I also had chosen it for myself; and my intention has all along been to serve God in the ministry, even when I was already professor at Halle, until at length against my will I was led away from it, God having arranged circumstances in such a manner that I could not carry out this intention. But having lived in my native place, Breslau, among the Catholics, and having perceived from my very childhood the zeal of the Lutherans and Roman Catholics against one another, the idea was always agitating my mind, whether it would not be possible so distinctly to show the truth in theology that it would not admit of any contradiction. When afterwards I learned that the mathematicians were so sure of their ground that every one must acknowledge it to be true, I was anxious to study mathematics, for the sake of the method, in order to give diligence to reduce theology to incontrovertible certainty." These words explain Wolff's whole system. He would make doctrine so plain by mathematical demonstration that it must be accepted. But the poison of his theory lay in the assumption that what could not be mathematically demonstrated was either not true or not fit to be taught. He sets out with the principle that the human intellect is capable of knowing truth. He divides his philosophy into two parts: *first*, the *theoretical*: *second*, the *practical*. The former he subdivides into logic, metaphysics, and physics; the latter into morals, natural right, and politics. He admits a revelation, and proves its possibility by maintaining that God can do whatever he wishes. But this revelation must have signs in itself, by which it may be known. *First*. It must contain something necessary for man to know, which he cannot learn in any other way. *Second*. The things revealed must not be opposed to the divine perfections, and they must not be self-contradictory: a thing is above reason and contrary to reason when opposed to these principles. *Third*. A divine revelation can contain neither anything which contradicts reason and experience, nor anything which may be learned from them, for God is omniscient,—he knows the general as well as the particular, and he cannot be deceived. Necessary truths are those the contrary of which is impossible; accidental truths, those of which the contrary is impossible only under certain conditions. Now, revelation could not contradict necessary truths; but it may appear to contradict those which are accidental. Geometrical truths are necessary; and therefore revelation could not oppose them; but as accidental truths refer to the changes of natural things, it follows that these may be apparently contradicted by revelation; though if we search minutely, we shall at last be able to lift the veil from the contradictions. *Fourth.* Revelation cannot command anything contrary to the laws of the nature of existence and of the mind, for whatever is opposed to the laws of nature is equally opposed to those of reason. *Fifth.* When it can be proved that he who declares that he has received a divine revelation has arrived at his knowledge by the natural use of his mental powers, then his declaration cannot be considered true. *Sixth.* In a revelation all things ought to be expressed in such words, or by such signs, that he who is the object of it can clearly recognize the divine action. For God knows all possible symbolical means of knowledge, and does nothing without a purpose.

These views Wolff taught from his university-chair in Halle, and disseminated throughout the land in publications under various titles. He aimed to reach not only the young theologians and all who were likely to wield a great public influence, but to so popularize his system that the unthinking masses might become his followers. He succeeded. Even Roman Catholics embraced his tenets, and he was accustomed to say, with evident satisfaction, that his text-books were used at Ingolstadt, Vienna, and Rome. The glaring defect of his philosophy was his application of the formal logical process to theology. He reduced the examination of truth to a purely mechanical operation. The effect was soon seen. When his students began to fill the pulpits the people heard cold and stately logic, extended definitions, and frequent mathematical phrases. Think of the clergy feeding their flocks on such food as the following: "*God—a being who supports all the world at one time;*" "*Preëstablished harmony—the eternal union of things;*" "*Ratio sufficiens—the sufficient ground;*" with many other arid definitions of the same class.

One preacher, in explaining the eighth chapter of Matthew, thought it necessary, when noticing the fact of Jesus descending the mountain, to define the term mountain by declaring it to be "a very elevated place;" and, when discoursing on Jesus stretching forth his hand and touching the leper, to affirm that "the hand is one of the members of the body." It is astonishing how quickly the popular principles and teachings of the followers of Wolff began to supplant Pietism. In the university and the pulpit there were sad and numerous evidences of decline. Perhaps no system of philosophy has ever penetrated the masses as did this of Wolff; for no one has been more favored with champions who aimed to indoctrinate the unthinking. Old terms, which had been used by the first Lutherans and Reformed in common, and by the Pietists with such effectiveness, were now abandoned for the modern ones of these innovators. Everything that had age on its side was rejected because of its age. Even the titles of books were fraught with copious definitions. The Wertheim translation of the Old Testament was published under the extended name of "*The Divine Writings before the time of Jesus, the Messiah. The First Part, containing the Laws of the Israels.*" The Wolffian adepts wrote for Moabites, *Moabs;* for the Apostle Peter, *Peter the Ambassador.*

Wolff's life was full of incident. The first publications he issued after his appointment to the mathematical professorship were on subjects within his appropriate sphere of instruction. Here he first acquired his fundamental principle of mathematical demonstration applied to theology, and henceforth his mind was bent on philosophical and theological themes. We are reminded of the same process of mental action in

Bishop Colenso. In a late catalogue of his works, we have counted twelve mathematical text-books. These are at least an index of his attachment to mathematical demonstration; and it is not surprising that an ill-regulated mind should fall into Wolff's error of applying the same method to the Scriptures. The Bishop's works find their exact prototype in the "*Reasonable Thoughts of God*," "*Natural Theology*," and "*Moral Philosophy*," of Christian Wolff. The mathematical professor at Halle was not long in exposing his views; and on more than one occasion gave umbrage to his Pietistic associates. His offence reached its climax when he delivered a public discourse on the Morals of Confucius, which he applauded most enthusiastically. The Rector of the university, Francke, requested the use of the manuscript, which the author refused to grant. Influence was brought to bear against Wolff at court; and when it was represented that if his teachings were propagated any further they would produce defection in the army, Frederic William I. issued a decree of deposition from his chair, and banishment from his dominions within forty-eight hours, on penalty of death. This occurred in 1723. After Frederic the Great ascended the throne, and began to countenance the increasing skeptical tendencies of the day, he recalled him, in 1740, to his former position. He was received, it is true, with some enthusiasm, but his success as a lecturer and preacher had passed its zenith. Of his reception at Halle after his long absence he thus writes, with no little sense of self-gratulation: "A great multitude of students rode out of the city to meet me, in order to invite me formally. They were attended by six glittering postillions. All the villagers along the roadside came out of their towns, and anxiously awaited my arrival. When we reached Halle, all the streets and market-places were filled with an immense concourse of people, and I celebrated my jubilee amidst a universal jubilee. In the street, opposite the house which I had rented as my place of residence, there was gathered a band of music, which received me and my attendants with joyous strains. The press of the multitude was so great that I could hardly descend from my carriage and find my way to my rooms. My arrival was announced on the same evening to the professors and all the dignitaries of the city. On the following day they called upon me, and gave me warm greetings of welcome and esteem. Among all the rest I was received and welcomed by Dr. Lange, who wished me the greatest success, and assured me of his friendship; of course I promised to visit him in return."

Verily this was an epoch in theological history. It proves how thoroughly the Wolffian philosophy had impregnated the common classes. They had learned its principles thoroughly, and the lapse of more than a century has not fully disabused them of its errors. The philosophy of Kant was the first to supplant the Wolfian in learned circles; but Kant has had no such popular interpreter as Wolff was of Leibnitz, and hence his influence, though deep where prevalent, was felt in a more limited sphere. Wolff cannot be termed a Rationalist in the common acceptation of the term, though his doctrines contributed to the growth of neological thinking. Had he been theologian alone, and applied his principles to the interpretation of Scripture, he would have done much of Semler's work. It was, therefore, the latter and not the former whom we would denominate the father of Rationalism. Moreover, Wolff manifested a strict observance of the ecclesiastical institutions of his day, and always professed the warmest attachment to the church,—which was anything but the fact, as far as the followers of Semler are concerned. Wolff wrote on a circular announcing some university celebration the following words, which indicate the habit of his life: "I see, and would like to be present. Yet as I have purposed to partake of the Lord's Supper on the same day I do not know whether I shall be able to be present, inasmuch as I should not like to change my intention; yet I will consider the matter with my minister. Signed, Christian Wolff, 1717."

Of the relations of the Wolffian philosophy to the theology of one century ago, and of its general Rationalistic bearing, Mr. Farrar says, "The system soon became universally dominant. Its orderly method possessed the fascination which belongs to any encyclopædic view of human knowledge. It coincided, too, with the tone of the age. Really opposed, as Cartesianism has been in France, to the scholasticism which still reigned, its dogmatic form nevertheless bore such external similarity to it that it fell in with the old literary tastes. The evil effects which it subsequently produced in reference to religion were due only to the point of view which it ultimately induced. Like Locke's work on the reasonableness of Christianity, it stimulated intellectual speculation concerning revelation. By suggesting attempts to deduce *à priori* the necessary character of religious truths, it turned men's attention more than ever away from spiritual religion to theology. The attempt to demonstrate everything caused dogmas to be viewed apart from their practical aspect; and men being compelled to discard the previous method of drawing philosophy out of Scripture, an independent philosophy was created, and Scripture compared with its discoveries. Philosophy no longer relied on Scripture, but Scripture rested on philosophy. Dogmatic theology was made a part of metaphysical philosophy. This was the mode in which Wolff's philosophy ministered indirectly to the creation of the disposition to make scriptural dogmas submit to reason, which was denominated Rationalism. The empire of it was undisputed during the whole of the middle part of the century, until it was expelled, toward the close, by the partial introduction of Locke's philosophy, and of the system of Kant, as well as by the growth of classical erudition, and of a native literature."[1]

Wolff was succeeded by a school of no ordinary ability. But his disciples did not strictly follow him; they went not only the length that he did, but much further. Their thinking and literary labor circled about inspiration. It was evident that they were intent upon solving the problem and handing the doctrine over to the world as entitled to respect and unalterable. Baumgarten was the connecting link between the Pietism of Spener and the Rationalism of Semler. He was the successor of Wolff in the university-chair of Halle, and, as such, the eyes of the people were turned toward him. His acquirements were versatile, for he studied every subject of theology with poetic enthusiasm. Nor was he a superficial student merely; and his opponents well knew that in him they had found no mean adept in philosophy, theology, hermeneutics and ecclesiastical history. His writings bear a strong impress of Illuminism, but he contributed most to the formation of Rationalistic theology by training Semler for his great destructive mission. He acknowledged the presence of the Holy Spirit in Scripture, but reduced inspiration to

[1] *Critical History of Free Thought*, pp. 215–216.

an influence which God exercises over the mental faculties. Both he and Töllner declared that the Spirit had permitted each writer to compose according to the peculiar powers of his mind, and to arrange facts according to his own comprehension of them.

Töllner was a follower of Baumgarten. He was not intent upon any innovating theories as much as he was desirous to harmonize the old ecclesiastical system with the new philosophy. He had some views in common with Wolff; but he totally differed from him in his conception of mathematical demonstration of theology, and maintained that theology cannot be mathematically demonstrated, but that its integrity and worth depend solely upon historical testimony. Does the Christian system have the authority of history for its defence? If so, it will stand the test of universal opposition; but, if not, it will fall of its own weight. The tendency of his deductions was negative, and hence we rank him as no ordinary agent toward the growth of historic doubt. Here we behold the germ of such thinking as developed in Strauss' *Life of Jesus* in the present century. Töllner held that Scripture is composed of two senses, the *natural* and *revealed.* That which is natural is subject to criticism; but the revealed or spiritual light is always clearer, and does not call for much inquiry. There may be differences between the two, but there can be no contradiction. "The revelation in Scripture," he says, "is a greater and more perfect means of salvation. Both the natural light and revelation lead the man who follows them to salvation. *Scripture only more so.*"

The historian cannot fail to observe a systematic and steadfast development of skepticism in the lands south and west of Germany. Many causes contributed to its growth in Italy, whose prestige in war, extensive and still increasing commerce, and ambitious and gifted rulers, were a powerful stimulus to vigorous thought. The classics became the favorite study, and all the writings of the ancients were seized with avidity, to yield, as far as they might, their treasure of philosophy, history and poetry. Leo X. was notoriously skeptical, and, as much from sympathy as pride, surrounded himself with the leading spirits of the literature of the times. With him morality was no recommendation. Two tendencies took positive form, as the result of the literary tastes of the court and thinking classes: *first*, a return to heathenism, produced by the study of the classics; and *second*, a species of pantheism, produced by philosophy.

We now come to the Deism of England, which not only succeeded in corrupting the spiritual life of France, but became directly incorporated into the theology of Germany. It was the so-called philosophy of common sense. The most thorough German writer on the subject, Lechler, has well defined it, "The elevation of natural religion to be the standard and rule of all positive religion, an elevation which is supported by free examination by means of thinking." It started on the principle that reason is the source and measure of truth; and therefore discarded, as its Rationalistic offspring in Germany, whatever was miraculous or supernatural in Christianity. There was much earnestness in some of its champions; nor was there any absence of warm attachment to the morality and religious influence of the Scriptures. Thus it differed widely from the flippancy and frivolity of the Deists of France. We cannot, however, consider Lord Herbert's serious reflections on the publication of his chief work as a fair specimen of the tone of his coadjutors. They were mostly inferior to him in this respect, though it would not be safe to say that their influence on the public mind of England was less baneful than his. Having finished his book, *Tractatus de Veritate*, he hesitated before committing it to the press. "Thus filled," he says, "with doubts, I was on a bright summer day sitting in my room; my window to the south was open; the sun shone brightly; not a breeze was stirring. I took my book on Truth into my hand, threw myself on my knees, and prayed devoutly in the words, 'O thou one God, thou Author of this light which now shines upon me, thou Giver of all inward light, I implore thee, according to thine infinite mercy to pardon my request, which is greater than a sinner should make. I am not sufficiently convinced whether I may publish this book or not. If its publication shall be for thy glory, I beseech thee to give me a sign from Heaven. If not, I will suppress it.' I had scarcely finished these words when a loud, and yet at the same time a gentle sound came from heaven, not like any sound on earth. This comforted me in such a manner, and gave me such a satisfaction, that I considered my prayer as having been heard."

Deism in England began with the predominance given to nature by Bacon. Locke contributed greatly to its formation by discarding the proof of Christianity by miracles and supernatural observations, but claimed that nature is of itself sufficient to teach it. Hence, man can draw all necessary faith from nature. Lord Herbert, of Cherbury, held that education is inconsistent with true religion, since the earliest pagan times manifested a higher state of morality than later periods of culture and refinement. Hobbes considered religion only a sort of police force, useful solely as an agent of the State to keep the people within bounds.

Shaftesbury, the disciple and follower of Locke, addressed himself by his style to the higher classes. He cultivated the acquaintance of the rising leaders of skepticism in France and Holland, and continued through life on terms of cordial intimacy with Bayle, Le Clerc, and others of kindred spirit. He was relentless in his attacks on revealed religion. His hostility may be inferred from the fact that Voltaire termed him even too bitter an opponent of Christianity. Warburton says, "Mr. Pope told me that, to his knowledge, *The Characteristics* have done more harm to revealed religion in England than all the other works of infidelity together." Collins contributed more than any other author to the rise of Deism in France. He applied himself to the overthrow of all faith. Ignoring prophecy, he held that nothing in the Old Testament has any other than a typical or allegorical bearing upon the New Testament.

Wollaston's creed was the pursuit of happiness by the practice of reason and truth. He was the epicurean of the system which he adopted, and sought to prove that religion is wholly independent of faith. He first published a brief outline of his views in a limited number of copies, but afterwards prepared a new and enlarged edition. Twenty thousand copies were sold, and six other editions found a ready sale between 1724 and 1738. Woolston strove to bring the miracles of Christ into contempt. Mandeville and Morgan, contemporaries of Woolston, wrote against the state religion. Of Chubb's views we can gather sufficiently from his three principles: *First.* That Christ requires of men that, with all their heart and all their soul, they should follow the eternal and unchangeable precepts of natural morality. *Second.* That men, if they transgress the laws of morality, must give proofs of true and genuine repentance, because without such repentance, forgiveness or pardon is impossible. *Third.* In order more deeply to impress these principles upon the minds of men, and give them a greater influence upon their course of action, Jesus Christ has announced to mankind, that God hath appointed a day wherein he will judge the world in righteousness, and acquit and condemn, reward or punish, according as their conduct has been guided by the precepts which he has laid down. With Bolingbroke's name closes the succession of the elder school of English Deists. He wrote against the antiquity of faith, showing bitter hostility to the Old Testament. His aim, in addition to this antagonism to revelation, was to found a selfish philosophy.

Many of the works by these writers were ill-written and lacked depth of thought. Some were, however, masterpieces of original thinking and writing. The style of Mandeville, for example, has been eulogized extravagantly both by Hazlitt and Lord Macaulay.

It cannot be expected that a movement so extensive as this, and participated in by the leading literary men of the day would be without its influence abroad. Its first effect was to elicit great opposition ; and numerous replies poured in from every quarter. Toland's *Christianity Not Mysterious* was combated in the year 1760 by fifty-four rejoinders in England, France and Germany. Up to the same period, Tindal's *Christianity as Old as the World* was greeted with one hundred and six opponents. The Germans repulsed these tendencies bravely at first, and among others was the gifted and versatile Mosheim, who delivered public lectures against the influx of Deistical speculations. But gradually translations were made, and the Germans were soon able to read those works for themselves. All the Deists were rendered into their language, and some were honored with many translators. True, there were replies from the theologians of England immediately upon the appearance of the works of the leading Deists; but many of them were very feeble, the puny blows doing more harm than good. When these rejoinders came to be translated they had almost as deleterious an influence as if they had been panegyrics instead of well-meant thrusts. John Pye Smith says, "Translations were made of our Deistical writers of that time, and of a large number of vindications of Christianity which were published by some English divines of note in reply to Collins, Tindal, Morgan and their tribe; and which, in addition to their insipid and unimpassioned character, involved so much of timid apology and unchristian concession that they rather aided than obstructed the progress of infidelity." Through the influence of Baumgarten and others Deism now gained great favor in Germany. Toland was personally welcomed, flattered and honored at the very court—that of Frederic William I.—which had banished Wolf, and made adherence to his doctrines a bar to all preferment.

There was a speedy adoption of English Deism by France, though the French had manifested strong attachment to skepticism as far back as the illustrious reign of Louis XIV., whose court had dictated religion and literature to Europe. It was in 1688 that Le Vasser wrote: "People only speak of reason, good taste, the force of intellect, of the advantage of those who put themselves above the prejudices of education and of the society in which they were born. Pyrrhonism is now the fashion above everything else. People think that the legitimate exercise of the mind consists in not believing rashly, and in knowing how to doubt many things. What can be more intolerable and humiliating than to see our pretended great men boast themselves of believing nothing, and of calling those people simple and credulous who have not perhaps examined the first proofs of religion?" The condition of things was no better in the reign of Louis XV., nor indeed at any time during the eighteenth century. It could not be expected that Rousseau would overpaint the picture; yet in his *La Nouvelle Héloïse* we find this language: "No disputing is here heard—that is, in the literary coteries—no epigrams are made; they reason, but not in the stiff professional tone; you find fine jokes without puns, wit with reason, principles with freaks, sharp satire and delicate flattery with serious rules of morality. They speak of everything in order that every one may have to say something, but they never exhaust the questions raised; from the dread of getting tedious they bring them forth only occasionally, shorten them hastily, and never allow a dispute to arise. Every one informs himself, enjoys himself, and departs from the others pleased. But what is it that is learned from these interesting conversations? *One learns to defend with spirit the cause of untruth, to shake with philosophy all the principles of virtue, to gloss over with fine syllogisms one's passions and prejudices in order to give a modern shape to error.* When any one speaks, it is to a certain extent his dress, not himself, that has an opinion; and the speaker will change it as often as he will change his profession. Give him a tie-wig to-day, to-morrow a uniform, and the day after a mitre, and you will have him defend, in succession, the laws, despotism, and the Inquisition. There is one kind of reason for the lawyer, another for the financier, and a third for the soldier. Thus, no one ever says what he thinks, but what, on account of his interest, he would make others believe; and his zeal for truth is only a mask for selfishness."

This was the basis upon which Voltaire and Rousseau built in France. What wonder that the one with his pungent sarcasm, popular style and display of philosophy, and the other with his morbid sentimentalism, should become the real monarchs not only of their own land, but of cultivated circles throughout the Continent? There was not the slightest sympathy between these two men, for they hated each other cordially, and each was jealous of the other's fame and genius. Voltaire said one day to Rousseau, who was showing him an *Ode Addressed to Posterity*, "This is a letter which will never reach the place of its address." At another time, Voltaire having read a satire of his own composition to Rousseau, the latter advised him to "suppress it lest it should be imagined that he had lost his abilities and preserved only his virulence." But Voltaire was inordinately ambitious; he longed to rise to fame, as on the wings of the eagle. "How unworthy, and how dull of appreciation is sluggish France," thought he. For her rewards he had toiled, and thought, and racked his brain for years. But she was stern, and would not honor him. He therefore became disgusted with his native land, and set out for England, whose scientific and theological literature had already fired his mind. George I. and the Princess of Wales, afterward Queen Caroline, distinguished him by their attentions, and relieved his poverty by securing large subscriptions to his works. It was here that he commenced to lay up a princely fortune; but it was not until the close of his long and stirring life that he forswore his miserly habits. He found in the deistical literature of England everything that could suit his taste and ambition. "Here," reasoned he to himself, "I find what I never dreamed of before. France would not tolerate these thoughts if her own sons had given birth to them; but this is England, and we Frenchmen respect the thinking of the English mind. I will not translate much, but I will go to work with hearty earnestness, and reproduce in French literature what I find worthy of it in these free-thinking masters. May be, after all, I shall become a great man." The plan succeeded. Voltaire, on his return, became more outspoken in his infidelity. His star ascended; and he ruled, not by original but by borrowed lustre.

Frederic the Great of Prussia was captivated by the skeptical and literary celebrity of Voltaire. The latter was not long back again in France before his selfish sensitiveness imagined that all the literary men of his country had entered into a cabal to deprive him of his fame and hurl him from the throne of his literary authority. He was therefore ready to be caught by the most tempting bait; and when Frederic offered him a pension of twenty-two thousand livres, it was more than the miserly plagiarist could resist. Of his reception by the king he thus speaks in his usual style: "I set out for Potsdam in June, 1750. Astolpha did not meet a kinder reception in the palace of Alcuia. To be lodged in the same apartments that Marshal Saxe had occupied, to have the royal cooks at my command when I chose to dine alone, and the royal coachman when I had an inclination to ride, were trifling favors. Our suppers were very agreeable. If I am not deceived I think we had much wit. The king was witty, and gave occasion of wit to others; and what is still more extraordinary, I never found myself so much at my ease; I worked two hours a day with his majesty; corrected his works; and never failed highly to praise whatever was worthy of praise, though I rejected the dross. I gave him details of all that was necessary in rhetoric and criticism for his use: he profited by my advice, and his genius assisted him more effectually than my lessons."

But matters did not move on a great while thus harmoniously, for Voltaire, becoming complicated in personal difficulties with greater favorites of Frederic, received the frown of the man he had so much flattered, and whose purse had been enriching his coffers. The skeptic returned to France, wrote other works, settled near the romantic shore of Lake Geneva, and returned honored, great, and feasted to Paris. Indulging in unaccustomed excesses, his frail and aged body sank beneath the weight. But Frederic and Voltaire maintained a correspondence many years after the flatterer's disgrace. Full of trouble, haunted by dreams of conspiracy and of poverty, successful in achieving more evil than usually falls to the lot of a single mind, Voltaire passed from the society of men to the presence of God. It has been truthfully said of him in proof of his inconsistency, that he was a free thinker at London, a Cartesian at Versailles, a Christian at Nancy, and an infidel at Berlin.

Rousseau sought to establish the proposition that the progress of scientific education has always involved the decay of moral education. With Lord Herbert he held that barbarism has ever been the condition of greatest moral power. A sentiment from his *Émile* furnishes the key to his creed: "Everything is good when it comes forth from the hand of the Creator; everything degenerates under man's hand. In the state in which things now are, a man who from the moment of his birth would live among others, would, if left to himself, be most disfigured. Prejudices, authority, constraint, example, all social institutions which now depress us, would choke nature in him, and nothing would be put in its stead. He would resemble a young tree which, growing up accidentally in the street, would soon pine away in consequence of the passers-by pushing it from all sides, and bending it in all directions." Rousseau wrote with great earnestness, and possessed the faculty of inspiring his readers with an enthusiastic admiration of his theories. His romances misled many thousands, and were the most popular productions of his times. Though he and Voltaire were the exponents of French Deism, they were greatly aided in the dissemination of skeptical doctrines by Diderot, d'Alembert, Helvetius, d'Argent, de la Mettrie, and others. Bayle, in his Dictionary, appealed to the learned circles; and, not content to give only historical facts, he ventured upon the origination or reproduction of those new skeptical opinions which captivated unthinking multitudes.

The Deism of France was now a coadjutor with that of England in the devastation of Germany. The throne of Frederic II. was the exponent and defender of the hollow creed. The military successes of that king gave him an authority that few monarchs have been able to wield, while his well-known literary taste and capacity enlisted the admiration of men of culture throughout the Continent. Born to bear the sword, he surprised his subjects by the same felicity in the use of the pen;

and the man who could leave to his successors a treasury with a surplus of seventy-two millions of thalers, an army of two hundred and twenty thousand men, a kingdom increased by twenty-nine thousand square miles, and a people grown since his accession from two millions to thrice that number, was not a king who could be without great moral weight among his own subjects. And it was known that he was a skeptic, for he made no secret of it. No traces of the old Pietism of his harsh father were visible in the son. Gathering around him such men as Voltaire, La Mettrie, Maupertuis, and others whom his gold could attach to him, he was the same king in faith and literature that he was in politics. Claiming to be a Deist, it is probable that he was a very liberal one. It is more than likely that he was truthful in his description of himself when he wrote to d'Alembert that he had never lived under the same roof with religion. He claimed for his meanest subjects the right to serve God in their own way; but all the power of his example was at work in drawing the people from the old faith. He hesitated not to supplant evangelical professors and pastors by free-thinkers, and at any time to bring ridicule on any religious fact or custom. That thin-visaged man in top boots and cocked hat, surrounded by his infidels and his dogs at Sans Souci, dictated faith to Berlin and to Europe. He would have no one within the sunshine of royalty whom he could not use as he wished; and just as soon as Voltaire would be himself he became disgraced. But Frederic lived to see the day when insubordination sprang up in his army, and in many departments of public life. It came from the abnegation of evangelical faith. And it is no wonder that when the old king saw the disastrous effects of his own theories upon his subjects, he said he would willingly give his best battle to place his people where he found them at his father's death. But the seed had been sown, and Prussia was destined to be only a part of the harvest-field of tares.

CHAPTER V.

SEMLER AND THE DESTRUCTIVE SCHOOL.

1750—1810.

THE foreign influences being fairly introduced, it now remained to be seen what course the German church would adopt respecting them. The process of incorporation was rapid. A remarkable activity of mind was observable in the theological world, and men of great learning and keen intellect began to apply the deductions of foreign naturalism to the sacred oracles. No one can claim that the interpretation of the Scriptures rested at this time on a pure and solid basis; and it is therefore not remarkable that those men who had no special predilection for the doctrine of inspiration should silently submit to the views of the orthodox believers of their time. The divine origin of Hebrew points and accents was rigidly contended for; and Michaelis only fell in with the accustomed current when, in his early life, he wrote a work in their defence. The theory that errors of transcription might possibly have crept into the text, was totally rejected. No such thing could, by any contingency, occur. The fable of Aristeas was still considered worthy a place in the canon. The sanctity of the Hebrew language, and other Rabbinical notions, were defended. Christ was discovered in every book of the Old Testament; the perfect purity of the Greek of the New Testament was held; and fabulous accounts of early martyrs and miraculous legends were elevated to the same standard of authority with the gospels. What wonder, then, that when such absurdities were entertained by the evangelical portion of the church the temptation of others to skepticism was so great? Men like Ernesti could not resist the enticement to combat such a state of criticism; and he gave himself to the task with all the ardor of his nature.

He was the classic scholar of his day. The purity of his diction and the fertility of his authorship gained him a hearing among the educated and refined. His word became law. In his case, as with many others of his countrymen both before and after him, his theological tastes gave him far more authority than his merely linguistic and literary attainments could have gained for him. He was distinguished as a preacher not less than as a scholar. Enamored with the old classic times, the atmosphere of Greece in her glory of taste and culture, and of Rome in her lustre of victory and law made him impatient of the dull theology of his day. He lived not in Germany, but in the temples and bowers of paganism. His Latinity was scarcely inferior to the flowing utterances of his heathen masters. He edited many classical works, and succeeded in regenerating the humanistic studies of Europe. For this all honor be given him; but he did not rest here. He examined the New Testament with the critic's scalpel, and applied the principles of ordinary interpretation to the word of God. He held that Moses should receive no better treatment than Cicero or Tacitus. Logos was *reason* and *wisdom* in the Greek writings; why should it mean Christ or the Word when we find it in the gospel of

John? Regeneration need not be surrounded with a saintly halo; it is absurd to suppose that it can mean any more than reception into a religious society. The Holy Spirit does not communicate divine influences, but certain praiseworthy qualities. Unity with the Father is mere unity of disposition or will. The Old Testament is very good in its way, but it certainly cannot be intended for all mankind; since many parts can have no salutary influence whatever on the heart and life. It might be of some use to the Jews, but since we are so far beyond them it is quite out of place for us.

Both Grotius and Wetstein had been the forerunners of Ernesti in this method of interpretation. What he wrought against the New Testament had its counterpart in the mischief effected by John David Michaelis against the Old. This theologian was profoundly learned in the Oriental languages, but he was a reckless and irreverent critic. He made light of many of the occurrences of the Old Testament, and whenever the students applauded one of his obscene jokes, he was tickled into childishness. He made no claim to an experimental acquaintance with the operations of the Holy Spirit, and used his position as theological professor and lecturer only as the stepping-stone to money and fame. He would make Moses a very good sort of statesman, but took care to cast censure upon him whenever the feeblest occasion was offered. Still he did not go so far as to cause great offense to his Jewish readers, who were very numerous at that time, for that would have endangered the pecuniary profits from his books. He lectured on every subject that came in his way, and discussed from his chair natural science, politics, agriculture, and horse-breeding, with as much respect and reverence as the song of Moses or the utterances of Isaiah. He carried Ernesti's principles a step farther than that scholar had done. He held that it is necessary not only to understand the situation and circumstances of the writer and people at the time and place in which the books were written, and the language and history of the time, but all things connected with their moral and physical character. The critic must also be conversant with everything relating to those nations with whom the Jews associated, and know just how far the latter received their opinions and customs from abroad.

There have been few men who have shown greater boldness in assaulting the Christian faith than Semler, the father of the destructive school of Rationalism. Reared in the lap of the sternest Pietism, he found himself a student at Halle pursuing his theological curriculum. He was one of the charmed disciples at Baumgarten's feet, but it was reserved for the pupil to accomplish far more than the master had ever anticipated. Gradually the old faith claimed him only by a slight hold; and when, while yet a student, he drew the subtle distinction between theology and religion, he, in that act, gave the parting hand to evangelical faith. Then step by step he descended, until he looked at the oracles of God with no more credence in their inspiration and divine claims than his master before him. In his turn he became professor; and that was a dark day for Germany and Protestantism when he read his first lecture to his auditory. He studied the Scriptures while laboring under the conviction that people worship the Bible instead of the universal Father; and he seemed to say within himself: "I will destroy this vain idolatry, if it take bread from my wife and children: if life be lost in the effort." So he set himself to work with a will. He was in a difficulty concerning the want of understanding as to the number of sacred books. He consulted the Jews of Palestine, and they replied "twenty-four;" he went to the Alexandrians, and they answered "a greater number than that;" and to the Samaritans, who stoutly held "that only the five books of Moses have a just claim to divine authority." With such difference of opinion among those who ought to know all about the Holy Scriptures, Semler, confounded and defiant, esteemed himself a judge on his individual responsibility. He consequently began to examine the merits of each part. And first of all, he must determine what is the proof of the inspiration of a book. This he decided to be the inward conviction of our mind that what it conveys to us is truth. Certainly, reason cannot be sunk so low as to discard its functions of judgment. And did not Christ use his natural faculties? Letting reason, therefore, be umpire, he concluded that the books of Chronicles, Ruth, Ezra, Nehemiah, Esther, and the Song of Solomon must be rejected; that Joshua, Judges, the books of Samuel, Kings, and Daniel, are doubtful at best; that the Proverbs of Solomon may be *his* or the joint production of a number of tolerably gifted men; and that the Pentateuch, and especially Genesis, is a mere collection of legendary fragments. The New Testament has some good qualities, which are wanting in the Old; but there are parts of it positively injurious to the church. The Apocalypse of John, for example, can only be held by every calm critic as the work of a wild fanatic. As to the gospels, their authenticity and integrity are very doubtful, and that of John is the only one in any wise adapted to the present state of the world; since he alone is free from the Jewish spirit.

The general epistles were written solely for the unification of the struggling parties into which the early church had unfortunately split.

We now come to the famous *Accommodation-Theory.* Christ and his apostles taught doctrines of such nature and by such method as were compatible with the peculiarities of their condition. They adapted themselves to the barbarism and coëxistent prejudices of the people; and hence we can only reconcile much that they taught by their disposition to cater to the corrupt taste of their time. The Jews already possessed many notions which it would not be policy in Christ to annihilate; hence, said Semler, he reclothed them, and gave them a slight admixture of truth. Thus he reduced Christ's utterances concerning angels, the second coming of the Messiah, the last Judgment, demons, resurrection of the dead, and inspiration of the Scripture, to so many *accommodations* to prevailing errors. Semler had some indistinct faith in these revealed truths, but the stress which Christ laid upon them was, in his opinion, a mere stroke of policy. This theory he had been maturing for some time, and he first made it public in the preface to his *Paraphrase of the Epistle to the Romans.*

Another distinction which Semler drew in connection with his new method of criticism, and somewhat allied to the details of his accommodation-theory, was between the local and temporary, the permanent and eternal, in the Scriptures. A large portion of the Bible, he held, is only ephemeral, and was never intended to be anything else. There was a local interest in the accounts of the writers; but after the change of government, or the lapse of a generation or two, they had no further application to mankind. Nor do they now meet the wants of the world; they are only the obsolete machinery of a superseded civilization. Semler bitterly complained of Ernesti by charging him with failing to fix the time and locality of the circumstances of the Scriptures. A few specimens will show how the latter strove to meet the great want. The coming of our Lord Jesus, 1 Cor. i. 7, is only the dawn of a temporal kingdom; "Christ is a stumbling-block to the Jews," because he would not throw off the Roman yoke as his countrymen had fondly hoped; the Apostle's determination "to know nothing but Jesus Christ crucified," meant that he knew nothing whatever of the second coming of Christ; "the Spirit searching the deep things of God" leads us to know that we can understand the dark things of the Prophets; "the creature which is made subject to vanity" is the Roman world still pursuing its idolatry; the demoniacs are mad men whom it was only necessary to bind in order to render perfectly harmless. With such a system of interpretation as this, no one who adopted it could pretend to assign for himself a limit to his skepticism. Whatever defied the critic's acumen or the believer's spiritual grasp was unraveled on the principle that it was local and temporary. Surely Rationalism was making a bold stroke for supremacy, and it had the rare fortune of possessing a man of Semler's versatile taste and boldness of utterance.

In one aspect he came into harmony with the English Deists, though his praise of them was extremely moderate. He maintained that they had done more good than harm; but it was only the best of them whom he really admired. He silently repudiated the volatile French school, the learned Bayle being the only one of the number whom he mentioned with any degree of satisfaction. The view by which he came into nearest relation to the free-thinkers of England was, that the Bible is but the republication of the religion of nature. He held that the world had been taught religion long before the Scriptures were written; though he confessed that in them we find it more clearly stated and more rigidly enjoined than anywhere else. Among the mass of natural teachings in the Bible we occasionally come across a modicum of eternal truth; but the seeker is very seldom rewarded with a real gem of permanent value. The Jews were grossly ignorant of all important spiritual light. Their chief idea of Jehovah was that he was their national God; and their religion was purely one of circumstances and ceremonies. Moses had some idea of the soul's immortality, but his countrymen were not so highly favored as himself. The Messiah of the Old Testament was a very vague personage; and indistinct indeed must have been the Jewish idea of a coming Redeemer.

But it was not here that Semler won his greatest victories. His chief triumph was against the history and doctrinal authority of the church. His mind had been thoroughly imbued with a disgust at what was ancient and revered. He appeared to despise the antiquities of the church simply because they were antiquities. What was new and fresh, was, with him, worthy of unbounded admiration and speedy adoption. His prejudice against the Fathers may have been imbibed in part from the Reformers; but, however derived, his distaste and censure knew no bounds. All the early Christian writers, he believed, were brimful of imperfections. Tertullian was fanciful, and Augustine captious. Sc persistent were his efforts against the traditional authority of the church that they endangered the very foundations of German Protestantism. One would have thought him at times exhausted of strength; but no sooner did the thinking public recover from one surprise than it was startled by another attack. The church reeled beneath his invasion of her doctrinal and historical authority. But there was a limit to her patience. To call those heroic standard-bearers of her early faith fanatics and visionaries was quite too much for her to endure.

It now remained to be seen whether Semler's boldness would overleap itself, or prove the ruin of the religious spirit of the Continent for generations. The result, whatever it might be, was soon to be decided. For such views as he was propagating throughout the Protestant church of Germany could not fail to determine speedily the drift of the public sentiment of his day.

His work, though destructive, was in conflict with the pure beauty of his private life. And here we look at him as one of the enigmas of human biography. True to his tenet that a man's public teachings need not influence his personal living, he was at once a teacher of skepticism and an example of piety. His Moravian origin and Pietistic training he could never forget; nor do we believe he attempted it. No doubt the asperity that he witnessed at Halle did much to repel him from the harsher side of Pietism. When he heard his room-mate praying aloud three hours a day upon his knees; and when he was advised to lay aside all extensive studies, because he would never be converted while pursuing them, he began to question whether intellectual progress were compatible with deep piety. The conclusion at which he arrived was against the intellectuality of the creed of Spener, but in favor of the spiritual purity of the life of his disciples. Through Semler's entire career we can find traces of that devoted spirit which had shined so brightly in his early youth, and which, in late life, he was not ashamed to confess. "There was no corner in the whole house," said he, "where I did not kneel, and pray, and weep alone that God might, out of his infinite mercy, pardon my sins. I felt that I was under the bondage of the law. Moravian songs seemed to be of very little help to me. I examined myself carefully to see whether or not I clung to any sin either consciously or ignorantly. I reproached myself several times for only giving one penny to the poor-collection when I had several pence in my pocket. My father would give me more the next time to make up my deficiency, and this was a great delight to me. It is now one of the pleasantest memories of my university-life that I used to give pieces of money to the poor."

His domestic life was very beautiful. He did not remain alone in his study, where most literary men love to be. But wherever his children were playing, or his wife knitting or spinning, he was most happy to pursue his studies and write his books. He gives the following picture: "We had the children continually about us, when they were not under the care of their teachers. Then we would have them read, or in turn sing a Psalm or a hymn, or learn some passage from a good book. We sang with them, and asked them questions in what they had been studying. They knew Gellert's songs by rote. There was nothing but peace and contentment in our circle. The servants never saw or heard anything unpleasant. Every little disturbance was hushed at once; and all the family felt the power of my wife in our household arrangements; and our reciprocal love was apparent to every one. I put all the money matters into her hands; she paid the debts and received the revenue. Thus passed on twenty years of beautiful uniformity; and parents and children felt that we were dearer to each other than was all the world besides. We all met faithfully our duties to each other. But little had then been written on domestic training, yet we created our ideas from the pure fountain of religion; and though we were deprived of much of the glitter of human life, we enjoyed its necessities and its beauty."

When such ties unite a family we are not surprised at the spirit with which death is met by a carefully nurtured child. The account is from Semler's own pen. His daughter, then twenty-one years of age, was on her death-bed, hastening to join her mother, who but shortly before had been borne from the threshold. "About nine o'clock," wrote the bereaved father, "I again pronounced the benediction upon her. With a breaking heart I lay down to sleep a little. She sent for me, and addressed me thus: 'Pardon me, my dear father, I am so needy; and do help me to die with that faith and determination which your Christian daughter should possess.' My heart took courage, and I spoke to her of the glories of the heavenly world which would soon break upon her. She sang snatches of sweet songs, following which I said but little. When I addressed her, 'My dear daughter, you will soon rejoin your noble mother,' she answered, 'Oh, yes, and what rapture will I enjoy!' I fell down at her bedside, and again committed her soul to the almighty and enduring care of God. Then just before I went to my lecture I went to see her again: I asked her if she still remembered the hymn, 'Thou art mine, because I hold thee;' when she said, 'Oh yes,' and repeated the verse, 'O Lord my refuge, Fountain of my Joys.' 'Yes, eternal,' I added.

I left her, thinking that she might last considerably longer. But I was suddenly called from my lecture, when I again committed her grand spirit to God who gave it, and closed her eyes myself. My bitter grief now subsided into calm affliction, and a sweet acquiescence with the wise will of God. Now I know what the real joy is of having seen a child die so calmly, and of feeling that I had some share in the training that could end so triumphantly. And I still publicly thank those of her teachers who have contributed to the formation of her character. Therefore, when some would in our days advocate an unchristian education, I can speak with the light of experience, when I earnestly recommend to all pious and provident parents to give their children a good Christian training. Thus Christian-like and beautifully have Christian-trained people been dying these many centuries."

It is astonishing that a man could live as purely and devotedly as Semler, and yet make the gulf so wide between private faith and public instruction. We attribute no evil intention to him in his theological labors; these were the result of his own mental defects. He was a careless writer, and not a close thinker. He read history loosely, and the philosophy of the Christian system was unperceived and unappreciated by him. He looked at single defects, and magnified them to such an extent that they obscured whole mines of truth and virtue. Having conceived a vague idea of his theme, he wrote hurriedly upon it. He was impelled by his previous notions and the excitement of the hour. He had a very retentive memory, but it was no aid to correct reasoning. When he saw one evil of the Fathers, a mistake of the church, or a defect in her doctrine, he generalized it until he believed error to be the rule instead of the exception. It has been said that, toward the close of his life, he regretted his theological instructions; but in a conversation two days before his death he betrayed the same skeptical views that had distinguished his life. His method of skeptical-historical criticism was the poison which, having been once introduced into the literature and pulpits of the church, produced wide-spread and long-seated disease.

Semler was not the founder of a school, for he advanced no elaborate system and possessed no organizing power. Great as were the results of his labors, no one was more surprised at them than himself. Two or three immediate disciples, who had heard him lecture, were enamored of his theories, but as they were men of moderate capacity their activity produced no permanent effect upon the public mind. It was in another respect that he was mighty. Some of his contemporaries who taught in other universities seized upon his tenets and began to propagate them vigorously. They made great capital out of them for themselves. Semler invaded and overthrew what was left of the popular faith in inspiration after the labors of Wolf, but here he stopped. His adherents and imitators commenced with his abnegation of inspiration, and made it the preparatory step for their attempted annihilation of revelation itself. Soon the theological press teemed with blasphemous publications against the Scriptures; and men of all the schools of learning gave themselves to the work of instruction. Göttingen, Jena, Helmstedt, and Frankfort-on-the-Oder were no longer schools of prophets, but of Rationalists and Illuminists.

Griesbach pursued his skeptical investigations for the establishment of natural religion and others aided him in his undertaking. But the men of this class were not the principal agents of the complete ruin of the religious vitality of the people. We turn to Edelmann and Bahrdt, two of the most decided enemies of Christianity who have appeared in these later centuries.

The former was the better man, but his career brought discredit on private virtue and public morality. In the early part of his life he was blameless, but he subsequently betrayed all the personal weakness which his skepticism tended to engender. We get a fair portrait of him from the pen of one of his countrymen, Kahnis: "What Edelmann wished was nothing new," writes this author; "after the manner of all adherents of Illuminism, he wished to reduce all positive religions to natural religion. The positive heathenish religions stand, to him, on a level with Judaism and Christianity. He is more just toward heathenism than toward Judaism, and more just toward Judaism than toward Christianity. Everything positive in religion is, as such, superstition. Christ was a mere man, whose chief merit consists in the struggle against superstition. What he taught, and what he was anxious for, no one, however, may attempt to learn from the New Testament writings, inasmuch as these were forged as late as the time of Constantine. All which the church teaches of his divinity, of his merits, of the gracious influence of the Holy Spirit, is absurd. There is no rule of truth but reason, and it manifests its truths directly by a peculiar sense. Whatever this sense says is true. It is this sense which perceives the world. The reality of everything which exists is God. In the proper sense there can, therefore, not exist any atheist, because every one who admits the reality of the world admits also the reality of God. God is not a person—least of all are there three persons in God. If God be the substance in all the phenomena, then it follows of itself that God cannot be thought of without the world, and hence that the world has no more had an origin than it will have an end. One may call the world the body of God, the shadow of God, the son of God. The spirit of God is in all that exists. It is ridiculous to ascribe inspiration to special persons only; every one ought to be a Christ, a prophet, an inspired man. The human spirit, being a breath of God, does not perish; our spirit, separated from its body by death, enters into a connection with some other body. Thus Edelmann taught a kind of metempsychosis. What he taught had been thoroughly and ingeniously said in France and England; but from a German theologian, and that with such eloquent coarseness, with such a mastery in expatiating in blasphemy, such things were unheard of. But as yet the faith of the church was a power in Germany!"

From Edelmann the transition is easy to the reckless and vicious Bahrdt. This man stands among the first of those who have brought dishonor upon the sacred vocation. What Jeffreys is to the judicial history of England, Bahrdt is to the religious history of German Protestantism. Whatever he touched was disgraced by the vileness of his heart and the satanic daring of his mind. He heard theological lectures. Thinking that in this field he could infuse most venom and reap a greater harvest of gold than in any other, he stripped for the undertaking. While a mere youth he gained, by his tricky management, a professor's chair. He blasphemed to his auditors by day, while at night he surrendered himself to the corruptions of the gambling-room, the beer-cellar and the house of prostitution. The slave of passion and of doubt, he was, of all his contemporaries, the most loud-spoken against the claims of God's truth, and adherence to the canons of the church. His mind was quick, active, and penetrating. Seizing the pen, he invaded the sanctity of every doctrine that stood in the way of his corrupt theories. He took up the Bible with sacrilegious purpose, and made it the plaything of his vicious heart. He sneered at what was revered by the church and the good men of past ages, with the kind of levity that should greet the recital of the stories of *Sinbad the Sailor* and the *Wonderful Lamp*.

He published many works, the aim of all being to infuse into the masses a contempt of the received Scriptures. He issued a travesty of the New Testament under the title of *The New Testament*, or *The Newest Instructions from God through Jesus and his Apostles*. He did just what he pleased with the miracles and words of Christ. He would convert dialogue into parable, and make any passage, however grave in import, minister to his unsanctified purpose. He banished such expressions as 'kingdom of God,' 'holiness,' 'sanctification,' 'Saviour,' 'Redeemer,' 'way of salvation,' 'Holy Ghost,' 'name of Jesus,' and all other terms that could leave the impression of inspiration and divine presence.

But corrupt as the church was, it was not ready for this fearful leap; therefore Bahrdt received a torrent of abuse. Banished and hunted by opposition, he gained many adherents from the force of the very arrows discharged against him. He had fallen from the height of faith which he occupied when he went to Giessen, a fact which he refers to in his autobiography: "I came to Giessen," says he, "as yet very orthodox. My belief in the divinity of the Scriptures, in the direct mission of Jesus, in his miraculous history, in the Trinity, in the gifts of grace, in natural corruption, in justification of the sinner by laying hold of the merits of Christ, and especially in the whole theory of satisfaction, seemed to be immovable. It was only the manner in which three persons were to be in one God, which had engaged my reason. I had only explained to myself a little better the work of the Holy Spirit, so as not to exclude man's activity. I had limited a little the idea of original sin; and in the doctrine of the atonement and justification, I had endeavored to uphold the value of virtue, and had cleared myself from the error that God, in his grace, should not pay any regard at all to human virtuous zeal. That in the doctrine of the Lord's Supper I was more Reformed than Lutheran, will be supposed as a matter of course."

But in due time he dropped these points of belief, one by one, until he indulged in all the illicit extravagances of the radical skeptics of France. The opposition he met with was a sore rebuke, but it failed to cure him. He set out for a journey to England and Holland with but three florins in his purse, and he suffered much by the way. He came home again only to find new edicts against him. On arriving at Halle, where he had once been honored, he was met with the following repulse from the faculty, at whose head stood Semler, the father of his doubt: "Our vocation demands not only that we should prevent the dissemination of directly irreligious opinions, but also that we should watch over the doctrines which are contained in Holy Scripture, and, in conformity with it, in the *Augsburg Confession of Faith*."

He labored as an educator, preacher, professor, and author. He made all his enterprises subservient to the dearest object of his life,—money. He wrote plain books for the masses, and his writings were perused alike in palace and cottage. While a resident in Halle he established an inn in the suburbs of the city where his depraved nature was permitted to indulge in those nameless liberties unbecoming, not only the theologian, but the rational man. His *liaison* with the servant-girl in his employ made his wife an object of public pity, and we can easily understand his injustice to the latter when he tells us himself that he had never loved with passion. His death was of a piece with his life. Having been a public frequenter of brothels and the associate of the loosest company, he died like the libertine. He was taken off by syphilis.

It is not necessary to enlarge upon the lesson of Bahrdt's life. He was the German crystallization of all the worst elements of French skepticism. He began his work with an evil purpose, and never sought the wisdom of God who promises to give liberally to all who ask him. The infamy of his life was soon forgotten, and only his teachings remained to corrupt the young and injure the mature of the land. While his love of money controlled his matrimonial alliances and literary labors, his hatred of revealed religion distorted his whole moral and intellectual nature. He is illustrative of the certain doom which awaits the man who commits himself to the sole guidance of his doubts. Semler's moral life was *in spite* of erroneous opinions; Bahrdt's was in *conformity* with them. And what the latter was in his career and death is the best comment that can be written on the natural effect of Rationalism. Would that he had been the only warning; but he had his followers when his creed became the fashion of the German church. The depth of his infamy is only aggravated by the holy sphere in which he wrought fearful havoc upon the succeeding generation. The Old Play says truly:

> "That sin does ten times aggravate itself,
> That is committed in an holy place;
> An evil deed done by authority
> Is sin and subornation; deck an ape
> In tissue, and the beauty of the robe
> Adds but the greater scorn unto the beast;
> The poison shows worst in a golden cup;
> Dark night seems darker by the lightning's flash;
> Lilies that fester smell far worse than weeds;
> And every glory that inclines to sin,
> The shame is trebled by the opposite."

CHAPTER VI.

CONTRIBUTIONS OF LITERATURE AND PHILOSOPHY.

THE views of Semler, possessing great power of fascination, soon gained popular strength. As a result, the strictly literary tastes of the people took a theological turn and the Bible became the theme of every aspirant to authorship. As no system had yet been advanced by the Rationalists, there was wide range for doctrinal and exegetical discussion. The devoted Pietists, who were now in the background, looked on in amazement as they trembled for the pillars of faith. They knew not what to do. Many of their number had proved themselves fanatics and brought odium upon the revered names of Spener and Francke. Their enemies were traveling in foreign lands, ransacking the libraries of other tongues to bring home the poisonous seeds of doubt. At home, the University was the training school of ungoverned criticism. History, science, literature, and philology were only prized according to the measure of strength they possessed to combat the great claims of the orthodox church. Besides, the Rationalists seemed to be impartial inquirers. They set themselves to understand the Scriptural lands and languages, while their progress in recent Biblical literature gained for them the respect of many who, though less learned, were more evangelical. The masses have always paid homage to learning, and in this case, it was the attainments of the Illuminists which gave them a standing denied to the friends of the Bible.

The times were all astir with the evidences of mental progression. There was now a resurrection of European activity. Look whither you will, there was nowhere either the spirit of sleep or of sloth. The science of government, the beauties of æsthetic culture, the discoveries of the material world, and the long-sealed mysteries of philology, were each the centre of a host of admirers and votaries. As in the fourteenth and fifteenth centuries Europe arose from the torpidity of the Middle Ages, so did the eighteenth century witness a new revival from the darkness and sluggishness of Continental Protestantism. There appeared to be a universal repudiation of old methods, and a new civilization was now the aim of every class of literary adventurers. Semler had struck the key-note of human pride. He had so flattered his race by saying that the Bible was not so sacred as to be exempt from criticism, that his contemporaries would not willingly let his words fall to the ground. The temptation was too strong to be resisted, and soon the Scriptures became a carcass around which the vultures of Germany gathered to satisfy the cravings of their wanton hunger. We do not say that the destructionists desired to injure the faith of the people, or to cast odium upon the pages that Luther and Melanchthon had unfolded to the German heart. But believing as they did that the popular respect for the Bible was sheer Bibliolatry, and that therefore the dignity of reason was compromised, they bestirred themselves to show every weak point in the faith of the church. They hastened to expose the defects of the Scriptures with as much frankness as they would brand a sentence in Cicero or Seneca to be the interpolation of an impostor.

In no nation has theology, as a science, absorbed more literary talent and labor than in Germany. In America and Great Britain the theologian is the patron of his own department of thought. But in Germany, poets, romancists, and scientific men write almost as many works connected with religious questions as on topics within their own chosen vocation. The Teuton considers himself a born theologian. So it was after the announcement of the destructive theories of Semler. All classes of thinkers invited themselves to discuss the Scriptures and their claims with as much freedom as if God had told them it was the true aim of their life.

What was the consequence? Semler, having left so much room for doubt, and having rather indicated a direction than supplied a plan, a great number of men adopted the accommodation-theory and each one built his own edifice upon it. But the conclusions arrived at by them were very unlike, and generally incongruous. And such a result was very natural; for, all claiming the unrestricted use of reason, the issue of their thinking was the work of the individual mind. No two intellects are perfectly similar. Set a number of men to write upon a given subject and they will employ a different style, give expression to diverse thoughts, and perhaps reach antipodal conclusions. So when these writers against inspiration plied the pen, and burdened the press with their prolix effusions, there was no harmony in their thoughts. In one opinion they were firmly united, *that the Bible is a human book.* But how much of it was authentic; what was history and what myth; what poetry and what incident; these and a thousand kindred points divided the Rationalists into almost as many classes as there were individuals.

There were two principal tendencies which gave a permanence and efficiency to Rationalism quite beyond the expectation of its most sanguine friends and admirers. One was *literary*, and inaugurated by Lessing; the other purely *philosophical*, and conducted by Kant.

The literary despotism at Berlin was one of the most remarkable in the annals of periodical literature. We refer to the *Universal German Library*, under the control of Nicolai. Its avowed aim was to laud every Rationalistic book to the skies, but to reproach every evangelical publication as unworthy the support, or even the notice, of rational beings. Its appliances for gaining knowledge were extensive, and it commanded a survey of the literature of England, Holland, France, and Italy. Whatever appeared in these lands received its immediate attention, and was reproached or magnified according to its relations to the skeptical creed of Nicolai and his co-laborers. Commencing in 1765, it ran a career of power and prosperity such as but few serials have ever enjoyed. It terminated its existence in 1792, having inflicted incalculable evil upon the popular estimate of the vital doctrines of Christianity. Being the great organ of the Rationalists, it sat in judgment upon the sublime truths of our holy faith. With all the rage of an infuriated lion it pounced upon every literary production or practical movement that had a tendency to restore the old landmarks. Its influence was felt throughout Germany and the Continent. Every university and gymnasium listened to it as an oracle, while its power was felt even in the pot-houses and humblest cottages. Berlin was completely under its sway, and *Berliner* was a synonym of *Rationalist*. Oetinger wrote a curious passage in a volume of sermons, published in 1777, in which he descants *On those things of which the people of Berlin know nothing*: "They know nothing of the Lord of glory; they are sick of these shallow-pated Liebnitzians; they wish to know nothing of the promises of God; they have nothing to do with the salutations of the seven spirits; they form a mechanical divinity after their own notion. The Berliners know nothing of man so far as he is a subject of divine grace; nothing of angels or devils, nothing of what sin is, nothing of eating and drinking the flesh and blood of Christ, and still less of the communion of saints, and that the spirit can be communicated by the laying on of hands. They know nothing of the truth that baptism and the Lord's Supper are agents for a spiritual union with Christ; they know nothing of heaven and hell; nothing of the interval before the resurrection. Neither do they wish to know anything save what may harmonize with their own depraved views. But the time will come when Jesus will show them how they should have confessed him before the world." This was Berlin, and Berlin was Germany.

The position of Rationalism during the last quarter of the eighteenth century was surrounded with circumstances of the most conflicting nature. Had it been advocated by a few more such ribald characters as Bahrdt its career would soon have been terminated from the mere want of respectability. But had it assumed a more serious phase and become the protegé of such pious men as Semler was at heart, there would have been no limit to the damage it might inflict upon the cause of Protestantism. And there were indications favorable to either result. However, by some plan of fiendish malice, skepticism received all the support it could ask from the learned, the powerful, and the ambitious. Here and there around the horizon could be seen some rising literary star that, for the hour, excited universal attention. His labor was to impugn the contents of the Scriptures and insinuate against the moral purity of the writers themselves. Another candidate for theological glory appeared, and reproached the style of the inspired record. A third came vauntingly forward with his geographical discoveries and scientific data, and reared the accommodation-theory so many more stories higher than Semler had left it that it almost threatened to fall of its own weight. Strange that the poetic Muse should lend her inspiration to such unholy purposes; but in the poetry of that day there was but little of the Christian element, and he need not be greatly skilled in classic verse who concludes that the loftiest poetry of Rationalism was as thoroughly heathen as the dramas of Euripides or Plautus.

Immediately before the appearance of the *Wolfenbüttel Fragments* by Lessing, there was the significant lull before the storm. A single editorial in some religious periodical might decide the fate of Rationalism. In a few years more it might lie outside the lecture-halls and renowned churches as thoroughly discarded as a cast-off garment. Or it might rise to new power and bend all opposition before it. Every one seemed to be waiting to see what would come next. Would it be the hoarse thunder and the glare of lightning; or would the clouds be rent and the clear sky be seen through the widening rifts?

Lessing touched a chord which vibrated throughout the land. While in charge of the celebrated Library at

Wolfenbüttel he met with a manuscript production of Reimarus, bearing the title of *Vindication of the Rational Worshipers of God.* It can still be found in the Town Library of Hamburg. Between 1774 and 1778, Lessing issued seven *Fragments* from this work; and the result was, that Germany was electrified by the boldness and importance of the views there advanced. They cannot be considered the private opinions of Lessing, for in many places he appends notes stating his opposition to them. But he heartily approved the substance of the work, though his object in the publication of the *Fragments* was more to feel the public pulse than to instill theological doctrines into the minds of the people. Reimarus had been a doubter like many others of his countrymen. He committed his mental phases to paper, though he thought that it was not yet time to issue them for public notice. The *Fragments* published by Lessing contain the gist of his entire work, and contributed far more to the growth of skepticism than a larger production would probably have done. The historical evidences of Christianity and of the doctrine of inspiration, according to the *Fragments*, are clad in such a garb of superstition that they do not merit the credence of sensible men. The confessions framed at different periods of the history of the church have savored far more of human weakness than of divine knowledge. They bear but slight traces of Biblical truth. The Trinity is incomprehensible, and the heart should not feel bound to lean upon what Reason cannot fathom. Nearly all the Old Testament history is a string of legends and myths which an advanced age should indignantly reject. Christ never really intended to establish a permanent religion; the work of his apostles was something unanticipated by himself. His design was to restore Judaism to its former state, throw off the Roman yoke, and declare himself king. His public entry into Jerusalem was designed to be his installation as a temporal king; but he failed in his dependence upon popular support, and, instead of attaining a throne, he died on the cross. Belief in Scriptural records is perfectly natural to the Christian, for he has imbibed it from education and training. Reason is forestalled in the ordinary education of children; they are baptized before they are old enough to exercise their own reasoning faculties. Faith in Scripture testimony is really of no greater value than the belief of the Mohammedan or Jew in their oracles, unless Reason be permitted to occupy the seat of judgment.

We have said that the excitement raised by the publication of the *Fragments* was intense. There was in them more calmness of expression, and more apparent effort for truthful conclusions than many of the previously published works of the Rationalists had indicated. By and by, there sprang up a decided opposition to the work of Lessing; and from all quarters of the German church there came earnest and vigorous replies. It was surprising that there remained so much tenacity for the old faith. Lessing received the censure of many of the best and wisest men of his time; his publication of the *Fragments* was claimed to be a curse to the cause of truth. But he had accomplished what he wished, while his success was far beyond his expectation. He found that a large portion of his countrymen were not willing to cast loose from the old moorings of the Protestant teachings, and that, whatever the previous indications were, there was yet a deep undercurrent of attachment to the time-honored confessions of the church.

The movement employed by Lessing to find out what the people really believed is one of the shrewdest literary tricks on record. Without committing himself to what he issued, and watching carefully the effect of the *Fragments*, he began to publish his own views with no little assurance that he would prove successful. He learned that the Wolfian philosophy was becoming effete, and so he raised the cry, loud and clear, against its longer existence. He violently opposed the obliteration of all dependence upon the historical proofs of Christianity, and claimed that, in the matter of religion, the heart has a work not less than the reason. His principle was: overthrow this historical basis, and you endanger the whole edifice. He inflicted great injury upon the inflated, pompous Popular Philosophy, for he exposed its emptiness as but few were able to do. He opposed, with all the force of his rare satirical and logical power, the attempt of the Rationalists to substitute the intuitons of Reason for the dictates of the heart and for the promptings of faith. "What else," he asks, "is this modern theology when compared with orthodoxy, than filthy water with clear water? With orthodoxy we had, thanks to God, pretty much settled; between it and philosophy a barrier had been erected, behind which each of these could walk in its own way without molesting the other. But what is it that they are now doing? They pull down this barrier, and, under the pretext of making us *rational Christians*, they make us most *irrational philosophers*. In this we agree that our old religious system is false, but I should not like to say with you [he is writing to his brother] that it is a patch-work, got up by jugglers and semi-philosophers. I do not know of anything in the world in which human ingenuity had more shown and exer cised itself than in it. A patch-work by jugglers and semi-philosophers is that religious system which they would put in the place of the old one, and, in doing so, would pretend to more rational philosophy than the old one claims."

It was difficult to tell what Lessing believed. His publication of the views of a doubter was of itself a proof that he agreed, to some extent at least, with them. This we must grant as a concession to his honesty and common sense. And when assailed by Götze and others for thus attacking the faith of the church, he replied that, even if the Fragmentists were right, Christianity was not thereby endangered.[1] He rejected the letter, but reserved the spirit of the Scriptures. With him, the letter is not the spirit and the Bible is not religion. Consequently, objections against the letter, as well as against the Bible, are not precisely objections against the spirit and religion. For the Bible evidently contains more than belongs to religion, and it is a mere supposition, that, in this additional matter which it contains, it must be equally infallible. Moreover, religion existed before there was a Bible. Christianity existed before evangelists and apostles had written. However much, therefore, may depend upon those Scriptures, it is not possible that the whole truth of the Christian religion should depend upon them. Since there existed a period in which it was so far spread, in which it had already taken hold of so many souls, and in which, nevertheless, not one letter was written of that which has come down to us, it must be possible also that everything which evangelists and prophets have written might be lost again, and yet the religion taught by them, stand. The Christian religion is not

[1] Kahnis: *History of German Protestantism*, pp. 145–165.

true because Evangelists and apostles taught it; *but they taught it because it was true.* It is from their internal truth that all written documents must be explained, and all these written documents cannot give it internal truth when it has none. The Christian religion is distinguished from the religion of Christ; the latter, being a life immediately implanted and maintained in our heart, manifests itself in love, and can neither stand nor fall with the Gospel. The truths of religion have nothing to do with the facts of history.

With such opinions as these, expressed in great clearness and conciseness, who can fail to perceive that their tendency was to overthrow the traditional faith of the church in large portions of the Bible? Who is to be the judge of what is to be retained and what rejected? Indeed, if Lessing be right, the entire Scripture record might be abolished without doing violence to religion. The effect of his writings was decidedly skeptical. His view of Christianity was merely æsthetical, and only so far as the Bible was an agent of popular elevation, did he seem to consider it valuable. He did not dispute the facts of Scripture history because of the various accounts given of them by the inspired writers. Variety of testimony was no ground for the total overthrow of the thing testified. He retained the history of the resurrection in spite of the different versions of it. "Who," he asks, "has ever ventured to draw the same inference in profane history? If Livy, Polybius, Dionysius, and Tacitus relate the very same event, it may be the very same battle, the very same siege, each one differing so much in the details that those of the one completely give the lie to those of the other, has any one, for that reason, ever denied the event itself in which they agree?"

We may examine the entire circle of Lessing's literary productions, and we shall see, scattered here and there through them, sentiments which, taken singly, would have a very beneficial effect upon the popular faith in inspiration and the historical testimony of the Scriptures. But, unhappily, these were overshadowed by others of a conflicting nature, and though he did not array himself as a champion of Rationalism, he proved himself one of the strongest promoters of its reign. He considered his age torpid and sluggish. It was his desire to awaken it. And he did succeed in giving to the chaotic times in which he lived that literary direction which we now look back upon as the starting-point of recent German literature. The chief evil that he inflicted was due to the position in which he placed himself as the combatant of the avowed friends of inspiration. He was honest in his love of truth, but he loved the search for it more than the attainment. The key to his whole life may be found in his own words: "If God should hold in his right hand all truth, and in his left the ever-active impulse and love of search after truth, although accompanied with the condition that I should ever err, and should say, 'Choose!' I would choose the left with humility, and say, 'Give, Father! Pure truth belongs to thee alone!'"

The revolution which Lessing wrought in literature was only equaled by that achieved by Kant in the domain of philosophy.

It has been one of the historical features of German theology that it has ever affiliated with philosophy. The mathematical method of Wolf has been a severe blow to orthodoxy, and it was but partially counteracted by the work of Pietism. But the influence of that copyist of Leibnitz is only of a piece with the impression made upon theology and faith by every respectable innovation in philosophy. But Kant threw all others in the shade. He was the agent of a change in philosophical thinking, which was destined not only to reform the old systems of Germany, but to wield a universal power over modern thought. He had looked to England for his masters, and succeeded in gaining a thorough acquaintance with the grave skepticism of Hume and kindred minds. He shut himself up in his native Königsberg, and, in all his life, never traveled more than thirty miles therefrom. He had the memory of a pious Christian mother ever present to him, and no one can conjecture the probable influence that her example exerted upon his mental processes. The astute philosopher wrote of her with the deepest feeling of his nature when he said, "My mother was an amiable, sensitive, pious, and devoted woman, who taught her children the fear of God by her godly teachings and spotless life. She often led me outside the city, and showed me the works of God; she pointed me with devout feelings to the omnipotence, wisdom, and goodness of God; and inspired my heart with a deep reverence for the Creator of all things. I shall never forget my mother, for it was she who planted and strengthened my first germ of goodness; she opened my heart to the impressions of nature; she awakened and advanced my conceptions; and it has been her instructions that have exerted a permanent and wholesome influence upon my life."

First an undergraduate and afterward a professor in the University of Königsberg, Kant quietly matured his principles, and was in no haste to communicate them to the world. He delivered his philosophy to his students in the form of lectures, and was extremely careful not to publish it until he was sure that his mind had arrived at its final conclusions. A student named Hippel, who had enjoyed his intimacy, was the first to give publicity to his opinions. He employed the medium of a novel. He forestalled their real author, and Kant was compelled to explain the matter openly as a breach of faith. Gradually the lecture-hall at Königsberg became full of hearers, who, in a little time, could gain admittance only with difficulty. The professor of philosophy was a magnet that drew to that bleak northern city students from all parts of the Continent. Finally the opportune moment arrived. Having written, rewritten, altered, and abridged until he looked upon his work as beyond his power of improvement, he now deemed his convictions permanently formed. So the *Critique of Pure Reason* entered upon its career of victory. The literary and thinking world had learned but a little of it in Hippel's book; and now there seemed to be no inclination to probe the concise language of the master's work, for the task appeared greater than the fruits would justify. This hesitancy was a glaring testimony to the loose thinking and careless literary habits of those days. But the haste with which Kant prosecuted the authorship of his work, apart from the thoughts employed in its elaboration into a system, furnishes some ground of apology for the failure of the public to fathom it. "I wrote," he says in a letter to Moses Mendelssohn, "this product of at least twelve years of diligent reflection within a period of from four to five months, paying indeed the greatest attention to the contents, but unable, borne away, as it were, upon the wings of thought, to bestow that care upon the style which might have promoted a readier insight into my meaning on the part of the reader."

Several years now pass by, and the great work is still neglected. Perhaps it is false, or mayhap it is ill-timed. Finally Schulze hits upon the difficulty when he conjectures that, if men only knew what was in the book they would not only read it, but be ravished with its contents. Thereupon he issues his *Elucidations of Kant's Critique of Pure Reason.* Now people begin to open their eyes. The work of Schulze is read by everybody, and in turn it serves as an introduction to the work of Kant. Soon the universities and reading circles demand it, and the whole land is suddenly transformed into a race of philosophers. The popularity of the work is boundless. It is written in a style adapted only to systematic thinkers; but no matter, it becomes a fashion to read it. It is the topic in stage-coaches and drawing rooms. Failure to have perused Kant's book is a mark of ignorance which receives rebuke on every hand. In self-defense every one feels bound to read it, if the continued respect of friends can reasonably be expected. The work itself is interlarded with new terminology and pruned expressions that betray the constant impress of the author's mind. So, in a short time, writers on the various sciences employ these very terms as at once the best vehicle for the conveyance of their thoughts and for accession to popularity. It has its opponents in Hamann, Jacobi, Reimarus, Tiedemann, and others; yet he is a bold spirit who dares to attack this object of universal favor. But the opposition is insufficient, and the *Critique of Pure Reason* is too strong for these hastily-conceived rejoinders. Every department of inquiry is powerfully affected by it. Religion, logic, metaphysics, law, psychology, æsthetics, and education are alike molded by its plastic touch. Holland and all the north of Europe are vocal with its praises.

And now we may ask, why such favor shown toward this new apparition? Let us delay a moment and examine the hard-wrought thoughts of this bachelor-son of an obscure saddler. Kant had been profoundly disgusted with the want of harmony in philosophical speculations. The disagreements that he saw in his own time were but the continuation of what, he had learned from history, was the fact in the days of the heathen sages. Following close upon the footsteps of Hume, he asked: "How far can human reason go? Where is its limit?" His *Critique* was the answer. He showed that, if the loose methods of thought were to be continued, philosophy, instead of being the hand-maid of religion, would be unworthy the attention of the most unlettered man. Hence he would recall reason from its lofty flights, and direct its attention solely to self-consciousness. Only by studying the powers of the mind as a datum, he held, can any positive results be gained. Using his own illustration of his work, he would do for philosophy what Copernicus had done for astronomy—reverse metaphysics by referring classes of ideas to inner, which before had been referred to outer, causes. He granted that, for some things, man's reason is sufficient. The existence of God, the doctrine of original sin, and the soul's immortality need no Scripture to reveal them. They are intuitive subjects of knowledge. But these truths are extremely limited; man needs what nature has not given him. Kant's distinction between practical and speculative reason was in favor of the former, since its aim was wisdom. But speculative reason is often exerted for its own gratification. Hence its results are frequently useless and ephemeral. His grand conclusion is, that no object can be known to us except in proportion as it is apprehended by our perceptions, and definable by our faculties of cognition; consequently we know nothing, *per se*, but only by appearances. Our knowledge of real objects is limited by experience.

With regard to the general character of the critical system of Kant, an acute author says: "It confined itself to a contemplation of the phenomena of consciousness, and attempted to ascertain by analysis, not of our conceptions but of the faculties of the soul, certain invariable and necessary principles of knowledge; proceeding to define their usage, and to form an estimate of them collectively with reference to their *formal* character; in which investigation the distinctions and definitions of those faculties adopted by the school of Wolf were presumed to be valid. It exalted the human mind by making it the centre of its system; but at the same time confined and restricted it by means of the consequences deduced. It discouraged also the spirit of dogmatic speculation, and the ambition of demonstrating all things by means of mere intellectual ideas, making the faculties of acquiring knowledge the measure of things capable of being known, and assigning the preeminence to practical Reason rather than to speculation, in virtue of its end—wisdom; which is the highest that reason can aspire to, because to act virtuously is a universal and unlimited, but to acquire knowledge only a conditional, duty. It had the effect of mitigating the dogmatical and speculative tendencies of the mind, and the extravagant attempt to prove everything by means of conceptions of the understanding. It proscribed mysticism and circumscribed the provinces of science and belief. It taught men to discriminate and appreciate the grounds, the tendency, the defects, and partial views, as well as the excellencies of other systems; at the same time that it embodied a lively principle for awakening and strengthening the interest attaching to genuine philosophical research. It afforded to philosophy a firm and steady centre of action in the unchangeable nature of the human mind. In general it may be observed that the theory of Kant *constructed* little; and rather tended to destroy the structures of an empty dogmatism of the understanding and prepare, by means of self-knowledge, the way for a better state of philosophical science; seeking in reason itself the principles on which to distinguish the several parts of the philosophy."[1]

Kant had but little to say concerning the positive truths of Christianity. He respected the character of Christ, and spoke reverently of the church and her doctrines. Morality, with him, was developed into religion, not religion into morality. The so-called revelation was only the mythical copy of the moral law already implanted in our nature. He believed in a universal religion. Everything peculiar and won by struggle should be given up; all strife of opinions should cease at once. Kant designed, in the main, to curb the illicit exercise of Reason, but his failure to indorse the great doctrines of our faith, because revealed, threw him on the side of the Rationalists. His adoption of God's existence, the soul's immortality, human freedom, and original sin, was not due to his belief in these doctrines as revealed, but as intuitive. He gradually became a devotee to his own method of thinking, and it was his aim not to teach *what* but *how* to think. He often told his students that he had no intention or desire to teach them philosophy, but how to philosophize. It was through Kant that the terms *Rationalist*,—one who

[1] Tennemann, *Manual of History of Philosophy*, pp. 407–408.

declares natural religion alone to be morally necessary, though he may admit revelation,—*Naturalist*—one who denies the reality of a supernatural divine revelation,—and *Supernaturalist*—one who considers the belief in revelation a necessary element in religion, came into use, and Rationalism and Supernaturalism became the principal division of theological schools.[1]

As Descartes had broken up the scholastic philosophy by considering man apart from his experience, so Kant now gave the death-blow to the philosophy of Protestant Germany by looking at the mind apart from its speculations. "The moral effect of his philosophy," says Mr. Farrar, "was to expel the French Materialism and Illuminism, and to give depth to the moral perceptions; its religious effect was to strengthen the appeal to reason and the moral judgment as the test of religious truth; to render miraculous communication of moral instruction useless, if not absurd; and to reäwaken the attempt which had been laid aside since the Wolfian philosophy of endeavoring to find a philosophy of religion."[2]

Among the antagonists of Kant, Jacobi was perhaps the most powerful. He was not content that, in these metaphysical speculations, reason should reign supreme. His belief was that feeling was of as much importance as the deductions of the intellect. He mastered the various systems of philosophy and rejected them, Kant's among the rest, as unfit for the acceptance and pursuit of responsible beings. The two principles which furnish the key to his views were that religion lies in the feeling, and that this feeling, which exists in every man's heart, is not reflected, but original. His dissatis-

[1] Appleton's *Am. Cyclopædia*—Article *German Theology.*

[2] *Critical History of Free Thought*, p. 230.

faction with all systems induced him to term himself the *Unphilosophical*, and it was with utter disgust that he was led to declare the foundation of all speculative philosophy to be only a great cavity, in which we look in vain, as down into an awful abyss. With him, as with Coleridge, Faith begins where Reason ends.

The two bright stars after Kant were Fichte and Schelling. The former commenced with the system of the great Königsberg teacher, and developed it on the negative side, contending that the whole material world has no existence apart from ourselves, and that it only appears to us in conformity with certain laws of our mind. He aimed to found a system which might illustrate, by a single principle, the material and formal properties of all science; establish the unity of plan which the critical system had failed to maintain; and solve that most difficult of all problems regarding the connection between our conceptions and their objects. His views of God are the most glaring defect of his sytsem. He contended that we cannot attribute to the Deity intelligence or personality without making him a finite being like ourselves; that it is a species of profanation to conceive of him as a separate essence, since such a conception implies the existence of a sensible being limited by space and time; that we cannot impute to him even existence without compounding him with sensible natures; that no satisfactory explanation has yet been given of the manner in which the creation of the world could be effected by God; that the idea and expectation of happiness is a delusion; and that, when we form our notions of the Deity in accordance with such imaginations, we only worship the idol of our own passions,—the prince of this world.[1]

[1] Tennemann, *Manual of History of Philosophy*, pp. 429–430.

Schelling was a man of ardent, sanguine temperament, and it was his natural proclivities that gave rise to his system of philosophy. He attributes a real existence to the material as well as to the immaterial world, but permits it a different mode of existence. He makes history a necessity. This natural philosophy conveys to us no knowledge of God, and the little it does reveal appears opposed to religion. What God performs takes place because it *must be.* Schelling created two opposite and parallel philosophic sciences, the transcendental philosophy and the philosophy of nature. He was a pantheist in identifying the Deity with nature, and in making Him subject to laws. He clothed his ideas in the beautiful fancies of his own vivid imagination, and in him we find the poet, not giving forth verses from his lyre, but delivering philosophical oracles.

What Schleiermacher was to theology Hegel became to philosophy. He was the turning-point from doubt and fruitless theories to a more positive and settled system of thinking. He was, when young, a decided Rationalist; and his *Life of Christ*, though yet unpublished, is said by one who has seen it to be a representation of the Messiah as a divine man, in whom all is pure and sublime, and who made himself remarkable chiefly by his triumphs over vice, falsehood, hatred and the servile spirit of his age. He endeavored to explain the reason for Christianity in the world. He longed for a positive religion. His philosophy is reducible to a philosophy of nature, which has quite a different meaning from that of Schelling, for, with Hegel, it is only the expression of the passage to another being; and to the philosophy of the mind, which considers thought reflecting itself on itself, and showing itself by the mind in the sciences of law and morality, in the state, history, religion, and the arts. The religion which is deduced from this system may be said to consist of the objective existence of the infinite mind in the finite, for mind is only for mind; consequently God exists only in being thought of and in thinking. In the philosophy of nature intelligence and God are lost in objective nature. Hegel allows them a distinct and separate existence, but refers them to a common principle which, according to him, is the absolute idea, or God. In this case, objective nature is only the absolute idea going out of itself, individualizing itself, and giving itself limits, though it is infinite. Thus the intelligence of all men, and external nature, are only manifestations of the *absolute idea.* It is a mournful tribute that M. Saintes pays to his memory when he says, as the sum of his labors, that "he perverted all the Christian opinions which he attempted to restore." As little flattering is M. Quinet's testimony, that "he saw in Christianity no more than an idea, the religious worth of which is independent of the testimonies of history."

This was indeed a race of thinkers who have been equaled in strength in but few periods of history. Coming in regular succession, their systems sprang from Kant's philosophy, and constituted the growth of his wonderful achievement. They tended to withdraw the flippant spirit of criticism to a more serious and modest path of inquiry, and to make men look more at their own weakness than at their greatness. But what a mass of subtleties do we have to pass through to get at the substance of their speculations! There is something so unsatisfactory in the study of them, that we find relief only in the knowledge that the Bible contains the true basis of all sound thinking on the great themes connected with the well-being and destiny of man. The plainest statements of the word of God are more valuable than all these vaporings about the non-*Ego*, the *Ideal*, and *Self-hood.* Simplicity is bliss.

> "Yon cottager who weaves at her own door
> Pillow and bobbins, all her little store,
> Content though mean, and cheerful if not gay,
> Shuffling her threads about the live-long day,
> Just earns a scanty pittance, and at night
> Lies down secure, her heart and pocket light;
> She for her humble sphere by nature fit,
> Has little understanding and no wit;
> Receives no praise, but though her lot be such,
> Toilsome and indigent, she renders much;
> Just knows and knows no more, her Bible true;
> And in that charter reads with sparkling eyes
> Her title to a treasure in the skies."

But yet we grant to these men the meed of having meant well, and of reforming the philosophy and literature of their times. The immediate effect of their views was decidedly in favor of Rationalism, because they almost uniformly deny the absolute authority of the Scriptures. They grant too much to reason. While Kant would drive the truant mind back to self-contemplation, he terminates by giving to reason a value and dignity so great that it becomes entitled to decide upon matters of faith. Their theories, spun out at such length and concluding in so little satisfaction, make us rejoice that we have not to depend upon philosophy for guidance in matters of either the intellect or heart. They thought independently of the Bible, and here lies the ground of all failure to obtain positive results in metaphysics. The Scriptures furnish everything noble and real, and when philosophy aims to supply a substitute for them it always labors in vain.

We wonder at the tropic luxuriance of Schelling's thoughts, but we are soon convinced of their little practical purpose when we recall the fact that he considered the revelation of the gospel as no more than one of the accidents of the eternal revelation of God in nature and in history. If Schelling and all these strong minds had commenced their investigations with the word of God as their basis, there is no telling how far they might have ministered to an immediate and thorough revival of faith. But failing to do this, their work has been more doubtful and tardy. It is a very plain fact that the church cannot look to any other than to a Christian philosophy for the conservation or regeneration of her torpid powers. Never has she been thoroughly benefited by the immediate agency of any other system.

There is one way, however, in which speculative philosophy has indirectly proved the aid of religion. It has strengthened and quickened the mental action of the people, and they have through its agency, been able to look with clearer ken upon the truths of Scripture. However, after it has reached the goal of its task, we see so little that is truly valuable and worth preserving, that we are compelled to fall back upon the Christian revelation as our only chart on the troubled sea of metaphysical discussion. When we look at the field opened for thought in the word of God we find it ample and safe. It would be well for every young mind about entering upon the uncertain mazes of philosophical speculation, to ponder deeply over these golden words from Isaac Taylor's *Saturday Evening:* "That portion of Heavenly Wisdom which, under such circumstances, survives and is cherished, will be just the first articles of belief,—the Saving Rudiments of Spiritual Life. Of these the Head of the church himself takes care lest faith should utterly disappear from the earth. But beside the inestimable jewel of elementary knowledge—

the price of which can never be told—does there not rest within the folds of the Inspired Book an inexhaustible store, which the industry of man, piously directed, ought to elicit; but which if men neglect it, the Lord will not force upon their notice? It is this hidden treasure which should animate the ambition of vigorous and devout minds. From such at second hand, the body of the faithful are to receive it, if at all; and if not so obtained for them, and dealt out by their teachers, nothing will be more meager, unfixed, almost infantile, than the faith of Christians."

CHAPTER VII.

THE REIGN OF THE WEIMAR CIRCLE—REVOLUTION IN EDUCATION AND HYMNOLOGY.

THE systems of the great philosophical minds whom we have contemplated were remarkable for their harmony. As we now look back upon them we do not see shapeless and unfitting fragments, but a superstructure of rare symmetry and grace. Jacobi was the leaven of improvement, and it was the mission of that devout man to continue to some extent the habit of respectful regard for God's word among intelligent circles of society. All who were unwilling to become votaries of reason were his careful readers and enthusiastic admirers.

What we thus see developed in philosophy was equally manifest in regard to literature. There arose, as if by the enchanter's wand, a group of literary giants at Weimar, an insignificant town on the outskirts of the Thuringian Forest, who wielded an influence which was destined to be felt in coming ages. Through a combination of circumstances, Weimar became their common home. It grew into a modern Parnassus, and to this day bears the name of the German Athens. Karl August, imitating the example of Augustus Cæsar, gathered around him as numerous and powerful a cluster of literary men as his scanty revenue would allow. He paid but little regard to their theological differences; all that he cared for was their possession of the truly literary spirit. His little principality, of which this was the capital, could not possibly be elevated into either a second or third rate power. All hope of great influence being cut off in this direction, he secured the presence of those chiefs of letters who gave him a name and a power secured to but few in any age. The town of Weimar possesses a calm rustic beauty by which the traveler cannot fail to be impressed. You see only a few traces of architectural taste, but the memory of the departed worthies who once walked the winding streets is now the glory of the place. There, the church where Herder preached now stands; near by, the slab that covers the dust of Wieland; yonder, the humble cottage of Schiller, with the room just as it was when the mute minstrel was borne from it to his home in the earth; across the brook is Goethe's country villa; and back in the grove, the table whereon he wrote. There is a quiet sadness in the whole town, as if nothing were left but the mere recollection of what it once was. How different the picture sixty years ago, when all the literary world looked thither for the last oracle from one of these high-priests of poesy! Book-publishers went there to make proposals for the editorship of magazines, or for some other new literary enterprise. Napoleon himself craved an audience with Goethe, and it is the strongest grudge held by the Germans against the master of their literature that the oppressor of the fatherland was not denied his request. Young men went to Weimar from all parts of Europe to kiss the hand of these great transformers of æsthetic taste. There was not a sovereign within the pale of civilization who did not envy

Karl August's treasures. The story of the literary achievements, of the Platonic friendships, and of the evening entertaiments of Weimar, forms one of the most remarkable chapters in the whole history of letters.

The name of Herder demands our prominent notice because of its intimate connection with the theological movement we have been tracing. He was eminently adapted to his times. Perfectly at home with his generation, he looked upon his contemporaries as brethren, and aroused himself manfully to serve them in every interest. We notice in all his works a careful study to meet the emergency then pressing upon society. We will not say that Herder wrote every work just as it should have been, and that he was evangelical throughout. This he was not, but he was greatly in advance of his predecessors. Amid the labyrinth of philosophical speculations it is interesting and refreshing to meet with an author who, though endowed with the mind of a philosopher, was content to pass for a poet, or even for an essayist. His was a mind of rare versatility. What he was not capable of putting his hand to scarcely deserved the name of study. In philosophy, practical religion, literature, church history, education and exegesis he labored with almost equal success. He was the instrument of God, not to raise each of the crushed elements of Christian power to a lofty vitality, but to contribute to the moderate elevation of nearly every one of them. It might be expected that his later writings would not abound in such hearty tributes to devout religious life as we find so glowingly expressed in his earlier productions. The atmosphere of Weimar favored a perverted growth. The personal acquaintance of the men who surrounded him increased his literary power but did not make his religion more fervent and powerful. His training had been in the old purifying furnace of Pietism. His father had been a rare specimen of that class of devout householders, who, back in the days of Spener and Francke, were the real glory of the German people. Young Herder was accustomed to family worship every day, when the hard duties of temporal life were forgotten by those engaged in singing, in the leisurely reading of the Scriptures, and in prayer. One of the first books that had fallen under his notice was Arndt's "*True Christianity.*" It was this work that inspired him with that respect for religion which never left him in subsequent life.

Herder's creed was the improvement of man. He expressed it in one word, *humanity.* But by this term he meant more than most men conceive in whole volumes. With him, it was that development and elevation of the race for which every true man should labor. We do not come into this life with a perfect humanity; but we have the germ of it, and therefore we should contribute to its growth with unceasing energy. We are born with a divine element within us, and it is for the maturity of this personal gift that all great and good men, such as lawgivers, discoverers, philosophers, poets, artists and every truly noble friend of his race, have striven, in the education of children, by the various institutions designed to foster their individual taste. To beautify humanity is the great problem of humanity. It must be done; man must be elevated by one long and unwearied effort, or he will relax into barbarism. Christianity presents us, in the purest way, with the purest humanity.

Herder was greatly interested in the poetic features of the Bible. His work on *Hebrew Poesy* is full of his warm attachment to the inspired pictures of early oriental life and history. Whatever divested the Scriptures of this eastern glow received his outright indignation. He censured Michaelis for having criticised all the heart out of the time-honored and God-given record. He compared the critical labors of the Rationalists to squeezing a lemon; and the Bible that they would give, he said, "was nothing save a juiceless rind." He totally rejected the scientific reading of the Bible for common purposes; and maintained, with great ardor, that the more simple and human our reading of God's word is, the nearer do we approach God's will. We must make use of our own thoughts, and we must imagine living scenes, with the inspired words as our thought-outlines. The whole policy of the new class of critics, he believed, was a thoroughly mistaken one. Instead of discarding the pictorial Biblical beauties, as they did with a few hasty dashes of the pen, he would elevate them to a loftier status, and lead the rising generation to imbibe their spirit as a useful element for later life. In his opinion, many of the Rationalists had not the keen insight into the marvelous beauty of the Bible which all should possess who would undertake to elucidate its language and doctrines. They were, therefore, not competent to decide upon it. The only proper method of studying the Scriptures for the instruction of others is by the exercise of a fine poetic sentiment. Hence the best poet makes the best exegete. This reminds us of Schiller's idea of historiography. Schiller said that, in his writing of history, he did not intend to feel continually hampered by the sequence of events, but that he would write as his own imagination approved. High above facts would he place æsthetic taste. A beautiful fancy! But heaven be praised that all historians are not Schillers, and that all commentators are not Herders.

From this representation of Herder's tenacity for the records of inspiration, and particularly for the Mosaic accounts, one would be led to infer that his attachment was due solely to his lofty views of the supernatural origin of these revelations. But we cannot think this was the fact. A careful estimate of his underlying sympathies leads us to conclude that he loved the Bible, not because it was inspired, as much as because it was the highest, earliest, and simplest embodiment of poetry,—for it traces out those things in our history which we are most interested in knowing. The poetic beauty of the Scriptures entranced him. Had each chapter of our canon been written in stately prose, Herder would have been one of its coldest admirers. He ransacked the myths and legends of various nations, and dwelt upon the stories of giants and demi-gods with scarcely less enthusiasm than if discoursing on the building of Babel or on the gift of the law on Sinai. Herder disliked the theories of Kant with cordial aversion. Of course the Königsberg sage had nothing in common with the Weimar rhapsodist. Had Herder only given a prominence to his belief in the *fact* of inspiration equally with an admiration of the *method* of it, his service to the cause of practical religion would have been incalculable. Yet, in his views of the person of Christ, he was far in advance of the times. He conceived Christ not as a mere innovating teacher, but as the great centre of faith. His belief in the sufficiency of the atonement stands out in bold contrast with the barren faith of his Weimar associates, who had such lofty ideas of human excellence that they thought man needed only one thing more to complete his perfection,

—his emergence from ignorance into taste and knowledge. But Herder could see an abyss of depravity in the heart along with the germ of excellence. He held that Christ alone was able to annihilate the former and develop the latter. He believed that the first three evangelists gave the human side of Christ's character, and that it was John who revealed his divinity. With these four accounts before us we cannot be at a loss to form a sound opinion on the mission of the Messiah. He came to seek and save the lost. What he accomplished could have been effected by no other agency. Herder's own words are: "Jesus must be looked upon as the first real fountain of purity, freedom, and salvation to the world." Of the Lord's Supper he said, on his entrance upon his pastoral duties at Weimar, "The Lord's Supper should not be a mere word and picture, but a fact and truth. We should taste and see what joys God has prepared for us in Jesus Christ when we have intercourse with him at his own table. In every event and accident of life we should feel that we are his brethren and are sitting at one table, and that, when we refresh ourselves at the festival of our Saviour, we are resting in the will and love of the great King of the world as in the bosom of the Father. The high, still joy of Christ, and the spirit which prevails in the eternal kingdom of heaven should speak out from ourselves, influence others, and testify of our own love." It is a lamentable reflection, however, that Herder's lofty views of the mission of Christ, which had been formed in the paternal home, were, in common with many other evangelical views, doomed to an unhappy obscuration upon the advance of his later years by frequent intercourse with more skeptical minds.

One of the chief services rendered the church by

Herder was his persistent attempt to elevate the pastoral office to its original and proper dignity. He held that the pastor of the church should not be solely a learned critic but the minister of the common people. In his day, the pastor was considered the mere instrument of the state, a sort of theological policeman;—a degradation which Herder could hardly permit himself to think of without violent indignation. In his *Letters on the Study of Theology*, published in 1780, and in subsequent smaller works, he sought to evoke a generation of theologians who, being imbued with his own ideas of humanity, would betake themselves to the edification of the humble mind. He would eject scholasticism from the study of the Bible, and show to his readers that simplicity of inquiry is the safest way to happy results. He would place the modern pastor, both in his relations to the cause of humanity and in the respect awarded him by the world, close beside the patriarch and prophet of other days. And that man, in his opinion, was not worthy the name of pastor who could neglect the individual requirements of the soul. According to Herder, the theologian should be trained from childhood into the knowledge of the Bible and of practical religion. Youths should have ever before them the example of pious parents, who were bringing them up with a profound conviction of the doctrines of divine truth. To choose theology for a profession from mercenary aims would preclude all possibility of pastoral usefulness. "Let prayer and reading the Bible be your morning and evening food," was his advice to a young preacher. Some of the most eloquent words from his pen were written against the customary moral preaching which so much afflicted him. "Why don't you come down from your pulpits," he asks, "for they cannot be of any advantage to you in preaching such things? What is the use of all these Gothic churches, altars, and such matters? No, indeed! Religion, true religion, must return to the exercise of its original functions, or a preacher will become the most indefinite, idle, and indifferent thing on earth. Teachers of religion, true servants of God's word, what have you to do in our century? The harvest is plenteous, but the laborers are few. Pray the Lord of the harvest that he will send out laborers who will be something more than bare teachers of wisdom and virtue. More than this, Help yourselves!"

The counsel given by Herder to others was practised first by himself. He lived among critical minds, who spurned humble pastoral work, but he felt it his duty, and therefore discharged it to the best of his ability. His preaching was richly lucid, and not directed to the most intelligent portion of his auditors. He took up a plain truth and strove to make it plainer. Yet, while the masses were most benefited by his simplicity of pulpit conversation, those gifted men who thought with him arose from their seats profoundly impressed with the dignity and value of the gospel. A witty writer of the time, Sturz, gives an account of Herder's preaching that throws some light upon the manner in which the plain, earnest exposition of God's word always affected the indifferent auditor. "You should have seen," says this man, "how every rustling sound was hushed and each curious glance was chained upon him in a very few minutes. We were as still as a Moravian congregation. All hearts opened themselves spontaneously; every eye hung upon him and wept unwonted tears. Deep sighs escaped from every breast. My dear friend, nobody preaches like him. Else religion would be to every one just what it should be, the most valuable and reliable friend of men. He explained the gospel of the day without fanaticism, yet with a grand simplicity which needed not to ransack the world for its wisdom, its figures of speech, or its scholastic arts. It was no religious study, hurled in its three divisions at the heart of stony sinners; nor was it what some would call a current article of pulpit manufacture. It was no cold, heathen, moral lecture, which sought nothing but Socrates in the Bible, and would therefore teach that we can do without both Christ and the Scriptures. But he preached the faith which works by love, the same which was first preached by the God of love, the kind which teaches to suffer and bear and hope, and which, by its rest and contentment, rewards bountifully and independently of all the joys and sorrows of the world. It seems to me that the scholars of the apostles must have preached thus, for they did not tie themselves down to the hard dogmatics of their faith, and therefore did not play with technical terms, as children with their counting pennies." William von Humboldt said of Herder's sermons that they were "very attractive: one always found them too short, and wished them of double length." Schiller spoke of his sermons as plain, natural, and adapted to the common life, and adds that Herder's preaching was "more pleasing to him than any other pulpit exercise to which he had ever listened."

Herder was the great theological writer of Weimar, and as such, his impression upon theology and religion in general was decided. Though he opposed the Kantian philosophy, because of its petrifying tendency, his antagonism was counteracted by others of the Weimar celebrities. Goethe and Schiller eclipsed all other names in their department of thought, and were the culmination of the new type of literature. Herder might preach, but it was only to a comparatively small world. Goethe and Schiller were, on all points of literature, the oracles of Europe. Like Kant, they stamped their own impress upon theology, which at that day was plastic and weak beyond all conception. Under the Königsberg thinker it became a great philosophical system as cold as Mont Blanc. Then came Poetry and Romance, which, though they could give a fresh glow to the face, had no power to breathe life into the prostrate form.

Schiller shares with Goethe the loftiest niche in the pantheon of German literature. But the former is more beloved than the latter, for the reason that his countrymen think that he had more soul. Schiller endeared himself to his land because of his ardent aspirations to political freedom. The poet of freedom is long-lived, and France will no sooner forget her Béranger, nor America her Whittier, than the German fatherland will become oblivious of Schiller. Like Herder, Schiller had been trained carefully in household religion. In his earliest outbursts of religious feeling there prevailed that ardent and devout spirit which, had it been fostered by a healthy popular taste, might have matured into something so transcendently brilliant and useful, that the writer of *The Robbers* would have proved one of the reformers of his people. If his education had reaped its appropriate harvest, his probable bearing upon the regeneration of Germany can be but faintly imagined by the aid of Klopstock's example. These were the sincere thoughts of Schiller's over-burdened soul when, one Sabbath in 1777, he addressed himself to the Deity: "God of truth, Father of light. I look to thee with the first rays of the morning sun, and I bow before thee. Thou seest me, O God! Thou seest from afar every pulsation of my praying heart. Thou knowest well my earnest desire for truth. Heavy doubt often veils my soul in night; thou knowest how anxious my heart is within me, and how it goes out for heavenly light. Oh yes! A friendly ray has often fallen from thee upon my shadowed soul. I saw the awful abyss on whose brink I was trembling, and I have thanked the kind hand that drew me back in safety. Still be with me, my God and Father, for these are days when fools stalk about and say, 'there is no God.' Thou hast given me my birth, O my Creator, in these days when superstition rages at my right hand and skepticism scoffs at my left. So I often stand and quake in the storm; and oh, how often would the bending reed break if thou didst not prevent it; thou, the mighty Preserver of all thy creatures and Father of all who seek thee.

"What am I without truth, without her leadership through life's labyrinths? A wanderer through the wilderness, overtaken by the night, with no friendly hand to lead me and no guiding star to show me the path. Doubt, uncertainty, skepticism! You begin with anguish and you end with despair. But Truth, thou leadest us safely through life, bearest the torch before us in the dark vale of death, and bringest us home to heaven, where thou wast born. O my God, keep my heart in peace, in that holy rest during which Truth loves best to visit us. The sun refuses to reflect itself in the stormy sea, but it is down into its calm mirror-like flood that it beams its face. Even thus keep my heart at peace, O God, that it may be fit to know thee and Jesus Christ whom thou hast sent; for this alone is the truth which strengthens the heart and elevates the soul. If I have truth then I have Christ; if I have Christ, then have I God; and if I have God, then I have everything. And could I ever permit myself to be robbed of this precious gem, this heaven-reaching blessing by the wisdom of this world, which is foolishness in thy sight? No. He who hates truth I will call my enemy, but he who seeks it with simple heart I will embrace as my brother and my friend.

"The bell rings that calls me to the sanctuary. I hasten thither to make good my confession, to strengthen myself in the truth, and to prepare myself for death and eternity. O lead me in such a path, my Father, and so open my heart to the impressions of truth that I may be strong enough to make it known to my fellow men. They know that thou art their God and Father, and that thou didst send Jesus thy Son, and the Holy Spirit who was to testify of the truth. They can therefore have strength for every grief of this life, and for the sorrows of death a bright hope of a happy immortality.

"Now, my God, thou canst take everything from me, yea every earthly joy and blessing; but leave me truth, and I have joy and blessing enough!"

It was the young Schiller who wrote these ecstatic words at a time when he contemplated entering the ministry. A few years passed by, and all was changed. He grew into a sincere admirer, we might say worshiper, of the heathen faith. He complained that all the life and spirit were taken out of the Bible by the Rationalists, but he did nothing to remedy their error. He became absorbed in the spirit of classic times. The antiquity of Greece was far dearer to him than that of Palestine, and his poetic fancy was excited to a greater tension by the tales of heathen deities than by the histories of the Bible. He was a devotee of Kant, and his poetry was largely made up of that philosopher's metaphysics. Yet, in Schiller's hand, abstractions became living pictures. He knew how to speak clearly, and his popularity is evidence to the fact that his generations of readers have plainly understood him.

While Schiller represented Kant in verse, Goethe did the same thing with Schelling's philosophy. The influence of the latter poet on religion was very pernicious. He expressed himself favorably of the Bible, but he claimed that it could only educate the people up to a little higher stage of intelligence and taste. He was intensely egotistic, and totally indifferent to all religious belief. His false idolatry of art and his enthusiasm arrayed for heathendom, in all the beautiful charms of the most seductive poetry, had a tendency fatal to the cause of Christianity and to all public and private virtue.[1] He expressed himself sometimes as very favorable toward the Roman Catholic worship, and the adherents of that faith quote his words of approbation with evident pride. In his *Autobiography* he pays some high compliments to the seven sacraments of the Romanists. He made several visits to the beautiful little Catholic church dedicated to St. Roch, situated just above Bingen on the Rhine. He presented it with an altar-piece, and on one occasion said, "Whenever I enter this church I always wish I were a Catholic priest." But Goethe's love and admiration of Catholicism were due rather to his attachment to the old works of art than to, that particular system of faith and worship. The Romish church was the conservator of the art-triumphs of the Middle Ages. She laid great store by her paintings and statuary, and had been the patroness

[1] Möhler's *Symbolism:* Memoir of Author.

of the arts ever since the wealth of noblemen and kings began to be poured into her lap. Goethe loved her because she loved art. The key to this only evidence of religious principle lies in his own words, as he once expressed himself on contemplating a painting of the old German school. "Down to the period of the Reformation," he said, "a spirit of indescribable sweetness, solace, and hope seems to live and breathe in all these paintings—everything in them seems to announce the kingdom of heaven. *But since the Reformation, something painful, desolate, almost evil characterizes works of art; and, instead of faith, skepticism is often transparent.*"

Our plan precludes an estimate of Goethe's literary achievements. But the influence of his productions on theology was, in the main, as destructive as if he had written nothing but uncompromising Rationalism. He was the head of the Weimar family. He had a cool, careful judgment. Schiller was excitable and impulsive; but Goethe was always stoical, regarding holy things as convenient for the more rapid advance of civilization, but not absolutely necessary for the salvation of the soul. He directed the literature of Europe. In popularity Schiller was his peer, yet in real power over the minds and lives of others no one was a match for Goethe. Other men at Weimar, such as Wieland, Knebel, and Jean Paul, were admired, but Goethe was the cynosure of all eyes. He was always thinking what next to write, and when he issued a new play, poem, or romance, a sensation was made wherever the German and French tongues were spoken.

Contemporaneously with these literary influences, which greatly increased the power and prestige of Rationalism, there was a gradual transformation of the training and instruction of the children of Germany. A thorough infusion of doubt into the minds of the youth of the land was all that was now needed to complete the sovereignty of skepticism.

It cannot be disputed that there were serious defects in the educational system already prevalent. The Latin schools instituted by Melanchthon were still in existence, but they had become mere machines. Children were compelled to commit the dryest details to memory. The most useless exercises were elevated to great importance, and years were spent in the study of many branches that could be of no possible benefit in either the professions or the trades. The primary schools were equally defective. There was no such thing as the pleasant, developing influence of the mature over the young mind. The same defect had already contributed to the spread of Rationalism, but the Rationalists were now shrewd enough to seize upon this very evil and use it as an instrument of strength and expansion.

Basedow was the first innovator in education, and, glaring as his faults were, he succeeded in effecting radical changes in the entire circle of youthful training. Sprung from a degraded class, addicted to vulgar habits, and dissipated beyond the countenance of good society, this man educated himself, and then set himself up as a fit agent for the reformation of German education.[1] He undertook, by his publication of the *Philalethy*, and of the *Theoretical System of Sound Reason*, to infuse new spirit into the university method of instruction. But he had taken too large a measure of his own powers, and therefore made but little impression upon the circle to which he had addressed himself. But, with that restless determination which distinguished

[1] Schlosser, *History of the Eighteenth Century*, vol. 2, pp. 33-41.

him through life, he began to appeal to the younger mind, and contended boldly for the freedom of children from their common and long-standing restraints.

From 1763 to 1770 Basedow deluged the whole land with his books on education; and, uniting his appeals for educational reform with strictures upon the validity of the Scriptures, he incurred the sore displeasure of Götze, Winkler and others of their class. They replied to him, but he was always ready-witted, and the press groaned under his repeated and sometimes ribald rejoinders. He told the nation, in an *Address to the Friends of Humanity*, that the old excesses would soon be done away with, since he was about to publish a work and commence an educational institution which would rid the children of the shackles of customary instruction. He solicited subscriptions for the issue of his elementary book, as it would require numerous plates, and be attended with other unusual expenses. His manifesto was freely circulated. Replies soon came to him, with liberal subscriptions from all parts of Europe. Princes and people became infatuated with his great plans and wrote him their warm approval. They remitted large contributions for his assistance. A specimen of his *Child's Book* appeared, and all classes were pleased with it. Whatever he promised was accepted with avidity, because his promises were at once so flattering and exaggerated. Schlegel and other educators tried in vain to make the multitude believe that the vulgar mountebank could never fulfill their expectations. Basedow proposed to parents, that if they would observe his system, all languages and subjects,—grammar, history, and every other study—could be learned, not in the tread-mill style, but as an amusement; that morality and religion, both Jewish and Christian, Catholic as well as Protestant, could be easily taught; that all the old bonds of education were henceforth to be broken; and that every great difficulty would hereafter be a pastime. Finally a part of the elementary work appeared. But one plan creating the necessity for another, he soon found himself immersed in the conception of a great philosophical school, in which not only children but also teachers were to be trained for the application of his new system to the appalling wants of the people. Every family became possessor of the elementary book, and all eyes were turned toward the *Philanthropium* in Dessau. Compared with Basedow's wishes, this was but a fragment of an institution. But upon its existence depended the solution of his lauded problems.

Just at this time Germany was stirred by the reading of Rousseau's works on popular education. Neither in Switzerland nor France had they effected the purpose for which they were written, but among the Germans their success was complete. Many persons, earnestly favoring Rousseau's doctrine of freedom from all conventional restraints in families, desired even his *Idyls of Life* to be introduced into the schools. Basedow and Rousseau thought in harmony; recommended that nature, not discipline, should be our guide in education; and that only those stories should be taught, of the utility of which the children are themselves conscious. Subscriptions came in profusely, and the *Philanthropium* in Dessau commenced its existence. It was opened without pupils on the twenty-seventh of December, 1774, and in the following year it was attended by only fifteen. It threatened to decline, but rallied again; and in 1776 a great public examination was held. Then Basedow retired from its curatorship;

but, returning once more, his institution suffered under his care, and finally met with total extinction. The great bubble of his plans burst. People awoke to their mistake, and many of his dupes began to confess that, after all, the old system of education was the best that had been devised.

But there were men who had lighted their torches at Basedow's flame. Some who had been temporary in. mates of his *Philanthropium* went to work with great perseverance to write juvenile books. Though the institution had tumbled to ruin, and public notice began to be turned from it, the excitement of the popular mind on the training of youth had been so intense that the subject could not soon cease to receive attention. For this reason, the writers of books for children found a large circle to read them, and become impressed by them. Herder had called attention to the subject of education in some of his most eloquent periods. He contended zealously for the development of the young mind. His own words were, "that it should be the chief aim of the teacher to imbue the child with living ideas of everything that he sees, says, or enjoys, in order to give him a proper position in his world, and continue the enjoyment of it through every day of his life." Jean Paul, in his *Levana, or the Doctrine of Education*, called attention to the necessity of the personal training of children by their parents in opposition to the old stiff method which, instead of quickening, only stupefied the intellect. Campe and Salzmann had been students in Basedow's *Philanthropium*, and subsequently each of them commenced a similar institution, but of more humble pretensions. Yet it was not so much as practical educators as by their writings, that they were instrumental in effecting a powerful impression upon the young mind of Germany. Campe's *Children's Library* had a fascinating influence upon children. It encouraged their literary taste to the exclusion of religious development. The author advocated morality, but only that which is taught by the common dictates of nature. He stoutly rejected the old *Catechism* of Luther as unfit to be drilled into a youthful mind, and, unhappily, he found many sympathizers. His *Robinson the Younger* was to the Germans what *Robinson Crusoe* was, and still is, to the English-speaking world, and from the time that the children read its wonderful stories they looked with disgust upon the less exciting histories of the Bible. From 1775 to 1785 it captivated every boy and girl who could collect groschen enough to buy a copy. When they had ceased reading it they were filled with the idea that they were naturally perfect.

Pestalozzi belongs rather to the present than to the last century, but he stands highest in the catalogue of the educational reformers who arose during the meridian strength of Rationalism. He was a Swiss by birth. In 1798 he went to Stanz and labored for the amelioration of the orphan children whose parents had fallen in the French wars.[1] His idea was, to make the school an educating family, into which the ease and pleasure of home should be introduced. He, too, believed in man's natural goodness, and held that true education is not so much the infusion of what is foreign to, as the educing of what is native in the child. But he warmly encouraged youthful acquaintance with the Bible, and said that the history of Christ is an indispensable ingredient in the education of every young mind. But while these few men, both by their active

[1] Kahnis: *German Protestantism*, p. 216.

life and facile pen, contributed their share to the improvement of the youth of Germany, there was a large class of writers for the young, whose productions became as plentiful as autumn leaves. Some were sentimental, having imbibed their spirit from *Siegwart*, *La Nouvelle Héloïse*, and similar works. Young men and women became dreamers, and children of every social condition were converted into premature thinkers on love, romance, and suicide. Whoever could wield a pen thought himself fit to write a book for children. There has never been a period in the whole current of history when the youthful mind was more thoroughly and suddenly revolutionized. The result was very disastrous. Education, in its true import, was no longer pursued, and the books most read were of such nature as to destroy all fondness for the study of the Bible, all careful preparation for meeting the great duties of coming maturity, and every impression of man's incapacity for the achievement of his own salvation.

The teachers in the common institutions of learning having now become imbued with serious doubts concerning the divine authority of the Scriptures, their pupils suffered keenly from the same blight. In many schools and gymnasia miracles were treated with contempt. Epitomes of the Scriptures on a philosophical plan were introduced. Ammon, in one of his works, tells the young people that the books of the Old Testament have no divine worth or character for us, except so far as they agree with the spirit of the gospel. As to the New Testament, much must be figuratively understood, since many things have no immediate relation to our times. Christ is a mere man. Dinter was a voluminous writer on theological subjects, and in his books tells children of imperfect notions of former times as to God, angels, and miracles. He gives teachers directions how to conduct themselves cleverly in such matters, and afterwards, in agreement with the principles he recommends, he lays down plans of catechizing. For example, there are to be two ways of catechizing about Jonah; one before an audience not sufficiently enlightened, and where all remains in its old state; another for places which have more light. In the prophecies concerning the Messiah a double explanation is given for the same reason. One is the old orthodox way, the other a more probable neological plan. A clever teacher is to choose for himself; a dull one may ask the parish clergyman how far he may go.

As a fair specimen of the kind of Biblical instruction then imparted to the children of Germany, we may adduce the example of Becker's *Universal History for the Young.* A second edition was issued in Berlin in 1806. Speaking of the person and character of Christ, the author says, "Jesus probably got the first notion of his undertaking from being a friend of John, and going often to his father's, who was a priest; and from the Gospel it appears that the sight of feasts and of the crowd of worshipers had a great effect upon him. It is doubtful whether Jesus and John were sent into Egypt for their education, or were taught by the Essenes, and then sent into Palestine as ambassadors of that sect, with secret support and according to arranged plan. . . . The indications of the Messiah in the Old Testament had produced great effect on Jesus and John who were both hot-heads, such as destiny raises for some great purpose. We are in danger, therefore, of judging them unjustly, especially from the great mixture of high and low, clear and obscure in them."

Becker had the modesty to say that he would not undertake to fix the character of Jesus, but merely collect the fragments of it from his *wretched* biographers. The friends had great mutual esteem, but John saw in Jesus a higher spirit than his own. Both had the same hatred of the priests, their pride and hypocrisy; both thought the Mosaic law no longer fit for the time, and that the notion of a national God was the source of all the evil in Judea. After long meditation they decided that Jesus must be the Messiah; and John found the part of a precursor fixed for himself. Christ, partly from his power of attraction, and partly from the hope of future power, made his disciples depend blindly on him. It was only with great caution that he could undertake his great work of destroying the priests. The people were divided into sects; and the characteristics of his plan were, his choice of the lowest people, and his withdrawing himself frequently from public view, that the priests might not nip his plan in the bud. As all the prophets had worked miracles, and many were expected from the Messiah, he too was obliged, according to Becker, to undertake them or renounce his hopes. No doubt he performed miracles; for the power of the mind on the body is such that we need not doubt his curing the melancholy and the nervous. As to the miraculous meals, raising the dead, curing the blind and deaf, these things must be attributed to the calculation of his historians; and we need not hesitate to do so after observing such tangible fabrications as Christ's walking on the sea, his blasting the fig tree, devils driven into the swine, and virtue going out of himself. In the story of Lazarus we cannot help suspecting some secret concert. Christ did perform some uncontested miracles, however and there was in his manner that inexpressible something which makes greatness irresistible. The mystic obscurity thrown over his future kingdom, the many parables he used, and his assured manner of speaking of future things, begot reverence. The prudence of his judgment and the strictness of his life are praiseworthy. He could pursue the destruction of old usages but very slowly; first he allowed the neglect of the Sabbath, and at last made open war with the priests, "*on whom he lanced all the thunder of a Ciceronian eloquence.*"

"John's death," continues this model writer for youth, "made Christ very timid. He got away into the desert and ordered his followers not to call him Messiah in public. In his last journey to Jerusalem, the multitude protected him by day, and he escaped by night. His answers, made to several questions at this time, for example, John viii. 3, are still admired. He had always suspected Judas; and as he had a presentiment that he would come to a bad end, he became very uneasy, and yet was able to exhort his disciples. He did not really die on the cross. Whenever recognized by his disciples afterwards, he went away directly, and came back unexpectedly and for a short time. At last he disappeared quickly, and let himself be seen no more. This end, like that of Lycurgus, produced many followers. By degrees all the tales of the crucifixion were extended and a Christian mythology erected."[1]

Becker was not more extreme in his inculcation of doctrine than many others. Even Gesenius, in the preface to his *Hebrew Reading Book*, tells the students of the Bible that Gen. i. 2, 3, contains the description of the origin of the earth by a sage of antiquity; that the narrator has a very imperfect knowedge of na-

[1] Rose, *State of Protestantism in Germany*, pp. 178-181.

ture, though his description is sublime, that he can hardly be the first inventor of the description, as the principal outlines of it and even the six works of creation are to be found in other religions of the East; and that probably he only accommodates the general tradition of the East to the national opinions of the Hebrews,—a remark which applies especially to his ascribing a mystic origin to the Sabbath, a festival peculiar to the Jews.

Such was the kind of theology in which the German youth were trained during a period extending through the latter part of the eighteenth and the beginning of the nineteenth centuries. It is no matter of astonishment, then, that when those children became adults they were rigid Rationalists from the mere force of training.

We now come to one of the most inexcusable deeds with which Rationalism stands charged. We refer to the general destruction or alteration of the time-honored German hymns.

Both the great branches of the Protestant church had always highly prized their rich hymns, of which there were eighty thousand in existence. Some of the finest lyrics of any tongue were among the number. The sacred songs now used in our American churches are not solely of English origin, or of our own production; but many of the sweetest of them are free versions from the German hymnists. The Rationalists, not being content with their present laurels, began in great earnestness to despoil the hymn-books of the Protestant church of everything savoring of inspiration or of any of the vital doctrines already rejected. They looked upon those songs of devotion as composed during the iron age of truth, and therefore unfit to be sung by the congregations whose lot had been cast in the golden period. Should these verses continue to be sung by the church, they would remain a strong tie holding the masses to the pitiable days of effete orthodoxy. The Rationalists reasoned correctly, for, in Germany, music is a power which has at times defied the authority of popes and kings. It was, therefore, with a sort of savage satisfaction that these destroyers of truth began the work of denuding those earnest and evangelical hymns of all their vigor and nationality for the purpose of placing in their stead cold and heartless moral verses.

Klopstock commenced the work of alteration, though with a good intention, by remodeling twenty-nine old church hymns. Cramer and Schlegel followed in his steps. Soon the devout and animating songs of Gellert, Bach, and their brother minstrels were despoiled of the spirit that had ever made them dear to the popular heart and familiar to the common ear. By and by, everybody who could make a tolerable rhyme seized some of the master-pieces of hymnology, and set them up on stiff philosophical stilts. New hymn books were introduced into many of the churches, and the people sang Rationalism. General superintendents, consistorial counselors, and court preachers, rivaled each other in preparing a new volume of religious songs for the territory under their charge. Individual towns and churches had their own selections. Some portions of Germany, especially Würtemberg, refused awhile to give up the old hymns, and certain writers of the sterling character of the poet Schubert, raised a loud and indignant voice against the wretched vandalism. But they could accomplish nothing, and the old hymns suffered that fearful mortality which the Rationalists had by this time become so able to inflict on almost everything of value. It is a lamentable scene to see those reckless doubters sit down with scalpel in hand to dissect as pure and inspiring hymns as are to be found in the devotional literature of any nation. For a good sacred song is only complete just as its author finishes it. If an authorized hymn committee attempt to alter it, they fill it at once with icicles. They can no more improve it by emendations than they can improve a rose by the use of a penknife. Each clipping or puncture destroys some natural charm.

But the music accompanying the hymns was doomed to a like fate. The old chorals, which had been lingering in those renowned gothic temples ever since the days of Luther, were so altered as to stand upon the same footing with the hymns themselves. All sentiment was extracted, as quite out of place, and sublimity was made to give way to a more temperate and stoical standard. In due time the Rationalists effected their purpose. Secular music was introduced into the sanctuary; an operatic overture generally welcomed the people into church, and a march or a waltz dismissed them. Sacred music was no longer cultivated as an element of devotion. The oratorios and cantata of the theatre and beer-garden were the Sabbath accompaniments of the sermon. The masses consequently began to sing less; and the period of coldest skepticism in Germany, like similar conditions in other lands, was the season when the congregations, the common people, and the children sang least and most drowsily.

We now behold Protestant Germany in the full possession of a shrewd, powerful, and aggressive system of infidelity. The most thorough student of church history must conclude that no other kind of skepticism has received more aid from external sources. Everything that appeared on the surface of the times contributed its mite toward the spiritual petrification of the masses. Hamann, Oetinger, Reinhard, Lavater, and Storr were insufficient for the great task of counteraction, while Rationalism could count its strong men by the score and hundred. Literature, philosophy, history, education, and sacred music were so influenced by increasing indifference and doubt that when the people awoke to their condition they found themselves in a strange latitude and on a dangerous coast. But they thought themselves safe. They could not see how each new feature in politics, literature, and theology was affecting them in a remarkable manner; and how so many influences from opposite quarters could contribute to the same terrible result,—the total overthrow of evangelical faith.

CHAPTER VIII.

DOCTRINES OF RATIONALISM IN THE DAY OF ITS STRENGTH.

THE church now presented a most deplorable aspect. Philosophy had come, with its high-sounding terminology, and invaded the hallowed precincts of Scriptural truth. Literature, with its captivating notes, had well-nigh destroyed what was left of the old Pietistic fervor. The songs of the church were no longer images of beauty, but ghastly, repulsive skeletons. The professor's chair was but little better than a heathen tripod. The pulpit became the rostrum where the shepherdless masses were entertained with vague essays on such general terms as righteousness, human dignity, light, progress, truth, and right. The peasantry received frequent and labored instructions on the raising of cattle, bees, and fruit. The poets of the day were publicly recited in the temples where the Reformers had preached. Wieland, Herder, Schiller, and Goethe became more familiar to the popular congregations than Moses, David, Paul, or even Christ. By this time we might reasonably expect the harvest from Semler's favorite theories. There was no school as yet by which he worked upon the public mind, but the greater portion of theologians caught up scrap-thoughts from his opinions and now dealt them out in magnified proportions to the masses who, like their Athenian predecessors, were ever anxious to learn what was new. That so many influences as we have seen in force should completely subdue orthodoxy is not wonderful, when we consider first the minds that originated them, and then the dull and frigid condition of the church.

But, as the fruit of these influences, there was no common system of theology adopted by the Rationalists. The reason is obvious. Rationalism was not an organism, and therefore it could have no acknowledged creed. Its adherents were powerful and numerous scouting-parties, whose aim was to harass the flanks of the enemy, and who were at liberty, when occasion required, to divide, subdivide, take any road, or attack at any point likely to contribute to the common victory. One writer came before the public, and threw doubt on some portions of the Scriptures. He was followed by another who, while conceding the orthodox view of those very passages, would discard other parts, even whole books, as plainly incredible. A third discussed the character and mission of Christ, and imputed a certain class of motives to him. A fourth attributed to him totally different, if not contradictory, impulses. There is no one book, therefore, in which we find an undisputed Rationalistic system, for the work that may represent one circle will give but a meagre and false view of another. Besides, what the most of the Rationalists might agree upon at one stage of the development of their skepticism, would be rejected by others, living a few years after them. The only means, therefore, by which we are enabled to arrive at some understanding concerning their opinions is to fix upon the time of their meridian strength, and then to hear what their representative men of that period say of the truths of revelation.

Now it cannot be doubted that Rationalism was most powerful after the decided impression made upon theology by the philosophical direction commenced by Kant, and by that of literature inaugurated by Lessing and followed by the Weimar poets. We are consequently under the necessity of hearing the statements of acknowledged Rationalists who flourished during this time, and, out of the chaos, arrive at the most probable and general views entertained by the people.

We shall see that the scene of spiritual desolation was repulsive enough to make every servant of Christ wish, with Wordsworth,—

> "I'd rather be
> A pagan, suckled in a creed outworn;
> So might I standing on this pleasant lea,
> Have glimpses that would make me less forlorn—
> Have sight of Proteus rising from the sea,
> Or hear old Triton blow his wreathed horn."

Religion. All religion was held by the Rationalists to be mere morality. As to any such thing as conversion, they were agreed that it could be only a work of the imagination. All the regeneration at which we may reasonably expect to arrive is an inclination to obey the dictates of reason. He who follows the teachings of his own intellect cannot go astray, for this is the light that lighteth every man that cometh into the world. The Scriptures give a high coloring to religion, and represent it as necessary; but those writings are not as reliable as the innate revelation which every son of Reason enjoys.

Existence of God. With this view of religion in general, all the other vital doctrines of Christianity suffered an equal depreciation. The existence of God is conceded, but the proof is impossible. His personality cannot be affirmed; it is confounded with the soul of the world. Of course, the doctrine of the Trinity cannot be accepted; for reason sheds no light sufficiently clear to establish it. A high dignitary of the church, Cannabich, wrote a book in positive denial of the Trinity, original sin, justification, satisfaction of Christ, baptism, and the Lord's Supper. As for the Trinity, the early Christians had no such tenet, and it was never concocted until after the lapse of several centuries of the Christian era. Both philosophy and nature are as capable of establishing the evidence of God's existence as the Scriptures themselves. The idea we have of God is due to prejudice and education. The mass of the Rationalists said, with Lichtenberg, that instead of God making man after his image, man had made God after his human image.

Doctrine of Inspiration. The Rationalists were fond of reasoning by analogy, and they used that method of argument freely in their discussions on the inspiration of the Scriptures. God never pursues the plan of operating immediately upon nature. His laws are the mediate measures by which he communicates with man. Gravitation is an instrument he employs for the control of the material world. Thus, in some way, does God impress upon man's mind all that he wishes to reveal, without any necessity of direct inspiration. The doctrine was, therefore, rejected because there was no need of it, and from this step it was easy to assume the position that there is no inspiration. This the Rationalists did assume. "Grant inspiration," said they, "and you bind us down to the belief that all the contents of the Scriptures are true. You force us to believe what our reason does not comprehend. The doctrine of inspiration opens the floodgate for the belief of a mass of mythical stuff which we will no more grant to be historically true than Niebuhr will admit the validity of the legends of early Rome." The poets of every land have enjoyed a sort of rhapsody when in their highest flights. This rhapsody or ecstasy is all that these idolaters of reason will concede. Doederlein's views of inspiration were much more elevated than those held by many of his *confrères;* but he too speaks of poetical excitement, and draws a line of distinction between the inspired and uninspired parts of Scripture. But Ammon represents this subject better than Döderlein. It was his opinion that the idea of a mediate divine instruction is applicable to all human knowledge. He rejects the notion peculiar to revelation. Inspiration cannot for a moment be accepted as an immediate divine impression, because it would compromise the supremacy of reason, and destroy man's intellectual and moral liberty. The diversity of style perceptible in the writers of the Scriptures is a proof that they were not influenced by immediate inspiration. "These writers themselves," say the Rationalists, "never claimed such extraordinary functions as those with which orthodox believers would now clothe them."

Töllner, a theological professor in Frankfort-on-the-Oder, wrote very fully on inspiration, and his work was held in great repute by many of the Rationalists who were inclined to supernaturalism. He held that the will, the matter, the words, and the order of both the matter and the words, might be objects of inspiration. But there are several degrees of inspiration. Some books were written without inspiration of any kind, and were only confirmed by God. In the Old Testament, Moses might have been directed to a choice of subjects, and his memory might have been strengthened. So of the Psalms and Prophecies. There is no such thing as inspiration of the historical books. It cannot be determined what degree was employed in the New Testament. In the Acts there was nothing more than natural inspiration. Luke and Mark were approved by the apostles, hence their writings may be received. Morus held that inspiration was sometimes only the inducing to write; sometimes an admonition to do so; sometimes revelation; and sometimes only a guarding from error.[1] Granting the Rationalistic denial of inspiration, we have no solid ground for any portion of the Bible. We find, therefore, that after this view had become prevalent the popular mind attached no importance to God's revealed will. Interpolations were imagined at every point of difficulty. Schröckh gives a sketch of the deplorable state of opinion on inspiration, when he says, "Inspiration was given up—interpolations in Scripture were believed to exist. In the oldest and partly in more recent history, instead of historical facts these writers saw only allegories, myth, philosophical principles, and national history. Where appearances of God and the angels, or their immediate agency, are related, nothing was seen but Jewish images or dreams. The explanation of all biblical books was pursued on new principles. The *Song of Solomon* was not mystical. The *Revelations* contained no prophecy of the fortunes of the church."

Bitter indeed must have been the emotions of the devout Christian on seeing the departure of inspiration from the opinions of the theological leaders of that day. Infinitely more exquisite must have been his pain than was that of the poet, who, sighing for the haunted and credulous days of olden time, said:

[1] Rose, *State of Protestantism in Germany*. Notes on Ch. iv.

"The intelligible forms of ancient poets,
The fair humanities of old religions,
The power, the beauty, and the majesty,
That had their haunts in dale or piny mountain,
Or forest, by slow stream, or pebbly spring,
Or chasms and watery depths: all these have vanished."

Credibility of the Scriptures. Schenkel affirms that Rationalism consists in giving up all the historical characteristics of Christianity and of Christian truths, and in the reduction of religion to the universal conclusions of reason and morality. The accuracy of this definition is very perceptible when we consider the wantonness of the assaults of the Rationalists upon the Scriptures as the canon of faith and practice. This period was marked by desperate attempts to overthrow the early history of all countries, and to convict historians of stating as fact what was only vague tradition. As the Bible was alleged by the supernaturalists to be the oldest historic record, great pains were taken to dissipate the mist from its accounts of supposed verities. The writers of the Scriptures, the friends of Rationalism held, were only men like ourselves. They had our prejudices and as great infirmities as we have. They were as subject to deception and trickery, and as full of political and sectarian rancor as partisans in these times. All through the Old Testament we find traces of biased judgment, Jewish national pride, sectional enmity, sectarian superstition, and rabbinical ignorance. It is but little better in the New Testament, for the disciples of Christ and the writers of the gospels were as susceptible of error and bigotry as their predecessors.[1]

The writers of the Scriptures were utterly destitute of any such great designs as the orthodox attribute to

[1] Von Ammon: *Biblische Theologie.*

them. They had no intention of writing for posterity, and were the mere chroniclers of what they had heard from others and seen for themselves. The Bible is, like the essays of Seneca, an excellent book for elevating the people by its moral tone. As a revelation of God's will it only takes its place beside others which God had previously made, and has been making in a natural way, ever since.[1] All ages and nations have their communications of knowledge, and the setting forth of any truth in a clearer light is a revelation.[2] There are many steps necessary for the education of the race and for its intellectual and moral development. The Scriptures are a very good aid to such a great consummation.[3] But they are full of errors, which we must leave for the supremacy of pure Reason to dissipate forever.[4]

We cannot forbear to give Wegscheider's testimony on the scanty measure of Scriptural credibility and authority in his own words. "But whatever narrations," he says, "especially accommodated to a certain age and relating miracles and mysteries, are united with the history and subject-matter of revelation of this kind, these ought to be referred to the natural sources and true nature of human knowledge. By how much the more clearly the author of the Christian religion, not without the help of Deity, exhibited to men the ideas of reason imbued with true religion, so as to represent, as it were, a reflection of the divine reason, or the divine spirit, by so much the more diligently ought man to strive to approach as nearly as possible to form that archetype in the mind, and to study to imitate it in life and man-

[1] Daub. [2] Herder. [3] Lessing: *Menschengeschlecht.* Rosenmüller: *Stufenfolge der Göttlichen Offenbarungen.* [4] Wegscheider: *Institutiones Dogmaticæ.*

ners to the utmost of his ability. Behold here the intimate and eternal union and agreement of Christianity with Rationalism. . . . The various modes of supernatural revelation mentioned in many places of the sacred books, are to be referred altogether to the notions and mythical narrations of every civilized people; and this following the suggestion of the Holy Scripture itself, and therefore to be attributed, as any events in the nature of things, to the laws of nature known to us. As to theophanies, the sight of the infinite Deity is expressly denied: John i. 18—1 John iv. 12—1 Tim. vi. 16. Angelophanies, which the Jews of a later date substituted for the appearances of God himself, like the narrations of the appearances of demons found amongst many nations, are plainly destitute of certain historic proofs; and the names, species, and commissions attributed to angels in the sacred books, plainly betray their Jewish origin. The business transacted by angels on earth is little worthy of such ministers. . . . The persuasion concerning the truth of that supernatural revelation, which rests on the testimony of the sacred volume of the Old and New Testaments, like every opinion of the kind, labors under what is commonly called a *petitio principii*."

The Bible is, in fact, of no more authority and entitled to no further credence than any other book. It is not worth more, as an historical record, than an old chronicle of Indian, Greek, or Roman legends.[1] The evangelists did not get their accounts of the doings of Christ from observation, but from a primitive document written in the Aramaic language. The gospels were not intentional deceptions; but that they are as well the work of error as of wisdom, no candid interpreter

[1] Eichhorn: *Einleitung*.

can deny. The life of Christ which they contain is but an innocent supplement to the *Metamorphoses* of Ovid.[1] Tittmann went so far as to affirm that the Scripture writers were so ignorant that they could not represent things as they really happened. Of course he excludes their capacity for inspiration.

DOCTRINE OF THE FALL OF MAN. While some Rationalistic writers conceded that Moses was the author of the whole or parts of the Pentateuch, his version of the origin of sin was universally rejected. The temptation by the serpent was, with them, one of the most improbable myths ever drawn up from the earliest traditions of nations. Whether Moses wrote much or little of the books attributed to him, his sources of knowledge were monuments and tales which he saw and heard about him. It is likely that he derived his idea of the fall of man from some hieroglyphic representation which he happened somewhere to see. As for the entrance of the serpent into Paradise, it is just as improbable as the rabbinical notion that the serpent of Eden had many feet. In the opinion of some, the whole narrative is only an allegory, or "a poetical description of the transition of man from a more brutish creature into humanity, from the baby-wagon of instinct into the government of reason, from the guardianship of nature into the condition of freedom."[2] Kindred to this theory is Ammon's; that at first man obeyed instinct only, and that his desire to eat the forbidden fruit was the longing of his mind to understand truth. But the great injury which these men thought they had visited on this doctrine was their assumption that man had not fallen, and that instead of being worse than he once was, he is every year growing purer and holier than at

[1] Paulus: *Kritische Commentar über das Neue Testament.* [2] Kant.

any previous stage of his history. This was flattering to their inflated pride, and their wish became father to their creed. With Eichhorn, the narrative of the fall was only a description of Adam's thoughts.

MIRACLES. It was no surprise to the wise disciples of Reason that there should be found numerous records of miracles in the Bible. It was just what might be expected from such writers in that gray morning of antiquity. The first chroniclers seized upon tradition; and their successors, seeing how well their fathers had succeeded, merely imitated them by catching up new ones, or enlarging upon the old account. By a sort of infection, therefore, we find what purports to be a revelation. Whatever harmony there is, was the result of an aim which was not lost sight of for a moment. Nature was the first teacher; and though she was competent, we have been poor disciples. She is instructing us all the time, though we have listened less to her than to the other auditors who sit about us. Lichtenberg says in poetical language, that "When man considers Nature the teacher, and poor men the pupils, we listen to a lecture and we have the principles and the knowledge to understand it. But we listen far more to the applause of our fellow-students than to the discourse of the teacher. We interlard the lecture by speeches to the one who sits next us; we supply what has been poorly heard by us; and enlarge it by our own mistakes of orthography and sentiment."

No branch of Scriptural faith attracted more of the wrath and irony of the Rationalists than miracles. They saw how important their service was to the authority of the Bible, and therefore bent all their energies for their overthrow. They denied their possibility in the strongest terms, averring that they degrade the character of God, and violate that noble nature of the human mind, which is necessarily bound to the most certain laws of experience, and can discern no positive marks of supernatural agency.[1] The miracles of the New Testament receive no better treatment than those of the Old. In every case they have no foundation in history. Various reasons are assigned for their presence in the Bible; in some cases they are only legends of mythologic days; in others, the pure fancy of the writer; and in others, hyperbolical descriptions of natural occurrences. Thus, while there was a diversity of opinion concerning the narratives, there was perfect union as to the purely natural character of the events.

We may particularize, in order to present more clearly the Rationalistic method of interpreting miracles. When Korah, Dathan and Abiram, with their fellow-unfortunates, were swallowed up, they only suffered what many others have done since,—destruction by a natural earthquake. This was the opinion of Michaelis. Others, more ingenious, thought that Moses had taken care to undermine privately the whole of the ground on which the tents of the sinners were; and, therefore, it was not surprising, either that they fell into the cavity, or that Moses should know this would be their fate. Eichhorn held that the three offenders, with their property, were burned by the order of Moses. Dinter explained Jacob's struggle with an angel by relating a recent dream. His brother having lately died, Dinter dreamed soon after that a man, with a little peep-show, presented to his view all sorts of pictures, and at length showed him his dead brother. The vision said, "To show you that I am really your brother, I will print a blue

[1] Wegscheider: *Institutiones Dogmaticæ.*

mark on your finger." The dreamer awoke and found not a blue mark but a pain which lasted some days. This profound exegete then asks, "Could not something similar have happened in Jacob's case? Even the less lively occidentalist sometimes relates as real what only happened in his mind. Why should we be surprised at a similar occurrence in the warmer fancy of the Eastern man?"

But of all the critics of miracles we must give the palm to Paulus. Let us hear how he accounts for the tribute-money in the mouth of the fish. "What sort of a miracle," he asks, "is that we find here? I will not say a miracle of about sixteen or twenty groschen, for the greatness of the value does not make the greatness of the miracle. But it may be observed, that, as Jesus generally received support from many persons, in the same way as the Rabbis frequently lived from such donations; as so many pious women provided for the wants of Jesus; and as the claim did not occur at any remote place, but at Capernaum, where Christ had friends; a miracle for about a thaler would certainly have been superfluous. But it would not only have been superfluous and paltry,—it would have taught this principle; that Peter, even when he could have remedied his necessities easily in other ways, might and ought to reckon on a miraculous interference of the Deity,—a notion which would entirely contradict the fundamental principle of Jesus, or the interference of the Deity. There is nothing of a miraculous appearance in this narrative, nor was there to Peter himself. Had there been, the fiery Peter would not have been cold-blooded at such a miracle, but would have expressed himself as in Luke v. 8. There is nothing more meant here, than that Christ designed to give a moral lesson; namely, that we should not give offence to our brethren, if we can avoid it by trifling circumstances. Hence, Christ said to him in substance, 'Though there is no real occasion for us to pay the tribute, yet as we may be reckoned enemies of the temple, and may not be attended to when we wish to teach what is good, why should not you, who are a fisherman, and can easily do it, go and get enough to pay the demand? Go then to the sea, cast your hook and take up the first and best fish. Peter must, therefore, have caught either so many fish as would be worth a *stater* at Capernaum, or one large and fine enough to have been valued at that sum. The opening of the fish's mouth might have different objects, which must be fixed by the context. Certainly, if it hang long, it will be less salable. Therefore the sooner it is taken to market, the more probable will be a good price for it."

Paulus and Ammon coincide in the following interpretation of one of the miracles of the loaves and fishes. There were always large caravans traveling near the time of the feasts, and they carried a plenty of meat and drinks on camels and in baskets. Now it is not according to Eastern hospitality to see your friends near you when you are eating, without asking them to join you. All that Jesus meant by saying they were without food was, that they had not a regular meal; and that therefore he collected them, arranged them in parties, and set those who had food the example of giving to those who had none, by doing so himself with the small portion which he had. As long as eating was going on, Christ made the twelve go about with their baskets and give what they had to all who wished it. The baskets were not entirely emptied, nor was any one left hungry; otherwise the needy would have applied to the stock of the Apostles. Jesus, pleased to have done so much with so little, desired them to collect what there was in the different baskets into one.

Our wise critic, the daring Paulus, finds as little difficulty in explaining away the miracle of Christ walking on the sea. When Christ saw that the wind was contrary, he did not wish to sustain the inconvenience of such a voyage; but walked along the shore and resolved to pass the disciples, as the wind was against them. From the state of the weather they coasted slowly along, and when they saw him walking on the land they were frightened. On their calling out, Christ desired Peter, who was a good swimmer, to swim to the shore and ascertain that it was he. Peter ran around to the proper side of the ship and jumped into the sea. When he was frightened by the violence of the waves, Christ who was standing on the shore, put out his hand and caught him. The boat put to land and they both got in!

Such was the common method of explaining miracles. The Rationalists were so opposed to the idea of the supernatural, that each was accounted for in some other than the Scriptural way. Many volumes were written on this subject alone, until the people became thoroughly imbued with the opinion that the Scriptures are nothing more than a well-intended and exhaustive Jewish mythology. It became a mark of superstition to credit a miraculous event, and the few who still adhered to this pillar of the Christian faith found themselves pitied by the learned and derided by their equals.

PROPHECY. The adventurous men who could deal thus with miracles would not be supposed to be more lenient to the prophecies of the Scriptures. We, therefore, observe the same skeptical rejection of the prophets. We have not dwelt at length upon the particular books which received their thrusts, for this would be quite too lengthy a task for the present volume. It is probable, however, that there is not a book of Scripture, or even a chapter, which these men would have remain just as we find it in the canon. "Something must be done with it," they argued, "no matter what it is. It is older or later than we have been accustomed to think. It was, of course, written by some one else than the accredited author."

A large share of these criticisms centered on the works of the prophets, for it was one of the most persistent efforts of Rationalism to destroy popular faith in them. Ammon discoursed boldly against them and attempted to convert every prophetic expression into a natural remark. He held that Christ himself directly renounced the power to prophesy, Mat. xxiv. 36; Acts i. 7; and that there are no prophecies of his in the New Testament. Prophecies are recorded in the Bible as uttered by men of doubtful character. Many of them are obscure, and were never fulfilled. Others were made after the events, and all were reckoned imperfect by the Apostles. These accusations apply to all the prophecies of the Old and New Testaments. The argument for them needs whatever excuse it can find, in the delirium of the prophets who were transported out of their sobriety, in the double sense in which they are quoted in the New Testament, or in the remarkable variety of interpretation. In fact, there is a moral objection to them, to say nothing of their historical character. They would favor fatalism, take away human freedom, and be irreconcilable with the Divine perfection. What Christ said concerning the destruction of Jerusalem is not a prophecy, because not stated with sufficient clearness. Jesus followed the style of interpretation found in the Talmudic and Rabbinical writings, and transferred to himself many things in the Old Testament, which really referred to future changes in the state of the Jews. He used the Jewish ideas of a Messiah to further his own notions of founding a spiritual kingdom. The prophecies in the Old Testament merely give a poetical dress to affairs occurring in the prophet's or the poet's life time.[1] Even the prophets made but little if any claim to the great gift ascribed to them. They were good politicians who had made a study of their subject; and, from the mere force of natural shrewdness and long experience, could see coming events. Paulus argued at length against Christ's prophecy of his own resurrection. His first proof is that the apostles did not so understand him, as is clear from the women seeking to embalm him; and from the apostles not believing at first the story of his resurrection. Then Christ had no notion of returning shortly. He would not have thought it necessary to cheer his disciples as he did before his death if he could have prophesied that in three days he should join them again. All the promises of meeting again refer to his joining them in a future life. Wegscheider adds that Christ, though he reproaches his disciples with their want of faith, does not allude to their distrust of any prophecy of his; and that the phrase *three days* is often used of what will soon happen. Scherer, a clergyman of Hesse-Darmstadt, represented the prophets of the Old Testament as so many Indian jugglers, who made use of the pretended inspiration of Moses and of the revelations of the prophets to deceive the people. He treated those who still have any regard for the prophecies of the New Testament as enthusiasts and simpletons; called all the

[1] Eichhorn: *Die Hebräischen Propheten.*

predictions respecting the person of the Messiah, nonsense; accused the prophets of being cunning deceivers; and said that the belief of those prophets has preserved incredulity on the earth.

THE PERSON OF CHRIST. The historical method of interpretation was applied by the disciples of Reason to the Gospel narratives of the character and atonement of Christ. The various circumstances surrounding the writers, the prejudices probably actuating them, the customs they witnessed, and their ignorance and consequent impressibility by a stronger mind, were all taken into the account. The Rationalists, therefore, place Christ before us as we would naturally expect him to appear after taking everything into consideration. They do not show him to us as he is, but as the nature of the case would lead us to expect him to be. There were many who charged him with unworthy motives and national prejudices. Reimarus accused him of rebellious, ambitious, and political views. "Afterward," says Stäudlin, "came out writings enough in Germany in which Christ was said to have performed his miracles by secret arts or by delusions. All proofs of the truth and divinity of his religion were taken away. He was exhibited either as a deceiver or self-deceiving enthusiast; and every possible objection to Christian morality as well as to the form of Christian worship was violently urged. Among the writers of these works were even theologians and preachers! What could be the consequence, except that they who still held somewhat to Christianity should set it forth as pure Rationalism, and that others should endeavor to extinguish it, and to introduce a pure religion of reason quite independent of Christianity and separated from it."

An anonymous publication appeared in 1825,

entitled *Vindiciæ Sacræ Novi Testamenti Scriptuarum*, in which Christ was declared to have deceived himself! Thereupon the Christians were obliged to elevate their founder's mean condition by wonderful stories. The first myth is concerning John the Baptist. Then follow the wonderful stories of Christ's birth, the advent of the wise men, the baptism, temptation, death, resurrection and ascension of Christ. There are doubts and difficulties connected with the resurrection, and though the apostles constantly assert its truth, the probable story is that the followers of Jesus, enraged at his death, gave it out that, being taken from the power of the wicked, he lived with God and enjoyed the reward of his virtue. They represented the life of their master to themselves and others in the most glowing colors, and so by degrees, said that he was still living, raised from the dead, and rewarded. Then all these things were told and believed, and it was not easy to contradict them or even examine their value.

Paulus affirmed that Christ did not really die but suffered a fainting fit. Bahrdt conjectured that he retreated after his supposed death to some place known only to his disciples. According to Henke, Christ was a remarkable teacher, distinguished and instructed by God. Inspiration was what Cicero ascribes to the poets; the doctrine of the Trinity came from Platonism; the name "Son of God" is metaphorical, and describes not the nature but the qualities of Christ; and personality is ascribed to the Holy Ghost through a prosopopœia not uncommon in the New Testament. The chief service of Christ was his doctrine. As a Divine Messenger it was his business to bring forward new and pure religion adapted to the wants of all mankind, and to give an example of it. His death was necessary to prove his confidence in his own doctrines, and to present an illustration of perfected virtue. Wegscheider took the position that Christ was one of those characters raised up by God at various periods of history to repress vice and encourage virtue. All notions of his glorification, however, are groundless, and the atonement is a mere speculation of the orthodox.

One of the most popular and direct of all the writers on the opinions of the Rationalists was Röhr, the author of the *Briefe über den Rationalismus*. He dwells at length upon nearly all the opinions we have mentioned, but his portrait of Christ demands more than a passing notice. He assumes a position, not very lofty, it is true, but yet much more favorable than some of the authorities to which we have referred. Christ had a great mission, and he felt that a heavy burden was upon him. Still he was only a great genius, the blossom of his age and generation, and unsurpassed in wisdom by any one before or after him. His origin, culture, deeds and experience, are yet veiled, and the accounts we have of him are so distorted by rhapsody that we cannot reach a clear conception of him. He had a rare acquaintance with mankind, and studied the Old Testament carefully. He possessed a large measure of tact, imagination, judgment, wisdom, and power. His wisdom was the product of unbiased reason, a sound heart, and freedom from scholastic prejudices. He knew how to seize upon the best means for the attainment of his human purposes. He embraced in his plan a universal religion, and to this he made all things minister. All his doctrines were borrowed from the Old Testament; and the most admirable can be found as far back as the time of Moses. He performed no miracles; but they seemed miracles to the eye-witnesses. He uttered no real prophecies, but his mind was so full of the future that some of his predictions came to pass because of the natural foresight possessed by him. His cures are all attributable to his skill as a physician, for every Jew of that day had some medical knowledge. His apostles propagated Christianity because of the influence wrought upon them by their master. Fortunately for his fame, Paul published him far and wide. Had it not been for that apostle, Christianity would never have gone further than Palestine. There is nothing more remarkable in the spread of this religion than in that of Mohammedanism, which has made such great inroads upon Arabia, Egypt, Northern Africa, and Spain. Röhr, however, reaches the climax of skeptical praise when he says of Christ that he was a "Rationalist of pure, clear, sound reason; free from prejudice, of ready perceptions, great love of truth, and warm sympathies,—an exalted picture of intellectual and moral greatness. Who would not bow before thee?"

The Rationalists made each act of Christ the subject of extended remark. Whenever they came to a serious difficulty they boldly attempted its solution by a few dashes of their unscrupulous pen. We may take the temptation in the wilderness as an example. One writer says that Christ, after his baptism, went into the wilderness full of the conviction that he had been called to a great work. He was hungry; and the thought came to him whether or not he was able to change the stones into bread. Then the conviction arose that his authority was not great enough to enchain the affections of the people. He wondered if God would not support him if he fell; but Reason answered, "God will not sustain you if you disobey the laws of nature."

Then, standing on the top of a mountain, he conceived the idea of possessing the surrounding lands, and of placing himself at the head of the people to overthrow the Roman power. The whole affair was a mere individual conflict.

From what we have now said, the opinions of the Rationalists on all points of Christian doctrine become apparent. The sacraments are only symbols of an invisible truth. Baptism is merely a sign of the purity with which a Christian ought to live. The Lord's Supper is but a memorial of the death of Jesus, and unites us with him only morally. The church is a human institution, whose teachings may be very distinct from the will of God. It gives therefore only relative aid. The future judgment is only a Rabbinical vision. Every one receives retribution for his faults in this life; and there is no eternity save that of God, in whom all beings are absorbed.[1]

By this barren creed all foundation for a holy life was taken away. The people, believing such absurdities, were transported from a period which is declared by the word of God to be blessed by the "dispensation of the Spirit" to a cold age in which the excellence of the intellect was measured by the ingenuity of its thrusts at the Scriptures, and in which the highest piety was the strictest obedience to the dictates of natural reason. The inspired advice given to the seekers of wisdom was travestied and made to read, "If any of you lack wisdom, let him ask of *Reason* that giveth to all men liberally and upbraideth not; and it shall be given him." The Christian of that day had but little to minister to his spiritual growth. All the endeared in-

[1] Von Ammon. Quoted from his *Magazine* in Saintes' *Histoire du Rationalisme.*

stitutions of his church were palsied by the strong arm of the Rationalists, who had nothing to put in their place. Their time was spent in destruction. They would pull all things down and erect nothing positive and useful. The doctrines which they professed to be lieve were mere negatives,—the sheer denial of some thing already in existence.

CHAPTER IX.

RENOVATION INAUGURATED BY SCHLEIERMACHER.

The commencement of the nineteenth century found the German people in a state of almost hopeless depression. They saw their territory laid waste by the victorious Napoleon, and their thrones occupied by rulers of Gallic or Italian preferences. They had striven very sluggishly to stem the current of national subjection and humiliation. The star of France being in the ascendant, the Rhine was no longer their friendly ally and western limit. No stage in the history of a people is more gloomy and calls more loudly for sympathy than when national prestige is gone, and dignities usurped by foreign conquerors. Though the apathy of despair is a theme more becoming the poet than the historian, we find a vivid description of the sadness and desolation produced by the French domination given by one who deeply felt the disgrace of his country. This writer says:

"The Divine Nemesis now stretched forth her hand against devoted Germany, and chastened her rulers and her people for the sins and transgressions of many generations. Like those wild sons of the desert, whom in the seventh century, heaven let loose to punish the degenerate Christians of the East, the new Islamite hordes of revolutionary France were permitted by Divine Providence to spread through Germany, as through almost every country in Europe, terror and desolation.

"What shall I say of the endless evils that accompanied and followed the march of her armies, the desolation of provinces, the plunder of cities, the spoliation of church property, the desecration of altars, the proscription of the virtuous, the exaltation of the unworthy members of society, the horrid mummeries of irreligion practised in many of the conquered cities, the degradation of life and the profanation of death. Such were the calamities that marked the course of these devastating hosts. And yet the evils inflicted by Jacobin France were less intense and less permanent than those exercised by her legislation. In politics the expulsion of the ecclesiastical electors, who, though they had sometimes given in to the false spirit of the age, had ever been the mildest and most benevolent of rulers; the proscription of a nobility that had ever lived in the kindliest relations with its tenantry; and on the ruins of old aristocratic and municipal institutions that had long guarded and sustained popular freedom, a coarse, leveling tyranny, sometimes democratic, sometimes imperial, established; in the church the oppression of the priesthood, a heartless religious indifferentism, undignified even by attempts at philosophic speculation, propagated and encouraged; and through the poisoned channels of education the taint of infidelity transmitted to generations yet unborn. Such were the evils that followed the establishment of the French domination in the conquered provinces of Germany. Doubtless, through the all-wise dispensations of that Providence who bringeth good out of evil, this fearful revolution has partly become, and will yet further become, the occasion of the moral and social regeneration of Europe." [1]

The patriot saw his country degraded; but the Christian wept for his absent faith. Rationalism was strongest when national humiliation was deepest. These formed a fitting twinship. It is a scathing comment on the influence of skepticism upon a people that, in general, the highest feeling of nationality is co-existent with the devoutest piety. It is the very nature of infidelity to deaden the emotions of patriotism, and that country can hardly expect to prove successful if it engage in war while its citizens are imbued with religious doubt. If lands are conquered, it knows not how to govern them; if defeated, skepticism affords but little comfort in the night of disaster. We do not attach a fictitious importance to Rationalism when we say that it was the prime agent which prevented the Germans from the struggle of self-liberation, and that the victory of Waterloo and the Congress of Vienna would never have been needed had those people remained faithful to the precedents furnished by the Reformers.

When Fichte was in his old age, and had completed his system of philosophy, he published his *Addresses to the German People.* Political writing was a new field for him, and yet, whoever will take the pains to study the fruits of his thinking, will easily perceive that the spirit animating the *Addresses* was the same which pervaded his entire philosophy. He saw the degradation of his country. Though at a time of life when youthful fervor is supposed to have passed away, he became inflamed with indignation at the insolence of the conqueror and the apathy of his countrymen, and addressed himself to the consciousness of the people by

[1] Möhler's *Symbolism*, Memoir of Author.

calling upon them to arise, and reclothe themselves with their old historic strength. His voice was not disregarded. The result proved that those who had thought him in his dotage, and only indulging its loquacity, were much mistaken. He wrote that enthusiastic appeal with a great aim. He had spent the most of his life in other fields, but posterity will never fail to honor those who, whatever their habits of thinking may have been, for once at least have the sagacity to see the wants of their times, and possess the still higher wisdom of meeting them. Fichte died in 1814; but it was at a time when, Simeon-like, he could congratulate himself upon the prospects of humanity. He still felt the rich glow of youth when, in his last days, he could say: "The morning light has broken, and already gilds the mountain-tops, and gives promise of the great coming day."

After independence had been achieved and the downfall of Napoleon had become a fact, there appeared evidences of new evangelical life. When the German soldiers recrossed the river which their ancestors had loved to call "Father Rhine," and felt themselves the proud possessors of free soil, not only they, but all their countrymen living in the Protestant principalities, manifested a decided dissatisfaction with that skepticism which had paralyzed them. Moreover, the memory that France had been the chief agent in introducing Rationalism was not likely to diminish their hatred of all infidelity. The masses breathed more freely, but they were still imbued with serious error. Restoration was the watchword in politics; but it was soon transferred to the domain of religion and theology.

But great as was the influence of the wars of freedom in bringing back the German heart to an intense desire for a more elevated nationality, we must not be unmindful of the great theological forces which were preparing for a thorough religious renovation.

They met in Schleiermacher. When quite young he was placed, first at Niesky and afterward at Barby, in the care of the Moravians. It was among these devout people that he became inspired with that enthusiastic love of inner religious feeling which characterized his entire career. The traces of Moravian piety are perceptible in all his writings. His own words concerning his early training are very touching. "Piety," says he, "was the maternal bosom, in the sacred shade of which my youth was passed, and which prepared me for the yet unknown scenes of the world. In piety my spirit breathed before I found my peculiar station in science and the affairs of life; it aided me when I began to examine into the faith of my fathers, and to purify my thoughts and feelings from all alloy; it remained with me when the God and immortality of my childhood disappeared from my doubting sight; it guided me in active life; it enabled me to keep my character duly balanced between my faults and virtues; through its means I have experienced friendship and love."

He became a student at Halle, and thence removed to Berlin, where he was appointed chaplain to the *House of Charity.* While in that metropolis he had rare opportunities for the study of his times. He saw that the indifference and doubt which centered in the court and the university, controlled the leaders of theology, literature, and statesmanship. He drew his philosophy largely from Jacobi, exhibiting with that thinker his dissatisfaction at the existing condition of metaphysics and theology. Schleiermacher could not look upon the dearth around him without the deepest emotion. He asked himself if there was no remedy for the wide-spread evil. The seat of the disease appeared to him to be the false deification of reason in particular; and the general mistake of making religion dependent upon external bases instead of upon the heart and consciousness of man. His conclusion was that both the friends and enemies of Rationalism were mistaken, and that religion consists not in knowledge but in feeling. It was in 1799 that he wrote his *Discourses on Religion addressed to its Cultivated Despisers.* Striking at the principal existing evil, which was indifference, he aimed to show the only method for the eradication of them all.

The late Mr. Vaughan, in speaking of the position of this work, says: "In these essays Schleiermacher meets the Rationalist objector on his own ground. In what aspect, he asks, have you considered religion that you so despise it? Have you looked on its outward manifestations only? These the peculiarities of an age or a nation may modify. You should have looked deeper. That which constitutes the religious *life* has escaped you. Your criticism has dissected a dead creed. That scalpel will never detect a soul. Or will you aver that you have indeed looked upon religion in its inward reality? Then you must acknowledge that the idea of religion is inherent in human nature, that it is a great necessity of our kind. Your quarrel lies in this case, not with religion itself, but with the corruptions of it. In the name of humanity you are called on to examine closely, to appreciate duly what has been already done towards the emancipation of the true and eternal which lies beneath these forms,—to assist in what may yet remain. Schleiermacher separates the province of religion from those of action and of knowledge. Religion is not morality, it is not science. Its seat is found accordingly in the third element of our nature—the feeling. Its essential is a right state of the heart. To degrade religion to the position of a mere purveyor of motive to morality is not more dishonorable to the ethics which must ask than to the religion which will render such assistance. . . . The feeling Schleiermacher advocates, is not the fanaticism of the ignorant or the visionary emotion of the idle. It is not an aimless reverie shrinking morbidly from the light of clear and definite thought. Feeling, in its sound condition, affects both our conception and our will, leads to knowledge and to action. Neither knowledge nor morality are in themselves the measure of a man's religiousness. Yet religion is requisite to true wisdom and morality inseparable from true religion. He points out the hurtfulness of a union between church and state. With indignant eloquence he descants on the evils which have befallen the church since first the hem of the priestly robe swept the marble of the imperial palace."[1]

Religion being subjective, according to Schleiermacher, there can be interminable varieties of it. As we look at the universe in numerous lights, and thereby derive different impressions, so do we acquire a diversity of conceptions of religion. Hence it has had many forms among the nations of the earth. There is in each breast a religion derived from the object of intellectual or spiritual vision. Christianity is the great sum resulting from the antagonism of the finite and the infinite, the human and divine. The fall and redemption, separation and reunion, are the great elements from which we behold Christianity arise. Of all kinds of religion this alone can claim universal adaptation and rightful supremacy. Christ was the revelator of a system more

[1] *Essays and Remains.* Vol. 1, pp. 61-62.

advanced than Polytheism or Judaism. Only by viewing his religion in the simple light in which he places it can the mind find safety in its attempts to seek for a basis of faith. But, important as Christianity is, it will avail but little unless it become the heart-property of the theoretical believer.

The *Discourses* produced a deep impression. They inspired the class to whom they had been directed with what it needed most of all, *a sense of dependence.* One could not read them and close the volume without wondering how reason could be deified and the feeling of the heart ignored. There were multitudes of the educated and cultivated throughout the land who, having become unfriendly to Christianity through the persistence of the Rationalists, were equally indisposed to be satisfied with a mere destructive theology. Something positive was what they wanted; hence the great service of Schleiermacher in directing them to Christianity as the great sun in the heavens, and then to the heart as the organ able to behold the light. His labor was inestimably valuable. His utterances were full of the enthusiasm of youth, and, years later, he became so dissatisfied with the work, that he said it had grown strange even to himself. As if over-careful of his reputation, to a subsequent edition he appended large explanatory notes in order to harmonize his recent with his former views. It would have been more becoming the mature man to leave those earnest appeals to reap their own reward. The times had changed; and the necessity which had first called forth his appeal to the idolaters of doubt was sufficient apology. Schleiermacher wrote other works, of which he and his disciples were much prouder; but we doubt if he ever issued one more befitting the class addressed, or followed with more beneficial results. Since his pen has been stopped by death, those very discourses have led many a skeptic in from the cold storm which beat about him, and given him a place at the warm, cheerful fireside of Christian faith. Severe censure has been cast upon them because of their traces of Spinoza. It is enough to reply that their author, in the fourth edition, repudiated every word savoring of Pantheism. Of books, as of men, it is best to form an estimate according to the purpose creating them, and the moral results following them. Neander, who could well observe the influence of the *Discourses*, gives his testimony in the following language: "Those who at that time belonged to the rising generation will remember with what power this book influenced the minds of the young, being written in all the vigor of youthful enthusiasm, and bearing witness to the neglected, undeniable religious element in human nature. That which constitutes the peculiar characteristic of religion, namely, that it is an independent element in human nature, had fallen into oblivion by a one-sided rational or speculative tendency, or a one-sided disposition to absorb it in ethics. Schleiermacher had touched a note which, especially in the minds of youth, was sure to send forth its melody over the land. Men were led back into the depth of their heart, to perceive here a divine drawing which, when once called forth, might lead them beyond that which the author of this impulse had expressed with distinct consciousness."

In the year following the publication of the *Discourses on Religion*, Schleiermacher issued his *Monologues*. Here he gave the keynote to the century. While, only the year before, he would cultivate the feeling of dependence and turn the mind inward, in the *Monologues* he would lead man to a knowledge of his own power, and show how far his individuality can go upon its mission of success. Here he lauds independence. Hence the latter work exerted the same kind of influence which attended Fichte's *Addresses*, and it had no small share in the reäwakening of the people to their innate power. There might appear an antagonism between these two works of Schleiermacher, but, while the *Discourses* were the exposition of his religious views, the *Monologues* were merely the annunciation of his moral opinions subsequently developed in his *System of Christian Ethics*. The latter production was not destitute of enthusiasm. In fact, the *Monologues*, cultivating the spirit of independence, were far more capable of arousing and invigorating the mind and heart. The author would have no one blind to the native strength secreted in every breast, nor fail to cultivate sympathy and love through every period of life. The consciousness should be a world in itself; not even seeking an external support, but satisfied with its own introspection; not watching the storm without, but satisfied with surveying the gilded halls of its own castle-home. Thus there becomes, instead of old age, continuous youth. This was his own pure experience. "For," said he, "to the consciousness of inner freedom, and acting in accordance with it, correspond eternal youth and joy. This I have got hold of, and shall never give it up again; and with a smile I thus see vanishing the light of mine eyes, and white hairs springing up among my fair locks. Whatever may happen, nothing shall grieve my heart; the pulse of my inner life shall remain fresh until I die."

A strong evidence that the German people were learning well the lessons now impressed upon them, was the increasing fondness for the institutions of purer times and a growing taste for history. The mind found no comfort in the present, and it was therefore driven back upon the past for solace. Poets began to start up, clothed with the spirit of independence, and singing of bygone days in such a way that they were understood as saying, "Now you see what our fathers did; how they believed and fought; go you and do likewise." This new race sprang from the Romantic School, led by Tieck, Schlegel, and others; but while it possessed that enthusiastic admiration of the past which these men indulged, their literary offspring exhibited a more earnest christian faith. It was in that day of distress that Uhland first poured forth his notes of awakening; that Körner sounded the bugle-call of freedom; that Rückert molded sonnets stronger than bullets; and Kerner sighed for a world where there is no war, and no rumors of war.

Thus, when liberation came, no one class could claim to be the sole agent of its accomplishment. But it is certain that if the religious spirit of the people had not been appealed to and aroused, all literary and æsthetic efforts would have been in vain. It was the religious consciousness of the masses east of the Rhine which, being thoroughly awakened, drew the sword, and gained the victory of Waterloo. If we view that great crisis in European history in any light whatever, we cannot resist the conviction that its importance in the sphere of religion was equally great with its political magnitude.

The King of Prussia, Frederic William III., began the work of ecclesiastical reconstruction. There were three questions of great delicacy, but of prime importance, which he attempted to solve; the constitution of the Protestant church; the improvement of liturgical forms;

and the union of the two Protestant confessions. Whatever course the king might adopt could not fail to make many enemies. But he belonged to a line of princes who had been aiming at the unity of the church for more than two centuries, and who, with the single exception of Frederic II., had endeavored to preserve popular faith in the Scriptures. Preparations were being made for the three hundredth anniversary jubilee of the Reformation. The land being now redeemed, it was hoped that the occasion would inspire all hearts with confidence in the future of both state and church. The king deemed it a most favorable opportunity to bring the two branches of the Protestant church together, not by one coming over to the territory of the other, but by mutual compromise, by the rejection of the terms Lutheran and Reformed, and by the assumption of a new denominational name.

There was really no reason why the two confessions should not be united, for it was very plain that the adherents of both were not rigid in their attachment. The Calvinists were no longer tenaciously devoted to their founder's views of absolute predestination, while the Lutherans, having departed from the doctrine of the real presence in the Lord's Supper, had adopted the Zwinglian theory. The rigid authority of the symbolical books was but loosely held by Lutherans and Calvinists. Frederic William III., seeing that the separation was more imaginary than real, wrote a letter on the second of May, 1817, to Bishop Sack and Provost Hanstein, in which he said: "I expect proposals from you concerning the union of the two confessions, which are in fact so similar; and as to the easiest method of effecting the same." On the twenty-seventh day of the same month he addressed a circular to all ecclesiastical functionaries within his dominions, calling upon them to exert their influence for the union of the two churches, and to give notice that the approaching jubilee would be the signal for it to take place. The thirty-first of October was the anniversary, and the plan was so far successful that in many places the people and ministry of both confessions met on that day for divine worship and partook of the Lord's Supper together. The fruit of the movement was highly satisfactory to the Prussian King. Very soon after the anniversary of the Reformation, the terms *Lutheran* and *Reformed* were stricken from official documents, and the united State Church was henceforth known as the Evangelical Church.

Beyond the limits of Prussia the Union gave rise to animated discussion; but within the space of five years it was effected in Nassau, Rhenish Bavaria, the Palatinate, Rhenish Hesse, and Dessau. It encountered the most decided opposition in the person of Harms, a pastor of the city of Kiel. He was not opposed to any movement which he thought would conduce to the advantage of Christ's kingdom, but it was his opinion that a return to the old Lutheran orthodoxy was more needed than the union of the two churches. The faith of the fathers, and not the union of Rationalistic divines, was, in his view, the only method of deliverance. Harms was little known outside his own province until the publication of his ninety-five *Theses* in connection with the original ninety-five nailed by Luther to the door of the Schlosskirche in Wittenberg. He was the son of a plain Holstein miller, and had been indoctrinated into the Lutheran catechism during his early youth. His first lessons in Latin and Greek were received at the hands of a Rationalistic pastor in his native town, but he assisted his father in the mill until he was nineteen years of age. He then visited the university of Kiel, and in due time entered upon the pastoral work. He scorned the customary dry method of preaching, and aimed to reach the hearts of his hearers by any praiseworthy method within his power. He made use of popular illustrations and ordinary incidents. His congregations increased, not only in the attendance of the middle and lower classes, but of the gentry and wealthy. His earnest plainness was so novel and unexpected that those who had long absented themselves from the sanctuary were rejoiced to attend the ministrations of a preacher who seemed to believe something positive and Scriptural, and who had the boldness to say what he did believe.

This was the man who came forth on the occasion of the anniversary of the Reformation as the champion for a return to the spirit of the olden time. He held that reason had totally supplanted revelation in the pulpits, universities, and lower schools, and that, until faith was crowned with supremacy, there was no hope of relief. The *Theses* exhibited great directness and clearness of appeal, and a keen insight into the methods of popular address. As a specimen of their style we introduce the following extracts: "III. With the idea of a progressing Reformation, in the manner in which this idea is at present understood, and especially in the manner in which we are reminded of it, Lutheranism will be reformed back into heathenism, and Christianity out of the world. IX. In matters of faith, reason; and as regards the life, conscience, may be called the Popes of our age. XI. Conscience cannot pardon sins. XXI. In the sixteenth century the pardon of sins cost money, after all; in the nineteenth it may be had without money, for people help themselves to it. XXIV. In an old hymn-book it was said, 'Two places, O man, thou hast before thee;' but in modern times they have slain the devil and dammed up hell. XXXII. The so-called religion of reason is destitute either of reason or religion, or both. XLVII. If in matters of religion, reason claims to be more than a layman, it becomes a heretic; that avoid, Titus iii. 10. LXIV. Christians should be taught that they have the right not to tolerate any unchristian and un-Lutheran doctrine in the pulpits, hymn-books, and school-books. LXVII. It is a strange claim that it must be permitted to teach a new faith from a chair which the old faith had set up, and from a mouth to which the old faith gives food. LXXI. Reason, turned head, goes about in the Lutheran church: it tears Christianity from the altar, casts God's works out of the pulpit, throws dirt into the baptismal water, receives all kinds of people as godfathers, hisses the priests; and all the people follow its example, and have done so for a long time. And yet it is not bound. On the contrary, this is thought to be the genuine doctrine of Luther, and not of Carlstadt. LXXIV. The assertion that we are more advanced and enlightened can surely not be proved by the present ignorance as regards true Christianity. Many thousands can declare, as did once the disciples of John, 'We have not so much as heard whether there be any Holy Ghost.' LXXV. Like a poor maid, they would not enrich the Lutheran church by a marriage. Do not perform it over Luther's bones! He will thereby be recalled to life, and then—wo to you! LXXVII. To say that time has taken away the wall of separation between Lutherans and Reformed is not a clear speech. LXXXII. Just as reason has prevented the Reformed from finishing their church and reducing it to unity, so the reception of reason into the Lutheran church would cause nothing but confusion and destruction. XCII. The Evangelical Catholic church is a glorious church; she holds and forms herself preëminently by the Sacrament. XCIII. The Evangelical Reformed church is a glorious church; she holds and forms herself by the Word of God. XCIV. More glorious than either is the Evangelical Lutheran church; she holds and forms herself both by the Sacrament and the Word of God."[1]

The appearance of the *Theses* of Harms created a great sensation. At a time when the union of the two churches became so desirable to many, they seemed to be a firebrand of destruction. Plainly, it would be best to return to the faith of the Reformers, but some of the most evangelical men claimed that the speediest method of return was through the Union. There appeared replies to the *Theses* from all quarters of the country, almost every theologian of distinction assuming the character of the controversialist. As many as two hundred works appeared on the subject, the most of them bearing strongly against Harms. In Kiel and Holstein, where he was best known, the excitement was intense. Even churches and clubs were divided, and the rancor went so far as to invade private families, and create domestic divisions and heart-burnings. Seldom has a theological topic caused such a blaze of tumult. Harms was declared guilty of heinous offenses. He was charged with Catholicism, and reminded that attention to the mill would be much better employment than wielding the pen. He was accused of aiming at the protracted division of the sects, and ministering in all possible ways to the devices of Satan. His was the fate

[1] Quoted from Kahnis, *History of German Protestantism*, pp. 224-225.

of the partisan. He did a great work, for the controversy arising from his *Theses* hastened the settlement of those points which the times required should be solved as speedily as possible. Indeed, this very discussion was a hopeful indication; for it proved that, long and terrible as the sway of Rationalism had been, there was still some interest felt among the people on the themes most intimately connected with faith and practice. It was a bright ray of the morning of renovation when the mere fact of vital religion was powerful enough to enlist public attention.

CHAPTER X.

RELATIONS OF RATIONALISM AND SUPERNATURALISM.
1810—1835.

THE task imposed upon the new state church taxed its powers to their utmost tension. Much that had been achieved was now no longer useful, for the stand-point of parties was totally changed. The Calvinist had written against Rationalism with one eye upon heresy and the other upon Lutheranism. The Lutheran had betrayed more spleen toward his Reformed brethren than toward the disciples of Semler and Ernesti. But when the union was effected there occurred the immediate necessity of new methods of attack upon the enemies of orthodoxy, and a steadfast cultivation of friendly feelings between newly-formed friends. As the adherents of the two confessions were now united, why might not their conjoined strength be wielded for the overthrow of skepticism? What was there, then, to prevent these great branches of the church from coming forward in perfect unison, and dealing strong blows against the system which had well nigh been the ruin of them both?

The devotees of reason saw their danger, for the day of the union was an evil one for them. But they did not become so alarmed as to take to flight and give up the contest. On the other hand, they no sooner perceived the awakening of the German people to a sense of patriotism and independence, than they predicted a similar disposition to return to the old faith; and being thus convinced of their danger, they wrote very vigorously, and attempted to be fully prepared for the onset. We therefore behold the anomaly of a system which had almost run its race before arriving at a formal exposition.

Rationalism never attained to the dignity of a clear and cogent elucidation until the publication of Röhr's *Letters on Rationalism*, and of Wegscheider's *Institutes*. It had reached the acme of its prosperity at the beginning of the century, yet the former work was not written until 1813, and the latter not until 1817. There was power in both these productions. The former was bold, popular, startling, and not without a show of learning. It was intended for the masses. The latter was a complement of the former; more heavy, but by virtue of its weight adapted to that class of people, everywhere abundant, who suspect either danger or puerility in every earnest sentence. The author held that it was the province of Protestantism to develop Christianity and Christian theology to a pure faith of reason. Issuing his work in the year of the Reformation jubilee, he dedicated it to the shades of Luther. But Röhr and Wegscheider, as far as their capacity to injure Christian faith was concerned, stood at the wrong term of the history of Rationalism. Had they written a half century earlier their works would have been much more injurious to the Christian Church. But the system they would now strengthen and propagate was beginning to decay, and it was beyond their power to save it from ruin. They built a house for an occupant who was too old to enjoy either the fascinating symmetry of its architecture or the gorgeous splendor of its furniture.

It was at the time of which we speak that we first find frequent use of the terms *Rationalism* and *Supernaturalism*. The more zealous friends of each school marshaled themselves for the final struggle. The conflict became hand to hand, and quick and direct blows were dealt by both combatants. One of the foremost among the champions of the old faith was Reinhard, who declared that there was an irrepressible difference between reason and revelation, Rationalism and Supernaturalism; that there was no possible point of compromise; that they had nothing in common; and that either the one or the other must exercise authority. Reinhard avowed himself in favor of the undivided supremacy of faith, and would have reason subordinate. The key-note of his active life and inspiring writings is found in his own language—words which, had he written nothing else, are sufficient to render him memorable. "While yet a boy," said he, "when I read the Bible I considered it the word of God to man, and never have I ceased to hold this view; so that now it is so holy to me and its utterances so decisive that a single sentence which would reproach its sanctity fills me with horror, just as an immoral sentiment would rouse my conviction of virtue."

Tittmann entered the lists with a work directed at the very heart of Rationalism. He charged it with being unimprovable, and merely temporary and unsatisfactory. His book, entitled *Supernaturalism, Rationalism, and Atheism*, went still further; for it aimed to show that if the Rationalists believe what they say, they are nothing less than atheists. Granting their premises, the conclusion must be that there is no God, and that if God be not the author of revelation, there is also no God of nature.

But while this war of books was going on with great bitterness on both sides, there arose a powerful band of mediators, who believed that no advantage could be gained for either combatant by continuing the strife, and that some point of union would have to be adopted before there could be peace and prosperity. Tzschirner differed from Reinhard in his view of the antagonism between Rationalism and Supernaturalism. He contended that there were features of sympathy between the two systems, and that the work of harmonizing reason and revelation was not impossible. He therefore attempted, in the present case, what Calixtus had formerly tried in behalf of the Calvinists and Lutherans. But the syncretism of Tzschirner was equally difficult of accomplishment. He conceded too much to the Rationalists: for he would unite them and their enemies on the ground that the aim of revelation is only to found a moral and religious institution through the personal agency of a Divine Ambassador; to strengthen the truths of the religion of reason; and to bring them so near to the consciences of men that the authority of reason to prove the origin and contents of revelation cannot be doubted.

But Tzschirner's influence did not consist so much in the particular plan he would execute as in the tendency toward union which he was the chief agent in creating. There were numbers who, having read his works on this subject, were loud in their demand for the union of reason and revelation on some basis that would compromise neither the value of the former nor the sanctity of the latter. Many books appeared whose sole theme was the possible harmonization of these elements, which heretofore had been deemed utterly incongruous.[1] Schott's *Letters on Religion and the Faith of the Christian Revelation* was directed to the same mark, and received great attention at the hands of both parties. According to their author, there was no opposition between the religion of reason and revelation, for Christianity is the mere expression of the highest reason. Both are derived from the same fountain, which is Divine reason. Nor is there any real difference between the purpose of Christianity and that of the religion of reason. Each one aims at the highest good.

But it soon became very evident that the Rationalists and Supernaturalists were unable to harmonize. The points of difference were so decided that it was vain to expect a union. Reinhard was correct in his opinion that one or the other would have to yield. Just at the crisis when these two systems were attracting greatest attention, Schleiermacher published his *System of Doctrines*, 1821. In this work he proved what had not been conceived by any writer save himself, that there was another road to progress. As soon as it gained a hearing the disputants saw that their arguments were no longer of value, that the ground of the discussion was altogether changed, and that the cause of faith must eventually triumph. The book was a complete surprise to all parties. It was a stroke of genius, destined alike to recast existing theology and to create a new public sentiment for the future.

The leading ideas developed in this master-piece of theology are Christ, Religion, and the Church. The Rationalists had ever held that reason is the criterion of truth, but Schleiermacher elevates Christian con-

[1] Baur, *Kirchengeschichte d.* 19 *Jahrhunderts*, pp. 180-181.

sciousness to the throne. They had reduced religion to a mere formal morality; yet he shows that religion and morality are very different, and that the former consists neither in knowledge or action, but in the sentiment or feeling of the heart. Thus he develops the opinion first published in the *Discourses on Religion*. He uses the term "piety" to designate religion. This piety should become the great spring of our life and the inspiring power of faith. There is no real inconsistency between knowledge and piety; they can harmonize beautifully when carried to their loftiest extent. The religious feeling, which judges truth, is characterized by absolute dependence. This is not degrading to man, but his true dignity consists in it. We have different conceptions of God, derived from the feeling of dependence, which is varied according to the nature of outward circumstances. Christ must be judged by us not so much according to the received accounts of his life as by his great relations to us as Redeemer and Saviour. Our view of him must be deeper than his mere incarnation. He was concerned in creation just so far as it was not completed until redeemed. If we would have communion with God we can enjoy it only through the medium of Christ. The peculiar value of redemption lies in its applicability to our necessity for salvation. The very sinlessness of Christ can be in a measure incorporated with our humanity, and we should aim after the mind that was in Christ. We are never fully united with Christ until we have a perfect spirit of dependence. When this occurs, the soul is passing into the glorious condition of the new birth. The church is the depository of that spirit of Christ which every believer must enjoy in order to inherit eternal life. The church, however, is not self-existent. Like the heavenly bodies, whose motions are constantly maintained by infinite power, the church is ever dependent upon Christ's agency for its very life. Christ is the spirit moving in history and controlling all things for the greatest good. The church is in some sense an organism of which Christ is the head. This fact is the central point of theology, for without Christ our faith is vain.[1]

Such teaching was what the times needed. The mind required to be directed to Christ as the only remedy for skepticism. But we must confess that, in the midst of some of the most evangelical expositions of divine truth, Schleiermacher gave expression to serious doubts. He disclaimed any great authority inherent in the Old Testament in the following style: "The Old Testament Scriptures are indebted for their place in our Bible partly to the appeals made to them by the New Testament Scriptures, and partly to the historic connection of Christian worship and the Jewish synagogue, without participating, on that account, in the normal dignity, or inspiration, of those of the New Testament."[2] As far as the inspiration of the Old Testament is concerned, there must be a distinction observed between the law and the prophets. The law cannot be inspired, for the spirit that could inspire it would be in conflict with that which God sends into the heart by virtue of our connection with Christ. Upon the law depend all the subsequent historical books; and both are, therefore, uninspired, according to the standard by which

[1] For summaries of Schleiermacher's views, see Herzog, *Encyclopædie*; Baur, *Kirchengeschichte, des 19 Jahrhunderts*; Vaughan, *Essays and Remains*; Gieseler, *Kirchengeschichte*, vol. vi.; Kurtz, *Church History*, vol. ii.; Saintes, *Histoire du Rationalisme*; Farrar, *History of Free Thought*; and Auberlen, *Göttliche Offenbarung*, vol. i.

[2] *Die Glaubenslehre.*

we judge the New Testament. The prominent portions of the prophetic writings proceed principally from the material spirit of the people, which is not the Christian spirit.

It is plain that Schleiermacher's views concerning the Trinity were defective. He despatches it thus: "The church doctrine of the Trinity demands that we should think each of the three persons equal to the Divine Being, and *vice versa;* and each of the three persons equal to the others. We are unable to do either the one or the other, but can only conceive the persons in a gradation; and in like manner the unity of the substance either less than the persons, or the contrary." He discourses eloquently of the Spirit; but, after all, he teaches that the Holy Ghost is only the common spirit of the Christian church as a corporate body striving after unity. The term "common spirit," which he employs, he understands to be the same that is used in worldly polity; that is, the common tendency in all, who form one moral person, toward the welfare of the whole. This beneficial sentiment is, in each, the peculiar love to every individual. The Holy Ghost is the union of the Divine Being with human nature, in the form of the common spirit animating the corporate life of the faithful. Schleiermacher did not reject miracles altogether as historical facts, but cast doubt upon their character by holding that, if they did occur, it was only in conformity with a higher nature of which we know nothing. His opinion concerning the doctrine of angels was not orthodox; for he rejected the existence of the devil, and the supposition of the fall of angels from heaven. Some of the most important events in connection with Christ were discarded by him as unnecessary to saving faith, namely, the miraculous conception, the resurrection, ascension, and return of Christ to judgment. In his opinion sin was hurtfulness, not guilt.

It is astonishing that we find so much truth and error concentrated in the same man. But Neander was nevertheless correct in the words in which he announced Schleiermacher's death: "We have now lost a man from whom will be dated henceforth a new era in the history of theology." In reading closely some of his false positions, we soon meet with something so deep and spiritually earnest that we are forgetful of the doubt, being attracted by the greater glow of the living truth. As life advanced he improved in his appreciation of doctrine, and his latest works are hardly recognizable as written by the same hand. He published several books, of which we have made no mention, but in all the fruits of his pen he revealed an unfailing love of a personal Redeemer. His sermons were the outflow of his genial nature, kindled by his stern view of Christ's communion with his living disciples Mr. Farrar eloquently sums up his work, though it must be acknowledged that the present generation stands too near the time of Schleiermacher's activity to bestow an impartial estimate upon either the theological position of the man or the influence resulting from him. "We have seen," says this author, "how completely he caught the influences of his time, absorbed them and transmitted them. If his teaching was defective in its constructive side; if he did not attain the firm grasp of objective verity which is implied in perfect doctrinal, not to say critical, orthodoxy, he at least gave the death-blow to the old Rationalism, which either from an empirical or a rational point of view, proposed to gain such a philosophy of religion as reduced it to morality. He rekindled spiritual apprehensions; he, above all, drew attention to the peculiar character of Christianity, as something more than the republication of natural religion, in the same manner that the Christian consciousness offered something more than merely moral experience. He set forth, however imperfectly, the idea of redemption, and the personality of the Redeemer; and awakened religious aspirations, which led his successors to a deeper appreciation of the truth as it is in Jesus. Much of his theology and some part of his philosophy had only a temporary interest relatively to the times; but his influence was perpetual. The faults were those of his age; the excellencies were his own. Men caught his deep love to a personal Christ without imbibing his doctrinal opinions. His own views became more evangelical as his life went on, and the views of his disciples more deeply Scriptural than those of their master. Thus the light kindled by him waxed purer and purer. The mantle remained after the prophet's spirit had ascended to the God that gave it."[1]

De Wette was, like Schleiermacher his friend and colleague at Berlin, a man in whom can be seen all the marks of a transition-character. There are two sides to his theological views, one bearing upon the old Rationalism and in sympathy with it, the other directly tending to revive faith and religion. Even before Schleiermacher became generally known, De Wette had openly declared that religion can be based upon feeling alone, and that a personal Saviour is the necessary centre of Christian faith. The entire theology of De Wette was the outgrowth of the cold, critical philosophy of Kant and the more earnest and living system of Fries. He was, therefore, a two-fold personage, and

[1] *Critical History of Free Thought*, p. 249.

it is not an easy task to harmonize his theories. One set of his opinions was based upon truth, the other on beauty. Religion has two elements, faith and feeling; doctrines and æsthetics. Religion may exist æsthetically, but it can only become vital in the feeling, or self-consciousness. Religious feeling embraces three shades: enthusiasm or inspiration, resignation, and devotion. Every history is, in a certain sense, symbolical. It is the mere reflection or copy of the human mind in its activity. So are the appearance of Christ, his life, and death, in some degree symbolical. In this symbolism consists the character of the Christian revelation. Here have appeared the eternal ideas of reason in their greatest purity and fullness; and Rationalism is nothing more than a philosophical view of the Christian revelation of faith, or the knowledge of the relations in which idea and symbol stand to each other in Christianity. Therefore, we must judge the miraculous accounts of the evangelists as symbols of the ideas existing in the early history of Christianity.

De Wette reflects somewhat on the moral character of John, perhaps without intention, when he supposes him to have written late in life—a time when his faith would naturally predominate over his love of facts. Strauss couples De Wette with Vater, as having placed upon a solid foundation the mythical explication of the history of the Bible.[1] According to De Wette, the narrator may intend to write history, but he obviously does it in a poetic way. The first three evangelists betray a legendary and even a mythical character. This explains the discrepancies in their histories, and also in the discourses and doctrines of Jesus. The miracle that took place at the baptism of Christ was a

[1] *Life of Jesus—Introduction.*

pure myth; and the resurrection and reappearance of Christ have their existence more in the mind than in history. With this view of the New Testament, it is not surprising that the Old should receive even more rigorous usage. The larger part of the Pentateuch was supposed to be taken from two old documents, the Elohistic and Jehovistic, and was compiled somewhere near the close of the legal period. The five books, purporting to have been written by Moses, are the Hebrew epic, and contain no more truth than the great epic of the Greeks. As the Iliad and Odyssey are the production of the rhapsodists, so is the Pentateuch, with the exception of the Decalogue, the continuous and anonymous work of the priesthood. Abraham and Isaac are equally fabulous with Ulysses and Agamemnon. A Canaanitish Homer could have invented nothing better than the journeys of Jacob and the marriage of Rebecca. The departure from Egypt, the forty years in the wilderness, the seventy elders at the head of the tribes, and the complaints of Aaron are each an independent myth. The character of myths is varied in different books; poetic in Genesis, juridical in Exodus, priestly in Leviticus, political in Numbers, etymological, diplomatical, and genealogical, but seldom historical, in Deuteronomy.

De Wette's theological novel, *Theodore, or the Doubter's Consecration*, 1822, was designed to banish the doubts of the skeptic by seeking refuge in the theology of feeling. Tholuck replied to it in his *Guido and Julius*, in which he proves that a deep appreciation and acceptance of Christ by the soul is the only remedy for infidelity. We perceive in De Wette a continual conflict between the longings of his heart and the theological creed to which he attached himself. The lines written by him just before his death touchingly declare the great failure of his life:

> "I lived in times of doubt and strife,
> When child-like faith was forced to yield:
> I struggled to the end of life,
> Alas! I did not gain the field."

With the name of the lamented Neander we hail the morning light of reviving faith. He was one of the purest characters in the history of the modern church. His influence was so great as to lead very many of the young men of Germany to embrace the vital doctrines of Christianity. His father was a Jewish peddler, Emanuel Mendel, and the boy was named David at circumcision. Various forces co-operated in directing his mind toward the Christian religion; of which we might mention the philosophy of Plato, the Romantic School, and above all, Schleiermacher's *Discourses on Religion*. When seventeen years of age he was baptized and received the combined name of his sponsors, John Augustus William Neander. In 1810 he began to lecture in the University of Heidelberg, and in 1813, owing to the publication of his *Julian the Apostate*, he received a call to Berlin. He was there brought into the society of Schleiermacher, Marheineke, De Wette, Fichte, Hegel, Ritter, Ranke and other celebrated men. It was very significant of the new life now beginning to be felt, that his lectures were numerously attended. Even Schleiermacher, his co-laborer for twenty years in the theological faculty, had a limited circle of auditors compared with the throngs who went to hear Neander.

His theological views were more positive and evangelical than those entertained by any of his associates. He shared, with the most orthodox of them, the opinion that religion is based upon feeling. The Christian consciousness was the sum of his theology. "By this term," said he, "is designated the power of the Christian faith in the subjective life of the single individual, in the congregation, and in the church generally; a power independent and ruling according to its own law,—that which, according to the word of our Lord, must first form the leaven of every other historical development of mankind." Neander was not a man of very strong prejudices; yet his disapprobation of the destructive nature of Rationalism was very decided. The reduction of religion to intellectualism received severe rebukes at his hand on more than one occasion. "I shall never cease," he declared, "to protest against the one-sided intellectualism, that fanaticism of the understanding, which is spreading more and more, and which threatens to change man into an intelligent, over-wise beast. But at the same time I must protest against that tendency which would put a stop to the process of development of theology; which, in impatient haste, would anticipate its aim and goal, although with an enthusiasm for that which is raised above the change of the days,—an enthusiasm which commands all respect, and in which the hackneyed newspaper categories of Progress and Retrogression are out of the question."

Neander's motto, "Pectus est, quod theologum facit,' unfolds his whole theological system and life-career. The Germans call his creed "Pectoralism," in view of the inner basis of his faith. With him, religion amounts to nothing without Christ. Nor must Christ be the mere subject of study; the soul and its manifold affections must embrace him. The barrenness of Judaism is done away in him, and the emptiness of Rationalistic criticism is successfully met by the fullness found in Christianity. Sin is not merely hurtful and prejudicial, but it induces guilt and danger. It can be pardoned only through the death and mediation of Christ. The illustrations of devout service to be found in the history of the church should serve as examples for succeeding times. Neander spent much of the careful labor of his life in portraying prominent characters; for it was his opinion that individuals sometimes combine the features of their times, the virtues or the vices prevalent; and that if these individualities be clearly defined the church is furnished with valuable lessons for centuries. The work published when but twenty-two years of age, *Julian the Apostate*, was the beginning of a series of similar monographs designed to show the importance of the individual in history, and to point out great crises in the religious life of man. He subsequently produced works entitled *St. Bernard*, *Gnosticism*, *St. Chrysostom*, *Tertullian*, *History of the Apostolic Age*, *Life of Christ*, and *Memorials of Christian Life*. To these may be added a few practical commentaries, essays, and a *History of Doctrines*.

But the great achievement of Neander was his *General History of the Christian Religion and Church*, embracing the period from the close of the apostolic age to the Council of Basle in 1430. Christianity is, in his conception, not simply a growth or development of man; it is a new power, a creation of God, a divine gift to the world. Therefore the history of the Church of Christ is the clear exhibition of the divine strength of Christianity; it is a school of Christian experience, a voice of warning and instruction for all who will hear it as it echoes down through the grand march of centuries.[1] The history of

[1] *History of the Christian Religion and Church. Preface to First Edition.*

the church, far from being the scholar's theme alone, furnishes nutritious food for the practical life of all the disciples of the Lord. If its history be permitted to exert its due influence upon the world, we shall behold a gratifying and widespread improvement in all things that increase happiness and lead heavenward.

It is quite too late to answer the charge against Neander's profundity. His achievements are his best defense, and the pen of censure is fast beginning to lose its bitterness. It is not time for him to be fully appreciated at home; for, as the beauty of the landscape is dependent on the sun to make it apparent, so Neander's character and labors must wait for an honorable and universal recognition until new evangelical light shall have overspread the land. A century hence he will be loved as dearly by the German people as he was by those weeping students who gathered around his grave to see his face for the last time. What Krummacher said on the occasion of his burial will yet be the testimony of the church, whose history was Neander's earthly Eden: "One of the noblest of the noble in the Kingdom of God, a prince in Zion, the youngest of the church Fathers, has departed from us."

Neander's relation to his times was most important. The various influences hitherto employed against Rationalism had proceeded as far toward its extinction as it was possible for them to go. Philosophy and doctrinal theology had spent their efforts. The history of the church having always been treated mechanically, it was now necessary that the continued presence and agency of Christ with his people should be carefully portrayed. The progress of his church needed to be represented as more than growth from natural causes, much as the force of civilization and education. It was necessary to show that a high superintending Wisdom is directing its path, overcoming its difficulties, and leading it through persecution and blood to ultimate triumph. Neander rendered this important service. He directed the vision of the theologian to a new field, and became the father of the best church historians of the nineteenth century. The child-like simplicity of his character was beautiful. Everything like vanity and pretense was as foreign to him as if he dwelt on a different planet. A recent German writer calls him a "Protestant monk or saint, whose world was the cloister of the inner man, out of which he worked and taught for the good of the church."

Of his remarkable personal appearance, Dr. Schaff, who enjoyed his friendship, says: "In his outward appearance Neander was a real curiosity, especially in the lecture-room. Think of a man of middle size, slender frame, homely but interesting and benevolent face, dark and strongly Jewish complexion, deep-seated, sparkling eyes, overshadowed by an unusually strong, bushy pair of eyebrows, black hair flowing in uncombed profusion over the forehead, an old-fashioned coat, a white cravat carelessly tied, as often behind or on one side of the neck as in front, a shabby hat set aslant, jack-boots reaching above the knee; think of him thus either as sitting at home, surrounded by books on the shelves, on the table, on the few chairs, and all over the floor; or as walking *unter den Linden*, and in the Thiergarten of Berlin, leaning on the arm of his sister Hannchen, or a faithful student, his eyes shut or looking up to heaven, talking theology in the midst of the noise and fashion of the city, and presenting altogether a most singular contrast to the teeming life around him, stared at, smiled at, wondered at, yet respectfully greeted by all who knew him; or as finally standing on the rostrum, playing with a goose-quill which his amanuensis had always to provide; constantly crossing and recrossing his feet, bent forward, frequently sinking his head to discharge a morbid flow of spittle, and then again suddenly throwing it on high, especially when aroused to polemic zeal against pantheism and dead formalism; at times fairly threatening to overturn the desk, and yet all the while pouring forth with the greatest earnestness and enthusiasm, without any other help than that of some illegible notes, an uninterrupted flow of learning and thought from the deep and pure fountain of the inner life; and thus with all the oddity of the outside, at once commanding the veneration and confidence of every hearer; imagine all this, and you have a picture of Neander, the most original phenomenon in the literary world of this nineteeth century."[1]

[1] *Germany—Its Universities, Theology, and Religion*, pp. 269-270.

CHAPTER XI.

THE REACTION PRODUCED BY STRAUSS' LIFE OF JESUS. 1835—1848.

It is related of Apelles, that, after finishing his pictures, he was in the habit of hanging them in front of his studio and then of concealing himself in order to hear unseen the criticisms of the passers-by. On one occasion, when a new picture was thus exposed to public inspection, a shoemaker stopped before it and observed that something was wrong about a sandal. After he had gone Apelles saw the justice of the objection and corrected the fault. The next day, when the shoemaker was passing again and saw that much importance had been attached to his opinion, he ventured to criticise a leg, but Apelles rushed out from behind the curtain, and, charging him with being hypercritical, told him that for the future he would do better to keep to his trade. The circumstance gave rise to the Roman proverb—"Ne sutor ultra crepidam."

The day was now near at hand when the criticism of the Scriptures, as conducted by the Rationalists, would go quite beyond the province of their authority and the bounds of moderation. When we read the cold, deliberate chapters of Ammon, Eichhorn, and Michaelis, we unconsciously identify ourselves with their generation, and exclaim, "Surely there will never be a step beyond this; the knife can have no edge for a deeper incision." As Neander toiled in his study, digging up the buried treasures of the past and enriching them with the John-like purity of his own heart in order that he might faithfully interpret the divine guidance of the church, he no doubt rejoiced in the conviction that the Rationalists had achieved their last great success, and that the work before him and those who believed as he did was to be henceforth more constructive than controversial. His co-workers were few in number, but they had pleasing indications in many quarters that their labors would have a triumphant issue.

It was very evident that, though there was a general rejection of the doctrine of inspiration in that elevated sense which it is the glory of the American church to entertain, there were great numbers who had become as captivated with Schleiermacher's word, *feeling*, as if it had been a harp-note from heaven. The people had thought so little about their own hearts within the last half century that they seemed to have forgotten their stewardship of the treasure. The whole land had been converted into a colossal thinking machine. And when the German people were told by a stentorian voice that man is emotional as well as intellectual they arose as from a long stupefaction. So, when Schleiermacher died in 1834, there were many who said with unfeigned gratitude, "He is gone, but sweet be his sleep, for he has told us that we have heart and soul."

Three years before Schleiermacher's death the spirit of Hegel had taken its departure. These were the two men who, though dead, were now speaking more authoritatively to the German mind than all others. Schleiermacher was represented by men more orthodox than himself, who gave every assurance of leaving the world far better than they had found it. Hegel had taught too long and thoroughly to be without influence after his eyes had ceased to look upon his entranced auditors at Berlin. It was not long after his death that his favorite theory of antagonisms had a literal fulfillment in the course adopted by the adherents to his opinions. His most ardent disciples found it difficult to tell what he had believed definitely, so varied are the expressions of his views in the eighteen volumes of his works. Even the same book was interpreted differently. His *Philosophy of Religion* was twice edited, first in a conservative sense by Marheineke, and afterward in a revolutionary light by Bruno Bauer.[1] Some passages in his *History of Philosophy* were written in defense of pantheism, while his later views have been brought forth in proof of his opposition to that error. Thus variously interpreted, and yet powerful in his hold upon the intellectual classes of Germany, it was impossible for his disciples to live in harmony. The chief points at issue were the personality of God, the immortality of the soul, and the person of Christ. Either side might be taken and the position defended by the master's own words. The result of this diversity of interpretation was a schism. Hegel's school was divided, after the model of the French Chambers, into three sections—the Right, the Centre, the Left. The Right asserted the orthodoxy of the Hegelian philosophy; the Centre held a position corresponding to their name; and the Left were unmitigated Rationalists. The last group were true to the skepticism inherited from their predecessors, and were radicals in church and state. They rejected

[1] Appleton's *New Am. Cyclopædia; Art. Hegel.*

the personality of God, a future life, and the credibility of the Gospel narratives.

Strauss was a Left Hegelian, and his *Life of Jesus* became the creed of his brethren in doubt. He was not in perfect harmony with all their extremes, but he co-operated with them, and gave them their chief glory.

The world has seldom seen a literary venture more remarkable in contents or in history than this meteor across the firmament of German theology. To say that it was unexpected is but a faint expression of the universal surprise occasioned by it. The Left Hegelians were a limited school and the current of theological thought had been against them. Therefore, when the *Life of Jesus* appeared, it was a bold thrust from an arm thought to possess but little strength. The author, David Frederic Strauss, was a young lecturer on theology in the University of Tübingen. He had experienced the several shades of opinion prevalent during his student life. Beginning with the Romantic School, lingering awhile with Schleiermacher, and finally passing through the gate Beautiful of Hegel's system, he tarried with that master as "lord of the hill." His stay was not brief, like that of Bunyan's pilgrim. But satisfied only by making greater progress, the philosophy of the great thinker became his Delectable Mountains, "beautiful with woods, vineyards, fruits of all sorts, flowers also, with springs and fountains, very delectable to behold."

Strauss was but twenty-eight years old when his cold, passionless, and pungent piece of skeptical mechanism was presented to the world. Who would suspect that quiet young man of possessing so much power over the minds of his countrymen? M. Quinet, speaking of a visit to him, said, "Beneath this mask of fatalism I find in him a young man full of candor, of sweetness and modesty; of a spirit almost mystical, and apparently saddened by the disturbance which he had occasioned." His book produced a universal impression in Europe. It was, to the moral sentiment of Christendom, the earthquake shock of the nineteenth century. Having been multiplied in cheap editions, it was read by students in every university and gymnasium, by passengers on the Rhine boats and in the mountain stages, and by a great number of private families. Even school children, imitating the example of their seniors, spent their leisure hours in its perusal. The most obscure provincial papers contained copious extracts from it, and vied with each other in defending or opposing its positions. Crossing the German frontier, it was published in complete and abridged forms in all the principal languages of Europe. Even staid Scotland, unable to escape the contagion, issued a popular edition of the exciting work.

Nor were the views advanced by Strauss in his *Life of Jesus* less extraordinary than its very flattering reception. He was diametrically opposed to Neander in the latter's estimate of the ideal and historical. According to Strauss the idea is the very soul of all that is valuable in the past; and history is the gross crust which envelops it. What is history in its early stages but so many faint legends? Happy are we if, within them, we can discover the seed-truth. The same neglect of the movements of history in their outward form led Strauss into still another tendency which proved to be in direct conflict with Neander. The latter, as we have seen, was devoted to his theory of the importance and power of personality in history. But Strauss rejected it as of small moment. He attached great importance to the issue involved, but regarded the persons engaged in bringing it to pass as mere machinery.

This contempt of the historical and the personal is the key to Strauss' work. The church, when it continued faithful, had always looked to the Gospels as the Holy Sepulchre of its faith, and was ever ready to make a crusade against the power which would wrest it from her grasp. But, amid the conflicts occasioned by the growth of the destructive criticism, the Gospels had received at its hands a treatment no less severe than had been inflicted upon the history of the Old Testament. Many theories had already been propounded by the Rationalists in order to account for them, but there was no general harmony among these men either on this or any subject of speculation. Wetstein, Michaelis, and Eichhorn were agreed that the Gospels were more human than divine, and the fate to which all the inspired records were consigned by those critics and their sympathizers has its analogy in the treatment bestowed by vultures upon the carcass of the exhausted beast that has fallen by the wayside. But, after all, the accounts of the Evangelists had suffered less severely than any other part of the Scriptures, and the injury they had sustained was owing more to the attacks made on the historical and prophetical portions of the Old Testament than to any immediate invasion. For the Bible is a unity. If but one book be mutilated the whole organism is disturbed.

The contest having been hitherto connected with other features of revelation more than with the person of Christ, it was no part of the design of the Rationalists to submit without staking a great battle upon the incarnation of the Messiah. Let them succeed here, and they can rebuild more firmly all they have lost. but if they fail, they will only bring to a more speedy ruin an edifice already in decay. Strauss undertook the work; and having written for the learned alone, no one was more surprised than himself at the popular success of the *Life of Jesus.*

According to him, the explanation of the mysterious accounts of Jesus of Nazareth can be found in the theory of the myth. Strauss held that the Holy Land was full of notions concerning his speedy appearance. The people were waiting for him, and were ready to hail his incarnation with rapture. Their opinons concerning him were already formed, owing to the expectations they had inherited from their fathers. Therefore, any one who answered their views would be the Messiah. There was much in both the character and life of Christ which approached their crude notions of the promised one. For this reason their hearts went out toward him, and they called him "Jesus." The world was already prepared, and since Christ best fitted it, he was entitled to all the honor of being waited for and accepted. All the prophecies of his incarnation were purely historical events. But the Jewish mind is very visionary and prone to allegory. Consequently, when Christ appeared among the Jews, it was not difficult to trace a resemblance between him and other marked personages in history.

Thus Christ did not organize the Church as much as the church created him. He existed and lived on earth, but very different was the real Jesus from that wonderful character described in the Gospels. The veritable Messiah was born of humble parentage, was baptized by John, collected a few disciples, inveighed against the Pharisees and all others who placed themselves in antagonism to him, and finally fell a victim to the cruelty of his foes. Years passed by after his death, and the popular imagination went wild with reports and exaggerations of the once obscure Nazarene. Great as the ideas of the people were before Christ appeared, they were infinitely magnified during the lapse of the thirty years between his death and the composition of the Gospels. These narratives are consequently not a representation of history, but of morbid popular fancies. The evangelists did not intend to deceive their readers; their picturesque sketches were only designed to clothe the ideal in the garb of the real. "Be not so unkind," Strauss says in effect, "as to charge these poor uneducated men with evil purposes. They were very unsophisticated, and did not know enough to have any extended plan of trickery. They heard wonderful stories floating about, just such as one meets with in all countries after a prominent man has died; and, as they had a little capacity for using the pen, they wrote them down to the best of their ability. Their writings are curious but very defective, since the authors were too unpractised in literary work to perfect a master-piece. How little they dreamed of the reverence which future generations would pay them! Poor souls, they hardly knew what they were doing. One caught one story, and his friend another; and it is a nice bit of mosaic which we find in their school-boy productions. No wonder their defenders are unable to harmonize their accounts. Let any four men who live among a legend-loving people transcribe the traditions they hear from the lips of childhood and garrulous old age, or read in the popular romances of the day, and it will surprise no one that they do not agree. How can they tell the same things in the same way, since the sources of each are so different? Nor, with only myths for warp and woof, is it at all surprising that we have nothing more than Homeric exaggerations when the fanciful fabric is once woven."

The introduction to the *Life of Jesus* consists of an essay on the historical development of the mythical theory. Having stated its present shape and great value, it is then applied to the life of Christ in the body of the work. This is the climax of destructive crititicism. Everything which Christ is reported by the Evangelists to have said or done shares the natural explanations of Strauss. From his very birth to his ascension, his life is no more remarkable than that of many others who have taken part in the public events of their times.

Beginning with the annunciation and birth of John the Baptist, Strauss considers the apparition to Zacharias and his consequent dumbness as actual external circumstances, susceptible of a natural interpretation. Zacharias had a waking vision or ecstasy. Such a thing is not common, but in the present instance, many circumstances combined to produce an unusual state of mind. The exciting causes were, *first*, the long-cherished desire to have a posterity; *second*, the exalted vocation of administering in the Holy Place and offering up with the incense the prayers of the people to the throne of Jehovah, which seemed to Zacharias to foretoken the acceptance of his own prayer; and *third*, perhaps an exhortation from his wife as he left his house, similar to that of Rachel to Jacob. Gen. xxx. 1. In this highly excited state of mind, as he prays in the dimly-lighted sanctuary, he thinks of his most ardent wish, and expecting that now or never his prayer shall be heard, he is prepared to discern a sign of its acceptance in the slightest occurrence. As the glimmer of the lamp falls upon the ascending cloud of incense, and shapes it into varying forms, the priest imagines that he perceives the figure of an angel. The apparition at first alarms him, but he soon regards it as an assurance from God that his prayer is heard. No sooner does a transient doubt cross his mind, than the sensitively pious priest looks upon himself as sinful and believes himself reproved by the angel. Now, either an apoplectic seizure actually deprives him of speech, which he receives as the just punishment of his incredulity, until the excessive joy he experiences at the circumcision of his son restores the power of utterance—so that dumbness is retained as an external, physical, though not miraculous occurrence—or the proceeding is psychologically understood; namely, that Zacharias, in accordance with a Jewish superstition, for a time denied himself the use of the offending member. Reanimated in other respects by the extraordinary event, the priest returns home to his wife, and she becomes a second Sarah.[1]

The original histories are adduced, and the parallels fully drawn between them and the gospel narratives in order to show the mythical character of the latter. The birth of John the Baptist is the mongrel product of the Old Testament stories of the birth of Isaac, of Samson, and of Samuel. Every event related by the evangelists is so strained as to make it analogous to other occurrences in Jewish history. The murder of the innocents by Herod is only a poetic plagiarism of the cruelty of Nimrod and Pharaoh; the star which guided the shepherds, a memory of the star promised in the prophecy of Balaam; Christ explaining the Bible when twelve years old, a gloss upon the precocity

[1] *Life of Jesus.* Ch. I. American Edition.

of Moses, Samuel, and Solomon; the increase of the loaves, a union of the manna in the wilderness and the twenty loaves with which Elisha fed the people; water changed into wine, a new version of the bitter waters made sweet; the cross, a reminder of the brazen serpent; the scene in the Garden of Gethsemane, the bloody sweat and the agony on the cross, poor copies from the Lamentations of Jeremiah; and the two thieves, the nailed hands and feet, the pierced side, the thirst, and the last words of Jesus, are borrowed narratives from the sixty-ninth and twenty-second Psalms.[1]

The same mythical explanation is applied to the conception and divine character of Jesus. By entertaining such notions of him as we find in the gospels we display a superstition worthy of the dim days of pagan legendry. In the world of mythology many great men had extraordinary births, and were sons of the gods. Jesus himself spoke of his heavenly origin, and called God his Father; besides, his title as Messiah was "Son of God." From Matt. i. 22, it is further evident that the passage of Isaiah vii. 14, was referred to Jesus by the early Christian church. In conformity with this passage the belief prevailed that Jesus, as the Messiah, should be born of a virgin by means of divine agency. It was therefore taken for granted that what was to be actually did occur; and thus originated a philosophical, dogmatical myth concerning the birth of Jesus. But according to historical truth, Jesus was the offspring of an ordinary marriage, between Joseph and Mary, which maintains at once the dignity of Jesus and the respect due to his mother. The transfiguration illustrates both the natural and mythical methods of interpretation. It is a reflection of the scene which trans-

[1] Cf. *Revue des Deux Mondes.* Vol. 16.

pired on Sinai at the giving of the law. The gospel account is an Ossianic fancy. Something merely objective presented itself to the disciples, and this explains how an object was perceived by several at once. They deceived themselves, when awake, as to what they saw. That was natural, because they were all born within the same circle of ideas, were in the same frame of mind, and in the same situation. According to this opinion, the essential fact in the scene on the mountain is a secret interview which Jesus had concerted, and, with a view to which, he took with him the three most confidential of his disciples. Paulus does not venture to determine who the two men were with whom Jesus held this interview; Kuinöl conjectures that they were secret adherents of the same kind as Nicodemus; and according to Venturini, they were Essenes, secret allies of Jesus. Jesus prayed before these arrived, and the disciples, not being invited to join, slept. For the sleep noticed by Luke, though it were dreamless, is gladly retained in this interpretation, since a delusion appears more probable in the case of persons just awaking. On hearing strange voices talking with Jesus, they awake, and see him—who probably stood on a higher point of the mountain than they—enveloped in an unwonted brilliancy, caused by the reflection of the sun's rays from a sheet of snow. This light falling on Jesus is mistaken by them in the surprise of the moment for a supernatural illumination. They perceive the two men whom, for some unknown reasons, the drowsy Peter and the rest take for Moses and Elias. Their astonishment increases when they see the two strange individuals disappear in a bright morning cloud —which descends as they are in the act of departing— and hear one of them pronounce out of the cloud the words, "This is my beloved Son in whom I am well pleased; hear ye him." Under these circumstances they unavoidably regard this as a voice from heaven.

The resurrection of Christ is regarded by Strauss as a psychological necessity placed upon the disciples, first to solve the contradiction between the ultimate fate of Jesus and their earlier opinion of him, and second to adopt into their idea of the Messiah the characteristics of suffering and death.

"When once the idea of a resurrection of Jesus had been formed in this manner," says Strauss, "the great event could not have been allowed to happen so simply, but must be surrounded and embellished with all the pomp which the Jewish imagination furnished. The chief ornaments which stood at command for this purpose were angels; hence these must open the grave of Jesus; must, after he had come forth from it, keep watch in the empty place, and deliver to the women,—who, because without doubt women had the first visions, must be the first to go to the grave,—the tidings of what had happened. As it was Galilee where Jesus subsequently appeared to them, the journey of the disciples thither, which was nothing else than their return home, somewhat hastened by fear, was derived from the direction of an angel; nay, Jesus himself must already before his death, and as Matthew too zealously adds, once more after the resurrection also, have enjoined this journey on the disciples. But the farther these narratives were propagated by tradition, the more must the difference between the locality of the resurrection itself and that of the appearance of the risen one be allowed to fall out of sight as inconvenient; and since the locality of the death was not transferable, the appearances were gradually placed in the same locality as the resurrection,—in Jerusalem, which, as the more brilliant theatre and the seat of the first Christian church, was especially appropriate for them."[1]

The ascension is claimed as a myth founded upon the Old Testament precedents of the translation of Enoch and the ascension of Elijah, and the pagan apotheosis of Hercules and Romulus.

The last part of Strauss' work is a dissertation on the dogmatic import of the life of Jesus. Here this merciless critic tries to prove that, though the belief of the church concerning Christ be thus uprooted by the theory of myths, nothing truly valuable is destroyed. He declares it his purpose "to re-establish dogmatically that which has been destroyed critically." He holds that all his criticism is purely independent of Christian faith; for, "The supernatural birth of Christ, his miracles, his resurrection and ascension, remain eternal truths, whatever doubts may be cast on their reality as historical facts." Thus, reliance is placed upon a difference between the import of criticism and christian faith—which subterfuge proved a broken reed when the masses read this mythical interpretation of the life of the Founder of Christianity. In vain did Strauss say, in the preface to his work, that it was not designed for the laity, and that if they read it, it must be at their own hazard. It was published—and therefore the public had a right to demand an examination. Let him who writes an evil thought never be deceived by the opinion that only those will read it who cannot be injured by it. "What is writ, is writ;" and then it is too late to wish it "worthier."

But the most remarkable feature of the work of Strauss yet remains to be traced. It was a compilation,

[1] *Life of Jesus*, 852-3.

and nothing more. Having ransacked every skeptical writer on the gospel history, he published their views at length in his *Life of Jesus*. He did not make many quotations. But the references at the foot of almost every page declare plainly enough the pains he took to put in force the incantation he had pronounced to all skeptical sprites,

> "Black spirits and white, red spirits and gray,
> Mingle, mingle, mingle; ye that mingle may."

No Rationalist escaped his notice. The English Naturalists reäppeared with all their original pretensions. Bolingbroke, Voltaire, Lessing, Kant, De Maistre, and all the representatives of skeptical thought communed in friendly society, regardless alike of disparity in particular opinions and of difference in the time when they flourished. On this very account M. Quinet infers the great popularity of the enterprise. Because it was a grouping of all heterodox doctrines of the person of Christ, the adherents of Rationalism saw whither their principles were leading them, and their opponents learned more of the desperate character of their foe than they had ever acquired from all other sources. It was a crystallization of the imputations and insults cast upon the gospels for more than seventy-five years. Then, for the first time, did the votaries of error, mass themselves. It was then, too, that the evangelical school were first able to count the number of their opponents.

The scene before the publication of the *Life of Jesus* was quite different from the one presented subsequently. Formerly the Rationalists said what they chose about Christ, and they suffered little from their rashness. But immediately after Strauss had issued his book, the attention of the church was profoundly attracted toward the consideration of the themes therein treated. The church seemed to say, "Strange, that I have given so little attention to this great pillar of Christian faith; now I see what reward I am receiving for my neglect. The like shall never happen again. No, I will not only quench this firebrand, but I will hurl back upon my enemies enough destructive missiles to reduce them to a disorganized band of homeless fugitives." This resolution was not the work of idle excitement, and soon to be forgotten. The replies to the *Life of Jesus* constitute a theological literature. They were very numerous, and written from as many points of view as there had been theological schools since the dawn of the Reformation. The first rejoinder came from the most distinguished theologian of Würtemberg, Steudel of Tübingen. He was superintendent of the very school where Strauss was tutor, and his work was written but a few weeks after the issue of the first volume of the *Life of Jesus*. It discussed the question whether Christ's life rested on a historical or mythical basis. The conclusion was an uncompromising decision in favor of the former view. Steudel represented the old Lutheran orthodoxy.

We now meet with the name of Hengstenberg, whom Providence designed to be an instrument of much good to the theology of the present day. He proved himself an unflinching hero when he dealt his first blows from his professor's chair in Berlin. His utterances soon acquired great importance wherever the current controversies attracted attention. He was the leader of the young orthodox school, and in his newly-founded *Evangelical Church Gazette*, he pictured his times in the language of desolation. His words were worthy of the dark days of Jeremiah. Adopting the exclamation of that prophet, he cried aloud, "Oh that my head were waters, and mine eyes a fountain of tears, that I might weep day and night for the slain of the daughter of my people!" Theologians, philosophers, and tradesmen seemed to him to be overwhelmed in skepticism. But he had a lion's heart, and fought steadily for the growth of the pure faith of the olden time. Nor has he grown tired of the warfare. He appears to have been born upon the battle-field, within sound of drum and cannon. He is as much the warrior to-day as when he entered the lists against Strauss nearly thirty years ago. His opinion of his great antagonist may be summed up in his own language. He says of him that, "He has the heart of a leviathan, which is as hard as a stone and as firm as the nether millstone; he assails the Lord's Anointed with composure and cold-bloodedness; and not a tear of pity flows from his eyes."

Harless and Hoffman followed in spirited criticisms on the *Life of Jesus*. Tholuck next appeared upon the arena in his *Credibility of the Gospel History*. This production was somewhat declamatory in style, but that was no barrier to its utility. It attacked Strauss in the weakest spot, namely, in his deductions against the authenticity and apostolic origin of the gospels. Tholuck defines a miracle to be an event which appears contrary to the course of nature, and has a religious origin and aim. He allows that inspiration is not total but partial, and that it is but fair to concede to his opponent the presence of Scriptural defects, such as mistakes of memory, and errors in historical, chronological, and astronomical details. We must be content to know and feel that, in the Bible, we find a basis of inspiration which is none the less substantial though surrounded by intruding weeds, or fragments of stone and mortar. But Tholuck's work is not a fair specimen of his writings. Besides its literary defects, the author concedes much more to the Rationalists here than he is accustomed to do in his many superior publications.

Again we meet with the revered name of Neander. His *Life of Christ* appeared in 1837. He published it not only as a reply to Strauss, but as an independent treatise upon the person of the Messiah. He announced himself as the mediator between those bitter partisans who, on the one side, would grant no rights to reason, and on the other, would leave no space for the exercise of feeling and faith. His work stands in the same relation to criticism which Schleiermacher's *Discourses* occupies to dogmas, and as the latter appears sometimes to lean toward Rationalism, so do we find in the former traces of concession to the destructive method of criticism. Neander's work, despite everything which he grants to his enemies, was the transition-agent toward a purer comprehension of the life of Christ. While we lament that he interprets the early life of Christ as a fragment derived from an evangelical tradition; that he believes the influence of demons in the gospel period susceptible of a psychological explanation, that the miraculous feeding of the five thousand is but the multiplication and potentialization of substances already at hand, that the feeding of the four thousand is a mistaken account of the former, and that the changing of the water into wine at Cana of Galilee was nothing more than an increase of power in the water, as we find sometimes in mineral fluids,—granting these and all the other interpretations which Neander makes on the score of nature or myths, we must attach an importance to his *Life of Christ* second only to his *History of the Christian Church.* One closes the reading of his account of the Messiah with a profound impression that the author had a true conception of the divinity and authority of the Founder of Christianity. We cannot doubt his sympathy with those words of Pascal which he quoted frequently with exquisite pleasure: "En Jesus Christ toutes les contradictions sont accordées."

Ullmann, in his treatise *Historical or Mythical*, will not accept the alternative that the life of Christ is all mythical or all historical. He enumerates the philosophical myth, the historical myth, mythical history, and history with traditional parts. It is to the last of these that he assigns the gospel history. He propounds the dilemma, whether the church has conceived a poetical Christ, or whether Christ is the real founder of the church? He accepts the latter, and invokes all history in proof of his argument. Weisse, in his *Gospel History treated Philosophically and Critically*, dwells upon the relative claims of the four gospels. At least one of the gospels is original and the authority for the rest. This is Mark's; and it is not mythical, but historical and worthy of credence. Matthew is a compilation of a later day; and Luke and John are of still less importance. But the miracles related by Mark are purely natural events. Christ's miraculous cures were owing to his physical powers. His body was a strong electric battery, which, in his later life, lost its power of healing. Else he would have saved himself from death. His early life is unadulterated allegory.

But there were numerous writers against Strauss, among whom may be mentioned Schweizer, Wilke, Schaller, and Dorner. Dorner's *History of the Person of Christ*, 1839, was an attempt to show the totality of

Christ as a universal character. The human conception of species is of a world of fragments, but in Christ we find them completely united. All single, individual prototypes coalesced in him. He is the World-Personality. Bruno Bauer wrote his *Criticism of the Synoptical Gospels* in reply to Strauss, though a few years afterward he changed his ground entirely. His position in this work was as mediator between reason and revelation. He brought into the conflict concerning Strauss' *Life of Jesus* an element of heated argument, and egotism, which ripened into his subsequent antagonism to the supernatural school. His entrance upon this field of strife may be comprehended by Schwartz's comparison of him with Carlstadt and Thomas Munzer, who had lived in the exciting period of the Reformation.

An enumeration of the titles of the works which appeared at frequent intervals during the ten years succeeding the issue of Strauss' *Life of Jesus*, indicates that toward the close of this period the controversy was directed more to the particular gospels than to the life of Christ as a unit. The many theories advanced exceeded all the ordinary illustrations of literary fecundity and extravagance in the department of theology. There was no theologian of note who did not take part in the contest. Pastors of obscure provincial churches, who did not venture upon a complete life of the Messiah, felt themselves competent either to originate a new view of one or more of the gospels, or to elaborate a borrowed one. The excitement was intense. There was no evidence of system in the rapid movement. But now that the battle is over we read the philosophy of the whole conflict. Strauss, without any intention on his part, had shown the church of the present century, its weakness in failing to comprehend the importance of the evangelical history. The numerous replies indicated a hopeful attention to the neglected compendium of divine truth. The friends who rushed to his aid declared by their impetuosity that their cause would have been better served had Strauss never penned a word about Christ. They saw their stronghold in ruins, and looked with tearful eyes upon the future of their creed. The language which Strauss had applied to his excited opponents upon the appearance of his work became severely appropriate to his own adherents, after that production had been faithfully answered. "Their alarm," said he, "was like the screaming of frightened women on seeing one of their cooking utensils fall upon the floor." Granting the appositeness of the illustration, we must add that the alarm mentioned by the critic was of brief duration; while that of the Rationalists and their adherents is like the long-standing despair of a circle of chemists, whose laboratory has been entered through a door left open by themselves, their carefully prepared combinations destroyed, and all their retorts and crucibles shattered into irreparable fragments.

After a long absence of twenty-nine years, Strauss has again appeared as the biographer of Christ. In his former work he wrote for the theological public, but we are now assured that he had ever kept in mind a purpose to do for the masses what he had achieved for critical minds. The last fruit of his pen is his *Life of Jesus Popularly Treated*, which, following close upon the issue of M. Renan's work, appeared in 1864, in the form of a large octavo volume of more than six hundred pages.

Strauss was induced to make his second work more

popular than the first, because of the gross injustice which the clergy had meted out to him in consequence of his former labors to establish the historical position of Christ. The " guild " of professional theologians are interested, he avers, in maintaining their own cause; of course, they would not loose their hold very willingly. The only italicized sentence in his preface is a thrust against this class, whom time has in nowise led him to esteem: " *He who wants to clear the parsons out of the church must first clear miracles out of religion.*" The spirit of the introduction, in which the German writer is always expected to announce his opinions and give the historical reasons therefor, is not materially different from the lengthy one in his *Life of Jesus.* It is divided into three parts. The *first* contains the important attempts which have been made to write the life of Jesus and represent it in its true light. They have all been failures. Hess, Herder, Paulus, Schleiermacher, Hase, Neander, Ebrard, Weisse, Ewald, Keim, and Renan must be content to lie in oblivion. Renan has done very well for a Frenchman; and as a work for France his book has some merit. The *second* treats of the gospels as sources of the life of Jesus. These accounts, not being authentic, are not of sufficient weight to be relied on. The *third* part contains certain explanations necessary to a proper appreciation of the remaining portion of the work. The following language indicates the author's unchanged opinion on the mythical character of Christ: " We now know for a certainty at least, what Jesus was *not* and what he did *not* do, namely, nothing superhuman, nothing supernatural; it will, therefore, now be the more possible for us to so far trace out the suggestions of the Gospels touching the human and natural in him as shall enable us to give at least some outline of what he was and what he wanted to do."

The body of the book is substantially an attempt to show that Christ, as represented by the Evangelists, is a mythical personage. Such a man lived; but his life is not remarkable; it is not what they described it; and not very different from the common life of ordinary men. We have *first*, an historical outline of the life of Jesus. Here Strauss makes himself, and not the Gospel narrators, the biographer of Christ. *Secondly*, we are furnished with the mythical history of Jesus in its origin and growth. The people were expecting some remarkable character, and they seized upon the first one who best answered their notions. John is as bad as his compeers. He is utterly untrustworthy. The only work of the New Testament from an immediate disciple is the Apocalypse of John. But this, too, is wholly unhistorical. Adopting the opinion of the radical Rationalists, Strauss holds that miracles are impossible, and that if God were to operate against natural laws he would be operating against himself. As a specimen of the method of criticism adopted to divest Christ's career of everything miraculous, we may instance Strauss' disposition of the resurrection of Christ. He confesses that if he cannot show that this is mythological, his whole work has been written in vain. Christ did really die, but his resurrection was a vision. His disciples were excited, and believed they saw their Master reappear. But it was a great mistake on their part. It was only an hallucination. Paul had his visions; so did Peter and John; and so did Mary Magdalene, who was subject to nervous disorders.[1]

The second life of Jesus has met with a cold reception. The "People of the Reformation," to whom it

[1] *New York Independent* and *New York Christian Advocate and Journal* —1864.

was flatteringly addressed, prefer a more substantial theology. The tide has turned since 1835, and no man feels the power of the new current more keenly than David Frederic Strauss.

The Rationalists, who gained nothing in the controversy concerning the first *Life of Jesus* by the tutor of Tübingen, were unfortunate in their organized, systematic, and well-sustained effort to regain lost ground. We have reference to the labors of the Tübingen school. Ferdinand Christian Baur was its founder. His works are numerous, and may be divided into two classes: *doctrinal* and *critical*. But there is consistency in all,—and, varied as his subjects of investigation are, they centre in a common focus. Baur sought the solution of the agitated question in the apostolic history rather than in the life of Christ. The Christianity about which so much discussion is elicited, is, according to him, not a perfect and divine production, but only a vital force in process of development. This is the principle which underlies the multifarious theories of the Tübingen school. In order to have a place where to stand and eliminate the theory, the epistles of Paul are chosen. But these are not all authentic. Hence a selection must be made, and, of course, only those must be chosen which are in harmony with the supposition that Christianity is but a dormant germ. Consequently, the Epistles to the Galatians, the Romans, and the Corinthians are favorites. They are made to dispel the darkness, and settle the question.

In them Paul exposes the fact that there were two parties in the early church, the Pauline and the Petrine. They struggled for supremacy, and the conflict was a long one. Peter was a thorough Jew,—and his side predominated even after the death of the principal com batants. Judaism was the cradle of Christianity; and the latter was only an earnest, restless, and reformatory branch of the former. But it was not an offshoot as yet, for Christianity was essentially Jewish all through its first historic period. The canonical writings of the New Testament, which constitute the chief literature of the first two centuries, are the literary monument of Christianity while it was yet undeveloped, and undetached from Judaism. These writings are the *mediating theology* of those distant days. The Petrine party was very strong, until the middle of the second century, when it was obliged to yield to, or rather harmonize with, the Pauline.

Many causes contributed to bring the two factions together. There was an absence of growth quite incompatible with their respective strength. Alone, they were almost unable to brave the storm of persecution. Finally, for the sake of security and propagation, they laid down their weapons, and united under one banner. From this union came the subsequent growth of Christianity. The canonical works so much revered by the church had been written in the interest of one or the other of the parties. Since the enmity has been destroyed, their literary productions must be considered in the light of history. The church is, therefore, much mistaken in attaching importance to the Scriptures, for they were written for a time-serving end, and are quite unworthy of the worth which we attach to them.

A numerous circle of disciples clustered around Baur, and they enjoyed his leadership until his recent death. But the writings of both the master and his school were answered by the best theologians of Germany. Some of the greenest laurels worn by Thiersch, Dorner, Lechler, Lange, Schaff, Bleek, Hase, and Bunsen, were won in the contest with the Tübingen school; and their united labors constitute a compendium of arguments which will not cease for centuries to be of inestimable value in the controversies of the church concerning Christ and the divine origin of Christianity.

The labors of the Tübingen school and of Strauss are two parts of the same effort to destroy the divine basis of Christian faith. We do not impugn the private opinions of the contestants, but we must judge them by their fruits. They wrote and taught against those departments of truth which it is necessary to preserve intact if we would have Christianity continue a vital power of the soul and an aggressive principle in the world. Objections will still be urged against the Gospel history, but it will still be blessed by the ceaseless oversight and unfailing ministrations of the Holy Spirit. Supposing the evangelical accounts to be purely human, we have even then the highest embodiment of truth in the history of man. Herder says, "Have the fishermen of Galilee founded such a history? Then blessed be their memory that they have founded it!" With the conviction that the writers of the Scriptures throughout were inspired men, and spake as they were moved by the Holy Spirit, we have a power demanded alike by the cravings of the soul and the aspirations of the intellect. Blessed with this sentiment, the individual and the church are thoroughly furnished unto every good work.

From Germany we turn to France. The latter country has been the traditional purveyor of revolutionary material for the rest of the Continent. No great popular movement west of the Rhine has been without its influence upon the eastern side. The July Revolution of 1830, which effected the overthrow of the Restoration represented by Charles X., set the German masses in commotion. They were henceforth restless, and ready, whenever occasion offered, to overturn the government and establish a national constitutional basis. The Rationalists were insurrectionary, and, the more rapid their decline in all religious sentiment the more decided was their opposition to constituted authorities. Strauss' *Life of Jesus*, great in its influence upon theology, was equally powerful over the political mind. Every new publication which befriended infidelity was not without its support of faction and discontent.

In connection with the revolutionary tendency, Rationalism assumed also a more pantheistic, and subsequently a more atheistic form. The second important work of Strauss, his *System of Doctrine*, was even more adapted than his first to sap the foundations of faith and social security. It was the embodiment of all the worst features of the Hegelian philosophy. It was frank and bold in all its statements. No man could mistake a single utterance. In it doctrines are traced to their genetic development, and held to be the luxuriant growth of the seeds of error. The truths of Christianity are surrounded by a halo to which it is no more entitled than the sagas of the Northmen. The old dogma was born of prejudice and error, hence the modern conception of it is sheer illusion. Faith and science are irreconcilable foes, for faith is the perversion, and science the development of human nature. Believing and knowing, religion and philosophy, are born antagonists, and man can make no rapid progress if he grovel in the errors of faith. The personality of God is not that of the individual but of the universal. The pantheism of Spinoza is the best solution of God's existence; "for," says Strauss, "God is not the personal, but the infinite personifying of himself."

The oracular responses of Feuerbach[1] were a step beyond even this skeptical usurpation. Religion is man's conduct to himself. Man, from time immemorial, has been buried in self-love, and become so far carried away by it that his religion is now one monstrous hallucination. Religion springs not from his intellect but from his imagination. He wishes to get to heaven; he desires to be comfortable; therefore he believes. He will put himself to no little trouble to propitiate the favor of one whom he considers divine. Here is the mystery of all sacrifices. They are offered by all people from the mere inner force of abject egotism. God has no absolute existence whatever. Christianity needs to be attacked historically. Its chief elements are Judaism and paganism. That it is a collection of absurdities, corruptions, and prejudices, can be perceived on its very face. But still man needs religion, though he can only gain it either by rejecting Christianity altogether or purifying it from its thick envelope of dross.

The *Halle Year-Books*, published 1838–'42, were the principal organ of the new atheistic doctrines. They commenced with the laudation of Strauss, then passed over into the service of Feuerbach, and finally served the cause of Bruno Baur and his fanatical adherents. They were under the chief editorship of Ruge; and, being popular and youthful in style, they wielded an unbounded influence on the dissatisfied and skeptical classes. They broke through all the restraints of religion, and propagated the wildest perversions of Hegel's opinions. Though short-lived, they gained an authority not often enjoyed by a periodical. They were

[1] In *Wesen des Christenthums*, Leipsic, 1841.

factious in the extreme, and became one of the principal agents in effecting the Revolution of 1848. They breathed mildew on everything stable in government and sacred in religion. But, Samson-like, they fell amid the ruin which they inflicted upon others.

Quite a new form of Rationalism was then presented in the popular conventions of the Protestant Friends. These individuals held that by a return to the spirit of the Reformation, Germany would be endowed with a new and living energy. But it must not be the Reformation as the church would have us understand it. It must be an impulse and spirit, not an outward attachment to form and compulsory authority. They were popularly called Friends of Light, and embraced all the schools of Rationalists throughout the land. Their convocation was the parliament of German infidelity. Professing adherence to some of the doctrines of Christianity, they so glossed them that even the atheist could be a member without violating his principles.

Their founder was Pastor Uhlich, who, in company with sixteen friends, held the first meeting at Gnadau, in July, 1841. The second convention met at Halle, and was numerously attended by clergymen, professors, and laymen of every class of society. The session at Köthen, in 1844, was a great popular assembly. It was addressed by Pastor Wislicenus, of Halle, whose lecture was subsequently issued as a reply to his antagonists, under the title of *Whether Scriptures or Spirit?* Not the letter, but the spirit, is the ground of true religion. The spirit permeates humanity, and hence there is no occasion for the observance of the law. The spirit comes with its own law; it is a law in itself. The Evangelical church stands safe only when resting upon freedom. The glory of the church is the absolute freedom of its members. The Scriptures are very good in their way. They are a witness of the faith of the first times, but were never intended for these cultivated days. The church is freed from the exterior law and elevated to the inner law of freedom.

Guericke, the church historian, called attention to Wislicenus in the *Evangelical Church Gazette.* Great surprise was manifested at once, and the sober mind of the nation became aroused to a sense of the danger now threatening the foundations of faith. In a short time the Saxon decree was issued against all assemblies which called in question the Augsburg Confession. The following month, August, 1845, the Prussian cabinet-order appeared, prohibiting all convocations of the Friends of Light. Protests appeared against Wislicenus and his followers, which were followed by counter-protests signed indiscriminately by all classes.

Another popular development of Rationalism occurred in Königsberg, in 1845. Pastor Rupp attacked the Athanasian symbol in his own pulpit, whereupon he was ejected by the consistory. He collected an independent congregation; and thus arose those Free Congregations, which contributed equally to the Rationalistic and revolutionary movements. Appearing in other parts of Germany, they became a formidable opponent of the church. While they held that the Scriptures were their rule of faith in the unity of God, they threw off their authority and that of all symbols. They adopted baptism and the Lord's Supper, and professed allegiance to the civil power. But their influence was against the government, and their two sacraments were odious corruptions. Their form of baptism is enough to determine their religious sentiment: "I baptize thee after the manner of the old apostolic baptism, that Jesus is the Christ; I anoint thy head with water as a sign that thy soul remains pure, pure as the water that runs down the mountain side; and as the water rises to heaven and then returns to the earth, so may you be continually mindful of your heavenly home." Their convocations were finally restricted by the civil authority. The supreme church council issued an excommunicatory order against them; the police broke up their meetings; and forty of the Free Congregations were closed in Prussia alone.

The leaders of the Revolution of 1848 were the organizers of these popular independent movements. When the people had gained the upper hand of their rulers, their very first action was to select the destroyers of their faith as their political champions and representatives. It was, therefore, a great triumph for those fanatical humanists to find themselves seated in the national parliaments of Frankfort and Berlin, and, wherever the revolution extended, to be the leaders of the excited masses.

What could be expected from a revolution conducted by such men as Wislicenus, Blum, Uhlich, Baltzer, Carl Schwartz and their adherents? It was a total failure. And when the restoration was completed in 1849, the reaction against Rationalism became so decided that the leaders had reason to tremble for their lives. The people were profoundly disgusted with a skepticism which could produce no better fruits than this one had matured. The indignation was even more intense than that toward French infidelity during the supremacy of Napoleon over the German States. In the latter case the people were disgusted with the efforts of foreign skepticism, but in the former, they saw and felt the sore evils of domestic Rationalism. Religious error had led them from peace and quiet into a dream-land. When the waking moment came, and the deception became apparent, the surprise at the delusion was overwhelming.

The doctrinal form of Rationalism had been arrested by Schleiermacher and his noble band of followers. Its exegetical prestige had been destroyed by the replies to the *Life of Jesus*. And, as if to make its defeat as humiliating as possible, the last blow was self-inflicted. It was the Revolution of 1848, and its consequent failure, which annihilated the political strength of German Rationalism. There is a God in history. And though one generation may fail to perceive the brightness of his presence, the following one may be favored with the vision. No skeptic should forget that the real philosophy of history is the march of Providence through the ages. But the infidel is the worst reader of history. The light shines, but he turns away from it. Or, as Coleridge expresses it:

> "The owlet Atheism,
> Sailing on obscure wings across the noon,
> Drops his blue-fringed lids, and shuts them close;
> And, hooting at the glorious sun in Heaven,
> Cries out, 'Where is it?'"

There is a deep principle underlying not only the miscarriage of the Revolution of 1848, but of all the popular movements toward independence which occur at a time when the people are involved in religious doubt. It is the spiritual status of a nation which commonly determines its love of law and order. A population adhering to an evangelical interpretation of the Scriptures can be forced to revolution only by evil and ambitious leaders, or by persistent oppression on the part of their rulers. The tardy movement of the American Colonies toward their revolt against the British Government betrayed a great unwillingness to inaugurate the struggle. At the beginning, the conflict was not designed to be a revolution but only a judicious expedient for the improvement of the colonial laws.[1] Wise rulers, governing for the best interests of their country, have generally found that the most discontented of their subjects are the most skeptical. Infidelity and error have systematically arrayed themselves against civil authority. This infidelity does not always assume the same type; for, while in Germany it was a general disbelief in the authenticity of the Scriptures, in France it was the rejection of the existence of God and of the immortality of the soul. Even Robespierre testified before the French National Convention of 1794, that "the idea of a supreme Being and of the immortality of the soul, was a continual call to justice, and that no nation could succeed without the recognition of these truths." A revolution in Christendom, which has its basis in the skeptical nature of man, or in an anti-scriptural idea, may succeed for a while, but it must eventually fail; because, like a vessel without compass, chart, or star, it lacks the cardinal elements and safeguards of progress and security.

[1] The hesitation to become independent was very decided, even as late as July, 1775.—Bancroft, *History of the United States.* Vol. 8: pp. 55-6.

CHAPTER XII.

THE EVANGELICAL SCHOOL. ITS OPINIONS AND PRESENT PROSPECTS.

THERE is a group of theologians who deserve to stand side by side with the immediate opponents of Strauss and his disciples. We mean the Mediation or Evangelical School. They represent the advance of German theology from Rationalism to positive orthodoxy. Beginning with able and irrefutable arguments for the Evangelists, they have extended their discussions to other important branches of Scriptural defence. As a consequence, they have built up a valuable apologetic literature which will occupy a prominent place in the theology of the church.

But, in order to portray the character of the Evangelical School, we shall need to dwell upon certain members in particular.[1]

Not least in honor and achievement is the late Karl Ullmann. He contributed to the *Studien und Kritiken*, a quarterly established by himself and Umbreit, an article on the sinlessness of Christ, which he subsequently elaborated into a volume. One of the most original

[1] For accounts of the later theologians of Germany, consult Schaff, *Germany: Its Universities, Theology and Religion.* Phila., 1857. Also, Schwarz, *Geschichte der Neuesten Theologie, Leipzig, Dritte Ausgabe,* 1864.

of his productions is his *Essence of Christianity*, which placed "him in the centre of the Mediation theology." He holds with Schleiermacher, that Christianity is not as much doctrine as vitality, and that it possesses the creative and organizing power of religion. Christianity is both divine and human; divine in its origin and essence, but human in its development and fulfillment. Without the person of Christ to stand in the very focus of Christianity, the latter becomes void and no more than any moral religion. We can have no proper conception of Christianity apart from its founder, for its whole essence exists in him. Christianity is Christ developing himself in humanity. Christ is God-man in so far as he represents in his own person the perfect unity and interpenetration of the human and divine. Christianity is that religion which neither deifies nor destroys nature. Without considering it essential to prove the facts of Christ's life, Ullmann showed that Christ, in the divine character which we attach to him, was necessary to Christianity just as the pillars are to the superincumbent edifice. The effect of this argument was most salutary, for it was so well timed that it could not be otherwise. There were two things to be established concerning Christ. One was the verity of the Gospel accounts of him; the other was Christ as a necessity for man's faith, the world's progress, and human salvation. The former having been treated by other hands, Ullmann undertook the latter and triumphed. He is one of the most pleasing of the German theologians. Partaking of the warm southern temperament—for he was a Bavarian by birth—he wrote in that easy, natural, and earnest style which renders him a popular writer not only in his own language but when translated into foreign tongues.

We find in Dorner one of the most acute speculative theologians produced by the later Protestant church. His style is as complex as Ullmann's is simple. It is amusing that, in one place, he even enters into a justification of his technical and abstruse writing. Applying himself to dogmatic investigations, the fruit of his labor is his *Doctrine of the Person of Christ.* Christianity was the world's great want, and all the religions of the natural man could not supply its place. But Christianity is vague unless the question be settled concerning the person of Christ. Here is the battle-ground where Christianity and reason must meet and decide the great issue. Hence Dorner passes by the personal ministry and history of Christ on earth and attempts the proper mode of construing his person. The Person of Christ is, in the trials and triumphs of individuals and the church, the central point of the Christian religion. He is the perfect Lawgiver, and also the Judge of the world. He controls the universe. Here he communicates the forgiveness of sins and the Holy Ghost, and in heaven, eternal felicity. The happiness of heaven is formed by perfect fellowship with his person. He has left his followers only in appearance, for, wherever two or three are assembled in his name, there he is in the midst of them. He is with his own always, even to the end of the world. To know Christ in his nearness belongs to the Christian worship; and this institution is appointed for the church as the highest means for the enjoyment of his nearness.[1]

According to Dorner, heathendom longed for the apotheosis of human nature. Judaism sought the fulfillment of the revelation not completed by the law, and

[1] *Doctrine of Person of Christ* (Clark's Foreign Theological Library, VI—VIII).

strained after the love of God as the consummation of the holy law. All these wants are met in Christ. He is the innermost revelation of the mystery, and the fullest condescension of God. For God has in Christ become man. Here is the point of unity between God and the world. But Christ did not appear in order to be the Son of God, as if this were the ultimate end; but the ultimate end was the glorifying of man, and therewith of God, in and through him. He is officially God's son.[1]

Was Christ possessed of sinless perfection? In both a physical and ethical point of view he was not absolutely complete from the first. He learned obedience. He *grew* in favor, not only with men but with God. Growth points backward to previous deficiency, or, what is the same thing, forward to the absolute goal which the reality approaches only by degrees. But deficiency in entire perfection is not sinfulness, for then all real humanity and sinfulness would be identical. Christ's temptations are explainable on this wise: he had a real moral task, not only external to himself, but in himself, which could not be solved at the beginning if he was to be like us. There was no disorder in him, but there were disorder and sin without him, which occasioned him the contests, temptations, and sufferings that filled his official life. These later conflicts were only assigned him because he remained the pure One, and had become morally harmonious in the midst of moral anarchy. But they were still inward and personal struggles; for he was to introduce the power of his harmony and of his sufferings, in order to overcome the disharmony in the world. He, the righteous one, must, by suffering, take upon himself disorder and dis-

[1] *Doctrine of Person of Christ*, Vol. 1, pp 80-81.

harmony, must live through it and taste it, in order to establish a power which is not only harmonious in itself, but so potent in harmony as to take the disharmony into itself, master it, and transform it into harmony. Christ was perfect man in growth and progress, in his temptations and conflicts, but without any historical trace of a flaw or blemish in his life. He was in all points made like us, without being necessitated to become like us as sinners. For, sin is the negation of the truly human. He laid claim to no exceptional law for himself as a privileged individual, but subjected himself to the universal human moral law. With this he was satisfied, and he fulfilled it in its purity, depth, and completeness. He knew nothing of a super-moral religious genius, and would have nothing to do with it. His religion is moral; his morality, religion.[1]

The name with which we are most familiar is the devout and laborious Tholuck. He generally takes higher ground than many of the Mediation-theologians. But he is sometimes at variance with evangelical sentiment. Inspiration, according to him, is not real and total, but only partial, and is to be determined in reference to the truths necessary to salvation. While there are many mistakes of memory, false citations, errors in historical, chronological, geographical, and astronomical detail, these need not depreciate our general estimate of inspiration. The Scriptures have a kernel and a shell. Upon the former there is the positive and direct impress of the Holy Spirit; but upon the latter it is indirect and relative.

In merely stating Tholuck's definitions, however, we do not measure out justice to him. He must not be tested by any special department of labor, but by the

[1] *American Presb. and Theolog. Review*, January, 1863.

spirit and totality of his service. In this light he is a remarkable personage, and his work is entitled to our highest eulogium. With him, Christ is not merely a person to be apprehended by the mind, but a Saviour to be received into the heart and henceforth to be a living power of the soul. He must be accepted by Christian faith, and the heart must undergo the transforming power of his Spirit. Without this preparation, all progress in science is but the worship of nature, and man, at the close of life, looks back upon a path of error and forth into a world of darkness.

"Tholuck has this characteristic," says one of his countrymen, "he cannot be classified; he belongs to no particular theological direction, because he belongs to all." This estimate is strictly true. He has gained his greenest laurels in exegesis; and his commentaries on Psalms, the Sermon on the Mount, Gospel of John, and Epistles to the Romans and Hebrews, have already taken their places in the theological libraries of English and American divines. But he has asked himself the question, "What can I do to lessen the hold which Rationalism has upon my country?" And he has given the answer by his life-career. All his productions centre in that thought, and it is not the least of his service that he has written sketches of the old Reformation theologians, as an incentive to the restoration of their spirit. It is not easy to estimate the benefit which his *Sin and Redemption* has conferred upon the young men of Germany. The Baron von Kottwitz is the real personage represented by the patriarch. Let us hear this venerable saint as he stands upon the border of the grave and anticipates a bright future for his loved church and country. His words are the key to Tholuck's life, and reveal the bright hope which burned within him ever since the day when he was welcomed to Halle by the hisses and threats of the Rationalists.

The aged man says: "The greater the crisis the more needful is it to unite the wisdom of the serpent with the simplicity of the dove. I therefore address you as such an one who, perhaps, will soon be engaged at the university as one of the instruments employed by God in that important period. The work of God's spirit is greater than either you or the majority can estimate. A great resurrection morning has dawned. Hundreds of youths on all sides have been awakened by the Spirit of God. Everywhere true believers are coming into closer union. Science herself is becoming again the handmaid and friend of the Crucified. Civil governments, also, though in part still hostile to this great moral revolution from a dread of its producing political commotions, are many of them favorable; and where they are not, the conflicting energy of the light is so much the stronger. Many enlightened preachers already proclaim the gospel in its power; many who are still in obscurity will come forward. I see the dawn; the day itself I shall behold not here, but from a higher place. You will live to witness it below. Despise not the words of a gray-headed old man, who would give you, with true affection, a few hints relative to this great day.

"The more divine a power is, the more to be deprecated is its perversion. When those last times are spoken of in Scripture, in which the gospel shall be spread over the whole world, it is declared that the truth will not only have to contend with the proportionably more violent counterworking of the enemy, but also with a great measure of delusion and error within the kingdom of light. Such is the course of things that every truth has its shadow; and the greatest truth is attended by the greatest shadow. Above all things take care that the tempter do not introduce his craft into the congregation of the faithful. There will be those for whom the simple gospel will not suffice. When a man has experienced the forgiveness of his sins, and has for a little while enjoyed the happiness of that mercy, it not unfrequently appears to his evil and inconstant heart too humiliating a condition to be constantly receiving grace for grace. There is no other radical cure for a proud, self-willed heart than every day and every hour to repeat that act by which we first came to Christ. Pray that you may have more of that childlike spirit which regards the grace of your Lord as a perennial fountain of life. Especially avoid the error of those who seek life for the sake of light, who would make religion a mere stepping-stone to intellectual superiority. Such persons will never attain to a vital apprehension of divine things; for our God is a jealous God, and will be loved by us for his own sake. The intellectual power, the mental enlargement arising from converse with the great objects of faith is always to be regarded as a secondary and supplementary benefit to that which it is the immediate object of the gospel to bestow. Despise not human greatness or talent or ability of any kind, but beware lest you overvalue it. I see a time coming—indeed it is already at hand—in which gifted men will lift up their voices for the truth; but woe to the times in which admiration and applause of the speaker shall be substituted for laying to heart the truth which he delivers! Perhaps in the next generation there will be no one in some parts of Germany who will not wish to be called a Christian. Learn to distinguish the spirits. The sum of my exhortations is humility and love!"

The most poetical and not the least penetrating of the evangelical school is Lange, once a farmer, but now a laborious professor at Bonn. How deeply he has imbibed the spirit of the Scriptures may be seen in the *Bible-Work*, which Dr. Schaff is now editing for the use of the American public. Religion, according to Lange, is subjectively a life-emotion of the human nature, and objectively a revelation of God. In the former case it may be termed natural, in the latter, revealed. The world is not a mere world, but a self-revelation of God in its fullest import. Creation is not simply creation, but a divine testimony. Nature is not nature alone, but a seed of life proceeding from the spirit and returning to the spirit. The proof of the true human conception of God, as well as of man, is their harmonious union in the conception of the God-man. This is the centre of all doctrine. The world is a progressive succession, developing the divine germ. History unites itself to revelation as a second creation, elevating man to continuous growth. God's providential changes unite with the active faith of man, and they do not constitute an isolated act of God, but a great historical combination of revelations. They rise gradually and find their completion in the God-man.

Miracles are the penetration of the absolute or new human-divine life principle into the sphere of the old natural human life. The revelation of the divine-human in Christ is the absolute miracle which manifests itself in a succession of single miracles. A miracle is supernatural and contrary to nature only in reference to the old life, and, in its highest meaning, is in conformity to a higher law. Therefore, miracles are the natural law of all natural laws taken together. Inspiration is in consonance with miracle; and there is à dissimilarity of inspiration observable in the Scriptures. The Old and New Testaments are very different, so also are the canonical and hagiographical writings. The word of God is contained in the Scriptures, and is there brought into living unity and operation with the mind of man. This union does not exclude human imperfections. But such imperfections are of a superficial character, and in no wise affect the kernel and religious centre of the Bible.[1]

The two most prominent divines in the department of dogmatical theology are Nitzsch and Twesten. The latter was Schleiermacher's successor at Berlin. Bright hopes were placed on him, but he has been a tardy author, and does not possess the brilliant gifts of his great prototype. Yet he is a clear and profound thinker, and, with a few points of exception, thoroughly evangelical. He is an ardent admirer of the old Lutheran theology, and, like his predecessor, places religion in feeling and dependence instead of in knowledge.

Nitzsch is also a disciple of Schleiermacher, and his doctrinal system bears distinct traces of the master's instructions. But it is a bold work, and has inflicted great mischief upon the doctrinal claims of the later Rationalists, who betook themselves to theory after their exegesis and history had failed them. The scope of his system is broad and clear. He commences by assigning Christian doctrine its proper place in theological study, a definition of the general idea of Christianity, a statement of the laws by which a knowledge of Christianity is acquired, and a history of the Christian system and its exhibition in the purest form. The three parts constituting the substance of Nitzsch's opinions, are *The Good, the Bad, and Salvation.* Chris-

[1] *Dogmatik*, 1849.

tianity is a determinate mode of man's life, and is so determined by conscious dependence on God, but in no wise by knowledge, conception, action, or the will. Religion does not arise from experience and sensation, but from an original self-consciousness. There is an intimate connection between doctrine and practice, truth and holiness. Redemption is not merely a restoration, nor a mere perfected creation, but one *through* the other. It is related to an original good, apart from which the bad itself would have no place, opportunity for existence, or continuance; since redemption is so closely connected with evil. Moreover, the good—in which evil has found opportunities for manifestation—cannot be the same which caused redemption. Hence, we safely presume the existence of an eternal God. This being is the foundation of Christian faith and life. A belief in the Redeemer cannot be separated from that in the Creator. But it is through a knowledge of the Redeemer that the Creator, with all his work, first becomes known in his perfect goodness and truth. The doctrine of salvation is more closely related to the degenerated condition of the world than to the original good, or to the right conduct of the creature towards God. Evil became possible with the creation of personality, though without being necessary. But it has become so very real that the heavenly Adam must needs come into the world to destroy the works of the devil,—which are sin and death,—and to renew the communion of the creation with the Creator. The effectuating cause of man's permitting himself to be seduced into sin, was not any fixed purpose or predestination of God, but man's perfect moral freedom. He chose the evil, and hence he inherits sin with all its dire results. Since then, sin has become a bias and righteousness requires an effort for its performance. But man is accessible to divine legislation by being the subject of fear, shame, and punishment. The church is an abiding testimony and a continued means for the redemptive ministry of Christ. It is the congregation of the sanctified.[1]

From these two useful professors in Berlin we pass southward to Heidelberg, and delay a moment with the celebrated Rothe. In his work on the *Primitive Church* he endeavors to explain the philosophy of the whole ecclesiastical system. He views the elements of the church in solution, and thence tries to deduce general principles. He advances the view, with Coleridge and Arnold, that the church will not be complete until absorbed in the state. Its present separate condition is provisional, and can only last during the time that Christianity is being developed. This period may be of long duration, but the development of our race is ever progressing. The church must exist on its own basis during the interval. Human deeds of righteousness tend toward the perfection of the church. Then will religion permeate the world. Yet it will not exist as something separate, but all-penetrative. It will not be absolutely divine, but superlatively human. Thus will the dualism of the human and divine, the religious and the moral, be destroyed. When the day of ecclesiastical perfection—which is really civil perfection—arrives, the state will perform the functions of the church. It will exercise church discipline for the purpose of religious and moral training. The divergence between religious and worldly science will be abrogated, and there will be no longer any conflict between the worship of God and nature. It is plain that these

[1] *System of Christian Doctrine.* Translated by Montgomery and Hennen. Clark's Library, Edinburgh, 1849.

views are based upon those of Hegel, who said of the state, that "it is the totality of moral purposes."[1]

The ethical system of Rothe is one of the most original and profound pieces of devout and reverent speculation in the entire range of theological literature. It has been termed "a work of art as well as of science; and the several stones of the ethical system are reared up here into a magnificent gothic cathedral by the skill of a master architect." It is based on the unity and identity of religion and morality. Here, as in the theory of the relations of church and state, the Hegelian philosophy is very perceptible. God's love is manifested in creation, and there existed the necessity of his creative activity in order to communicate himself to others. Hence, God's love is not a mere attribute, but one of the necessary conditions of his being. Creation is a necessary act of God. God is as truly creator as he is benevolent. There is, therefore, a correlation of God and the world. There is no God without also the world. God's creative activity is still continued by his providential movements, and these are the steps of man's development. Man's complete character is in some measure dependent on his discipline, and sin is the necessary ordeal or process through which he must pass in order to arrive at the highest development.[2]

Rothe has very recently published a volume of his essays, entitled *A Contribution to Dogmatic Theology*. It is occupied mostly with the consideration of the Scriptures. The author thus states his opinion: "The matters I handle in this volume inevitably place me in a most unfavorable position. The question is one in which I find myself in direct conflict with both the leading parties in the theology of the present day. My

[1] *Die Anfänge der Christlichen Kirche und ihrer Verfassung*, 1837.
[2] *Ethik*—1845-1848.

mode of regarding Holy Scripture runs directly counter to modern orthodoxy. My supernaturalism and firm belief in revelation are no less opposed to theological liberalism. This very antagonism encourages me to hope that I may be found to have spoken a word in season. On the one hand, it is my belief that the consciousness of the age will never thoroughly reässimilate Christianity till it can take courage to believe again in miracle and supernatural influence. I am no less firmly convinced, on the other hand, that miracle and supernatural influence will never find their way into the conscious belief of Christians in the form in which church-theology has allowed those ideas to be inoculated into it. That which is passed can never be recalled to life after history has once buried it. But there are not a few persons who long for the reconciliation of the old and the new. These are the persons to whom I would gladly be useful according to my small measure."[1]

Rothe regards the supernatural interference of the Deity in the stream of human history as a part of that history. It is not enough that the divine interposition has incorporated itself with the traditions of the race; it must be fixed in a written narrative. Not only must there be a book or writing, but that book must be of a historical character. As the revelation did not consist in doctrines, so the doctrine we require is not a creed or compend of doctrines. Besides vouching the facts, the doctrines must represent them in a vivid manner; that is, the writing must be such as can stand for long posterior generations in the place of the original revelation, and place us in the immediate personal experience of revelation. It is part of the extraordinary operation

[1] *Ethik*, *Preface*, p. 6.

of the Deity to provide such a writing. The document itself, as well as the facts it relates, are supernaturally produced. What the divine influences in the world are to its moral and human laws, the record of those influences is to ordinary narrative. The Bible is therefore what the old Protestant theology styled it, "The Word of God": but in a very different sense. It was meant by that phrase that the books, as we have them, were dictated by God in such a way that the sacred penmen contributed nothing but the letter-marks upon the paper. The dogma of inspiration current in the sixteenth century is not accepted. The inspiration which Rothe attributes to the Bible is the same by which he explains that peculiar impression received by the pious soul from its study of the book. It is the constant experience of the evangelical Christian, that, in his Bible, he possesses a direct means of grace. Scripture is to him an active medium of the saving work of God in his soul, and supernatural forces move within it. The Bible stands alone in all literature as this incarnation of a fresh, full, life-giving religious spirit. But the peculiar influence which it exercises upon minds indicates not merely a divine element in its pages, but a whole, complex, and sound human spirit side by side with that divine element; the two not crossing or interfering with each other, but forming together a unity of living truth. The books of the Bible must be regarded as the general product of the minds of their human authors. These authors have had their moments of inspiration, to which they owe much of the religious experience they have embalmed in their writings. But inspiration was not the normal condition of their minds, nor were their books written during the moments of such inspiration. Again, not every part of the Bible is an equally full and intense expression of this spiritual mind of the writer. We must assume degrees of inspiration according with the nature of the contents, and with their nearer or remoter bearing on the proper matter of the prophetical utterances.[1]

Passing over the names of Julius Müller, Ebrard, Hävernick, Hundeshagen, Umbreit, Gieseler, Olshausen, Hagenbach, and Jacobi, we pause at Schenkel and Hengstenberg.

Schenkel has been, until lately, a recognized evangelical theologian. The author of the *Essence of Protestantism*, he took his stand as an able defender of orthodoxy; and there was every reason to hope that he would be one of the chief agents in the final overthrow of Rationalism. As a proof of the high estimate placed upon his opinions, when the Baden government and church consistory were calling their strongest orthodox theologians into the various posts of prominence, after the Revolution of 1848, Schenkel was declared counselor, and director of the theological seminary of Heidelberg. From that time almost to the present his evangelical sentiments had not been questioned. But, when his *Picture of the Character of Jesus* appeared, the surprise was great throughout Germany. It seemed incredible that he could write a work in such direct antagonism to all his previous views. People were unwilling to censure it at first; the Rationalists rejoicing at the great accession, and the orthodox retaining too much respect for the author's past services to bestow harsh criticism upon him. But a book of importance need not wait long in Germany upon the publisher's shelf before it is weighed and assigned its proper position in literature. In due time the critics came forward, sifted its contents,

[1] *Westminster Review*, July, 1863.

and decided it to be skeptical. The theological periodicals abounded in lengthy reviews of it. Schenkel seemed as much astounded as any one else at the public judgment. He answered the charges against his orthodoxy by stoutly denying that he had turned Rationalist. He held that his critics were so obtuse that they could not understand him; and that if he were accused of heterodoxy it was their blunder and not his guilt. But it is needless to say that Schenkel makes a poor case for himself. His book stands against him. The miracles of Christ receive his severe comment. They are, in his opinion, the dark shade which has been cast upon the bright splendor of the public activity of Jesus. It was a matter of course that the idea of a life like that of the Redeemer should, soon after his death, be veiled by a multitude of tales. His disciples endeavored to represent his internal wonderful power of personal glory and greatness by the external miraculous occurrences which they ascribed to him. Their deeply excited imagination magnified the great hero whom they had loved and admired. Their enthusiastic religious fancy did him homage by ascribing to him the performance of miracles. The gift of working miracles was merely the endowment of nature. For Jesus was favored with the highest ability and rarest moral power, by which he worked beneficially upon sufferers and took them by surprise. Schenkel further rejects and denies the faith in Christ's personal and bodily resurrection from the dead, and his continuation of life in the glory of the Father. But he holds that Christ lives in his community, in which are his home and temple. The living Christ is the spirit of his community.

After the position of Schenkel's work had been fairly decided, numerous remonstrances appeared against it from the orthodox theologians. One hundred and eighteen clergymen sent in a formal protest to the consistory for his removal from his important office as director of the seminary. But the ecclesiastical council decided in favor of his continuance in discharge of his functions. They extenuated themselves by saying that the free examination of the Scriptures is the privilege of Protestant Christians. The Rationalists claim the result as one of the most signal of their recent victories.

Hengstenberg, the strongest and most heroic of the later opponents of Rationalism, commenced very early in life as both author and professor. It is now more than thirty years since he was elected professor of Old Testament exegesis at Berlin. He was chosen to that important position with a view to counteract the prevailing Rationalism, and, if possible, to raise up a new school of earnest evangelical men. He has not been without success. Having never swerved from his first avowed position, his antipathy to all kinds of skepticism is so sincere and active that he combats it without any regard to moderation or consequences.

Of all the members of the Evangelical school he takes the highest rank as controversialist, and defender of the Old Testament. He saw that it was the Old Testament which the Rationalists had assailed most vigorously, and that unless they were met upon their own ground they would claim the mastery of the field. Hence, he made the Pentateuch, Daniel, and the second part of the prophecy of Isaiah the theme of his defence[1]—for it was these that the Rationalists had long claimed as their collateral evidence. At that very time there was almost no orthodox theologian in Germany

[1] *Beiträge zur Einleitung in das alte Testamente.* Drei Bände, 1831-39.

who had confidence enough to contend for them. But the greatest apologetic achievement of Hengstenberg was his christological work.[1] Here he develops his theory that the Messianic prophecies extend through the entire Old Testament; that they can be traced in Genesis; that they increase in clearness as the scriptural history advances; that they become perfectly lucid in the later prophets; and that they are finally fulfilled in the Messiah himself.

But it was not by theological lectures or books that Hengstenberg achieved his greatest triumphs over Rationalism and Pantheism. Clearly perceiving the power of the periodical press, he commenced the publication of the *Evangelical Church Gazette*, which by its fearless spirit and marked talent, soon became the chief theological journal of Germany. Its aim was not only to overthrow skepticism but everything which ministered to its support. Its contributors have been among the leading men of the country, among whom we find such names as Otto von Gerlach, Professors Leo and Huber, and Doctors Göschel, Vilmar, Stahl, Tholuck and Lange. The *Gazette* has changed its tone according to the new demands of the times, but it has never abated its deadly antagonism to Rationalism. It has betrayed an increasing High Church tendency, especially since 1840. The editor, true to his earnest nature, believed that no moderate and conciliatory spirit was capable of successfully resisting the great enemies of the church. The relief which he relied upon was in fighting them with the heroic ardor of a crusader. Hence he claimed that an elevation of ecclesiastical power was necessary to meet the demand; and therefore he stands to day as the High Church

[1] *Christologie.* Drei Bände, 1829-35.

champion of Protestant Germany. For this course he has received quite as many maledictions as have been visited upon Pusey of England, but he is one of those men who care as little for the curses of foes as for the adulations of friends.

There have been other theological journals which have contributed greatly to the spread of vital Christianity in Germany.[1] They do not possess, on the one hand, the popular character of many of our religious papers, nor, on the other, do they deal so much in abstruse theological questions as to preclude them from large circles of readers. They possess popular adaptation without yielding to the demand for light religious reading. Many of their contributions having been written by far-sighted laymen, they have gained access to minds usually occupied in the absorbing interests of commercial and political life. The whole Protestant church owes a debt of profound gratitude to the men who commenced these enterprises and have zealously sustained them through the social changes which have convulsed Germany.

But in our estimate of renewed religious life we must not overlook the improved condition of the instruction now imparted in the gymnasia and universities.[2] Besides the names we have already mentioned there are professors and instructors of all grades who have drunk deeply of the spirit of the Gospel, and,

[1] Besides the *Evangelical Church Gazette*, semi-weekly, by Hengstenberg, established 1827, are the *Studien und Kritiken*, by Ullmann and Umbreit, 1828; the *Deutsche Zeitschrift für christliche Wissenschaft*, &c., by Neander, Nitzsch, and Müller, 1850; and the *Jahrbücher für Deutsche Theologie*, by Liebner, Dorner, and others, 1856.

[2] An invaluable account of the common and higher Schools of Germany is furnished in Horace Mann's *Seventh Annual Report*, published in the *Common School Journal of Boston*, under the title of *Education in Europe*, 1844.

having been taught and encouraged by such men as Hengstenberg and Tholuck, are now strengthening themselves for future victory. Young men have passed through their student life in Halle, Heidelberg, and Berlin, and are now scattered throughout the land, sowing the seeds of truth, and urging the people to espouse the good cause. Others are preparing to take their places when these are no more. The spirit of theological instruction has undergone such a thorough transformation that the old Rationalism which had so long prevailed is now taught by only a few gray-haired veterans, who, many years ago, listened to the lectures of Wegscheider and Gesenius. They are now bringing their days to a close in the midst of a narrow circle of auditors who hear from curiosity or indolence, and never expect to use their information to any future advantage. Devotional services are becoming more common among the students. The Scriptures are studied with a feeling of devout reverence, and are no longer subjected to that profane ridicule which has given an unenviable fame to many of the Rationalists.

Much of this improved evangelical spirit observable in the students of all the Protestant Universities,—for even Tübingen has been obliged to yield,—is due to the kindly intercourse between the professors and the students. In no country is education so much a matter of friendship as in Germany. The professors cultivate social and even intimate relations with the undergraduates, nor do they consider it beneath their dignity to invite them frequently to their homes, draw out their minds by discussing some important point, loan them books or periodicals, suggest subjects for essays or books, employ their service as amanuenses, and recommend them in due time for proper vacancies. Who would suspect that half-bent, sallow little man, wrapped up in his blue coat, and walking briskly a mile or two from Halle through the wintry storm, of being the patient and devout Tholuck? But he is not alone. Beside him is a youthful stripling who opens his heart to the professor, catches every word of response as if it were a priceless diamond, and treasures each utterance for future use. To-morrow, the same kindly teacher will be attended by one or two other young men, whom he is desirous to encourage, direct, and instruct.

Such intimacy does not lead to any disrespect toward the professors, but rather increases the reverence for their age and talents. The hours of profitable communion naturally become a fund of pleasant memories to the student in his subsequent life. Knowledge thus imparted is deeper-rooted than that conveyed in the lecture-room, and hence, in the literary and theological history of Protestant Germany, we find many illustrations of the consistent and steady prosecution, by a disciple, of a tendency or system which the master commenced but died too soon to finish. One of the prime agents in the rise of Pietism was Spener's child-like intimacy with young men. They imbibed his spirit and knowledge, and the fire burned after his departure.

As to the future, there is no room for discouragement. The leaven of faith has been penetrating the entire mass of German theology, and the prospect is to-day brighter than ever before. The bold and continued defense of Christianity, in all its vital relations, has accomplished great good during the entire interval between Schleiermacher's period of activity and the present time. The recuperation of German Protestantism from the polar frigidity of skepticism to the faith and spirit of the Gospel, is one of the most beautiful and forcible of all the illustrations of the indestructible and regenerating power of Christianity. The instruction imparted in the high-schools has long since lost its Rationalistic puerilities. The candidates for the pastoral office are not asked such questions as were propounded to their fathers and predecessors. Church history, written in clear and natural style, is no longer a collection of pointless anecdotes. Exegesis has ceased to be a word-play, and the companion of classical annotations. The sermons of the present ministry partake of Reinhard's earnestness and faith. Gallicisms and technical terminology are no longer proclaimed to the peasants, while the artisan is no more entertained with grandiloquent descriptions of the last night of Socrates, or with Ciceronian laudations of the Schoolmen.[1] The popular attendance at the public services is greatly on the increase, and the congregations are expressing in no doubtful terms their desire for the restoration of the thrilling evangelical hymns of other days.[2]

The masses, having tasted the word of God in its simplicity, will not be satisfied without deep draughts for many future years. The Protestant Church will yet be "fair as the moon, clear as the sun, and terrible as an army with banners." Then will Germany be what she was in the heroic age of the Reformation,—the instructor of the ignorant, the friend of the helpless, the dread of Romanism, and the mother of giants. The evil days are nearly numbered. "Good Friday is the precursor of a joyous Easter Morning."

[1] Hagenbach, *Kirchengeschichte d.* 18 *und* 19 *Jahrhunderts*, Vol. II., pp. 384-388.

[2] An instance of the new tendency is seen in the recent action of the Heilbronn Clergy, supported by the Stuttgart Consistory. For account of which, see *Christian Work*, Sept. 1863.

CHAPTER XIII.

PRACTICAL MOVEMENTS INDICATING NEW LIFE.

JEAN PAUL has wittily said of the providential distribution of the earth that the land was assigned to the French, the sea to the English, and the air to the Germans. Popular opinion is not much at variance with this sentiment as far as the last proprietorship is concerned. But Germany has been practical withal. Shade of Jean Paul! What if thy countrymen do live in the air; they have not therefore flown so far away from the gross nether earth as to lose sight of its misery, nor become deaf to its wail of sorrow.

German Protestantism has given birth to some of the greatest charities of the present age, whether we take into the account the number of the beneficiaries or the faith and self-sacrifice of the founders and their successors. Even during the period of religious indifference there were here and there celebrated institutions designed for the amelioration of the suffering classes. They contended against great opposition, but like a few stars amid surrounding clouds, their light appeared to all the greater advantage. Modern philanthropy has received a great impulse by the labors of Howard and Wilberforce. But the charitable institutions we speak of were in progress east of the Rhine years before the former commenced "his voyage of discovery, his circumnavigation of charity, to collate distresses, to gauge wretchedness, to take dimensions of human misery;" or before the latter could write in 1807, after so many labors for the extinction of the Slave Trade, "Oh what thanks do I owe to the Giver of all good for bringing me in his gracious providence to this great cause, which at length, after almost nineteen years, labor, is successful."

Philanthropy stands in intimate relations to revived christian faith. Sometimes it is its forerunner, at others its co-operator, and always its follower. Whenever a land is morally prostrate and helpless, the ministry skeptical or indifferent, and the sects arrayed against each other, if humane efforts can be discovered, there is hope of better times. Love of the body of man is the unfailing Baptist-herald announcing the speedy care of his soul. The only indications of evangelical faith in Germany at the closing period of the eighteenth century were the quiet labors of such devoted friends of humanity as Oberlin, Hamann, Lavater, and Claudius. And philanthropy assumed a more stalwart form in the same ratio as religion gained strength over the popular mind.

We have already spoken of the celebrities of Weimar. Students and aspirants to fame from all parts of the Continent went thither, hoping to enjoy at least a few conversations or perhaps a subsequent correspondence with one of the ruling literary divinities. To have a word of advice from Goethe, and to hear Schiller read an ode in his own study was a memory of life-long value. Among the most venturesome of this class was John Falk, once the humble son of a poor wig-maker of Dantzic, but afterwards the Halle student, the novelist, satirist, and poet.[1] He received high compliments from Wieland, and was admitted into an intimacy with Goethe which resulted in his publication of the latter's *Conversations.* He gradually gained public favor, and his elevation to the society and attention of the literary regency of Weimar was no ordinary testimonial to capacity and prospects.

By and by the sound of war was heard in that town, and with war came its many evils. Napoleon having proved victorious at Jena, his legions were quartered on the poor and rich through all the surrounding country. The Duchy of Weimar, with its population of only one hundred thousand, were required to support for five months nine hundred thousand of the enemy's soldiers, and five hundred thousand horses. The air was rent with the cries of orphans and poverty-stricken widows. Sorrow reigned in every household, and the town of Weimar became a prominent part of the funeral scene. But, unaccountable as it may appear, the resident literati were not much disturbed. Living so near the top of Parnassus, they would not listen to the storms below. Goethe, the acknowledged prince, wrote as zealously as ever in his villa-garden, and it will be a lasting stigma on his fame in his own fatherland that he chose "the moment of his country's deepest ruin to write an exquisite classic story."

But Falk was touched by what he saw. He could not be contented with literary dreams while widows were dying around him of starvation, and children were growing up in wickedness. He remembered some words said to him by the burgomasters of Dantzic

[1] *Praying and Working.* By Rev. W. F. Stevenson, of Dublin. This is by far the best source of information on the leading charities of Germany. Our high appreciation of its value is indicated by the use made of its contents in the preparation of our account of Falk and other humanitarians treated in this chapter.

when they met one day in the town hall, and an old member arose and told him that they had concluded to send him to the University and pay his own expenses, adding at the close of his remarks: "One thing only, if a poor child should ever knock at your door, think it is we, the dead, the old, gray-headed burgomasters and councilors of Dantzic, and do not turn us away." At last the poor child was at his door. Henceforth Falk's life was spent in reforming criminal youth. "Come in," said he to the vagrants, "come in; God has taken my four angels, and spared me that I might be your father."

Falk established his Reformatory from a pure love of humanity, and of Him who came to seek and save the lost. His method was simple. The lads whom he sought out and who came to him were desperately wicked. No sooner were they within his institute than he treated them as his own children. The two words so often on his lips reveal the principle of his discipline: "Love overcometh." He used no harshness, and would have no locks on his doors. He said, "We forge all our chains on the heart, and scorn those that are laid on the body; for it is written 'If the Son shall make you free ye shall be free indeed.'" "His mind was hung all around with pictures," says Mr. Stevenson, who has furnished us with the following beautiful specimen of Falk's picturesque manner of teaching great truths to those who fell under his care.

When one of the boys, on a certain evening, had invoked this divine blessing on their supper, "Come, Lord Jesus, be our guest, and bless what thou hast provided," another boy looked up and asked,

"Do tell me why the Lord Jesus never comes? We ask Him every day to sit with us, and he never comes."

"Dear child," replied Father Falk, "only believe and you may be sure he will come, for he does not despise our invitation."

"I shall set him a seat," said the boy; and just then, a knock being heard at the door, a poor apprentice came for admission. He was received, and invited to take the vacant chair at the table.

Then said the inquiring boy again, "Jesus could not come, and so he sent this poor man in his place: is that it?"

"Yes, dear child, that is just it. Every piece of bread and every drink of water that we give to the poor, or the sick, or the prisoners, for Jesus' sake, we give to Him. 'Inasmuch as ye have done it unto one of the least of these my brethren, ye have done it unto me.'"

Falk's benefactions were of varied character. He organized a system for the cessation of beggary in Weimar; established a training institute, the *Johanneum*, for instructors of the youth under his charge; sent forth many hundreds of the inmates of his *Reformatory* to become useful members of society; wrote earnest religious songs which the people will sing for generations; died uttering the words, "God,—popular,—faith,—short, —Christ,—end;" and was borne to the grave by the children whom he had blessed. His resting-place is now marked by words which his own pen had written:

"Underneath this linden tree
Lies John Falk; a sinner he,
Saved by Christ's blood and mercy.

Born upon the East Sea strand,
Yet he left home, friends, and land,
Led to Weimar by God's hand.

When the little children round
Stand beside this grassy mound,
Asking, who lies underground?—

Heavenly Father, let them say,
Thou hast taken him away;
In the grave is only clay."

Other philanthropists followed in the footsteps of Falk. What he did for children has been succeeded by greater humanitarian movements in behalf of the criminal youth, and abandoned and helpless adults. Theodore Fliedner was pastor of a congregation of operatives in Kaiserswerth, in 1826. Very soon after his installation they were reduced almost to beggary by the bankruptcy of their employers. He refused to leave them in their distress, and devised plans for their relief. One step led to another. He became the friend of not only the poor of that town, but of all the adjacent country. To become more useful at home he traveled through foreign countries. He described his visit to London in the following brief but characteristic words, "*I have seen Newgate and many other prisons.*"

At last he matured a settled plan. It was the amelioration of the sick poor. The largest house in the town being for sale, he secured its possession, and on the 13th October, 1836, opened his *Deaconess Institute.* The enemies of Fliedner called it a hospital, and looked with aversion upon it. The beginning was very unpromising. But the founder never hesitated, and the close of the first year of the history of the *Institute* revealed the fact that it had received forty sick persons, and that these were nursed by seven deaconesses. Every day gave new strength to the enterprise; and soon there were more of a similar character springing up in Holland, Switzerland, France, and other countries, but all dependent upon the parent at Kaiserswerth for properly trained nurses and instructors. The organization of new institutes at a great distance, imposed severe labor on Fliedner, but it was cheerfully undergone for the sake of the great cause so dear to him. It was to advance its interests that he came to America, and afterwards went to Jerusalem, to superintend the establishment of branch Institutes of Deaconesses. They are now in prosperous existence in Constantinople, Smyrna, Alexandria, Bucharest, and Florence,—not to mention many more in the Protestant lands of the Continent.

But it is in Kaiserswerth that the Deaconesses are trained for their humanitarian life-work. Of this institution Mr. Stevenson says: "It consists of an Hospital for men, women, and children; a Lunatic Asylum for females; an Orphanage for girls; a Refuge for discharged female convicts; a Magdalen Asylum; a Normal Seminary for governesses; an Infant School; a Chapel; two shops; a publishing office; a museum; residence for the Deaconesses; and a Home for the infirm. Besides, as the property of the Institution, there are a home for maid-servants in Berlin; an Orphanage at Altdorf; the Deaconess Home at Jerusalem; the Seminary at Smyrna; the Hospital at Alexandria; and the Seminary at Bucharest. The number of these Christian women is about three hundred and twenty, of whom upwards of one hundred are at Kaiserswerth, or at private service, and the rest scattered over seventy-four stations in Europe, Asia, Africa, and America. Upwards of eight hundred teachers have been sent out to educate many thousand children. The number annually in hospital is over six hundred, and upwards of fifty families are supplied with sick-nurses; in the Asylum there are twenty-four; in the Orphanage, thirty; in the

Infant School, fifty; in the Refuge, twenty; in the Seminary, fifty. The number dependent on the Institution for daily bread is between seven and eight hundred."[1]

In addition to the enterprises of Falk and Fliedner there has recently arisen another, which, by virtue of the character of its organization and the number of its supporters, has not only promoted humanitarian movements, but has contributed largely to the restoration of a vigorous evangelical faith, the suppression of sectarian hostility, the stability of the civil government, and the decrease of the power of the state over the church. We refer to the Evangelical Church Diet which held its first session in 1848, and now occupies a wide field of operations.

While political revolution was imminent and no one knew when or where it would burst in violence, and while the atheistic and socialistic views of the living generation of skeptics were imbuing the minds of many of the young and gifted, it became a matter of serious concern whether or not the tide of religious and political destruction could be stayed. The prospect was forbidding. The state had its full burden in watching its own vitality; the church was already sore with the stripes of skepticism. The crisis was upon the land. The work of written apologies for Christianity had been faithfully discharged, and no one could find fault with those heroes who had rushed to the rescue of the evangelical and apostolic oracles. But the time for writing books was now past, and important concerted practical measures were necessary to be taken, or the day would be lost and generations might be required to repair the damage.

[1] *Praying and Working*, pp. 212–213.

For a number of years the Pastoral Conferences, composed of small circles of devoted ministers and laymen, had been in existence, and kept their attention carefully directed to the necessities of the times. The increased danger made the members doubly watchful. In view of the exigency, some of the leaders arrived at the conclusion to call a church assembly of all the leading evangelical sects, to take such action as the peculiar condition of theology, religion, and politics might require. During the first six months of the revolutionary year of 1848, three of these pastoral conferences held their sessions, during which the propriety of convening a general assembly was discussed. The conference at Sandhof, on the 21st June, was the occasion of serious embarrassment. It was well nigh concluded that the whole enterprise would prove a failure, but Dr. Bethmann-Hollweg arose, and by a few stirring words infused hope and zeal into every member. "It is the Lord, my friends," he said, "who builds the church. Never forget this. Whether the assembly spoken of will accomplish what we desire and hope, no one can tell. Our resolution must be an act of faith. Like Peter, we shall have to walk on the sea; but we know also that the Lord does not suffer any one to perish who trusts in him. If we look merely upon ourselves and upon the scattered, distracted, and weak members of the church, we would have indeed to despair. But if we raise our eyes in faith to him who is the Lord, we will venture it."

The conference yielded to this earnest appeal, and a general assembly was called, to convene at Wittenberg, in the following autumn. On the 21st of September, the appointed day, five hundred of the leading evangelical theologians and laymen of Germany were present, to adopt whatever measures might be thought best to avert existing and impending evils. They met in the same old gothic temple on whose door, three centuries previously, Luther had nailed his ninety-five theses. The exercises opened with prayer, and the singing of Luther's hymn, "Eine feste Burg ist unser Gott," which has been thus translated by Carlyle:

"A safe stronghold our God is still,
A trusty shield and weapon;
He'll help us clear from all the ill
That hath us now o'ertaken.
The ancient Prince of Hell
Hath risen with purpose fell;
Strong mail of craft and power
He weareth in this hour,—
On earth is not his fellow.

"With force of arms we nothing can,
Full soon were we down-ridden;
But for us fights the proper man,
Whom God himself hath bidden.
Ask ye, Who is this same?
Christ Jesus is his name,
The Lord Zebaoth's Son;
He, and no other one,
Shall conquer in the battle.

"And were the world all devils o'er
And watching to devour us,
We lay it not to heart so sore,
Not they can overpow'r us.
And let the prince of ill
Look grim as e'er he will,
He harms us not a whit,
For why? His doom is writ—
A word shall quickly slay him.

"God's word for all their craft and force,
One moment will not linger,
But spite of hell shall have its course,
'Tis written by His finger.

> And though they take our life,
> Goods, honor, children, wife,
> Yet is their profit small;
> These things shall vanish all,
> The Church of God remaineth."

The Church Diet, now in its first session, was in direct contrast with the revolutionary outbreaks in Frankfort and other cities. True and firm hearts were within the walls of the Schlosskirche. Earnestness, seriousness, humility, and faith were depicted on the countenances of the members. Those men had been steadfast in the past, and were now intent upon the immediate and utter destruction of the worship of reason. Doctrinal differences were laid aside and apparently forgotten. Men who had been contending with pen and paper for many years now grasped each other's hand in friendship, and, burying their doctrinal animosities, stood close together in a common effort to reconstruct the temple of evangelical faith for the benefit of their countrymen. The Lutheran could not be distinguished from his Reformed brother, nor the member of the United Church from the Moravian. That denominational union and fraternal intercourse which had been foreshadowed in 1817, were now thoroughly consummated for the first time.

Without, the heavens were dark with the portents of impending social convulsions. The signs were unmistakable. The masses were intoxicated with a wild frenzy seldom, if ever, surpassed. They were intent upon the destruction of all constitutional authority. Freedom from the restraints of law and religion, the ruling thought of the Continent during 1848, was their sole object. It was clear that if the populace could overthrow the governments they would not be long in putting an end to all the outward and traditional observances of religion. For the middle and lower classes had not as yet become permeated by the healthful leaven which had been introduced into the theological circles by the apologetic antagonists of Strauss and his compeers. The wisest statesman could not foresee one day's deeds of that skeptical, revolutionary rabble, which had already lost its self-control. Blood had actually been shed. Barricades had been reared in the streets of the larger cities. The universities were pouring forth their hundreds of students and professors, to take part in the conflict. The revolutionary crowds were choosing their leaders; the royalist forces were everywhere fortifying; princes were concealing their plate and strengthening their hiding-places. This was the social and political scene while the five hundred were praying, singing, counseling, and comforting each other over the sleeping dust of Luther and Melanchthon.

In the days of the imprisoned Peter, fetters were strong, prison doors well-barred, and the four quaternions of soldier guards faithful; but all these safeguards could not resist the force which lay in the unceasing prayers of the church. So with the revolutionary movements of the people in 1848, as opposed to the Christian faith of the members of the Church Diet. That assembly contributed more than all other human agencies to save the German states from utter political and social ruin, and the German church from a longer night and a fiercer storm than any through which it had passed.

The practical result of the session was an invitation to all the Protestant churches of Germany to observe the fifth of the coming November, the Sunday following the anniversary of the Reformation, as a day of humiliation for past unfaithfulness and prayer for the revival of true religion throughout the land. It was resolved to form a confederation of all the German churches adhering to the confessions of the Reformation, in order to promote denominational unity, be a mutual defense against Rationalism and indifference, advance social reforms, protect the rights of the church against the encroachments of civil authority, and secure a more intimate fellowship with evangelical bodies outside of Germany.

The Church Diet has steadily enlarged its sphere of operation and gathered strength and influence. Besides attracting great throngs of spectators from the surrounding states, its members have attained to the number of two thousand on more than one occasion. The providential prosperity which has attended its history is the best proof of the real demand for its institution and for the valuable purposes it has already served. At every session the most important questions of the day are discussed with freedom and always with great ability. Among other themes which have come up for careful attention, we may mention the relation of church and state, the sanctity of the Sabbath, divorce and the oath, the relations of Protestantism to Romanism, all forms of skepticism, and the inner organization of the church,—such as the renewal of the diaconate, the possession of church estates, and the abrogation or retainment of ecclesiastical discipline.[1]

During the first session of the Church Diet a man arose to speak, who indicated by his earnest manner that he had been thinking deeply, and that the subject of his remarks was a matter of no ordinary importance.

[1] Schaff, *Germany, &c.*, pp. 200-212.

It was John Henry Wichern, founder of the Rough House, near Hamburg. He had just returned from his laborious tour through the districts of Silesia, which, in addition to the demoralizing revolutionary excitement, were stricken by famine and fever. Whole villages were depopulated, not enough inhabitants being left alive to bury the dead. Grief and despair reigned everywhere. The number of orphans had grown so large that Wichern and his few assistants, with all their experience and organizing power, were unable to remedy their immediate wants. The scene having made a profound impression upon his mind, he unburdened his heart to the assembly. He described what he had witnessed, pictured the evils of his people in their true light, and declared that the church must either do more Christian missionary work at home, or God's curse would rest upon it. He therefore called upon the Diet to incorporate the Inner Mission into its system as a necessary measure to improve the religious and social prosperity of the country. He spoke as one sent from God. The assembly was mastered, and the reformer's plan adopted. In all the subsequent meetings of the Diet, about one half of its session, or two whole days, have been occupied in the management of the Inner Mission, and in discussions on the best means to secure its increased effectiveness.

But Wichern was not a stranger to the members of the assembly. The beneficial results of his labors at the Rough House had already been felt throughout Europe. An old thatched cottage, about three miles from Hamburg, was the nucleus of his work. He sought out wild, abandoned boys, and aimed to bring them within the fold of domestic Christian influence. He solicited no contributions, but, adopting the method of Müller, of Bristol, England, prayed to God that funds necessary for his great purpose might be forthcoming by voluntary benefactions. An associate was so struck with the repeated bestowal of the needed supply that he exclaimed, "Just look! We no sooner make our purchase in faith, than the Lord stands behind us with the purse to pay the bill." Gradually the Rough House was surrounded with other buildings, while the managers and those under their care became very numerous. The institution was no longer a local but a national charity. It was a centre of light for the abandoned of all lands. In 1856 there were two hundred and sixty of its reformatories in existence, and the work of establishing new ones was going on rapidly in Europe and other parts of the world.

Of the gratifying results of the training at the Rough House, Wichern says: "A glance round the circle of those who were children of the House carries us into every region of the world, even into the heart of Australia. We find them in every grade and social position; one is a clergyman, another a student of theology, and a third a student of law; others are, or were, teaching. We find among them officers in our German armies, agriculturists, merchants in Germany, and at least in two other European countries, partners in honorable firms. They are presidents of industrial institutions, skillful landscape-gardeners, lithographists, and xylographists; artisans scattered through many towns, and wandering apprentices in every conceivable craft. One is a sea captain, some are pilots, others sailors who have taken one voyage after another and seen all the seas of the world. They are colonists in America and Australia, and both there and at home there are happy fathers and mothers, training their children righteously, and building up their family life after the fashion they have learned here. And there are men-servants and women-servants and day laborers; and, besides those who are better off, there are also the poorer, and such as are burdened by care either with or without their own fault. Besides, a considerable number have died at home and abroad (very many, in proportion, of its earlier girls); and some of those who went out to sea have never returned; probably many have found a sea-grave; some have disappeared; some suddenly turn up after long years have passed. I recall one who left this House twenty years ago, and of whom I heard nothing for the last ten years, until he has now notified himself as a well-doing master-artisan, and a happy father, in a distant town."

The Inner Mission, of which the Rough House was the origin, is not simply a philanthropic institution. Wichern distinctly discards this limitation, by saying that its object is to do within the sphere of Christendom what the church is endeavoring to accomplish in heathen lands, "the propagation of pure evangelical faith and the relief of physical suffering,"[1] as far as it may be possible to reach these ends. "It aims at a relief of all kinds of spiritual and temporal misery by works of faith and charity; at a revival of nominal Christendom and a general reform of society on the basis of the gospel and the creed of the Reformation. It is Christian philanthropy and charity applied to the various deep-rooted evils of society, as they were brought to light so fearfully in Germany by the revolutionary outbreaks of 1848. It comprises the care of the poor, the sick, the captive, and prisoner, the laboring classes, the traveling journeyman, the emigrants, the temperance movement,

[1] Herzog's *Real Encyclopædie*. Art. *Inner Mission.*

the efforts for the promotion of a better observance of the Lord's day, and similar reforms, so greatly needed in the churches of Europe."

But while the German church has been attentive to its work at home, it has not been negligent of its duty toward those beyond the pale of Christendom. As long ago as the beginning of the present century there was a missionary school organized by Janicke at Berlin. Others have been established at brief intervals since that time, while missionary societies under the auspices of both the Lutheran and Reformed churches have arisen in a number of the cities and larger towns.

One of the pioneers of the foreign mission enterprise was Gossner, whose life, at first full of reverses and disappointment, has lately come to a triumphant and brilliant close. He was originally a Roman Catholic priest, but his Pietistic inclination precluded him from the favor of his less devout brethren. He went from one city to another, tarrying only a few years in each. From St. Petersburg he went to Berlin, thence to Hamburg, and afterwards to Leipzig. While in the last city he quietly left the Romish fold and took orders in the Protestant church. He became pastor of the Bethlehem chapel in Munich. His effective life began there, though he was then fifty-six years of age. His ministrations were fascinating, and the people came from all sides to hear him preach.

On a certain occasion a few young men, who were animated by a missionary spirit, went to him for counsel. They had been turned away from the missionary seminary as unfit for the service. He declined to encourage them in their views. Still they came in increasing numbers. Finally he asked them, "What shall I do with you? Where shall I send you? I don't know;

I can do nothing for you." Their reply was, "Only pray with us; that can do no harm; if we can't go we must even stay. But if it is God's work, and his holy will that we go, he will open the door in his time."

Gossner yielded, and instructed them. But their number enlarged so rapidly that he was compelled to secure teachers for them. Though he was then at that time of life when most men think of bringing their labors to a close, he laid his plans as if he were exempt from death for centuries. He founded his first mission when sixty-five years of age. In 1838 he sent out eleven missionaries to Australia. The following year some were despatched to India; since which time this zealous servant of God has established missions among the Germans in the American Western States; on the islands of the Southern seas; in Central India; on Chatham Island near New Zealand; among the wild Kohls at Chota Nagpore; on the Gold Coast; and in Java, Macassar, and New Guinea. He employed no agencies; was his own corresponding secretary; superintended the instruction of all his missionaries; and died at the age of eighty-five, as full of youthful feeling and perseverance as when a student at Augsburg. The instructions he gave to his missionaries declare the sources of his own success. "Believe," said he, "hope, love, pray, burn, waken the dead! Hold fast by prayer. Wrestle like Jacob! Up, up, my brethren! The Lord is coming, and to every one he will say, 'Where hast thou left the souls of these heathen? with the devil?' Oh, swiftly seek these souls, and enter not without them into the presence of the Lord." Gossner's beautiful motto, found in his diary, was, "Pereat Adam! Vivat Jesus!"

The missionary labors of Louis Harms, of Hermannsburg, kingdom of Hanover, demand the serious attention of every friend of humanity. The small beginning of his enterprise, the unexpected and unsolicited means placed at his disposal, the zeal with which a plain rural parish has devoted itself to the missionary work, and the remarkable fruits attending every new step, prove both the power of a single heart when imbued with a great thought, and the sad truth that the church has hitherto buried in a napkin some of the most valuable talents committed to her keeping. Harms labored among his own congregation until every family became earnest and active in the service of God. By and by their awakened fervor craved new avenues of usefulness. In 1849 twelve men presented themselves to their pastor for the missionary work. This was the beginning, and God has so provided for every emergency that the entire enterprise has been favored with marked prosperity.

Missionaries having been sent out from time to time, —all previously trained under the careful superintendence of Harms himself,—it was at last suggested that a missionary ship be built by the Hermannsburg congregation. The timbers were soon on the stocks, the vessel completed, and its charge on board. That boat has since become a messenger of light to many heathen minds. The missionary work of Harms has cost nearly one hundred and nineteen thousand crowns. It is still in vigorous prosecution, the parish increasing every year both in its gifts and in its capacity to give. The stations established in heathen lands, especially New Hermannsburg in Africa, have been judiciously selected, successfully conducted, and are now centres of truth to large areas of unevangelized territory.

The return of spiritual life to the German church is

indicated by other useful agencies than those immediately connected with humanitarian and missionary work. Societies for the distribution of Bibles and cheap religious literature have been organized in Berlin, Hamburg, Frankfort-on-the-Main, and all the larger cities.

The Gustavus Adolphus Union was instituted for the extension of Protestantism without regard to sectarian differences. Deriving its name from the illustrious Swedish champion of Protestantism, who died on the victorious plain of Lützen, its constant object has been to continue what he began. Its principal scene of labor has been among the dispersed Protestants who are living in abject poverty and wretchedness throughout Roman Catholic countries. The Union seeks them out, brings them to the light, and supplies their necessities. Then it bands them into a congregation, and, whenever the laws permit, supplies them with the gospel and religious literature. It goes into every open door, contributing the renewal of religious vitality both by forming new churches and strengthening feeble ones. For a time it was seriously impeded by the participation of radical Rationalists; but they having been judiciously sifted out, it has since pursued a steady career of usefulness.

Prelate Zimmermann became superintendent in 1849, since which time its receipts have increased and its field of operation widened. Its twenty-second session was held in 1865, in Dresden, Saxony. The receipts of the previous year amounted to one hundred and ninety-five thousand thalers, which were expended for the relief of seven hundred and twenty-three churches or communities. One of the late reports shows that of the societies benefited by its agency, one was in Portugal, two in Italy, one in Algiers, four in the United States, four in Switzerland, sixteen in France, thirty-four in Poland, fifty-six in Hungary, one hundred and nine in the upper provinces of Austria, and the remainder in the other German states.

These enterprises do not interfere with each other. Every one has its own path of duty and its individual attractions. But the amount of good effected, not only by those we have mentioned, but by others which are every year taking form, is of incalculable influence upon indifference and Rationalism. Their ministry is beautiful in the extreme, for they are restoring what has been nearly destroyed. One night, while John Huss was awaiting martyrdom in the dungeon at Constance, he dreamed that he had painted pictures of Christ around the walls of his little Bethlehem oratory in Prague. By and by he saw them all erased by the violent hands of the angry pope and his bishops. While in great distress at his ill fortune, he dreamed again. But this time there entered a large number of accomplished artists, who restored all the pictures to more than their original beauty. Then there came a great concourse of people, who, having surrounded the painters, cried out: "Now let the popes and bishops come; they shall never efface them more!"

The German church is now using its artist-hand in reproducing the long-erased images of beauty and faith. Every believer within her own fold and throughout Christendom should unite in the solemn protest that no bright color shall be erased again.

CHAPTER XIV.

HOLLAND: THEOLOGY AND RELIGION FROM THE SYNOD OF DORT TO THE COMMENCEMENT OF THE PRESENT CENTURY.

THE only country whose national existence and independence are due to the Reformation is Holland. To be the first to break the triumphant power of the Spanish army would have been glory enough for any ordinary ambition, but no sooner was her independence declared than she gave signs of great commercial and intellectual activity. Her Hudsons navigated every sea and planted the Dutch flag on shores not then traced on any map of the world; her manufacturers supplied all markets with the fruit of their labor and ingenuity; her soldiers were a match for any European force; her De Ruyters and Van Tromps knew how to contend with the Blakes of England; her William of Orange, whom she gave to her British neighbor, made as good a ruler as ever lived in Whitehall; her scientific men founded the systems which have continued in use to the present time; her philosophers revolutionized the thinking of the civilized world; her universities were the seat of the most thorough humanistic researches of the age; her painters founded new schools of art, and vied with the Italian masters; her theologians gave rise to controversies which brought all churches and their champions within the scene of conflict; and her pulpit orators acquired a celebrity which, in spite of the inflexibility of the language, was second only to that enjoyed by the most renowned preachers of France and Great Britain.

After Holland had fallen a victim to her political partisanship, she gradually disappeared from public observation. Her greatness in the past would have been well nigh forgotten if Prescott and Motley had not recalled it. But the judgment of the world concerning her, in her present state, is not more flattering than that of the author of *Hudibras*, who, in addition to venting his spleen against the people, employs his wit upon the irrational land, calling it,

> "A country that draws fifty feet of water,
> In which men live as in the hold of nature;
> And when the sea does in upon them break,
> And drowns a province, does but spring a leak."

But while the political status of Holland has been inferior and unobserved during the last century and a half, her important theological and religious career,—covering a much longer period than that,—is a theme of deep interest to every student of the history of the church.

Rationalism arose in Holland by means of some agencies similar to those which had produced it in Germany. The previous disputes and barren ministrations of the clergy made the soil ready for any theological error that might urge its claims with force. But the repulsive technicalities of Germany were not equally prevalent in Holland, and scholasticism refused to affiliate with the Reformed much longer than with the Lutheran church.

But when the synod of Dort, which held its sessions in 1618–1619, pronounced those dogmas by which the Arminians were excluded from the Dutch church, it established a standard of orthodoxy. In proportion as the synod gained the favor of the people, the Bible came into use, but more to serve the cause of polemics than of edification. Hugo Grotius, Erasmus, and other exegetical writers who had manifested independence in their interpretation of the Scriptures, were regarded with great suspicion and distrust. The door for the entrance of scholasticism was thrown wide open. To use the language of a writer of that day, "The doctrines were cut after the fashions of Peter Lombard, Thomas Aquinas, and Scotus; while the power of the word of God was denied, and the language of Babel was heard in the streets of Jerusalem." Theologians made an idle display of learning. Imaginary distinctions, definitions, and divisions became the food of the youth in schools of every grade, and of the congregations in all the churches. The books which have come down to us from that period are weapons against Atheism, Deism, Socinianism, and every other heresy that had arisen during the history of Christianity. Whether light was created on the first day; whether it was an attribute or a substance; whether Adam, after the formation of Eve, was a rib the worse; whether the knowledge of the unconverted may be called spiritual knowledge;—these were some of the topics of labored sermons. It was announced as a most gratifying result of accurate research that the soul of a boy was created forty days after conception, while that of a girl required eighty.

There were exceptions to the general sterility of the pulpit and lecture-room. Alting, professor at Groningen, enjoyed the sobriquet of "Biblical Theologian," because he made the Scriptures, and not scholasticism, the basis of his inquiries. Students from foreign lands flocked to his auditorium, and received the leaven of his earnest and reverent spirit. Yet his candidates were distrusted, and he had great trouble in defending himself against repeated charges of heresy.

But another important feature of the prevalent theology was the corruption of ethics. The doctrines of grace, of which the church of Holland had always been the defender, left no room for an ethical system. What the unconverted man does is nothing but sin; all are equally guilty; and all that we have of good is from God. If we be disposed to ask, "Does not this view make men careless and impious?" the answer comes back from the Catechism, "No; for it is impossible that those who are planted in Christ should be without the fruits of gratitude." This opinion had a strong tendency to isolate theology still more than scholasticism had done, from all practical interests. "What shall we do?" was an idle question, for, as a matter of course, man could do nothing. But "what must I be?" was the all-important and searching inquiry. Thus ethics glided into radical casuistry, and, in this form, became united with the scholastic theology.

The homiletic literature of that day indicates the unification very clearly. Besides being a tirade against schismatics of all classes, the discourse was often a discussion of grammatical principles, accompanied with a description of the spiritual condition of every hearer. After the singing of the hymn in the middle of its delivery, the people adjusted themselves to hear the application in which their cases were to be stated. There was *first*, an enumeration of "heretical sinners," divided into numerous groups; *second*, the "unconverted," separated into many subdivisions; and *third*, the many flocks of Christians. It was in this part of the sermon that the casuistry of the preacher had full play, and he who could subdivide his congregation in such a way that every auditor could not mistake his own proper position, received great honor from his brethren. The hearer waited until he "heard his name called," after which he might sink back again to his dreams. Even to this day, on leaving a Dutch church, it is a common question among the separating members to inquire of each other, "Have you heard the dominie call your name?" They mean by this, "Have you heard the pastor so describe people that you could not mistake the class to which you belong?"

We have now stated the two sources from which many of the troubles and defections of the Church of Holland have sprung. On the one hand was dogmatism, with its endless distinctions, begotten and fostered by Scholasticism. On the other, practical mysticism, cherished into strength by a disgusting system of casuistic ethics. The reaction against those prevalent errors was Rationalism. They were the domestic fountains of that species of error.

But there were men who, when they saw the evils their venerated Church was suffering, threw themselves into the breach, and contended for her deliverance.

Cocceius, the celebrated opponent of Scholasticism, was born in Bremen, in 1603. He studied all branches of theology; but having been instructed in Hebrew by a learned Rabbi of Hamburg, he applied himself especially to the Scripture languages. In 1629 he visited the Dutch University of Franeker, and wrote tracts on the Talmud, with extracts therefrom in German. He also composed Greek verses with great ability. Returning the same year to Bremen, he there became Professor of Sacred Philology. In 1636 he was called to Franeker, to take the Hebrew first, and afterward the Greek chair. Still later he taught theology. His exegetical works, being far in advance of any which had appeared at that time, acquired great renown for their author. In 1649 he was invited by the Curators of the University of Leyden to take charge of the department of theology in that seat of learning. His long-cherished antipathy to Scholasticism was well known, but he pursued his course in quiet until 1658, when he was daringly assailed.

Having developed his opinion that the Sabbath had not been instituted in Paradise, but in the desert, and was not therefore binding upon Christians, Cocceius was buffeted by a host of writings, in which he was charged with every imaginable species of skepticism. The literature of the Cocceian controversy abounds in as violent and harsh expressions as have disgraced theological history at any time. Yet Cocceius was not without ardent disciples and friends, who knew as well how to give as to receive severe thrusts. As an illustration of the method of the discussion, we mention the title of a book written in favor of Cocceius: "Satan's Defense of himself, on being questioned why he had instigated some persons to distort and vilify the orthodox, wise, and edifying Writings of the Blessed Professor Cocceius, &c., &c." In this work Satan, on being questioned whom he fears most, replies that "no one has done more harm to the power of darkness than Cocceius,—not even Calvin."

The States of Holland wrote to the Synod not to discuss the Sabbatarian question, and to forbid the combatants from further controversy. There were other charges brought against Cocceius, however, one of which was his distinction between *ἄφεσις ἁμαρτιῶν* and *πάρεσις ἁμαρτιῶν*, by which he held that the former was a complete pardon, but the latter incomplete, and only in force under the old dispensation. He placed the whole system of theology under the figure of a covenant. There were two covenants, one of works, and the other of grace. The latter had a threefold economy: before the law; after the law; and under the Gospel. The institutions under the first economy were symbolical of the second; and these again of the third. Everything was a shadow of some higher and future good. Forgiveness was no exception to the rule. That of the Old Testament was *πάρεσις* preparing the way for the complete *ἄφεσις* of the New.

There was one point of agreement between Cocceius and Des Cartes: their common aim of emancipation from Scholasticism. But the former strove by revelation, the latter by philosophy to secure the result. It has been charged that Des Cartes influenced Cocceius, since the school of that philosopher was growing into power at the very period of the Cocceian tendencies. But the charge is groundless. Des Cartes stood on the ground of reason alone, while Cocceius planted himself upon the Scriptures. Thus there was a world-wide difference between the two men at the very starting-point of their systems; a difference which becomes more apparent at every additional step in the study of their sentiments.

If Cocceius was opposed when he arrayed the Bible against Scholasticism, Descartes might be expected to meet with increased resistance when he used only the weapon of philosophy. "Aristotle," said the theological world of Holland, "was a heathen, it is true, but then he afterwards became soundly converted to Catholicism. In due time he was transformed into a most exemplary Protestant. Yet this Des Cartes is a downright Jesuit, and a very demon let loose from the infernal world. His whole system commences with doubt and is pervaded by it. How dangerous then to our orthodoxy is the attack of this Catholic Arminian! If his assumption concerning skepticism be correct our whole theology becomes overturned; for then the elect would have ground for doubting their own salvation, which would be opposed to the infallible doctrine of the final perseverance of the saints. And to crown the scene of this Des Cartes' audacity, he holds that the earth and not the sun turns round, which, as good father Brakel says, 'is a sure sign that the man's head is turned.'"

Voetius was the leader of the forces against the pretentious philosophy. A book, issued anonymously by a friend of Spinoza, applying a little more logic to the Cartesian idea of substance, caused him to obtain additional ground. For the new school which he was combating already rested under the imputation of Crypto-Atheism. The hand of the government interfered, and Cartesianism appeared to be extinguished. But it had its secret admirers, especially in the academies of Northern France, where its adherents occupied almost every chair of instruction. Its last representative was Ruard Andala, 1701, at whose death Newton and Leibnitz came into power.

The place assigned to reason by Cocceius led his foes to accuse him of Cartesianism. He made the intellect the interpreter of Scripture in this sense; that, since the words of the Bible are capable of many meanings, reason must decide which are proper and which improper, and not be forgetful to derive as much thought as possible from the sacred text; "for," said he, "the Scripture is so rich that an able expositor will bring more than one sense out of it." He aimed to find Christ and his church in each biblical book; but he interpreted every statement as allegorical, typical or prophetical. Reason as applied by him, became a light to expose many sides of truth which had never been perceived by the reigning dogmatism. The result of his labors was the overthrow, in many minds, of philosophical Scholasticism, but the enthroning of biblical Scholasticism in its stead. His allegorical method of exposition led his followers into gross aberrations.

The Cocceians and Voetians were now the two great theological parties which attracted to their standards nearly every man of promise or note throughout Holland. The former were the Progressives, the latter the Conservatives. The Cocceians favored the entrance of new ideas, and effected the junction of philosophy and theology. The Voetians professed to desire a reform, but their conduct was not in harmony with their avowal. While they agreed with their antagonists in calling the Bible the fountain of light and truth, they held that the fathers of Dort and the Reformers had digested its contents and explained its meaning in most excellent summaries, and that "it was for us to light our candles at those great lights of the church." They were very properly called "Traditionarians," a name of which they were proud. One of their writers said, "We have caught up the last voices and words of our ancestors, those Fathers of whom we are now glad to call ourselves the echo."[1]

[1] Owenusters.

The Cocceians studied the original text, and took leave to differ often from the authority of the translators. Their opponents attached great value to the translation, and sometimes called it "inspired." The former delayed not to appropriate the fruits of the latest researches in science and criticism, in certain cases laying aside fragments of the text in favor of the suggestions of the most recent editions of Cocceius. To the Voetians this conduct was not much better than atheism. They hurled all the curses and plagues of the Bible against every one who whispered that there could be a mistake in the transcription of a word or even of a Hebrew vowel-point. The Cocceian brought all his questions into the pulpit, where he preached them in a manner more adapted to addle the heads of his hearers than to edify their hearts. Hebrew grammars were published for the laity. Even women,—among whom was Anna Maria Schurmann, the adherent and friend of Voetius,—were able to read the Bible in the original tongues. Nor did they hesitate to take part in the angry disputes of theologians. The Cocceians ran wild with their principles of fanciful interpretation. Every prophecy was, in their view, a treasury of allegorical facts yet to come to pass, and to be heartily endorsed. The Voetians prided themselves on their literalism, and named Hugo Grotius as their master. Yet they held that they never could swallow his abominable Arminianism.

The history of hermeneutics in all times shows that there is but one step from the literal to the allegorical. So with the Voetians. They indicated a disposition to yield, and at length became more fanciful and allegorical than their adversaries had been. They sought the interior sense of the text, but would be limited by no rules. They spiritualized the entire contents of the Bible. He who could draw most profit and instruction from a word was the best teacher, for a scribe must bring forth from his "heart" both new things and old. Not reason, nor logic, but experience and feeling must explain every word of God. The Bible literally became all things to all men. The "inner light" was its great interpreter. Many people despised scientific students of the truths of revelation, calling them "slaves of the letter,"—a term which, singularly enough, is still in common use among the uneducated members of the church of Holland. The Bible, taken in its real character, was banished and an artificial volume placed in its stead. Practical mysticism was now fairly inaugurated. Even conventicles spread throughout the country, and ignorant men who knew how "to speak to the hearts of the people" were infinitely preferred to any educated minister.

The strife ran very high. While there was an assimilation of the Voetians to the Cocceians in the application of the allegorical principle of interpretation, there was a moral retrogression of the latter which greatly reduced their strength. This arose from the defective views of Cocceius on the sanctity of the Sabbath. His disciples carried his unfortunate opinion far enough to gain the favor of the worldly and immoral classes. The freest customs and gayest fashions were imported from France, and Cocceian ministers made it their boast that they designed to keep up with the times. More spiritual adherents became disaffected by the growing impiety. Koelman, a layman, and Lodensteyn, a clergyman, gave the alarm that the kingdom of Christ had become secularized and corrupt. The latter would not baptize the children of unbelievers nor hold any communion with them. De Labadie, formerly a Jesuit but afterward a French minister, blew the clarion of reform. The watchword on all sides was, "Separate ye my people." Nothing but the stringency of his rules and the counter-efforts of the government prevented the pious masses from joining the reformer. Mystical sects, influenced by Jacob Boehme and Spinoza, appeared here and there. Chiliastic ideas spread abroad in proportion as men despaired of the speedy regeneration of the church through natural instrumentalities. All was commotion and disruption, and, for a time, everything seemed to be on the downward course to ruin.

But the imminence of the danger brought a speedy and violent reaction. The persecution of the French Huguenots drove them across the boundary line. The Dutch true to their traditional hospitality, received them with open arms. The guests returned their welcome by diffusing new spiritual life through the hospitable country. The Coccëians laid off their worldly habits. Days of fasting and prayer were appointed by the civil and ecclesiastical authorities, while an increasing love for the church, as bequeathed by the fathers, was overspreading the land. The attachment to what was old and time-honored became a glowing enthusiasm. Sharp distinctions between parties disappeared. Men who had formerly been violently arrayed against each other now expressed a disposition to unite in one common effort to restore the church to her former purity. Brokel, Imytegeld, Groenewegen, Lampe, and Vitringa, representing different and opposing forces, united in a harmonious effort to reform the heritage of Christ. Their labors were fruitful, for the people greatly honored them and earnestly followed their good advice.

The theological candidate had previously been asked two questions, which had an important bearing upon his subsequent life. One was, "Do you fear God?" The other was, "To what party do you belong?" The latter inquiry was now abolished. In every university the long-prevalent partisanship subsided. But under the improved state of religion, a Voetian was invariably placed in the chair of dogmatic theology, a Cocceian in that of exegesis, and a follower of Lampe in charge of practical theology. The pulpits were likewise supplied with an equal number of ministers from the ruling parties.

After 1738 the religious progress of the church of Holland became more tardy. Attention to spiritual life decreased, while more care was bestowed upon the improvement of theological training. The department receiving greatest favor was the linguistic study of the sacred text. Professor Schultens was the first to apply himself to the Hebrew cognate languages, especially to the Arabic. The critical works of Mill and of Bengel found their way, in 1707 and 1734, into the Dutch universities. John Alberti, inaugurated professor at Leyden in 1740, made the Arabic his special branch, and in five years' time that study became so popular that Valkenaer found it necessary to warn young men against yielding too freely to its fascinations. The direction of theological taste to another department of inquiry increased the indifference to party distinctions. Henceforth the terms Voetian and Cocceian became more unfrequent and unimportant.

The theological tendency toward the study of the languages of the Bible had the single unfortunate result of increasing that puerile literalism which had appeared in only sporadic forms during several preceding centuries. It was the element antagonistic to the allegorical and spiritual interpretation of the text.

Peter Abrest, the Dutch Ernesti, taught in Groningen in 1773. His work on *Sacred Criticism as the best Safeguard of Theology*, showed the value he attached to a thorough grammatical and historical study of the Scriptures. His labors were in harmony with the long-standing literal interpretation of the text, though he would elucidate scientifically what had previously been treated mystically. Even before the Reformation, the Dutch theologians were preëminently textual in their habits of study, and in subsequent times, they built up their systematic and polemical theology by the stress laid upon the "words" of the inspired volume.

Nowhere was the proverb "Every heretic has his letter"[1] so common and yet so true as in Holland. The old quartos we have received from the seventeenth and former half of the eighteenth centuries will ever remain marvels of literalism gone mad. They were gotten up like a geometry, with theorems and propositions, followed by a lengthy array of texts transcribed without one word of comment. The sermons published at that time were divided and subdivided, their appearance being similar to a page of a dictionary. They were interlarded with Latin, Greek, and Hebrew letters and figures of various sizes, all being literal quotations from the Bible, and proving nothing except that the preacher had made free use of his Concordance. The consequence of so much textual citation in books and sermons was the increased popularity of theology.

The systematic works of the seventeenth century were familiar to the masses. What was said of the

[1] "Jedere Ketter heeft zyn Letter."

theological disputes of the third century, that bakers' and shoemakers' shops reëchoed the words '*homoousian*' and '*homoiousian*' might be applied to the period of which we speak. Even now, there exists in Holland a remarkably popular acquaintance with theology. "I have seen," says a clergyman, "fishermen who could pass examination for licentiate's orders at one of your American schools, and beat the best of the candidates in the handy use of texts and definitions."[1] The descendants of the Dutch settlers in the United States are still familiar with Brokel; while if you ask any Hollander what he thinks of John á Marck's *Marrow of Divinity*, he will probably indicate very soon that he has committed nearly the whole of it to memory. Francken's *Kernel of Divinity* is equally well-known to the masses, for he belonged to the Voetian party. He was eminently practical and ascetical. He was not without a vein of mysticism, as may be inferred by the title of one of his works: "*Earnest Request of the Bridegroom Jesus Christ to the Church of Laodicea to celebrate the Royal Marriage Feast with Him.*"

During the entire period, dating back to the Synod of Dort, there was an undercurrent of Rationalism, which, though sometimes daring to make its appearance, observed in general the strictest secrecy. Cartesianism made it bolder for a time, and in party struggles it ventured to take sides. But the keen eye which the church ever turned toward heresy made it timid. Yet it was a power which was only waiting for a strong

[1] Extract from a letter of Rev. P. J. Hoedemaker, dated September, 1864. The correspondence of this accomplished scholar, who has been some time in connection with the University of Utrecht and in intimate relations with the best minds of Holland, has been invaluable to us in the preparation of the Chapters on Dutch Theology.

ally in order to make open war upon the institutions which the heroes of Holland had wrested from Philip II. of Spain.

Balthazer Bekker, " a man who feared neither man nor devil," was the first Rationalist in the Dutch church. He was a disciple of Des Cartes, and an ardent lover of natural science, particularly of astronomy. He published a work on Comets, in which he combated the old notions, prevalent among his countrymen, that a comet was always the precursor of heresies and all manner of evils, and that it should be made the occasion for a general call to prayer and fasting. Bayle, of Rotterdam, a reputed atheist, harmonized with Bekker. Bekker separated between the sphere of reason and that of religion. Whenever they meet each other it should be as friends and co-workers. Religion has greater dignity, but that gives it no right to disregard the authority of reason. When the Scriptures speak in an unnatural way of natural things, it is high time for the operation of reason. This idea led to the accommodation-theory, which, applied to the doctrine of spirits in his book, *The World Bewitched* (1691), resulted in Bekker's excommunication. His Cartesianism, which had taught him to distinguish so rigidly between the two "substances," matter and spirit, as to deny all action of the one upon the other, led him to assert that spirits, whether good or bad, have no influence upon the bodies of men. The Jews ascribed all exertion of power to angels, through whom God worked mediately. Jesus adapted himself to these ideas of his times.

Bekker loved to trace all spirit-stories to some plausible origin, and then to hold them up to the ridicule of the masses. To give substantial proof of his disbelief in all spiritual influence, he passed many nights in graveyards, on which occasions he manifested a sacrilegious hardihood, which, besides making him the wonder of his time, could only be accounted for by supposing that he kept up secret correspondence with the devil. "For," reasoned the Dutch theologians, "is not all this one of Satan's tricks to make us believe that he does not exist, so that he may capture us unawares?" On account of Bekker's acknowledged merit, the government took his part, and at his death, paid his salary to his family. Voltaire said of him: "He was a very good man, a great enemy of the devil and of an eternal hell. . . . I am persuaded that if there ever existed a devil, and he had read Bekker's *World Bewitched*, he would never have forgiven the author for having so prodigiously insulted him." In the library at Utrecht there are ten quarto volumes containing reviews of this book, in which Bekker's personal appearance, said to have been very unprepossessing, receives a goodly portion of the censure. His body was believed by his contemporaries to be a most excellent portrait of the devil himself.

Professor Roell, of Franeker University, started from the Cocceian principle of freedom of thought. In his inaugural address, he announced it as his opinion, that Scriptures cannot be interpreted in any safe way except by the dictates of reason; that reason is the grand instrument by which we arrive at a knowledge of all truth; and that it is the great authority for the determination of all theoretical and practical religion. This author is best known to theologians by his ideas on the sonship of Christ. He held that Christ could not be a son, for then there would be a time when he came into being from nonentity. The term "son" could not signify unity of essence with the Father. "Brother" would be a more correct word. The only sense in which Christ could be son was as the divine ambassador. These assumptions brought upon Roell the charge that he was a Socinian and an Arminian. His principal opponent was Vitringa.

Rationalistic tendencies increased in both number and force in proportion as the church decreased in the zeal which it had possessed at the close of the Cocceian and Voetian controversy by virtue of the immigration of the exiled Huguenots of France.

Van Os, of Zwolle, attacked the accepted covenantal theory, and the doctrine of immediate imputation. The latter was a mere scholastic opinion, not accepted among the doctrines of the church, but yet maintained by the people as a requisite of orthodoxy. Having gone thus far, Van Os proceeded to deny a form of infralapsarianism, which was termed "justification from eternity." Many prominent but bigoted minds, having long entertained these ultra ideas he was endeavoring to refute, and some having gone so far as to attempt their introduction into a revised edition of the confession of faith, Van Os was censured for heresy. But he took the first opportunity to preach the Protestant doctrine that every one had the right to test the church-creed by the word of God. In the opinion of the people this course amounted to a total renunciation of the creed, and he was accordingly dismissed. Another dispute, which created attention and attracted the suspicion of the watchful church, was on toleration. All who dared to defend even the word, were stigmatized as unpardonable heretics, for Voltaire had just written in its favor. Pastor De Cock placed himself in danger of excommunication because he was so rash as to advocate it. He was only rescued by the interference of the government, and by luckily publishing that he distinguished between Christian and ecclesiastical toleration.

There were controversies concerning minor points of doctrine, but amid them all, it was very perceptible that there was a well-organized disposition to break through the stringent rules of order, and escape from the control of the vigilant guardians of the church. But whoever departed a hair's breadth from the doctrinal system laid down in the confession of faith was charged with skepticism. Van der Marck's employment of a single term cost him his professorship. But he was afterwards restored, and died in 1800. Kleman wrote a book, in 1774, on the *Connection between Grace and Duty*, in which he held that the right use of those intellectual and spiritual gifts which God has imparted to us is the condition of his further blessings. He was compelled to retract his heresy. Ten Broek, of Rotterdam, considered only the death of Christ expiatory, while his colleagues wished the same to be said of every act of his life. Because that rash theologian ventured to use the word " world," in John iii. 16, in its broadest sense instead of circumscribing it to " the world of the elect," he had the choice either to recant or give up his office. The government interfered and saved him.

But while all these influences were at work in the church of Holland, a still stronger current was setting in from England. The impolitic ecclesiastical rigor became an enemy to truth, and contributed powerfully to the development of Rationalism. Never have church and state presented a more complete contrast. The government of Holland was the most liberal in the world, but the ecclesiastical authorities have not been surpassed in bigotry during the whole history of Protestantism. Holland was the refuge and home of the exile of every land who could succeed in planting his feet upon her dyke-shores. But the church of that country was so illiberal that the use of a term in any other than the accepted sense was a sufficient ground of excommunication.

The intimate relations in which Holland stood to England by the accession of William and Mary to the British throne afforded an opportunity for the importation of English Deism. Nowhere on the Continent was that system of skepticism so extensively propagated as among the Dutch. The Deists took particular pains to visit Holland, and were never prouder than when told that their works were read by their friends across the North Sea. On the other hand, Holland supplied England with the best editions of the classics then published in Europe, some of which are still unsurpassed specimens of typography.

The works of Hobbes appeared in Amsterdam in 1668, his *De Cive* having been issued as early as 1647. Locke's *Epistle on Toleration* was translated into Dutch in 1689, while his *Essay on the Human Understanding* was rendered not only into that language, but also into the French. Collins and Chubb were read scarcely less by the Hollander than by the Englishman. Locke spent seven years in Holland, and Toland studied two years in Leyden. Shaftesbury resided among the Dutch during the year 1691, and made a second visit in 1699. The adversaries of the Deists enjoyed the same privilege, and did not hesitate to improve it. Burnet became a great favorite in Holland. Lardner, who spent three years there, was well known to the reading circles, for his works were translated into their tongue. Lyttleton, Clarke, Sherlock, and Bentley received no less favor. Leland enjoyed a cordial introduction by the pen of Professor Bonnet, while Tillotson had his readers and admirers among even the boatmen in the sluggish canals of Leyden, Rotterdam, and Amsterdam. But the Deists of England gained more favor in Holland than their opponents were able to acquire. The former were bold, while the latter were timid and compromising. Consequently a brood of domestic Deists sprang up, who borrowed all their capital from their English fathers. Patot, a follower of Lord Herbert of Cherbury, referred to Christ by asking, "What do we trouble ourselves about the words of a carpenter?" He wrote his *Fable of the Bees*, to ridicule the doctrines of the atonement and resurrection.

But as English Deism was reinforced by the atheism of France before the invasion of Germany by either, so did the same copartnership take place in reference to Holland.

The works of the French skeptics were as copiously distributed in Holland as at home. Many of them were issued by Dutch publishing houses. Des Sandes published his *Reflections on Great Men*, in Amsterdam; Toussaint's *Morals* gained the honor of more than one edition in the same city; and De Prades, who had been condemned by the Sorbonne on account of the thesis by which he tried to gain his baccalaureate, published his *Defense* in Amsterdam in 1753. It was in this work that he compared the miracles of Jesus to those of Æsculapius. Hase says that it was in Holland, and not in London, that the *Système de la Nature* first came to light. Rousseau's *Émile*, which had been burned by the sheriffs in France, had the largest liberty afforded it beyond the northern frontier. The Dutch would not be sated with Volney until they had published and read three editions of his works.

Voltaire was very popular throughout the country. A number of periodicals arose, having the avowed object of disseminating the views of himself and his friends wherever the Dutch language was spoken. La Mettrie, driven from France, here found a home. Voltaire barely escaped the Bastille by fleeing thither, though when he left the land which had given him shelter, he bade it the graceful farewell: "Adieu canals, ducks, and common people! I have seen nothing among you that is worth a fig!" But Voltaire had cause to cherish no very pleasant feelings toward Holland. Her great men had received him coldly. His excessive vanity was never so deeply wounded as by the sober Dutchmen. Desiring to make the acquaintance of Boerhaave, the most celebrated physician in Europe, he called upon him, stating that he "wished to see him." Instead of becoming rapturous at the Frenchman's compliment, the plain old Leyden burgher coolly replied: "Oh, sit as long as you please, sir, and look at me; but excuse me if I go on with my writing." On offering one of his philosophical books to Professor Gravesande, the latter returned it to Voltaire in a few days with only this comment: "You are a poet, sir; a very good poet, indeed!"

The chief disaster resulting from the French skeptical writings was not so much the skeptical indoctrination of the people as the general diffusion of a light and frivolous indifference to all religion. Through the influence of France the Dutch became enslaved to vicious customs, taste, modes of thought, and conversation. The etiquette of the Parisians was domesticated among their northern imitators. The works published in Holland were mere reproductions from the French, and many of them were written in that language. The simplicity, truthfulness, and attachment to old forms, which had so long existed, gave place to a general spirit of innovation. The reverential and determined spirit that had enabled their forefathers to gain their independence was no longer apparent in the children. Liberal to a fault, Holland was now paying the penalty of her excessive hospitality. Sensuality and superficial epicureanism were at once the taste and the destruction of many of the young minds of the country.

When the people of Holland began to awaken to their condition, they were seized with a spirit akin to despair. The coldness of the church amid all the attempts to destroy the basis of her faith appeared as the chill of death. When the learned societies offered a prize in 1804 for the best work on *The Cause and Cure of Religious Apathy*, they could not find one to crown with their medal. Holland, finding herself unable to keep pace with the quick step of French recklessness and irreligion, bethought herself of finding refuge in Gallic politics. "Our people," says Bronsveld, "then became a second-hand on the great dial of the French nation." Old men are now living who have not forgotten those days when all distinctions vanished, when the only name heard was "burgher," and when the skeptical and daring favorites of the people obtained seats in the national assembly. Religion was driven from the elementary schools and also from the universities. The chairs of philosophy and theology were united, for it was enjoined that no doctrine should be taught in future but natural theology and ethics. The Sabbath was abolished.

Then came Napoleon Bonaparte. He presented his plea, was received with open arms, and returned his thanks by draining the country of its treasures. It was only when the people felt the physical sting of his wars, and saw the indescribable moral dearth pervading their country, that they resolved to go back to the old paths and the good way, and to abandon all deference to French examples. On the occasion of the great jubilee of 1863, which commemorated deliverance from the yoke of France, there was heard throughout Holland but one note of joy: "Thanks be unto the Lord who hath delivered the nation from the ruin which it had prepared for itself, and into which infidelity had thrust it!"

CHAPTER XV.

HOLLAND CONTINUED: THE NEW THEOLOGICAL SCHOOLS, AND THE GREAT CONTROVERSY NOW PENDING BETWEEN ORTHODOXY AND RATIONALISM.

THE commencement of the new era in the religion and politics of Europe was the restoration of peace after the battle of Waterloo. Wherever the French bayonet had won territory to the sceptre of Napoleon, it opened a new and unobstructed sway for the propagation of the skepticism taught by the followers of Voltaire. But the same blow that repulsed the armies of France produced an equally disastrous effect upon her infidelity. A sincere desire began to animate many persons living in the subjugated countries that, with the restoration of their nationality, there should also be the return of the pure faith of their fathers.

Holland had passed through nineteen years of humiliating subjugation, and she did not possess religious vitality enough to take full advantage of the rare opportunity presented by the peace of 1814. The people turned from France to Germany, and thought they found relief in the Rationalism of Semler and Paulus.

Orthodoxy was inactive. The Mennonites had become so mystical that they rather aided than arrested the incoming error. All the Socinian elements gained strength. The discipline of the church was exercised with such laxity that immorality was unrebuked. The Constitution of 1816, by its reunion of church and state, threw a great weight in the balance with Rationalism. William of Orange wielded a power over the church which he dared not exercise upon any other corporation. The Synods and Classes were driven back to forms, and allowed almost no freedom. Then came the notorious Pastoral Declaration, established by the Synod of the Hague in 1816, which no longer required of candidates for the ministry an unqualified subscription to the ancient Confessions. Their adherence to them was to be "in so far as" these formularies of faith agree with the word of God, not "because" they thus agree. That little change—*quatenus* substituted for *quia*—cast off all restrictions from the future preaching of the Dutch clergy. The orthodox preachers became very indignant at the official measure, and a bitter theological controversy arose.

Previous to this outbreak, a rupture had occurred upon the introduction of the new hymns, ordered by the Synod of North Holland in 1796. When presented for approval in 1807, they were violently rejected by the orthodox, who held that the version of Psalms which they had been singing many years was all that was needed. Besides, there was a perceptible Rationalism in many of the new hymns. They were foreign to the Dutch heart. Such a one as

> "Yonder will I praise the Friend,
> Who here has shown me truth,"

was not likely to elicit a response from those who desired an improved religious spirit. To fill up the cup of their misfortunes, the use of the hymns was made obligatory. But they hoped that when the Prince of

Orange came back, he would restore the venerated Psalms. Yet on his return he not only issued an official recognition of the new Hymn-Book, but expressed his warm approval of it. The congregation had no choice left but to refuse to sing altogether, or to use but one and the same hymn from one Sabbath to another.

THE REVIVAL AND THE SECESSION. There was an under-current of deep religious feeling among the masses which was unsupported by theological education. The lectures in the universities were similar to those delivered by the old school of German Supernaturalists. The prevalent orthodoxy was moderate and equivocal at best. Not much hope of awakening could be derived from it. The Bible was held to be the supreme authority; the historical character of its accounts was confessed; and the infallibility of its communications was maintained. Miracles, and prophetical and apostolical inspiration were accepted. But there was a neglect of the nature of this authority, together with a manifest indifference to the paramount value of all the great doctrinal possessions of the church. There was no scientific defense of the pillars of faith, and no attempt to discuss the true ground of miracles, and their inherent accordance with divine laws. Christian philosophy was totally ignored. Such natural theology as had been produced by the school of Leibnitz and Wolf, and more recently improved by the moral arguments of Kant, was the chief object of study, and had been made obligatory since the restoration of the Dutch universities in 1816. There was a general compromise between revelation and the old philosophy.[1] Supernaturalism was stagnant, and gave no promise of future progress.

[1] D. Chantepie de la Saussaye. *La Crise Religieuse en Hollande. Souvenirs et Impressions*, pp. 24–29.

While the church of Holland was in this deplorable condition, God raised up a few men to be the instruments of new life. They were endowed with great talents, moral heroism, and a steady purpose to elevate every department of ecclesiastical organization. The Holy Spirit accompanied their labors. The leaders of the group were Bilderdyk, Da Costa, Dr. Capadose, and subsequently Groen Van Prinsterer.

The first stood at the head of the modern school of Dutch poetry, and was one of the greatest poets ever produced by Holland. His conceptions were vivid, his style impassioned, his diction unequaled by any of his predecessors, and his moral life irreproachable. Having a conservative mind, he opposed each indication of revolution with every weapon at command. He was profoundly learned in the classics, history, and jurisprudence. Apart from all his efforts for the religious awakening of the people, he was the representative of the old Holland nationality. An ardent despiser of the French spirit, imparted by the fatal principles of 1789, he was equally opposed to the Rationalism of Germany. He believed that if new life were kindled in the Dutch heart, it could not be derived from without, but by a return to the pure teachings of the fathers of the Reformation in Holland.

Da Costa and Dr. Capadose were Jews. The former looked upon the condition of the country from the Israelitish standpoint developed in his *Israel and the Nations*. He believed in the millennium, and saw in it the divine cheerfulness of history, and the relief from surrounding evils. He is well described by one of his countrymen as "the Israelite who raised himself above the church of the Gentiles; the Israelite who testifies against this church; the Israelite who announces the glory of this church." He was a popular and spirited poet, excelling even his friend Bilderdyk in the lyrical character of his verses. He hated Rationalism in every form, and resisted whatever would interpose any authority between the conscience of man and the word of God. His Israelitish view made him reject the secondary authority of the confessions of faith, and did not permit him to attribute anything more than a relative value to the church of the Gentiles, "the church before the millennium."

Groen Van Prinsterer appeared at a time when the revival had taken definite shape, but he attached himself to its interests and contributed more than any one else to its development. He is one of those decided characters who are mentioned by friends and enemies with great animation. Studiously rejecting the individuality taught him by the school of Vinet, and reticent of his personal opinions, he has incurred the animadversions of some of his warmest admirers. Being a man of continual literary and political activity, he has taken part in all the important movements of his times. He is the Guizot of Holland. Though banished for a time from his seat in the States General by the Catholics, Revolutionists, and Rationalists, he did not intermit his labors to lead back the masses to evangelical piety. His powerful influence has been in favor of home missions and similar agencies. He has comprehended the revival, in all its scope, more clearly than any one else. He says of it that "it was neither Calvinistic, nor Lutheran, nor Mennonite, but Christian. It did not raise for its standard the orthodoxy of Dort, but the flag of the Reformation, the word of God. And though it found the doctrine of salvation admirably expressed in our symbolical books, appreciated a rule of education so conformable to the Holy Scriptures, and opposed the doctrines of the church and the duty of her ministers to the usurpations of Rationalism, it never thought of accepting and imposing the absurd and literal yoke of formularies with an absurd and puerile anxiety. A spirit of Christian fraternity predominated over the old desires."

The direct associated result of the revival was the Reunion of Christian Friends. It was presided over by Groen Van Prinsterer, and held semi-annual sessions in Amsterdam from 1845 to 1854. Its monthly journal, *The Union, or Christian Voices*, was conducted by Pastor Heldring, a warm-hearted man who has made himself illustrious in the annals of beneficence by his labors for home missions, by his foundation of an asylum for little neglected girls, and by similar charitable works.

Other pastoral associations sprang up in consequence of the new life, but some of them failed in a few years because of the want of a common symbol of faith. Groen Van Prinsterer hailed with joy every indication of Christian unity. He hoped that by this unity the church might be built up in its holy faith. From 1850 to 1855 he edited *The Netherlander*, a political and ecclesiastical review. It was in this periodical that he eulogized the revivals of other countries, and ranked the leaders of them among the greatest ornaments of history. The labors of the French and Swiss theologians, MM. Bost, Malan, Merle d'Aubigné, Gaussen, Grandpierre, and Monod find in him a most appreciative admirer.[1]

[1] Da Costa, in his biography of Bilderdyk, enumerates other participants in the revival in the Dutch Church; among whom were the two brothers Van Hogendorp, Nicolaas Carbasius, J. T. Bodel, Nyenhuis, Brugmans, Elout, Ran Van Gameren, Baron Van Wassanaer, Willem de Clercq, the poet, and author of a work on the *Influence of Southern Literature on that of Holland;* Van der Kemp, author of an admirable *Biography of Maurice of Nassau;* and Kœnen, author of an historical work on the *Refugees in Holland.*

The movement inaugurated by Bilderdyk, Da Costa, and Capadose led to an important secession from the Church of Holland. There were men who saw the necessity of revival on a large scale, but in their zeal for Confessionalism, they went far ahead of their leaders. Their cry was, "Let us leave Babel, and build up a new Church." De Cock and Scholte were the first to sound the note of secession. They were joined by such men as Brummelkamp, Van Reeh, Gezelle, and Van Velsen. This party rallied around the old Calvinistic symbols, and De Cock stood in their van. As early as 1829, when he became preacher in the little village of Ulrum, he distinguished himself for his zealous ministry. People came from a distance of eighteen miles to hear his sermons. He soon indoctrinated them so thoroughly that they would no longer permit their children to be baptized by "unbelievers." This brought him immediately into conflict with the rules of the Church. Two pamphlets appeared against him, which he answered in his *Defense of the True Reformed Doctrine, and of the True Reformed; or, the Sheepcot of Christ attacked by two Wolves.* Another pamphlet appeared with his approval, in which the new hymns were called "*Siren's Songs.*" The result was that he was suspended, and in 1835 excommunicated. In the same year he published his curious book, entitled "The so-called Evangelical Hymns, the Eyeball of the misguided and deceived Multitude in the Synodical-Reformed Church: Yes, of some Children of God, in their blindness, and while they have become drunk by the wine of their whoredom, tested, weighed, and found wanting: Yes, opposed to all our forms and doctrines, and the word of God; by H. De Cock, under the Cross because of Christ."

The expulsion of De Cock attracted many new

friends to his standard. At the close of 1834 a Separation Act was devised at Ulrum, by which all his adherents dissolved connection with the Church. They were said to number eighty thousand, but it is probable that the estimate was an exaggeration. By request of the Synod, the Separatists were prosecuted by the government, who used as a pretext an article in the *Code Napoléon*, which forbade the assembly of more than twenty persons for worship without the consent of the civil authorities. They were defended by many lawyers of the school of Bilderdyk. Foremost of the number was Groen Van Prinsterer. " the conscience of the Legislative Assembly, the right arm of religion in the State, and the defender of the principle of religion in the school." They were assailed by mobs who called them the "New Lights."

The schism was not a success. What promised to be a great and honorable Church, like the Free Church of Scotland, with which it now stands connected, carried with it much of the prejudice and bigotry of the land. It did not identify itself with scientific progress, and paid little regard to education. Any man of piety and utterance could become a preacher in one of its pulpits. It has at present a Seminary at Kampen, with a small faculty of three professors. Its course of study will compare favorably with that of any institution in the United States. The young men of talent, who now grow up in its fold, are prejudiced against its ultraism, and stand ready at any moment to unite with some new movement which will combine the piety of their fathers and the scientific demands of the present day. The radical defects of its initial steps were narrow-mindedness and fanaticism. The Separatists utterly ignored the elements of good in the mother-church. They could have done infinitely better service by casting all their influence with Bilderdyk and his followers in the Church, instead of arraying themselves against it, and becoming an enemy from without. Some of the leaders have organized colonies, which greatly weakened the power and prestige of those who remained at home. The emigrants came to America and settled, for the most part, in the Western States.

THE GRONINGEN SCHOOL. Each of the two tendencies prevalent in the Church of Holland had its decided defects. While one was zealous for theological training, it was nevertheless cold, indifferent and Rationalistic. While the other was burning with religious fervor and a practical evangelism, it was deficient in culture, scientific grasp, and a capacity to meet the wants of the time. There was a call for a third party, which would unite the best features of the two others, and develop them into a new progressive power. Hence arose the Groningen School. Its immediate origin was the attempt of Professor Van Heusde to modernize Platonism and adapt it to the nineteenth century. Hofstede de Groot, Pareau, and Muurling have been its leaders. Its organ is the periodical entitled, *Truth in Love.*

The characteristic of this school is, that there is in human nature a divine element which needs development in order to enable humanity to reach its destination. This destination is conformity to God. All religions have aimed and worked at the same problem, but Christianity has solved it in the highest and purest manner. Still, there is only a difference in degree between that and other religions. This is the germ of what the Groningens call the "Evangelical Catholic Theology." Conformity to God, they say, has been reached in Jesus Christ; but Plato, Zoroaster, and Confucius strove to attain to it. They failed because their task was too great for the means at command. God has fulfilled the desire of man, whom he had prepared for salvation by sending perfection embodied in Christ. We may not attach ourselves to any system or effort as absolutely true or good, nor condemn any as utterly false. All knowledge and arts are related to religion. They refine man and aid him in his emancipation from whatever is sinful and sensual.

The correspondence of ideas between Hofstede de Groot and Pareau was so intimate that they published a joint work on dogmatic theology, which contains a complete exposition of the principles of the Groningen School. Jesus Christ constitutes the centre of religion. In him we see what is God, what is man, the relations of one to the other, and how we can be so delivered from sin and its power as to become God's children by faith and love. In Christ's death we find love even for sinners, and learn that suffering is not an evil. In his glorification we perceive the aims and results of suffering. In him is the Theanthropos, not God *and* man, but God *in* man. There is but one nature in Christ, the divine-human. Jesus being the focal point of the interests of man, we must know, *first*, what he is outside of us, objectively; *second*, how he appears within us, subjectively. To know Christ we need the exegetical study of that preparation of man for Christ, which is furnished by the Old Testament. The New Testament is the fulfillment. The latter contains the sayings of Jesus and the conclusions of the Apostles. The writers of the Scriptures were not infallible, though they did not often err. Revelation is continued in the history of the church, which is the third principle of development. Augustine stood higher and went further than Paul, Luther than Augustine. If our development be partial and imperfect we must go back and begin anew.

The Groningen School is distinguished for its ethical system. How does Christ live in us? This is the question it proposes to answer. There is a distinction between the nature of man, which is divine, and his condition, which is sinful. Sin is the point where man, misusing his liberty, surrenders himself to his sensuous nature, which is not sinful in itself. God educates man by Jesus Christ in three ways; *first*, by revelation of truth; *second*, by manifestation of love; *third*, by education of the church. The high aim of the Church is to lead man to a consciousness of the unity of his origin and destiny, and to bring all to a knowledge and love of Christ, and of God in Christ. Christ was educated before his life on earth for the work designed for him, and he established the church by leaving his glory and leading a life full of love and truth. His death was the highest manifestation of his love and truth, for by it he showed God to man, and man to himself. His resurrection makes our hope of eternal life a certainty.

In the Groningen system there is no place for the doctrine of the Trinity. The influence of the sacraments is merely external, while Calvinism and the "blood-theology," are subjects of abhorrence. It would be unjust to place the Groningens beside the German Rationalists, though the influence of both has been similar. The former class, like the latter, have one fatal defect; they consider sin a mere inconvenience. They hold that man needs a Teacher but not a Redeemer, since all sinners will be eventually holy and happy. The Groningen tendency, as related to Dutch theology, is similar to that applied by Channing to the orthodoxy of the American church. Human nature is declared worthy of our attention and development. True humanity is pure piety. God can be found everywhere, even in the heart of man. The philosophical theology of Schleiermacher has stamped the Groningen system with its own signet. They both proceed from the same starting-point,—not reason, but the heart. Theirs is the religion of feeling.

The Groningens have done important service to the Dutch church. Their elevation of ethics to a proper position in theological instruction has been a national boon, while their unwavering zeal for the education of the masses and of children will always remain a monument to their honor. While they were the first to establish Sunday Schools in Holland, they have given a new impulse to missions. They defend religion against skepticism, and picture the latter in all its deformity.

But the Groningen system has almost totally failed of its object. It did not unite the zeal of the fathers with the science of the present day. Though opposed to Rationalism, it is more negative than positive, and is less distinguished for its doctrines than for its absence of them. It claims that the Church neither possesses nor needs doctrines. Therefore, it destroys the line of demarcation between the various confessions and that confessional Latitudinarianism, which is the direct offspring of the destructive principles of the Rationalism and Liberalism of the eighteenth century.

THE SCHOOL OF LEYDEN. In no theological system had any satisfaction been afforded to the joint feeling of attachment to the old confessions and of a desire to develop them in conformity with the requirements of the age. Many rejected the Groningen school because it depreciated the formularies of the church, and did not know how to value their scope or to elaborate them for immediate usefulness. The Leyden school filled the vacancy. Taking its origin in a disposition to establish a connection between the faith of the Reformers and our own, its aim has been to unite the old traditions with the new opinions.

The father and expounder of the School of Leyden is Professor Scholten, formerly of Franeker, but now of Leyden. He is well known as the author of historico-critical introductions, and of a *History of Philosophy*, but his reputation has been acquired mainly by his *Doctrines of the Reformed Church*, a work of great clearness, profound erudition, and romantic interest. As the reader peruses its fascinating pages he is bound by a spell which he cannot easily break. The remark of Dugald Stewart, on reading Edwards *On the Will*, occurs to him with peculiar appositeness, "There is a fallacy somewhere, but the devil only can find it."

There is, according to Scholten, a distinction between the principles and dogmas of a Church. The former are the norm and touch-stone of the latter. The Reformers were not always logical in their reasonings, and have left an unfinished task for the present day. Man arrives at a knowledge of the truth by the Holy Scriptures, but they must not be understood as containing the only revelation from God; He also reveals himself to the world through the hearts of all believers. The Bible is the source of the original religion. There is a difference between the Scriptures and the word of God. The latter is what God reveals in the human spirit concerning his will and himself. The writing down of the communication is purely human; therefore, the Bible cannot be called a revelation. We know, by the testimony of the

Spirit, that God's word in the Scriptures is truth. But Scriptural authority must not be accepted,—a liberty which would apply to a Jewish but not to a Christian age. Jesus and the apostles did not compel men to accept truth by a proclamation of authority, but by an irresistible moral power. Even in times when the liberty and individuality of faith have been lost in the Church, there were men who did not answer the question, "Why do you believe?" by saying, "Because the Church has spoken;" but by appealing to their interior consciousness.

Historical criticism must be called in, Scholten further holds, to prove the certainty of the facts of revelation. But the truth of the Christian religion cannot be established on this plan. With Rousseau, Lessing, and others, he opposes any attempt to make the best historical grounds the basis of a religious conviction. The truth of Scripture is testified by human nature itself, which, educated by Christianity, recognizes freely and personally the truth of the gospel. The natural faculty that performs this high office is reason, not feeling. Scripture is the touchstone of the Christianity of a conviction, but not of its truth. The Reformers very properly distinguished between a first and secondary authority, and allowed themselves complete liberty in their search after the origin of the books of Scripture. This was not a dangerous experiment, for he who has once come to know Christianity as the highest form of religion, can never fall into a negative criticism. If the religious contents of the Bible find their justification in the interior consciousness of man, then the question arises, "Can human reason attain to the supersensual, or is it limited to the sensuous experience?" The organ of all natural knowledge of God is reason; while its fountain is the physical, intellectual, and moral world. The first Adam did not possess that knowledge of God which was thoroughly enjoyed by the second. But can man attain to the knowledge of God while in a sinful condition, and while the light of his reason is darkened? Assuredly he may, for sin does not belong to the essence, but to the condition of man. The Reformed theologians built on the acknowledgment that Religion has her seat in the being of man, and sees in the Christian the expression of the reasonable religion. The material principle of the Reformed church is the doctrine of God's sovereignty and free grace. The weakness of the Reformation lay in its inconsistency, for it substituted the authority of the letter for that of the Church.

Scholten's abhorrence of authority has led him to a denial of miracles. From this point of view he can freely join hands with the Rationalists. In his latest work, the *Gospel of John*, he takes occasion to retract the favorable opinions formerly expressed concerning that portion of the New Testament. He has been fearlessly assailed by Oosterzee, La Saussaye, Da Costa, and other leading theologians. Unfortunately, he exerts more influence over the young theologians of Holland than any other Dutch theologian. He is ardently supported by Knenen, the exegete, his colleague at Leyden; and by Rauenhoff, the ecclesiastical historian. We close our estimate of Scholten with a word on his opinions of Christianity in general. It is neither superhuman nor supernatural. It is the highest point of the development of human nature itself, and, in this sense, it is natural and human in the highest acceptation of those terms. It is the mission of science to put man in a condition to comprehend the divine volume presented by Christianity.[1]

THE SCHOOL OF EMPIRICAL-MODERN THEOLOGY. The two leading representatives of this important branch of contemporary Dutch theology are Opzoomer and Pierson. The former, a professor in the University of Utrecht, left the sphere of theological instruction for a time, and took a prominent part in political debates in order to combat the claims of the anti-revolutionary party. He exerted little influence during the first years of his professorship in Utrecht, but since his publication of a manual of logic, *The Road of Science*, he has had a large share in founding the school with which he is now identified. In this work he maintains that observation is the only means of arriving at certainty, and that everything which cannot be proved by experience is uncertain, and has no right within the domain of science. This is the central thought of his whole system.

Pierson stands related to Opzoomer as Mansel does to Sir William Hamilton. The son of religious parents, he was at first rigidly orthodox. He is now pastor of the Walloon Church at Rotterdam. His early writings were touchingly beautiful and attractive, for it was in them that he laid open his inner life. But in his later works he assumes the air of the censor and scoffer. He was long the personal friend of La Saussaye, but, owing to doctrinal differences, they have parted and now pursue different paths. He is an orator of the American type. His opinions are elaborated in his two works, *The Origin of the Modern Tendency*, and the

[1] An article by Scholten on *Modern Materialism and its Causes*, may be found in the *Progress of Religious Thought in the Protestant Church of France*. London: 1861, pp. 10–48.

Tendency and Life. In the latter treatise we learn not merely the personal views of Pierson, but the creed advocated by all the adherents of the empirical-modern theology.

The New Theology, he holds, has an indisputable right to assume the epithet "modern," in distinction from "liberal." The latter term is borne by the Groningen school, which always opposes the church-creed. The principle of reform has not been fully carried out by the Protestants. The Protestant builds his faith on the Bible, but on what does he build his faith in the Bible? Is it not the testimony of the Holy Spirit? He has this support only through the Bible. Certain liberal theologians, like the orthodox, are extremely illogical in their conclusions concerning the word of God. The former will not accept of verbal inspiration, yet they call the Bible a divine book, which, fortunately, could be no better. Though they laugh at the story of Jonah and the whale, they accept every word of Christ, who quotes the story. They will not hear of present miraculous interpositions of providence, but accept some of the miracles of the Bible. There are Catholic priests who are affability itself, while there are orthodox Protestants possessed of ultra views. In contrast with all these classes stand the heroes of the *Modern Theology*, who possess the "passion for reality," and are endowed with the new cosmology of Galileo.

All true knowledge, argues Pierson, is self-knowledge. Reality comes to us in the impressions we receive of it. I see, I hear; and whether there is a reality outside corresponding to the impression, is a question never asked by a reasonable man. One who has a fever on a July day complains of cold. The bystanders deny his right to say it is cold. Now do they obtain their right from a comparison of their impressions with something objective? No. His knowledge is subjective in this sense; that it arises from sources which are in him alone, while theirs is objective, because they compare their impressions. Error is not in the impression but in the explanation. Man has more than sensual impressions. We have a faculty which brings us into contact with a spiritual world. The religious man is by necessity an anthropomorphist. He claims a personal God, a Father, a Redeemer, an Ideal. We need a sharp analysis to see the reflections of the contents of our religious feeling. Our mind seeks a conception of God, the basis of which must be the idea of the Absolute, Infinite Being. The Scriptures must be criticised by our reason. The first three gospels, which tell us what Christ said and did, are not authority for us. Their writers are unknown, in the main, and by no means original. But exact criticism may succeed in giving us a portrait of the Prophet of Galilee. He lived a life according to the spirit, and proclaimed a religion such as no one before or after him has been able to do. Is it not enough that he has glorified humanity, and made himself adored as king of humanity, even with a crown of thorns upon his brow? The hearts of men have been disclosed to him, and he has caused to well up therefrom streams of love, which none can turn aside. Is his name not glorious when we think that the penitence of a Magdalene, and the sorrow of a Peter, are flowers which have permanently sprung up from earth only after that earth had been drenched by his blood and tears? But the Church has made a mythological character of Christ. It has contemned the real Jesus who stood in opposition to authority and tradition. In his name the Church has enthroned and glorified this authority. It was not from a system but from a principle that he expected the regeneration of man. We have a safe revelation in the world about us. It is God's work in and around ourselves. Explore it; study yourself and man; but do it with such a spirit and purpose as Christ possessed.

As a specimen of Pierson's style, we give his portrait of a good preacher: "All elements are concentrated in him in such a way that men will, can, and must listen, for attention is as much a state as love. You cannot command, but you may deserve it. Paint for humanity, which, though despised by the formalists, terrified by the moralists, and condemned by the Pharisees, is yet the image of him who spoke not of its guilt, but of its sickness and sorrow; not of a judgment-seat, but of the open arms of the Father; not of damnation, but of regeneration. A Holland painter came from a foreign land, and painted a Dutch landscape. But everybody who saw it, said: 'He has been in Italy.' So let it be said of every Christian minister, 'He has been in Galilee, it is the color of Jesus.'"

The opinions entertained by the defenders of the Empirical-Modern Theology have few points of sympathy with evangelical Christianity. They stand above Rationalism, but not opposed to it. The system attempts a purification-process of Christian faith. It does not break with tradition and doctrine, but claiming the privilege of using its own eyes, it rejects the authority of both. It does not admit a supernatural origin of the Scriptures, but looks with suspicion upon many of the accounts contained therein. Taught by the philosophy of experience that everything has a natural source, even in the world of mind, it finds no room for free will. It cherishes a high regard for the individuality of man, and esteems it wrong to let the particular be lost in the universal. It discards any system of morals which does not do justice to this individuality. Its ethics are deterministic, but not fatalistic. It holds that the mysteries of orthodoxy are mystifications which insult the thinking man. It claims that its doubts are not sinful, for it says: "I have not doubted from a wish to doubt." But it furnishes nothing to take the place of that which it destroys by its negative criticism. This is its fatal weakness. With its principle, "no authority," it attacks the Bible, and finds it written neither by the supposed authors nor at the alleged dates. It destroys the sanctity of that which has become hallowed by our inner experience. It takes away Christ, in all his essential attributes, from the believer.

THE ETHICAL-IRENICAL SCHOOL. We have thus far seen, in the present state of theology in Holland, few indications of the vigorous progress of evangelical truth. But the Ethical-Irenical School, combining the principal orthodox minds, stands in manly and prosperous opposition to all parties which possess Rationalistic affinities. Chantepie de la Saussaye and Professor Van Oosterzee are its leaders. These men differ on minor points, but, in general, they are harmonious co-workers against skepticism in every form. They stand in the front rank of Dutch theologians, the former having no superior as a thinker, and the latter none as an orator.

La Saussaye is not a popular writer. His style is compact and his arguments intricate. He is sometimes eloquent, however, and a close thinker takes pleasure in reading his pages. He does not like the term "orthodoxy," for he thinks it too loud a profession. He has been charged with Hegelianism because of some expressions in his *Commentary on the Hebrews.* But the allegation is false, for he only applauded Hegel and Schelling as thinkers, without giving any sanction to their opinions. His views are as yet but little known to the people, only a few being willing to study his weighty thoughts. He is thoroughly imbuing his congregation in Rotterdam with his own spirit, and has now many followers, who are giving his ideas to the public in an attractive form. In 1851 he had a long and serious illness, after which he deemed it his duty to limit himself no longer to the functions of the pastoral office, but to raise his voice in ecclesiastical debates. In 1852 he took part in the formation of a society called "Seriousness and Peace" and was associated with Beets and Doedes in the editorship of their organ bearing the same name. The principle of the new organization consisted in the prominence given to science and its service in theology, in opposition to the school of Bilderdyk. It held that the Scriptures are of divine authority; that they are properly expressed in the confessions of the Reformed church of Holland; and that science must be subsidized for their explanation.[1]

Soon after the appearance of Renan's *Life of Jesus*, the Dutch theologians were surprised by a pamphlet entitled *History or Romance*, which, besides giving an admirable criticism on the new work, defined very clearly the points at issue, and lifted out of its poetic frame the picture deserving more serious study. The style was recognized as that of Professor Van Oosterzee. Like everything coming from his pen, it was easily read and as easily digested. It sounded the alarm, and

[1] *La Crise Religieuse en Hollande*, pp. 12–107.

warned the public mind against accepting Renan's romance as history. A few sentences in Professor Van Oosterzee's little work reveal his position in the present conflict with Rationalism. "Modern Naturalism," says he, "can be conquered only by a Christian philosophic belief in revelation, and by a powerful development of modern supernaturalism. . . . . . To some, nothing is easier than to lay all supernaturalism under condemnation, especially when it is opposed only in that form in which it appeared against the worn-out Rationalism of the past century, without attending to its further development, or taking the trouble to add to Renan's critical anathema a clear and intelligible exposition of his own point of view. Renan's *Life of Jesus* shows us what becomes of Christianity when we regard only the ethical-religious side of revelation, and not its supernatural character. You can hope for no victory as long as you know none but a subjective ground of faith, and do not meet Satan, coming as an angel of light, with a perspicuous and powerful, 'Thus it is Written.'"

Professor Van Oosterzee was called four years ago to the chair of Scriptural Interpretation in the University of Utrecht, now the centre of evangelical theology in Holland. He had been pastor of a church in Rotterdam, and his new appointment, made at the instance of the King and his ministers, was a great triumph of the orthodox party. He had already distinguished himself by his *Life of Christ and Christology*, in six volumes, and by his exegetical labors in connection with Lange's *Bible-Work*. But the oration he delivered on his assumption of office in the University added largely to his reputation, and obliterated any doubt which may have existed concerning his firm attachment to the faith of the fathers. Bearing the title, *The Skepticism which is anxiously to be avoided by the Theologians of our Day*,[1] it discusses the character, origin, rights, fruits, and remedy of the infidelity of the present time. The cardinal characteristic of this skepticism is, according to Professor Van Oosterzee, a denial of the great revelation of grace and truth in Jesus Christ, as the Son of God and of man, by whom salvation is made possible to us and to all the world. There are three fountains of the modern infidelity; a scholastic dogmatism, which has laid more stress on the formularies of the church than on the Gospel itself; a wild, revolutionary spirit in politics, not of native growth, but imported from abroad, which only satisfied itself by the overthrow of thrones, by the transgression of all established limits, and by its declaration of the supreme rights of reason and will; and a false philosophy, with its unholy brood of Empiricism, Idealism, Materialism, Rationalism, and Naturalism. The skepticism of the present day asserts rights to which it has no claim whatever, for it holds that the so-called mysteries of Christianity have no divine basis, and that there can be nothing supernatural in revelation. Neither can the labors of the skeptics produce substantial and permanent good in any department of theology. The only way to combat them is not by reviewing the opinions of departed thinkers and teachers, so much as by going directly back to the Bible itself, and looking at it with the aid of every new step in science. Such a weapon is a sound system. It may be termed the *Evangelical-Biblical, historical-philosophical, Irenical-practical theology.* If it be developed, all the shafts of infidelity will fall harmless at its feet.

Immediately after the appearance of Professor Van

[1] *Oratio de Scepticismo, Hodiernis Theologis Caute Vitando*, quam habuit Johannes Jacobus Van Oosterzee Theologis Doctor: Roterodami. 1863.

Oosterzee's reply to Renan, La Saussaye published his work entitled, *How must Modern Naturalism be attacked?* While he opposes Naturalism, he also takes exception to the usual orthodox method of assailing it. In this work, together with other treatises by the same vigorous writer, we find the Ethical-Irenical theology stated and defended.

The term *Ethical* is not, according to La Saussaye, the same as *moral*,—for morality, conscience, duty, and virtue are terms which find their home in the Kantian philosophy, and are now appropriated by the Groningen School. *Ethical* has application to the receptivities,—the inner wants, and states of the heart. It differs from *religion* just as want differs from supply. The Christian knows that religious truth, life, and action, are not the fruits of his subjective state of feeling, but of revelation, and of the communication of God to his spirit. The *ethical* is the natural, and the *religious* is the supernatural state of the heart. The Ethical theologians differ from the Supernaturalists on the following psychological ground: the former believe that the supernatural is communicated with human nature, and is so inseparable from it that a denial of it is a rejection of all that is most human in man. The latter hold that the supernatural, since it is an essential part of religion, is not necessary merely to accredit revelation, but to establish it.

While La Saussaye agrees with Van Oosterzee in application of the term *ethical*, he does not hold with him that the "*Thus it is written*" is an adequate reply to the Rationalist. Neither will his view of miracles harmonize with that of the professor, or with Vinet and De Pressensé, of whom he forcibly reminds us in many of his opinions. The supernaturalistic theory, La Saussaye contends, is incorrect. The Church has paid too much attention to the exterior features of miracles, but far too little to their ethical import, and to the connection between nature and spirit. Miracles can be defended only on the ground that the power to work them is still in the church over which Christ presides and to which he communicates his energy. The Naturalist who opposes the present power of miracles can be convicted by an appeal to his own personality; for he is not merely *nature*, but also supernatural, free, spiritual. He feels himself responsible; he has a conscience. Renan, in his picture of Christ and his apostles, places salvation on an equality with deliverance from sickness, and makes it mere socialism. If we would rebuke the skepticism of the present day we must return to first principles; not to the doctrines, but to the facts on which they rest. Revelation presupposes the ideas of God, law, responsibility, sin and judgment. We must recognize Israel's law, though national in form, as written on the hearts of all men. When you prove the ethical idea in religion you show at once its necessary factor. The life of the Church is a spiritual, supernatural, and therefore wonderful life. It is the great standing miracle which proves the truth of God. The first and all-important thing to be done by us is not to fight the naturalism outside of us, but that which is in us. Above all, let the church feel and show the power of the resurrection. The true method of gaining "the world" is by the awakening of the Church to a consciousness of those elements of truth in her possession. The enemy we fight is not men but a spirit,—the spirit of negation, destruction, and Satan. Let us believe in that Saviour who makes the soul at peace with God, reconciles man to the Infinite, and leads and encourages us to attempt to appropriate by our thoughts the undeveloped in our souls.

On what then depends the future of the Church? We hear La Saussaye describe in eloquent words the conditions of her success: "I do not hesitate to declare," he says, "that the future of a nation depends on a revival, in the very bosom of the Protestant Church, of a profound and enlightened piety, of an alliance of faith with science, an alliance which constituted the strength of our illustrious wise men, and to which we ought to devote whatever greatness there is yet left us. It is only by the payment of this price that the Netherland Church can reconquer that place which she once occupied among Christian people. But since she does not fill this position, since we are afraid of majestic science, and only employ our resources to treat of questions in detail, since the stream of our piety runs through a narrow channel, and since science only moves in the direction of a foolish liberalism, European Protestantism must suffer from the unhappy vacancy that is now left in the ranks of the Church of the Netherlands."[1]

The Church of Holland is now passing through the most important crisis in its history since the Arminian controversy. The orthodox party is vigorous, and many strong men are attaching themselves to it. But their foes are vigilant and bold, and the result cannot yet be seen. The crisis is a necessity created by the evil elements of the eighteenth century. When the mineral was in a state of fusion in the bowels of the earth, it became mixed with foreign and gross elements. But we cannot now disengage the impure accessory by breaking the mass with a hammer. If it be put into the crucible just as it is, the elements will separate of themselves. The theology of Holland, like that of every other Protestant country, is now in the crucible. The heat is intense,

[1] *La Crise Religieuse en Hollande*, p. 200.

but the intensity guarantees the destruction of the dross which has gathered about the truth. There are many good men in the Church who cannot see the connection and bearing of the gigantic efforts now making for the overthrow of faith in Holland. Looking upon them as abnormal, they become discouraged. Therefore they have cherished a warm attachment to the doctrine of the speedy coming of Christ. It is now a more common expression than ever before in that country, "Christ cometh!"

Next to the philosophical and religious causes of the present momentous crisis, stands the absence of popular thought and of Christian work. There had been a reliance on the symbols without proper meditation upon them, or a disposition to trace them back to their Biblical fountain. Men believed what their fathers had told them, or, as the French say, "*Parceque tout le monde le disait.*" The teachers of the young thought in the old routine. But the Rationalistic theologians are driving every friend of the Church and every firm believer in Scripture to reason for himself, with the Bible for his basis; and in no country is religion more rapidly christianizing science than in Holland. Young theologians preach more earnestly than their predecessors had done for a century. La Saussaye is an illustration of how an individual is influencing the tendency of the theological mind. He has never published a complete system, though his friends are anxiously awaiting the appearance of his *Psychology*. It is the man himself who has done so much for emancipating the individual, and placing him upon the immovable truth of the Bible.

Very recently the Church of Holland has applied herself to earnest, practical work. Her evangelizing efforts will now compare favorably with those of French Protestantism. In no country have the congregations been more attached to the clergy than in Holland. But the intimacy has diminished the development of individual labor and responsibility. Everything was left to the pastor. Religion consisted in being preached to and edified. Prayer meetings, and humanitarian and evangelizing associations were unknown. But, of late, many Sunday Schools have been organized; religious societies have been established; and missions have attracted profound attention.

The first missionary society ever formed in Holland was the Moravian Mission to Zeist, in 1732. Sixty-five years elapsed before a second one came into being. Not one was instituted from 1797 to 1851. Since that date twelve foreign missionary organizations have been established, and the religious people of the country are devoting a large portion of their means and labor to their prosecution. So great is the popular interest in missions that an Evangelical National Missionary Festival, held in the open air in July, 1864, attracted many from the surrounding country to take part in the exercises. It was a Christian Feast of Tabernacles. The assembly met in a large pine wood. Carriages, horses, and the rude vehicles of the peasantry lined all the roads leading thither. The singing of the old Dutch Psalms could be heard at a great distance. The assembly, numbering from ten to twelve thousand, gathered around the pulpits erected in various places, where returned missionaries and celebrated preachers from different cities were speaking on topics adapted to the occasion. The scene was deeply solemn, and highly calculated to awaken and quicken the conscience of every hearer.

Two Home Missions are contributing important service to the religious and physical improvement of the poor and neglected. One is the Society for National Christian Education, founded five years ago, and now under the presidency of that tireless Christian statesman, Groen van Prinsterer. Its centre is the Hague, but it has agents scattered throughout the country to seek out any locality that may need a school. It has normal schools in Rotterdam, Utrecht, Groningen, and Nymegen. It is educating many thousands of children who would otherwise go through life without any religious instruction. The other Home Mission, the Society for the Propagation of Christian Truth in Amsterdam, is more local in its character. Though very young, it has founded sixteen Sunday Schools, attended by two thousand children; a Christian lodging or boarding-house at the cheapest rate for homeless females; a room where the members of the society can regularly meet to attend Bible lectures, or to hear reports about home or foreign missions; an infant school; a drawing-school for boys; and knitting and sewing-schools for girls. A large popular religious library has been formed, which is constantly increased by the current useful literature. All of these institutions are under careful Christian direction.[1]

The leaven of Christian faith is at work. The masses are beginning to feel its permeating and purifying power. La Saussaye has despondingly said that "what the church of Holland is now wanting is faith in itself, in the genius which has distinguished it, in the mission which is confided to it,—faith in its future." She must have faith in God before she can have faith in herself. The one leads to the other. God's strength

[1] *Christian Work*, Sept. 1863, and July and August, 1864.

is never perfected except in weakness. It is from without that we receive new power. The disciples who met in the upper room of the temple were visited by an energy to which they had been total strangers. The Spirit came not from their own hearts, but descended from heaven. Yet their hearts were immediately illuminated, and they felt the force of the promise, "Ye shall receive power after that the Holy Ghost is come upon you." Real strength is not self-development alone, but reliance on that Love and Power which, now, as long ago, can save the burning bush from destruction.

CHAPTER XVI.

FRANCE: RATIONALISM IN THE PROTESTANT CHURCH—THE CRITICAL SCHOOL OF THEOLOGY.

SOME French clergymen, who were sojourning in Berlin in 1842, asked Neander, "What ought to be done to arouse the Protestants of France to thinking upon theological subjects?" "Give yourselves no trouble on that score," replied the professor; "Theology will yet have its good day among you. You have in France the soil in which true theology loves to germinate and grow—I mean Christian life. This has brought you your great theologians of the sixteenth and seventeenth centuries, and it is sure to do the same thing in the nineteenth." The present century has not yet run two-thirds of its course, and yet the prophecy has been literally fulfilled.

The spectacle presented to-day in France is highly interesting. The period of indifference has already terminated. The first step toward new vitality has therefore been taken. French theology is displaying an animation and seriousness which may well excite the notice of the whole civilized world. The great minds are bestowing upon sacred subjects an attention nowhere surpassed in vigor and acuteness. Important religious questions are taking their place beside political themes, and the circle of theological readers and thinkers is constantly enlarging. Each class is deeply engaged in the discussion of all the new phases of opinion. Every man chooses his party, cherishes his own convictions, and preaches them boldly. The traveler who may make only a brief stay in Paris will find the representatives of all the professions spending the whole evening in the criticism of the last books from the Liberal Party, and of the rejoinders of their orthodox opponents. Now, for the first time since the seventeenth century, a state of general religious inquiry and earnestness exists. It is not difficult to interpret this quickening of national thought on theological questions. It means that France will have no small share in the decision of the great points at issue between evangelical believers and their critical, destructive antagonists.

A half century ago the Reformed and Lutheran churches were sunk in skeptical formalism. They were divided into two parties, neither of which possessed spirit enough to defend its position, or grace enough to ask God for his blessing. One adhered to the cold Supernaturalism of the eighteenth century, the other to a system of philosophical Deism. The reduced state of piety was largely due to the oppression suffered at the hand of the state. The Revocation of the Edict of Nantes, which deprived Protestants of both religious and civil liberty, occurred in October, 1685, and it was not until 1808 that the law of the 18th Germinal once more recognized their rights, and placed Catholicism and Protestantism on an equal basis. The whole interval was marked by a stagnation of fearful character. At the time of the Revocation, the Reformed church had eight hundred edifices and six hundred and forty pastors, but when the restoration occurred it had but one hundred and ninety churches and the same number of pastors.

The apostasy of the Protestants went to a fearful extent. For example, at the very time of the infamous worship of the Goddess of Reason, a pastor and his elders carried their communion plate and the baptismal vessels to the mayor, to have them melted down for the nation. Improvement began about 1820. There were but three Protestant chapels in Paris, and the services were dull and unattractive. To the late Frederic Monod belongs the imperishable honor of commencing the renovation by means of his little Sunday school. "Never will the traces of his labors be effaced," says M. de Pressensé, "for he it is to whom we owe the first furrows in the vast field which now we rejoice to see white unto the harvest." A domestic evangelical spirit, embracing the most distant provinces, began to be apparent in the ministrations of the clergy and in the popular attendance at the services.

A foreign agency also contributed to the awakening. In 1785 a Wesleyan mission was commenced in the Norman isle of Guernsey, and in the following year Adam Clarke was sent to Jersey. It was designed to make the Channel Islands the beginning of French missions. Wesley predicted that they would be outposts for evangelizing efforts all over the Continent. In a short time Jean de Quetteville and John Angel went over into Normandy, and preached the gospel in many villages. Dr. Coke, the superintendent of the Methodist missions, went with the former preacher to Paris, where they organized a short-lived mission. But the labors of Mahy, who had been ordained by Coke, were very successful. Large numbers came to his ministry, and many were converted through his instrumentality. When peace was declared after the battle of Waterloo, three men, Toase, Robarts, and Frankland, sailed for

Normandy. In 1817 Charles Cook joined them. He went from town to town, stirring up the sluggish conscience of French Protestantism. He terminated his arduous toils in 1858, leaving behind him a French branch of the Methodist church, which embraces one hundred and fifty-two houses of worship, one hundred ministers, lay and clerical, and fifteen hundred members. Merle d'Aubigné has said of Dr. Cook that "the work which John Wesley did in Great Britain Charles Cook has done, though on a smaller scale, on the Continent." His death was lamented by all the leaders of French Protestantism. Professor G. De Félice, of Montauban, has affirmed that, of the instruments of the French awakening, "Dr. Charles Cook was not the least influential."[1]

The new religious interest arising from the native and imported influences was so fatal to the prevalent skepticism that Voltaire and his school have now but few adherents. Skeptics of France consider that type effete, and unworthy of their support. "The present disciples of Voltaire," says Pastor Fisch, "are compelled to deny his language if they would remain true to the spirit of their master. For, to deride Jesus Christ would manifest an inexcusable want of respectability."

But infidelity has only changed its position. Des Cartes, the apostle of Rationalism in France, had taught that God was only a God-Idea, or human thought continuing itself in divine thought and in infinity. He would make no greater admission than that God had put the world in motion. The principles of Des Cartes, clustering around this opinion, have never lost their hold upon the French mind, and are now influencing it to a remarkable degree.

[1] Stevens, *History of Methodism*, Vol. 2, pp. 331-339.

Cartesianism gained new power by the agency of the Eclectic School, whose champions were Royer-Collard, Maine de Biran, Cousin, and Jouffroy. Their great achievement was the unification of the philosophical sytems of Germany and Scotland. But the Eclectics are now in a state of dissolution.

Positivism, as a subordinate system, is the work of Comte alone. This, too, is every year losing its hold upon the land of its birth. Its fundamental principle is, that in virtue of an inner law of development of the mind, the whole human race will gradually emancipate itself from all religion and metaphysics, and substitute for the worship of God that of love of humanity, or a mundane religion. The law of development consists in the psychological experience that all the ideas and cognitions of the human mind have necessarily to pass through the three stages of theology, metaphysics, and positivism. It is only when it arrives at the standpoint of absolutely positive, or mathematically exact knowledge, that human thought attains its goal of perfection. The religion of mankind is divided into three stages; fetichism, polytheism, and monotheism. Its representatives are Judaism, Mohammedanism, and Christianity. Catholicism is better suited than any other form of religion to the perfect development of human society. The Christian world is now in the transitory stage of metaphysics, which, by and by, will lead to the golden age of Positivism. This is the absolute religion, or the worship of humanity, which needs no God or revelation.

While Comte has so deeply impressed the thinking circles of France that his opinions are still perceptible in the doctrines of the Liberal Party, another great agent has been operating upon the young, uneducated, and laboring classes. We refer to the light French novel, or *feuilleton* literature. Such writers as Sue, George Sand, and Dumas, father and son, have published many volumes which were issued in cheap style, and afterward scattered profusely over the land. These works have been extensively read, not only in France, but in all parts of the Continent, Great Britain, and the United States. A recent traveler has averred that he found many persons perusing them in the reading-rooms of Athens. But the public mind sometimes needs a path by which it can effect a transition from a skeptical to an evangelical condition. May it not be that, as far as France is concerned, the minds of the masses have, by this agency, been deflected to such an extent from the infidelity of Encyclopædism that popular evangelical literature will now find a readier entrance than it could otherwise have effected? If a taste for reading be once created, it may be won, under judicious management and by the aid of God's Spirit, to a purer cause than that which first excited it. The tendency of the works in question is indisputably pernicious, but, if we may think they will serve as a medium of passage for the French masses to the reading and adoption of the great truths of the Gospel, let us not be too slow to accept the consolation.

Such are some of the agencies which have been operating upon the French mind. It now becomes necessary to take a survey of the present theological movements, and to show in what relations the Rationalistic and evangelical thinkers stand to each other.

The Critical School of Theology is beyond all comparison the greatest foe of orthodoxy in France. The English Rationalists exhibit but little scholarly depth, having borrowed their principal thoughts from Germany. The

Dutch are too speculative to be successful at present, and the Germans have already grown weary of their long warfare. But the French School, claiming such writers as Scherer, Colani, Pecaut, Réville, Reuss, Coquerel, and Renan, is not to be disregarded, nor are its arguments to be met with indifference. It is, however, most gratifying to state that those ardent friends of the Gospel who resist the attacks of this school manifest a zeal, learning, and skill, quite equal to their ill-armed opponents.

By virtue of that principle of centralization which has long been in force in France, the Critical School of Theology makes Paris the chief seat of its influence. Availing itself of the advantage of the press, it now publishes an organ adapted to every class of readers.[1] The members of the Critical School are connected with the Protestant Church, yet they claim to teach whatever views they may see proper to entertain. They profess deep attachment to the Church, and in their journals advise every one to unite himself with the fold of Christ. If the Reformed Church, in which the most of the Rationalists are found, were not bound to the State by the Concordat and Budget it is probable that it would be divided. One branch would be the Reformed Church of France, founded in 1559, with a clearly determined creed, which none but a General Synod would have power to modify. The other would be the Church of the Future, which would proclaim the admission of no dogmas, no liturgy, and no discipline, and would give

[1] For thinking circles, it issues the *Revue de Théologie et de Philosophie Chrétienne*, founded fifteen years ago by Scherer and Colani. It influences the general public by the daily political paper, *Le Temps*, and the *Revue Germanique*. The Strasburg *Revue* and Paris *Lien*, are for the special benefit of Protestants in general; while the *Disciple de Jesus Christ* and *Piété-Charité* are designed for children and uneducated persons.

power to every one to preach contradictory and negative doctrines in its pulpits.[1]

The association of Rationalists in Paris is called the Liberal Protestant Union. It claims that Protestantism, as represented by the churches, has ceased to be progressive and civilizing. According to its platform, there is no religious authority but free examination; while hostility to all common symbols, and to all profession of faith, is a duty. The Union was immediately opposed. Among other indications of the ill-favor with which it was received was a Remonstrance, signed by some of the most distinguished laymen of Paris. Their language in defense of the Bible as authority for faith was unequivocal. "We do not believe," they said, "that righteousness is indifference; nor do we believe that there is, or can be, a church without a doctrine, a religious doctrine, which unites believers and forms the bond of the Church."

The opinions of the French Critical School of Theology, at which the Remonstrance was aimed, may be briefly stated.

No system is adopted. It professes none, and studiously avoids the embarrassment consequent upon any obligation. Colani says, "We do not present to our readers any fixed system; we have none; we are *asking for* one conscientiously, patiently; with all our contemporaries, we are in the midst of an epoch of transition. We call around us those who, dissatisfied with the forms of an antiquated system of dogma, and fully admitting salvation by Christ alone, desire to labor in raising the new edifice which is to be built on the solid basis of Him who is at once the son of man and the Son of God. . . . Not a school, not a system, but a tendency is that which we represent. The device

[1] M. De Coninck, *Christian Work*, April, 1863.

on our banner is 'The True Development of Christian Thought.'"[1] It is difficult to arrive at a knowledge of what this leader is so modest as to call only a "tendency." It claims to have the right of judgment concerning all the truths of the Bible; holds that the *Rochelle Confession* is a very good monument of the faith of the fathers, but should not now be imposed; that the Bible has no more authority than the books of Plato or Aristotle; that each man has a revelation in himself, free from the imperfections of the Mosaic and Christian revelations; that science, criticism, and examination open the only path to truth; that miracles should be discarded; that Protestantism has lost sight of its mission; and that a second Reformation, embodied in the Church of the Future, is needed to complete the first.[2]

An acknowledged leader of the liberal party has made some statements which more nearly approach the enunciation of a system than we have been able to find in any other authority of French Rationalism.

M. Réville says, "The modern Protestant theology [Rationalism] aspires not to deny the doctrines of the Reformation absolutely, but to preserve the truth that is in them by filtering them through a medium more conformed to our science and our reason. The dogmas of original sin, the trinity, the incarnation, justification by faith, future rewards, and the inspiration of the sacred writings, may serve as examples. On the first of these dogmas, renouncing the idea of an original perfection, the reality of which is contrary to reason, and to all our historical analogies, modern theology would insist on the evil influence which determines to evil an

[1] *Progress of Religious Thought in the Protestant Church of France*, pp. 8–9.

[2] *L'Église Réformée de France et la Théologie Nouvelle*, pp. 5–7.

individual plunged in society where sin reigns, on the necessary passage from a state of innocence to a state of moral consciousness and struggle, on the fall which man endures when he sinks from his higher nature to his lower, and renounces God's will to serve his own. As to the trinity, avoiding the scholastic and contradictory tritheism of the old creeds, intent on vigorously preserving God's essential unity, and at the same time his conscious or personal life, this theology attaches itself to the grand idea of the Divine Word pervading the world, as the uttered thought, the objective revelation of God, conceived as manifesting himself to himself in his works. In humanity this eternal word becomes the Holy Spirit, the light which lightens every man coming into the world, but which shines in all its splendor in Jesus Christ. In this series of ideas the incarnation loses that stamp of absolute contradiction which it takes from the orthodox idea of one and the same person, who is at the same time God and man, finite and infinite, localized and omnipresent, praying and prayed to, knowing and not knowing all things, and impeccable, yet tempted. The pure and real humanity of Christ is the basis of the system, and the system may be summed up in these words: The Son of Man is the Son of God. Man is justified by faith, not as the old orthodoxy taught, that is, because he believes that satisfaction was given to God in his place and on his behalf, but because he has confidence in the eternal love of God, and in his own destination for good, as evidenced by Christ in his life and in his death.

"The eternity of future sufferings gives place to an idea more in conformity with sound philosophy, and the revelation of infinite love, according to which, pain resulting from sin, can have for its object only the amelioration of the sinner, and special stress is laid on the spiritual truth that heaven and hell are much less different places than different states of the soul. The inspiration of the Scriptures, that dogma the truth of which consisted in the scriptural value of the Biblical books, as giving a sure basis for faith, as supplying aliment to piety, and elevating the heart, more and more loses its miraculous character to approach analogous phenomena drawn from religions in general, or from other fields where the mind of man reveals itself as inspired. The change of views, however, does not take from the Bible its character as a truly divine book; still does it remain in religion the Book of Books."[1]

It is unsafe to adduce the testimony of any member of this school as an absolute standard of the theological position of all the rest. There is a wide diversity of opinion among them, as any one will perceive who has attempted the comparison. But after examining the individual opinions of some of these men, it will not be difficult to form a correct judgment of their intellectual position as a whole.

One of the most laborious of the number is Edmond Scherer, formerly Professor of Theology in the University of Geneva. His first point of departure from orthodoxy was on the inspiration and authority of the Bible. He became absorbed in German Rationalistic criticism, and adopted its leading principles. His skeptical views caused such offense that he was led to resign his position, when he soon commenced the publication of his views in the new *Revue de Théologie* at Strasburg. He has subsequently kept aloof from all participation in the State Church and confined

[1] *Progress of Religious Thought in the Protestant Church of France*, pp. 89-90.

himself mostly to writing essays. Some of them have recently been collected into a volume, entitled *Miscellanies of Religious Criticism.*[1]

Protestantism, according to Scherer, has a right to free inquiry. Once give it the Bible as authority, and you drive it back to Catholicism. This is what has already been done by Protestants, whose religion has numbered its days. Authority has been its ruin, and now it has no liberty. The Evangelists contradict each other in many instances. The Apostles failed to quote the Old Testament correctly. Their gross errors are sufficient of themselves to overthrow all the claims of Scripture to authority. It is not certain that the Gospel of John is authentic; that the discourses of Jesus are correctly reported; that Jesus taught his consubstantiality with the Father; that the divinity of Christ involves his omnisicence; that Christ had any intention to decide questions of criticism and canonicity; that he believed in the inspiration of the Old Testament; that he acknowledged the divinity of the Canticles and Ecclesiastes; or that, if he sanctioned the inspiration of the Old Testament, he did the same thing concerning the New.

The New Testament, says Scherer, is full of errata. It contains different records of the same facts. Take as an example the conversion of Saul, of which there are three accounts in the Acts. The discourses of Christ are described in different contexts; the same discourses are not related in similar words; and there is no exactness in the narratives. There are differences in the Gospels, affecting the ideas and actions of Jesus, which sometimes amount to positive contradictions. They

[1] *Progress of Religious Thought in the Protestant Church of France. Biographical Notices*, pp. iii.-iv.

exist also between the first three Gospels and that of John. The last Evangelist gives a very different account of many points in the history of the passion and resurrection of Christ, especially in respect to the last Supper and the chronology of the whole passion-week. Christ announced his second coming as near at hand. Hence he, or the Evangelists in reporting him, were grossly in error. There are, in a word, serious objections to accepting the New Testament as authoritative; because we find in it the use of the Septuagint; quotations from the Old Testament in a sense not intended in the original; influence of Jewish traditions; Rabbinical arguments; uncertainty in reports of the discourses of Christ; contradictions between different accounts of the same facts; errors in chronology and history; and Messianic hopes and expectations not in accordance with external events. What right have we, therefore, to accept as infallible that in which we find such an admixture of error? It is the duty of religious science to reconcile revelation with the growing requirements of human thought, and to smooth over the transition from the dogma of the past to that of the future. Dogmatic exegesis does this by separating the substance from the form, faith from formulas, and by distinguishing and pointing out the religious element under the temporary expression which reveals it.

What then is the Bible which Scherer's exegesis presents to us? Faith in it rests on two bases; *first*, the inspiration and canon of Scripture; and *second*, the subjects or organs of inspiration. The first is untenable and false, for the stand-point of authority has already spoiled everything in our theology. Authority determines beforehand what we must believe, whereas reason alone should perform that office. There is a communicated revelation to our own minds which should claim the high office of authority. The Bible, in an objective sense, is a divine book, because it contains the remembrance of the most important events in the religious history of the world. Judaism and Christianity are there in their completeness. The Bible is therefore more than a book; it presents us with the living personality of those who founded Christ's Kingdom on earth. Inspiration, such as we find in the Scriptures, is not confined to them, for it is immanent wherever there is intelligence. The spirit of the Bible is the eternal spirit of God; but it is the same spirit which has inspired all good men in past Scriptural periods,—the Augustines, St. Bernards, Arndts, and Vinets. It is a falsehood of theology against faith to deny these men the same kind of inspiration which we find in the Scriptures. Biblical inspiration differs in different writers. They wrote from diverse stand-points. The chroniclers of Scripture told all they knew, but not much could be expected of them. Who would dare to speak of the inspiration of the books of Samuel, Ruth, Kings, and Chronicles?

But let us hear what Scherer says of the miracles of Christ. No evangelical facts should be taken as points of departure in testing Christianity. It is absurd to speak of Christ's miracles as being designed for manifestations of his divinity. Conceding them to be prodigies, they are far below those of Moses and Elijah. Christ did not work miracles in attestation of his power. He performed them in connection with his own words or expressions of other persons. When he gave miraculous power to his disciples, he simply did it as a means of beneficence. Miracles, in their true sense, are opposed to both the Jewish and Christian notions of them. Those of Christ are not the attestation and recommendation of his ministry; they are acts of that ministry; acts which have not their value exterior to themselves; whose value is not in their argumentative character, but in their own intrinsic nature. They constitute an integral part of the gospel, but nothing more. Christ's cures are not solely the symbol, they are the counterpart of the spiritual redemption brought by him unto the world. The authenticity of miracles is another question, and belongs altogether to exegesis.[1] Taking the Scripture narrative as a whole, we greatly err in attaching any authority to it. Mohammed and the false prophets should be placed side by side with Moses and Jesus Christ; for the religion of Christ is a purely human one, like that of Buddha and the Arabian prophet. The Mosaic account of creation is evidently absurd; for man was at first a monkey.

M. Larroque contends that the time has now come for a total departure from the last pagan tradition. Christianity has passed its alloted time, and is now in its death-pangs. Material interests claim minute attention. All we want is the assertion of a pure, rational religion. It was a great misfortune that Marcus Aurelius did not popularize the theism which he expressed in his writings. It would not then have been possible for Constantine to establish the Christian religion, and the world would have been spared the irruption of the barbarians, and the many subsequent periods of darkness.[2]

M. Rougemont adheres to the accommodation-theory. It is the only method of relief in this day of darkness. God, in revelation, has only addressed him-

[1] Essays: *Theological Conversations; Errata of the New Testament; What the Bible is; The Miracles of Christ.*

[2] *Examen Critique des Doctrines de la Religion Chrétienne; Renovation Religieuse.*

self to the physical man. He communicated his spirit —not the Holy Spirit—to the prophets. But that was exterior action. The sacred volume is the historic witness of revelation, and is merely a relative necessity. The Church has existed before the Scriptures, and could still live if they were extinguished.[1]

M. Colani is prominent both as preacher and writer. A pastor of Strasburg being sick, he was urged to supply the pulpit for a few Sabbaths. Though he accepted with great reluctance, he was successful in pleasing the congregation. He was chosen permanent pastor, and has continued the functions of his office, together with the chief editorship of the *Revue de Théologie*. His opinions are to be found in that periodical, and in several successful volumes of sermons. He professes to be neither satisfied with Rationalism in its destructive sense, nor with orthodoxy. He is confessedly one of the champions of the Critical School. Skepticism, he contends, is perfectly legitimate. We are authorized to doubt; our opinions are fallible; we must be prepared to change them whenever we think we can find better ones. The Bible is intended to reveal to us a life, not a dogma. We find in it no effort to describe dogmas; no theological criticisms; no system of morality.[2] Religious inspiration is nothing but an extraordinary kindling of the divine spirit inherent in human nature. The Scripture writers are imperfect and limited by their own intelligence. The only way to reconcile religion and science is by history. We must study man not as an individual or nation, but as to his human nature. By doing this we will not take a characteristic for the man himself. Man is, by the testimony of history, a religious being, and history reveals his destiny.

[1] *Christ et ses Témoins.* [2] *Revue de Théologie.* Oct. 1853.

Immortality is accepted. We have a personal life going into the infinite. Humanity develops itself by the action of the individual genius, and the individual only successfully unfolds himself by not breaking the bond which unites him to the general development of his species. We must consider the Bible as a collection of documents, over which criticism has absolute rights. We must distinguish between the thought of Christ and that of his historians. They insisted on what seemed to them miracles. Christ is in open conflict with the principle which would make miracles the necessary sign of a true revelation. He has taught the world to recognize God in the regular operation of natural laws. He never lays down any dogmatic conditions, and does not make religious character dependent on the reception of any class of doctrines. We must have faith in him alone, and not in his words. To be a Christian is to participate in the general life of the Christian church, and to take part with others in the labor of the Christian mind.[1]

M. Pecaut affirms that the present position of the French Protestant church is no longer tenable, for its principle of doctrinal faith restrains free examination. It is, however, in a transition-period, and there is an indication of progress in the present interest in great questions of theology. For the doctrines of Protestantism we should substitute a pure, simple Deism; we should substitute philanthropism for morality. The Bible is not entitled to authority, for it has no trace of inspiration. There is no such thing as mediation. We must not attach too much importance to the Messianic idea, for this would imply a special revelation. The

[1] Essay: *Views and Aims.* Sermons: *What there is in the Bible; The Simplicity of the Gospel.*

Gospels rest on a very insecure basis. The theses of Paul betray a continued oscillation between the mys tic and Jewish conceptions. As a whole, the Bible is not divine, and we should at once discard faith in its authoritative character. The only way by which Christ now acts upon persons is by the force of his example and ideas, just as Moses, Mohammed, and Socrates now influence men. Religious faith is not necessarily faith in Christ. He was not free from sin in a moral sense; he had a natural sinfulness by virtue of his humanity.[1]

M. Grotz, pastor at Nismes, was once under the influence of A. Monod, but owing to the withdrawal of Scherer from orthodoxy, he joined the Rationalists. He holds that revelation is not peculiar to the Scriptures. There are many kinds of revelation, and we find them continually in history. Every manifestation of God is a revelation. We must always examine freely and critically; nowhere does Christ enjoin the contrary. We need to use our intellectual faculties and conscience. The greatest revelation is Christ,—not his doctrines, but himself. We should always keep prophecy and miracles in the background, for they are minor questions and should occupy an humble position.[2]

Of all the members of the Critical School, Renan is the best known to the English and American public. He has written a number of works on various topics,[3] but it is by his *Life of Jesus* that he has gained greatest celebrity. God, Providence, and immortality are, with him, dull words about which philosophy has long played and finally interpreted in the most refined sense.

[1] *Le Christ et la Conscience.*

[2] Essay: *What is Revelation?*

[3] *Studies of Religious History; On the Origin of Language; Averroes and Averroism; History and comparative System of the Semitic Languages; Book of Job; Essays on Morals and Criticism; Solomon's Song.*

There is no reason why a pappoose should be immortal. Religion is a part of man's nature, and, in return, he is benefited and elevated by it. God's revelation is in man's innate consciousness. There is no necessity for miracles; all that we need in this life is the mere result of the operation of natural forces. The present age is one in which we should freely criticise whatever comes up for acceptance; but it is wrong to assume the propagandist. Let men have their own views; we have no right to force others upon them. Man is very much attached to the theories contained in the world's first religion. He has given it symbolical expression, for it is thus that religion will always embody itself. Man wants some way by which to tell how and what he thinks of God.[1]

The Gospels were all written, Renan contends, in the first century. The Jews were anticipating somebody who would prove a means of their improvement. Christ fitted the ideal, and the way was smoothed for his success by their visions, dreams, and hopes. The beautiful scenery of lake, valley, mountain, and river developed his poetic temperament. Then the Old Testament made a deep impression on him, for he imagined it was full of voices pointing him out as the great future reformer. He was unacquainted with Hellenic culture, and hence it was his misfortune not to know that miracles had been wisely rejected by the schools which had received the Greek wisdom. In course of time a period of intoxication came upon him. He imagined that he was to bring about a new church which he everywhere calls the Kingdom of God. His views were Utopian; he lived in a dream life, and his idealism elevated him above all other agitators. He found-

[1] *Miscellanies.*

ed a sect, and his disciples became intoxicated with his own dreams. But he did not sanction all their excesses: for instance, he did not believe the inexact and contradictory genealogies which we find in his historians.

Yet he was a thorough thaumaturgist and sometimes indulged a gloomy feeling of resentment. His miracles are greatly exaggerated. He probably did some things which, to ignorant minds, appeared prodigies, but they were very few in number. He never rose from the dead; he had never raised Lazarus. By and by, the love of his disciples created him into a divinity, clothed him with wonderful powers, made him greater than he had ever pretended to be. Hence Christianity arose. It was love like that of Mary Magdalene, "a hallucinated woman, whose passion gave to the world a resurrected God."[1] Renan's position will explain all that he says of Christ. He looks at him from the stand-point of naturalism. Christ is no mediator. As an American writer has well said: "From this life of Christ no one would ever infer that there was sin in the world and that Christ came to save sinners."

The reception of the *Life of Jesus* was most hearty throughout France. Criticism from every side was employed upon it. Over a hundred thousand copies were soon sold, and translations were made into all the European tongues. Its greatest success was in Roman Catholic countries. In France, Italy, Austria, Belgium, and Spain it has found a warm reception, but in the north of Europe, Protestant Germany, and England, it has had less success. As to the ultimate effect of the work, we have every reason to value the opinion of M. de Pressensé, who has surveyed the whole ground, and also written the best criticism upon Renan that has

[1] *Life of Jesus.* American Edition.

appeared in any country. He says: "I am persuaded that the results accomplished by it will be, in the main, good; that it will not shake the faith of any true believer; that it will produce, with many of those who were wavering, a good reaction, which will bring them back to a positive faith; and that the common sense of the people will not fail to see that it is not thus that history is written, and that the problem of the origin of Christianity still remains unexplained in its grandeur." It is likely that an advantage will accrue to Renan from the recent action of the Government. He occupied the chair of Oriental Languages in the College of France, but was deposed by the Minister of Public Instruction. Boasting that he would still retain his title, he continued to teach in his private house. He lost his salary, but claimed the martyr-crown. When last heard from, he was traveling in the countries described in the New Testament as the scene of the labors of the apostles. His avowed purpose is to publish an attack upon the apostolic history.

Athanase Coquerel, jr., editor of the *Lien*, and a celebrated preacher, justly takes rank among the leaders of the Critical School. He has recently been the subject of an excitement of little less absorbing interest than the sensation occasioned by Renan. Fourteen years ago, Martin Paschoud, one of the Rationalistic Reformed pastors of Paris, selected him as his suffragan or assistant. The Consistory ratified the appointment.

In the Reformed church the assistant pastors do not hold their office by the same title as the titular or regular pastors. The continuance of the former is subject to renewal every two or three years by the Presbyterial Council. But the regular pastors, when first nominated by the Consistory, are afterwards confirmed by the Government. They cannot be removed except by the action of the state. This is the reason why so many Rationalistic pastors are now in full possession of prominent Protestant pulpits in France. No synod, consistory, or presbytery has power to try them for heresy. In fact, there is no standard of doctrine by which heresy can be tested. There being no General Assembly, with power either to establish new standards of doctrine or to give vitality to the old ones, the pulpits of the Reformed church are open to every form of teaching that may profess to be Christian.[1]

Coquerel's last renewal expired about the end of 1863, when his re-appointment became necessary. But his decline into Rationalism had been so rapid that the Presbyterial Council refused to renew the mandate, and he lost his position as suffragan by a vote of twelve against three. He subsequently published a confession of his faith, addressed to his former catechumens, in which the only point of real defense which he substantiates is the charge of Pantheism. He strongly affirms his belief in the personality of God. From M. Coquerel's essays we can derive a correct view of his Rationalistic principles. He affirms that his opinions on the trinity, original sin, the atonement, inspiration of the Scriptures, and other doctrines, called fundamental, are not a little, but *altogether* different from the orthodox views. He does not consider the Bible inspired, and has therefore written a work in defense of Renan, his "dear and learned friend." As for the Gospels, he finds in them the sublimest of all histories on the one hand, and traces of legends on the other; doctrines and precepts of eternal validity in one place, and stains of the errors of the age in which the books were written,

[1] McClintock, Letter of March, 1864, in *New York Methodist.*

in another. Reason has the right of judging all the truths of revelation. The Confession of Faith of the sixteenth century is a very good monument of the faith of our fathers, but should not now be imposed. The Apostles and Evangelists never made any claim to infallibility. There are two groups of views concerning Christ in the New Testament: *First*, that contained in Paul's epistles, especially in Hebrews. Paul did not identify Christ with God, nor did he misconceive the humanity of Christ, and attribute preëxistence to him. *Second.* All the second group, consisting of the epistles of James and Peter, the Acts, and the Apocalypse, rest on a purely historical view. To the writers of the latter, Jesus seemed the Messiah; hence we have from them all that is extraordinary in his history. Christ meant in Matt. xi. 27, that he had received his knowledge from God. He did not refer to his own essence. Literal interpretation of Scripture does not bring us to a knowledge of Christ. His humanity, being all that is valuable in his character, contains the mystery that belongs more or less to every individual. His commission from God does not differ from that of other men. That which distinguishes him from his species was his knowledge of humanity and of the future. He had not omniscience, nor infallibility; nothing but superior knowledge. He had his gross defects; for example, his belief in the power of evil spirits. Yet Christ was not a real sinner, and he represented and realized progress without any arrest. Thus he is the ideal and model of humanity.

That which distinguishes Coquerel's views from Socinianism is his Christology. Contending for the moral purity of Christ, he holds that he was the second Adam. But Christ was not the Son of God. He was so denominated just as we term a hero the Son of Mars. We must look at the Scriptures in the light of reason; then we shall behold the fabulous element. Many parts differ in quality, while some are not authentic. The Second Epistle of Peter, for example, was neither written by that apostle nor was it a product of his age. But authority does not rest in the letter, or in the leaves of Scripture. The divine spirit acts in the soul freely and independently of the letter. It is high time that we renounce the püerile, disrespectful, and contradictory worship of the letter. The letter killeth.

The French Critical School numbers among its adherents many young and talented theologians, some of whom are already distinguished for profound learning and literary activity. But the history of Skepticism discloses the fact that religious error has always attracted the young to its embrace. One half of the triumphs of infidelity are attributable to the flattering promises which it makes to those who have not lived long enough to know that infidelity is nothing but a colossal structure of egotism. The deluding voice says to the young man, "You live in a progressive age, and why are you not progressive yourself? Your fathers believed the old Confessions, imagined Christ to be divine, and the Scriptures inspired. We do not blame them much, for they knew no better. But, if you follow in their footsteps, the world will never give you any credit for originality; your slow chariot will move on in the old rut; you will never accomplish anything; your generation will be in advance of you. Be a man! The field of usefulnesss, prominence, and honor, opens before you. Think for yourself! The Bible is a book of the past, and you should have more manliness and independence than to be guided by its declarations."

It is not surprising that the temptation to fall into this snare is, for many, too great to be resisted. This is true not only of many young Frenchmen, but also of large numbers of Englishmen and Americans, who are casting about for a permanent creed. When they yield, they little dream of the unhappiness in store for them. They never have the consolation derived from settled opinions; life passes without a fixed faith; old age becomes miserable; and death, however much it may appear to be a relief, is a step into darkness and uncertainty.

CHAPTER XVII.

FRANCE CONTINUED: EVANGELICAL THEOLOGY OPPOSING RATIONALISM.

THE influences operating against the integrity and progress of the Protestant church of France are opposed by vigorous agencies. From the clergy and laity men of eminent endowments have arisen who, in ecclesiastical councils, and through the press, have defended evangelical Christianity with a spirit worthy of their Huguenot ancestors. Their task has been herculean. At every point of the horizon infidelity has appeared, and sought to gain a hearing in Paris. Romanism has crippled the advance of truth among the masses. The priesthood enjoy the favor of the government. But the faithful and learned adherents to orthodoxy in all parts of the empire are able to cope with their antagonists. Inspired by such men as Vinet and Monod, they do not stand merely on the defensive, but are constantly aggressive.

Foremost of the modern reformers of France stands the name of M. Edmond de Pressensé. He is a vigorous writer, takes an active part in public religious movements, and edits the *Revue Chrétienne*, a theological monthly, which, in both the ability and orthodoxy exhibited in its contents, has no superior in the world. Through this medium M. de Pressensé is able to keep up a constant attack upon his adversaries, and to dis cover all their subterfuges as fast as they may appear. We do not look to this theologian for a system, because he publishes his views mostly as replies to the assaults of Rationalism. Yet, by an analysis of his writings, we shall find him entertaining such opinions as do equal honor to his devout spirit and gigantic intellect.

M. de Pressensé believes that it is the duty of the Church not to create a moderate Rationalism to take the place of the bolder system, but to engage anew in a vigorous warfare against a school that would contest the divine basis on which Christianity rests. Such, he holds, is the task of the Christian philosophy of the present day. Evangelical Protestantism is everywhere manifesting a necessity of reorganization. And it has need to do so. The Church of the present day is engaged in an inner crisis, which, in one respect, is legitimate; for it has the great burden of expurgation and reconstruction upon it. The burden consists in separating the immortal truth of the gospel from human imperfections, and in finding in it a more complete expression. The present crisis has dangers and temptations which, in our day, render moral and intellectual life very difficult, and multiply shipwrecks before our eyes. "We wish," M. de Pressensé declares for himself and his co-laborers, "to serve the cause of evangelical theology, and nothing else. We do not lift a standard which would summon all opinions and systems without distinction. We stand upon the position that there is a positive revelation, which is not the most distinguished product of human reason, but a divine work of redemption by him whom we appeal to as the Son of Man and the Son of God, who 'died for our sins and rose again for our justification.' It is in the Holy Scriptures that we find the revelation which supplies the immortal wants of our conscience. Apostolical Christianity does not come to us as the first theological elaboration, the first system in a series. It is Christianity itself, and consequently the primitive type, from which we ought never to wander. It is the norm and rule of theology. Within these limits we freely admit the liberty of thought. Variety of opinions has nothing which frightens us; and we would regard uniformity and unanimity on secondary points as a fearful evil."[1]

The purity of the Protestant theology of France is an aim constantly before M. de Pressensé. He holds that, notwithstanding the diversity of its formulæ, this theology is distinguished by two features: *first*, it accepts the authority of the Holy Scriptures, and considers them alone as containing the normal type of Christian thought; *second*, it believes firmly in redemption, and that is in the salvation of ruined humanity brought about by the sacrifice of the Man-God. Though the fall of man was great, it was not absolute. Man was ruined by apostasy, but he was not left destitute of all higher life. He retained some vestige of his primal nature. A sense of the divine, a religious aptitude, and the longing to return to God, subsist in his heart. These render his redemption possible; for the moral law, which had been vindicated by the terrible consequences of the fall, is maintained in all its integrity in the restoration of the fallen creature. A certain harmony was necessary between man and God in order to salvation. Had our nature been thoroughly perverted, no contact would have been possible. We would not have had the capacity to receive from God that great gift which was the only mode of repairing the

[1] *Revue Chrétienne*, Feb., 1861.

fall of beings created in his image and formed to possess him.[1]

This being the condition of man, M. de Pressensé maintains that the result of this divine teaching was to convince him of his weakness and evoke the desire of salvation. Therefore Christianity comes in to supply a felt want of human nature. Here is the first point of contact between conscience and revelation. The Cross is not simply a testimony to the Father's love, like the flowers at our feet, or the starry sky above our head. It is the altar of the great sacrifice which restores man to God and God to man. Christ is for us a Saviour as well as a Revealer.[2] There is one perfection which can be perceived by neither the eye of the body nor by that of the soul, unless it be revealed by a supernatural fact. We mean the mercy of God. Pardon does not consist in the pure and simple abrogation of condemnation; nor can it restore guilty humanity to communion with God while the state of revolt lasts. Humanity can only be saved by returning to God, and it will not return to God until the divine law has been perfectly filled by it. Christ alone is capable of completely carrying out the divine law. The obedience must go as far as sacrifice, for the fall of man demands it. By coming here, Christ took upon himself the wrath of God. He who was without sin was treated like a sinner. He suffered and died, but his sufferings and death rose to the height of a free sacrifice of love and obedience. Condemnation, thus accepted, is no longer condemnation. It is an act of union with God, *un acte réparateur*,—a redemption.

The Bible, according to M. de Pressensé, is not a

[1] *Religions before Christ*, T. & T. Clark, Edinburgh, 1862.
[2] *Le Redempteur*, Paris, 1854.

metaphysical geometry, but a description of the struggle of Divine love with human liberty. This great Bible history, if we consider it at the time when the Redeemer accomplished our salvation, stands before us as the most striking consecration of the moral idea. Redemption is the painfully reëstablished agreement between the human and the divine will by a mysterious sacrifice. It is the most perfect reciprocal penetration of the divine and human by means of liberty. If the moral idea be consecrated by Christ, it will lead to the Gospel. No one will become a Christian unless he has determined to listen to his conscience, and never question concerning moral certainty. We know of no other corner-stone in morality or in religion. But, in order to bring the truths of the Gospel home to the heart, there must be religious liberty. Christianity is the religion of love, but to what could a reconciliation amount which is not free? It is the religion of freedom; and God, in order to save us, has need of freedom.

M. de Pressensé, in his recent discussion on the religious bearings of the French Revolution, proves from an historical stand-point the absolute necessity of the separation of Church and State. His excellent work is entitled, *The Church and the French Revolution; a History of the Relations of Church and State from* 1789 *to* 1802. The motto upon the title-page, derived jointly from Mirabeau and Cavour, will indicate the spirit of the book: "Remember that God is as necessary as liberty to the French people—The Free Church in the Free State." We trust the day is distant when M. de Pressensé will be compelled to lay aside the pen. He is engaged in a contest of momentous issues. That he has violent enemies might be expected; yet he has also the sympathy and prayers of many warm supporters. Hopeful and ardent, he sees indications of success where others imagine darkness and failure. And why not? He has God and truth on his side.

The Evangelical School has an able defender from the laity, the distinguished scholar and statesman, M. Guizot. No one has taken a deeper interest in the present controversy from its inception to the present time than that venerable man. It had been supposed for some time that he was meditating a reply to Renan's *Life of Jesus*. We now have, as the latest fruit of his graceful and prolific pen, the first instalment of the *Meditations upon the Christian Religion*, a work which will prove not only a fitting answer to his countryman's attack on the Gospels, but will serve equally well as an antidote to the present skeptical tendencies of French theology.

According to M. Guizot, there is a great intellectual and social revolution now in progress. Its characteristics and tendencies are the scientific spirit, and the preponderance of the democratic principle and of political liberty. Christianity has submitted to tests and trials, and it must pass through those of the present day. It has surmounted all others, and so it will overcome this. Its essence and origin would not be divine if it did not adapt itself to all the different forms of human institutions. Christian people must not deceive themselves as to the nature of the present struggle, the perils which it threatens, and the legitimate arms with which to oppose infidelity. Skeptics attack the Christian religion with brutal fanaticism and dexterous learning. They appeal to sincere convictions, and the worst passions. Some contest Christianity as false, others reject it as too exacting and imposing excessive restraint.

Concerning the Church and its relations to the

enemies of evangelical faith, M. Guizot asks, "Does it comprehend properly and carry on suitably the warfare in which it is engaged? Does it tend to reëstablish a real peace, and active harmonious relations between itself and that general society in the midst of which it is living? In order to answer these inquiries, he defines the church. It is not one branch, but the whole body of Christ on earth. Therefore, when men deny the supernatural world, the inspiration of the Scriptures, and the divinity of Jesus Christ, they really assail the whole body of Christians—Romanists, Protestants, or Greeks. They are virtually attempting to destroy the foundations of faith in all the belief of Christians, whatever their particular differences of religious opinion or forms of ecclesiastical government. All Christian churches live by faith. No form of government, monarchical or republican, concentrated or diffused, suffices to maintain a church. There is no authority so strong, and no liberty so broad, as to be able in a religious society to dispense with the necessity of faith. What is it that unites in a church if it is not faith? Faith is the bond of souls. When the foundations of their common faith are attacked, the differences existing between Christian churches upon special questions, or the diversities of their organization or government, become secondary interests. It is from a common peril that they have to defend themselves, or they must be content to see dried up the common source from which they all derive sustenance and life.[1]"

In the *Meditation* already published, M. Guizot discusses the essence of Christianity, creation, revelation, inspiration of the Scriptures, God according to the Biblical account, and Jesus according to the Gospel nar-

[1] *Meditations on the Essence of Christianity.* Preface, pp. 6-10.

rative. In order to complete his work, the author designs to write three more parts. In the second, he will examine the authenticity of the Scriptures, the primary causes of the foundation of Christianity, the great religious crisis in the sixteenth century which divided the Church and Europe between Roman Catholicism and Protestantism, and finally those different anti-Christian crises which at different periods and in different countries have set in question and imperiled Christianity itself, but which dangers it has ever surmounted.

The third *Meditation* will be a survey of the present internal and external condition of the Christian religion. The regeneration of the Roman Catholic and Protestant churches at the commencement of the nineteenth century will be exhibited. The author will then describe the impulse imparted by the Spiritualistic Philosophy, and the opposition it met with in Materialism, Pantheism, and Skepticism. He will conclude by exposing the fundamental error of these systems as the avowed and active enemies of Christianity. In the *fourth* series there will be a characterization of the future destiny of the Christian religion, and an indication of the course by which it is called upon to conquer completely the earth and then to sway it morally. M. Guizot, having spent his life in political excitement, now resolves to occupy his remaining years in aiding the cause of religion. "I have passed," says he, "thirty-five years of my life in struggling, on a bustling arena, for the establishment of political liberty, and the maintenance of order as established by law. I have learned, in the labors and trials of this struggle, the real worth of Christian faith and of Christian liberty. God permits me, in the repose of my retreat, to consecrate to their cause what remains to me of life and of strength. It is the most salutary favor and the greatest honor that I can receive from his goodness."

We may now ask, What is the fruit of the labors of MM. de Pressensé, Guizot, and their heroic coadjutors? Is the spirit of French Protestantism against them, and are the majority of the clergy yielding to the insinuating arguments of the skeptical school? These questions are satisfactorily answered by the recent action of the French Protestant Conferences. The Conferences are not composed of members formally admitted, but of the pastors and elders who attend the spring anniversaries, and choose to participate in them. The General Conference includes all denominations of Protestants; the special, only the ministers of the Lutheran and Reformed churches who constitute together the National Protestant Church. Whatever action may be adopted by either body is a safe index of the sentiment pervading the entire mass of French Protestantism. In the General Conference which convened in Paris in the spring of 1863, there was a violent debate between the Rationalistic and Evangelical members. M. de Pressensé presided. Pastor Bersier made a remarkable speech, in which he declared that true science, light, liberty, and progress are on the side of earnest faith in revelation, the atonement, and the other great doctrines of Christian truth. At the conclusion of the discussion, the following protest was carried by an overwhelming majority:

"The Conference, considering that the faithful may be troubled by systems of the present day, attacking the very basis of Christianity and the Church; that these negations are produced in the name of science, and given as the definitive results of the elaboration of modern thought,—protests in the name of Christian faith, of Christian conscience, of Christian experience, of Christian science, against every doctrine which tends to overturn the existence of supernatural order, of the divine authority of the Scriptures, of the divinity of Jesus Christ, and all that touches the very essence of Christianity; such as it has been professed in all times, by all churches, marked with the seal of religious power and faithfulness. The Conference invites the faithful to beware of these systems of science, a thousand times contradicted by the incessant transformations of the human mind; and exhorts the different churches to make efforts and sacrifices to favor the development and progress of Christian science."

The Rationalists hoped that by spending a year in the industrious promulgation of their opinions, they would gain some official recognition or power in the ensuing Conference. Accordingly, when the General Conference of 1864 convened, they demanded the passage of a resolution by which ministers would be freed from all authority, and permitted to preach any doctrine, no doctrine, or a denial of all Christianity, as they might choose. The debate was very animated, and lasted three days. But the result was all that the most sanguine friends of orthodoxy could desire. The Conference adopted the following declaration, by a large majority:

"*Whereas*, For some years, pastors and professors of theology have expressed opinions which affect not only the divine authority of the Holy Scriptures, but also the most elementary doctrines of Christianity; the Conferences declare that it is an abuse of power and a spiritual tyranny for a minister of Jesus Christ to take advantage of his position to propagate directly or indirectly, ideas contrary to the fundamental doctrines of

Christianity, such as the authority of the Bible, the divinity and redemption of Jesus Christ, which are contained in all the Protestant liturgies."

M. Guizot, who is an elder in the Reformed church, took a prominent part in the session of the special Conference in 1864. He introduced a declaration of principles, the character of which may be judged by the following extract: "We have full faith, 1*st.* In the supernatural power of God in the government of the world, and especially in the establishment of the Christian religion; 2*d.* In the divine and supernatural inspiration of the Holy Books, as well as in their sovereign authority in religious matters; 3*d.* In the eternal divinity and miraculous birth as well as in the resurrection of our Lord Jesus Christ, God-man, Saviour, and Redeemer of men. We are convinced that these articles of the Christian religion are also those of the Reformed church, which has plainly acknowledged them." "Gentlemen," said he, in support of his proposition, "I call your attention to one important fact. Look around you! The attacks against the bases of Christianity are seen everywhere, in Germany, Switzerland, Holland, England, and France. I fear nothing, provided aggression meets with resistance. . . . I have entire confidence in the cause of Christianity. But man is God's workman; it is by our faith and labor that the Christian religion must be defended. Gentlemen, we have before us a responsible position and great duties. We are the vanguard of all Christianity; we have behind us all the Christian communions. Let us show ourselves equal to this great task, and firmly resolve to accomplish it."

The debate resulted in the adoption of the declaration by a vote of one hundred and forty-one against twenty-three.

In addition to these proofs of the orthodoxy of French Protestantism, there is another of different character but of not less significance. We mean the successful working of the evangelizing agencies lately inaugurated in France. Forty years ago, A. Monod was in the midst of his small Sunday School in Paris. The government was in the hands of the Jesuits, and Protestantism had neither the political power nor spiritual disposition to labor for the conversion of Romanists. As M. Grandpierre has graphically said: "From 1810 to 1815 you could count on your five fingers those Protestant French pastors who preached faithfully and zealously the true principles of Christianity."

But improvement began, and between 1820 and 1830 several important religious societies were organized in Paris. The Methodist and Free Churches vied with the two National Protestant Churches in efforts for the conversion of the masses. In 1830, the Free Church possessed but one place of worship, but it now has a complete establishment for evangelizing purposes in almost every *quartier* of the great metropolis. In the same year there were but six Protestant pastors and five Churches; but in 1857 there were thirty-nine pastors and fifty-one sanctuaries. Including the whole of France, there are, under Protestant jurisdiction, about one thousand pastors, from fifteen to sixteen hundred churches, and from seventeen to eighteen hundred elementary schools. The official census previous to 1857 gives the total number of Protestants in Paris as thirteen thousand; and seven hundred and seventy thousand throughout the country. M. Grandpierre thinks these numbers are really double; for in Paris alone two pastors are omitted, and if they are left out what must be expected of the members under them? During 1862 twenty new

Protestant Churches were opened and consecrated to the worship of God. Twenty-five years ago there was but one Protestant bookstore in Paris, and it was threatened from time to time with bankruptcy. Now there are four, all of which are in a flourishing condition. There is a Sunday School in nearly every Protestant Church of the Empire.

Almost every year some new society is organized, having for its avowed object the conversion of souls and the relief of the suffering. Those now in prosperous existence will compare favorably with similar institutions in Great Britain and the United States. We mention the most prominent: The French and Foreign Bible Society, which sold eighty-eight thousand copies of the Bible in 1862; the Protestant Bible Society; the Tract Society; the Paris Missionary Society; the Primary School Society and the Protestant Sou Society. Each of these has its well-defined field of labor, one aiming to arouse slumbering Protestants, another to seek out wandering Protestants, and a third to educate homeless children. The Evangelical Society of France, whose secretaryship M. de Pressensé has held for thirty years, founded during the year 1862 nine new Churches; created six additional centres of evangelization; aided twenty churches; supported two Normal Schools; organized many others; cultivated two of the faubourgs of Paris; and expended three millions five hundred and eighty thousand francs for the purposes of evangelization. In addition to these societies, there are Orphan institutions, Schools, Asylums for the unprotected, destitute, fallen, sick, and infirm; some associations for the aid of those near at hand, and others for those at a distance. The press has been active in the same great cause. Weekly and monthly journals have been multiplied, and carry the good news of God not only through France but into all parts of the Continent. The theological schools are in a flourishing condition, and evangelical professors are everywhere in the majority. Of the seven teachers at Montauban, five are outspoken adherents of orthodoxy. The inability of M. Reville to be elected to a chair in that institution indicates the religious status of those in authority of it.

Neander said one day to M. de Pressensé, "This period in which we live is indeed a critical one. It is to be a dismal abyss or a rosy morning light. But, depend upon it, it is going to be whatever we have a mind to make it." The Evangelical Protestant clergy of France "have a mind" to do a good and permanent work. We do not apprehend an unfavorable issue from the present conflict, but that the prayers, proscription, and exile of eight hundred thousand Huguenots will yet reap their appropriate harvest, and that the Revocation of the Edict of Nantes will be avenged by the pure faith and permanent triumphs of Protestantism.

CHAPTER XVIII.

SWITZERLAND: ORTHODOXY IN GENEVA, AND THE NEW SPECULATIVE RATIONALISM IN ZÜRICH.

SWITZERLAND has failed to retain the influence over the theological thought of Europe enjoyed by her in the days of Zwinglius and Calvin. Impressions, instead of being given, have of late only been received. France and Germany have contributed their respective phases of theology, the French Cantons adopting the opinions emanating from the former country, and the German those from the latter. We must not therefore expect to find a very wide difference either respecting theology or practical religion between the Swiss and their two influential neighbors.

When the Skepticism of Voltaire and his disciples was penetrating the French mind the Reformed Church of Switzerland did not long remain unaffected by it. While that crafty man was enjoying his romantic retreat at Ferney, he was visited and even flattered by persons who had taken upon themselves the vows of the Christian ministry. The pastors of Geneva were regarded by the Encyclopædists as sympathizers and co-laborers in overthrowing the distinctive doctrines of the Gospel. In the early part of the nineteenth century there was in Switzerland, as in Germany, a strife between the old confessional faith and Rationalism. But in Germany

Reason attacked the contents of the Scriptures, while in Switzerland the attempt was made to reduce all revealed truth to a system of natural religion. Rationalism in the Swiss Church was Arianism and Socinianism revived.[1] It swept away the strong Calvinism of the old Genevan theology. The clergy were little better than the English Deists. D'Alembert says, "All the religion that many of the ministers of Geneva have is a complete Socinianism, rejecting everything called mystery, and supposing that the first principle of a true religion is to propose nothing to be received as a matter of faith which strikes against reason." Rousseau declares that those who filled the pulpits of that venerable city had no answer to the question, "Is Christ divine?"

Theological training was neglected. The professors, like the pastors, committed themselves to an undisguised system of Rationalistic Unitarianism. M. Bost, writing in 1825, says that, "for more than thirty years the ministers who have gone out of our schools of theology, to serve either the churches of our own land or those of France and other foreign countries, have not received one single lecture on the truths which exclusively belong to revelation, such as the redemption of mankind by the death of Christ, the justification of the Saviour by faith, the corruption of our nature, the divinity of our Saviour, &c. In theology we were taught nothing but what are called the dogmas of natural religion. The extent to which this practical incredulity was carried is clear from the fact, elsewhere unheard of, I suspect, in the annals of the Protestant churches, that, excepting for a lecture in the Hebrew language, when the Bible was used simply as a Hebrew book, and

[1] Hagenbach, *Kirchengeschichte d.* 18. *und* 19. *Jahrhunderts*, vol. ii., p. 416.

not for anything it contained, the word of God was never used throughout our course; in particular, the New Testament never appeared, either as a language-book or for any other purpose; there was no need of the New Testament, whatever, in order to complete our four years' course in theology; in other words, that book, especially in the original, was not at all among the number of books required in order to accomplish the career of our studies for the sacred ministry."[1]

The *Vénérable Compagnie*, comprising the clergymen and theological professors of Geneva, went so far, in 1817, as to impose upon all candidates for ordination to the ministry, the obligation not to preach on the two natures of Christ, original sin, predestination, and other received doctrines of their confession. As might be expected, practical piety was thrown into the background. Children were not instructed in the Scriptures, and the churches were attended by small congregations, who were favored with no better gospel than the combined opinions of Voltaire and the German Rationalists. There were here and there loud protests against this apostasy. The Canton Vaud was benefited by the labors of that excellent woman, Madame de Krüdener, who exchanged a life of Parisian gayety and affluence for humble labors among the poor and uninstructed Swiss. She loved to sit upon a wooden bench and teach all who came to her the truths of the Bible and the necessity of a regenerated heart. Her influence was powerful in Geneva after the commencement of the evangelical movement. Another counteracting agency was a sect of Methodists, nicknamed the "Momiers," who had gone thither from England, and were rebuking the prevalent Rationalism by every available means.[2]

[1] Alexander, *Switzerland and the Swiss Churches*, p. 194.

[2] Kurtz, *Church History*, vol. ii., p. 334.

From the outset Geneva had been the centre of the great religious decline. The Theological Academy founded by Calvin had become the nursery of as injurious errors as had emanated from Halle in the period of Wolf's triumphant career. Its chairs were occupied by the very teachers described by M. Bost, men in every respect unworthy to prepare students for the Christian pulpit. But, by the providence of Him who watches every juncture with a Father's care, a new influence was brought to bear upon the Academy, and through it upon the whole Protestant Church of Switzerland. Robert Haldane, having sold his large estate in Scotland, directed his attention to the moral dearth at Geneva by endeavoring to imbue the students with his own evangelical opinions and earnest spirit. His labors were eminently successful. Many of the young men became converted, and for the first time had a clear conception of the great work before them. It was through Haldane that Merle d'Aubigné, Adolphe Monod, Malan, and others of their school, were inspired with the spirit of the Gospel. Switzerland can never be too grateful to God for sending such a man at that important crisis.

The immediate issue of this awakening was the organization of the Evangelical Dissenting Church. All who had grown dissatisfied with the formalism and Rationalism of the National Church came to the new fold and co-operated in the work of reformation. A school of theology, established in Geneva, was visited by students who came seeking an education that might enable them to relieve the moral wants of the masses. Gaussen, the author of *La Theopneustie*, was one of the professors. The new Church soon found in him its leader. He has recently died, but his long life has been of valuable service to the kingdom of Christ. Besides reviving and reorganizing the Sunday School system in Geneva, and personally superintending the religious instruction of the children, for whom he wrote his inimitable *Catechisms*, he became the author of many theological works adapted to the wants of clergy and laity. In company with a few friends, he published the popular Swiss version of the New Testament. It occasioned him real joy when he witnessed late in life the improvement of the National Church of Switzerland. But it must be confessed that the parent has yet much to learn and accomplish before reaching the high evangelical status now occupied by the earnest daughter.

The name of Vinet belongs to the whole of Protestant Europe, and is identified with the revival of religious sentiment in Switzerland, Germany, Holland, and France. His excellent writings have familiarized him to the theological readers of Great Britain and the United States. The separation of Church and State was one of the leading aims of his life, and he eloquently contended for it whenever occasion offered. In 1837 he accepted the invitation of the government of his native canton to take charge of the professorship of Theology in the Seminary in Lausanne. Already profoundly impressed with the opinions of Pascal, he admired the more evangelical portion of Schleiermacher's theology. Combining these, he originated the only native theological system which Switzerland has produced since Calvin's day.[1] In all his works he manifests profound thought and erudition. His *Homiletics* and *Pastoral Theology* have already become text-books in many theological seminaries.

The spirit now dominant at Geneva clearly indicates the success of the late efforts toward reform. The congregations have largely increased; various humanitarian

[1] Farrar, *Critical History of Free Thought*, p. 444.

enterprises have been vigorously prosecuted; societies for the circulation of religious knowledge have been founded; and the laity have come to the assistance of the clergy in labors for the social and moral elevation of the masses. For a quarter of a century young men have been judiciously trained in theology, and Switzerland is now supplying many prominent French pulpits with her graduates.

The present sojourner in Geneva finds but few remnants of that skeptical preaching and general religious indifference so lamentably prevalent before the rise of the Evangelical Dissenting Church. M. Levalois, who is an avowed skeptic, looks upon a very different scene from that which once so delighted Rousseau. Coming from the source they do, his words are a valuable testimony to the religious growth of the mother-city of French Protestantism. "I now come," says this traveler, "to the essential characteristics of Geneva. Before being literary and liberal, the Genevan is Christian. In Geneva the free-thinking stranger is *advised* of Christianity. In the souls of men, instead of meeting with no resistance, no solidity,—as, for instance, among the greater part of our Parisian Catholics,—instead of finding himself in the face of a creed mechanically repeated, of a memory and not of a conscience,—you feel yourself in contact with an individual who will believe, who can believe, who is in full possession of the *why* of his belief. Nothing in the world is to me so sacred as sincerity in intelligent faith. Just as I despise certain time-serving Catholics, who are converted because they dread socialism, or because they dread the Empire, so much do I respect the man who freely attaches himself to the Gospel, devotes himself to Christ, and prays to Him. Does this imply that I return from Geneva a Protestant? No; I have not been *converted*, but, I repeat, *advised.* I have seen Christianity working, not only in churches, but, which is much more edifying, in individuals. Yes, I have seen it in turns the inspirer of language, the spring of actions, the spur and the discipline, rule and support of the future, impregnating, so to speak, the flesh and the spirit. Such a spectacle excites one to reflection. We have been in too great haste to exclaim, Christianity is dead! An hour's conversation with two or three Genevese, suffices to convince us that if Christianity is dead it is not yet buried."[1]

The course of lectures delivered in the Theological Academy of Geneva in the winter of 1862–'63, may be taken as an illustration of the character of the instruction imparted in that influential institution. M. Secretan delivered learned lectures on "Theism." He showed that the objections which can be raised, on the ground of natural religion, against the existence and personality of God, lose all their force on Christian ground; therefore Hegelianism has no base. M. Naville, in his course on "Spiritualism," summoned the resources of his learning and genius to aid him in his heroic combat with every form of current materialism. Pastor Coulin lectured on "Christian Works." It was an eloquent appeal for renewed Christian activity. MM. Bungener, Bret, and Rorich lectured on "Christian Life;" M. Gaberel on the "Part taken by Geneva at the time of the Reformation;" and also on the "Present Literary and Religious state of Germany;" M. Archinard on the "Ancient Religious Edifices of Switzerland;" M. Aug. Bost on the "First Fifteen Centuries of the History of Mankind;" and M. De Gasparin on

[1] *L'Opinion Nationale*, 1863.

the "Family Life, its Organization and Duties." In addition to these, there were lectures on detached subjects, such as religious prejudices, the study of the Bible by simple-hearted believers, drunkenness, the religious education of children, the instruction of catechumens, the dissipation of cities, and the duty of evangelization.[1]

Of the German cantons, Basle has been the only one which has successfully resisted the encroachments of Rationalism. The University has fully recovered from the influence of De Wette, and the professors now stand in the front rank of evangelical thinkers. The *Mission House* has been a highly useful agency. Though not a half-century old, it has already trained four hundred missionaries, nearly three hundred of whom are still living and actively engaged in evangelizing the dark places of the earth. The people are unwilling to permit any minister to occupy one of their pulpits whom they have reason to suspect of skeptical opinions. The infidel Rumpf was excluded in 1858 from the list of candidates for the ministry, and all his subsequent efforts for restoration have failed in the chief council. A similar occurrence took place in Berne in 1847, upon the calling of Zeller to the theological professorship.

We now turn to a less evangelical part of Switzerland. Zürich is one of the acknowledged centres of European Rationalism. Its spiritual decline has been rapid during the last twenty-five years. In 1839, Strauss, the author of the *Life of Jesus*, was invited by the chief council to take a theological chair in the seminary. But the people arising as one man against the measure, the appointment failed, the council was overthrown by a popular revolution, and the city still pays

[1] *Christian Work*, Aug., 1863.

a pension to the disappointed aspirant. But in lamentable contrast with that event is one of more recent occurrence. As late as 1864, when the little town of Uster was about to elect a pastor, the candidate declared himself "a friend of progress and light." Some religious men, unwilling to see their children placed under the instruction of a skeptic, took upon themselves the task of showing in what the "progress" consisted. They accordingly published a notice to their fellow citizens in which they set forth the avowed opinions of their candidate. The document asserted that he believed the Bible to be a tissue of fictions and fables; Jesus a sinful man like others, neither risen from the dead, nor sitting in the glory of his Father; no one can assert with positiveness a life beyond the grave; and the opinion that we are reconciled to God by Jesus Christ, merely a superstition and a day-dream. The authors of the circular besought the ecclesiastical council to deliver them and their children from the promulgation of such doctrines, and further reminded them that every pastor on entering upon his functions must swear to preach faithfully the word of God, both law and gospel, according to the fundamental principles of the evangelical Reformed church. The council took no notice of the remonstrance, though the candidate did not deny the charges. He was elected by eight hundred and sixty-five votes against one hundred and forty-five. In the church, where the result was proclaimed, the acclamations were so loud that they "shook the windows." In the evening there was a serenade, accompanied by rockets and blue lights.[1]

The only representative of evangelical doctrines in the theological faculty of Zürich is a tutor, placed there

[1] *Semaine Religieuse.* Geneva: 1864.

and supported by a private society. The most effective means by which Rationalism emanates from that city is periodical literature. The leading publications are, *The Church of the Present*, and *Voices of the Times*. The latter journal was commenced in 1859. Its editor, Lang, is a frequent contributor to prominent Rationalistic serials of Germany, particularly the *Protestant Church Gazette* of Berlin. He has published, besides other works, *A System of Doctrine*, and *A March through the Christian World*. Professor Biedermann, an instructor in Zürich, has embodied his skeptical opinions in a *Manual of Christian Doctrine*, for the use of the youth in Swiss colleges. Dr. Volckmar, another theological professor of the same city, has advanced in his numerous works on primitive Christianity, opinions even more radical than those of Strauss or the Tübingen School. All those men are members, in good standing, of the Reformed church of Switzerland.[1]

The Rationalistic works in question are studiously adapted to the common mind. They contain a complete system, which we term the New Speculative Rationalism. It declares a strong attachment to Protestantism, and professes to cultivate a much higher development of Christian life than was aimed at by its German predecessor. Like the Groningen school of Holland, it lays stress on the character of Christ. It proposes to establish a new church, which shall have a wider door for the entrance of Protestant Christians than that opened by the confessions. The present fold is entirely too small; the new Rationalism would organize one of colossal popular dimensions. "Our church," say these teachers of Zürich, "is truth and morality. Whoever

[1] Riggenbach, *Der Heutige Rationalismus besonders in der Deutschen Schweitz.* Basel: 1862.

thinks upon these things and strives for them shall find a place in it." Their opinions are the direct result of the Hegelian philosophy applied speculatively to the obsolete, destructive Rationalism of Germany.

The Holy Scriptures. Protestantism mistakes itself in treating the Bible as authority. Though the Scriptures declare our relations to God, they should not escape our free criticism and occasional censure. Every man has a right to interpret them for himself, and on his individual understanding of their contents he should feel bound to act. No man has a right to impose his opinion upon another, nor has any church a guarantee for obliging its members to subscribe to a fixed creed. All deductions from the positive statements of the Scriptures are mere human opinions, and should only receive the credit due to them as such. What are confessions but human opinions?

Christ. Strauss was wrong in taking his cold view of Jesus. There was a real historical personage whom we properly call Jesus. Nothing is gained, but everything lost by resolving all the statements of the gospels into myths. It is through Christ that salvation is attained, for Christianity is the reconciliation of God and man as revealed to us in the consciousness and life of Christ. He is the end of the law, the second Adam, the fulfilment of prophecy, the head of a renovated humanity. In him we find the revelation of a new religious principle in man, a real unity with God, a filial adoption, freedom from natural corruption, the pardon of sin, and victory over the world. Jesus became the one man who bore in himself the fullness of the godhead.

Important concessions to Christianity seem to be made; nevertheless subtle Pantheism underlies their statements. But one of their opinions subverts every thing they grant to orthodoxy. Christ was not, according to their view, the Messiah in the sense foretold by the prophets and preached by the apostles. We must judge him apart from all poetry, speculation, and human judgment. The Christ of the present church is the creation of theologians, not the character portrayed by the evangelists. Unfortunately for our correct view of him, Paul speculated entirely too much upon his nature and work. The resurrection of Christ never took place, because there was no necessity for it. It was a good thing for the apostles to believe that such an event took place, for it encouraged them. Christ never showed himself to any one after his death, and the belief that he did appear arose purely from the excited nerves, imaginative temperament, and strong desire of his followers to see him. His spirit did not die with his body, but entered upon another stage of existence.

Jesus did not work miracles, for he had not the power. He was eminently a moral man, the very personification of the truly religious character. Religion became flesh in him, and he was the exemplification of love. The salvation we find through him is by virtue of his example and inculcation of moral truths. The spirit of Christ still exists, but it does not live in a purely personal relation, nor does it operate as a personal existence. His spirit and example are with us, but he is not here himself. The good man is favored with the influence imparted to humanity by Christ's exemplary life, but he is nowhere actually present in the world.

God and his Miracles. No miracles, in the orthodox sense of the term, have ever occurred. The scientific examination of the Scriptures banishes them altogether. Neither are miracles possible, otherwise we should see them every day. They would be acts of arbitrary authority on God's part; and if he performed them he would destroy the harmony and connection of natural laws. Christianity was not introduced by miracles. It was inaugurated, and even originated, by underlying causes of a purely natural character. Miracle is only a creation of the imagination, and should be discarded as a human error.

The personality of God is freely spoken of, but his self-consciousness, in the strictest sense, is not allowed. Hence God is really deprived by them of all plan, aim, love, and favor. He is a spiritual being, but he is not a spirit. He is spirit, yet not a real, thinking, self-conscious, willing spirit. He is not a personality or individuality. "A person," these men appear to say, "must have a place to stand upon, and surely we would not say this of God? The fact is, we grossly misrepresent the great All-Father. We picture him in our sensuous forms, and almost imagine him to be like one of ourselves."

IMMORTALITY. The Speculative Rationalists attach less importance to individual immortality than their predecessors conceded. We might infer this, however, from the Hegelian point of view adopted by the former. They profess adherence to Schleiermacher's dictum: "In the midst of the finite to be one with the infinite, and to be eternal every moment." But they adhere to the doctrine of "eternal life," by which term they mean an existence commencing and terminating with faith. It is a life of such value that it should be called "eternal" life, although it ends with our last breath in this world. It consists in the attainment of the end of our existence and of conquest over sin. Thus, they reduce the eternal life of which the gospel speaks to a mere method and duration of stay in this world. This life, with them, exhausts life; the kingdom of God has not an eternal, but a present and temporal existence; there is, therefore, no new heaven and new earth.

SIN. The fall of man did not take place. It is an absurd superstition. Since the world is but a limited and imperfect representation of God, sin came into it immediately upon its origin. We err when we look at sin apart from a correct conception of the world. Sin has its seat in the natural weakness of man, for he is a temporal being, and in process of necessary development from impure naturalness to reason and freedom. It is the condition in which man finds himself before arriving at an idea of what he is or will be. If it be asked, "Why is sin in the world?" the rejoinder is made, "Why is not man, in the outset of his existence, what he is destined to be, and why must he stand in need of development?" Sin, in the beginning, was natural imperfection, but it never becomes a work of the will until man is developed. It is the melancholy result of an awakened consciousness. But, after man is once aroused to self-consciousness and begins his actual, sinful life, he never becomes a lost sinner.

FAITH. The gospel is not a compendium of principles. Its only value consists in its description of the moral and religious character of Christ, and every one must derive from it such opinions as seem most plausible and reasonable. But they err who excogitate from it those severe dogmas which express only dreams of the imagination and wishes of the religious spirit. Faith in the gospel is not a condition of salvation. For faith is the inner relation of the spiritual man to God, not the acceptance of fixed traditions. It is such a feeling, emotion, and relation as can exist independently of doctrine. Objective truth is not the measure of faith, and the salvation of man is not conditioned by his theoretical opinions. The human spirit in man is the agent of regeneration. Therefore, man, and not God, is the author of human regeneration. Justification by faith is produced by seeking God's favor, but Christ has nothing at all to do with the matter.

We cannot as yet foresee the complete result of the efforts of the New Speculative Rationalism to propagate itself. German Switzerland will be influenced by Germany, and because of the thorough improvement already inaugurated in the latter country no general resurrection of skepticism need be feared. The evangelical professors at Basle are eagerly watching every new movement, and we believe they have sufficient strength to meet every emergency. Christianity is aggressive. Sometimes it is obliged to halt and give battle. The carnage may last long, and the on-looking world may, in its ignorance, decide too speedily that the day is lost. But the victory of error is only temporary. The ark in Dagon's house was still the ark of God. Since good men are a perpetual power to a people, we may reasonably hope that the Swiss reformers will continue to animate the citizens of all the French and German cantons. May the pulpits and theological chairs of Switzerland ever be filled with men who can say what Zwinglius uttered one New Year's Day as his first words to the assembled multitude in the cathedral of Zürich: "To Christ, to Christ will I lead you,—to the source of salvation. His word is the only food I wish to furnish to your hearts and lives!"

CHAPTER XIX.

ENGLAND: THE SOIL PREPARED FOR THE INTRODUCTION OF RATIONALISM.

THE religious lesson taught by the condition of England during the eighteenth century is this: The inevitable moral prostration to which skepticism reduces a nation, and the utter incapacity of literature to afford relief. English Deism had advantages not possessed by the Rationalism of Germany. Some of its champions were men of great political influence; and in no case was there a parallel to the abandoned Bahrdt. The Deists were steady in the pursuit of their game, for when they struck a path they never permitted themselves to be deflected. But the Rationalists were ever turning into some by-road and weakening their energies by traversing many a fruitless mile.

The literature of England, during the most of the last century, presents a picture of literary ostentation. The Deists had toiled to build up a system of natural religion which would not only be a monument to their genius, but serve as an impassable barrier to all such claims as were urged by the zealous and loud-spoken Puritans. But early Deism lacked an indispensable element of strength,—the power of adapting itself to the people. Its best priests could not leave the tripod, though many of the oracular responses were heard some distance from the temple-doors. In time, there arose a group of essayists and poets, who, with a similar coterie of novelists, dictated religion, morals, politics, and literature to the country. Their influence was so great that when they flattered the heads of government, the latter were equally assiduous in playing the Mæcenas to them.

The writers of the eighteenth century, viewed in a literary sense alone, have never had their superiors in English literature. The works of Addison, Pope, Gray, Thomson, Goldsmith, and Johnson will continue to be classics wherever the English language is spoken. The British metropolis was pervaded with the atmosphere of Parnassus. It was a time when literature was the El Dorado of youth and old age. Those were the days when clubs convened statedly in the neighborhood of the Strand, and when, every night, the attics of Grub street poured out their throngs of quill-heroes, who were welcomed into the parlors of the nobility as cordially as to their own club-houses. The last new work engaged universal attention. Society was filled with rumors of books commenced, half finished, plagiarized, successful, or defunct. Literary respectability was the "Open Sesame" to social rank. There has never been a season when cultivated society was more imbued with the mania of book-writing and criticism than existed in England during at least three-quarters of the eighteenth century.

While many of the publications of that time were prompted by Deism, French society and literature were contributing an equal share toward poisoning the English mind. France and England were so intimately related to each other that the two languages were diligently studied in both countries. If the English adventurer in letters had not spent a few months in Paris, and could not read Corneille almost as readily as Spenser or Shakspeare, he was cashiered by certain Gallicists west of the Channel as a sorry aspirant to their coveted favor.[1] The rise of the French spirit in England was mainly due to Bolingbroke, who was as much at home in Paris as in London. He had numerous friends and admirers in the former metropolis, and at two different times made it his residence. Freely imbibing the skeptical opinions of the court of Louis XIV., he dealt them out unsparingly to his English readers. He was one of the most accomplished wits who frequented the *salon* of Madame de Croissy, and he developed his skeptical system through the medium of the French language, in a series of letters to M. de Pouilly.[2]

Bolingbroke accused the greatest divines and philosophers of leading a great part of mankind into inextricable labyrinths of reasoning and speculation. Natural theology and religion, he held, had become corrupt. In view of these results of mental infirmities, he applied himself to correct all errors. He proposed "to distinguish genuine and pure theism from the profane mixtures of human imagination; and to go to the root of that error which encourages our curiosity, sustains our pride, fortifies our prejudices, and gives pretense to delusion; to discover the true nature of human knowledge, how far it extends, how far it is real, and where and how it begins to be fantastical; that, the gaudy visions of error being dispelled, men may be accustomed

[1] For an excellent view of the relation of France and England in the eighteenth century, vid. *Revue des Deux Mondes*, 1 Dec., 1861.

[2] Schlosser, *History of the Eighteenth Century*, vol. i., p. 98.

to the simplicity of truth."[1] The Scriptures, according to Bolingbroke, are unworthy of our credence. They degrade the Deity to mean and unworthy offices and employments.[2] The New Testament consists of two distinct gospels; one by Christ, the other by St. Paul. The doctrine of future rewards and punishments is absurd, and contrary to the divine attributes.[3] Christianity has been of no advantage to mankind. "The world hath not been effectually reformed, nor any one nation in it, by the promulgation of the gospel, even where Christianity flourished most."[4] There is a supreme All-Perfect Being, but he does not concern himself with human affairs as far as individuals are concerned. The soul is not distinct from the body, and both terminate at death. The law of nature, being sufficient for the purposes of our being, is all that God has proclaimed for our guidance.[5]

There were other members of the English nobility who used their influence for the introduction of French infidelity, literature, morals, and fashions. Some did not equal Bolingbroke in repudiating the spirit of the gospel, but nearly all were willing students at the feet of their pretentious Gallic instructors. The house of Lady Mary Wortley Montague, at Wickenham, was the centre whither gravitated that large class of acknowledged chiefs in letters represented by Steele, Pope, and the Walpoles. They thought, spoke, and dressed according to the French standard, which, in respect to religion and morals, was never lower than at that very time. The attempt to rear a Paris on English

[1] *Works*, vol. iii., p. 328. London Edition of 1754. 5 vols., quarto.
[2] Ibid. p. 304. [3] Ibid. vol. v., p. 356. [4] Ibid. p. 258.
[5] Leland, *View of Deistical Writers of England*, pp. 307-308. London Edition of 1837, with Appendix and Introduction, by Brown and Edmonds.

soil was a complete success. The young were delighted with the result; the aged had been too ill-taught in early life to raise the voice of remonstrance. With the exception of the Puritan opposition, the gratification was universal; and that took place in religion and literature which, had it occurred in warfare, would have kindled a flame of national indignation in every breast: England fell powerless, contented, and doomed into the arms of France.

The attacks of Hume and Gibbon on the divine origin of Christianity take rank with the mischievous influences imparted by the elder school of Deists, and by French taste and immorality.

Hume was a philosopher who drew his inspiration directly from his own times. Attaching himself to the Encyclopædists, he played the wit in the *salons* of Paris. He became fraternally intimate with Rousseau, and brought that social dreamer back with him to England as a mark of high appreciation of his talents. He was a metaphysician by nature, but he erred in speculating with theology. That was the mistake of his life. He fell into Bolingbroke's error of excessive egotism. Standing before the superstructure of theology, he carefully surveyed every part of it, and deemed no theme too lofty for his reasonings, and no mystery beyond the reach of his illuminating torch. He lamented the absence of progress in the understanding of that evidence which assures us of any real existence and matter of fact. But this difficulty did not impede him from an attempted solution. He thought himself performing a great service when he addressed himself to the "destruction of that implicit faith and credulity which is the bane of all reasoning and free inquiry."[1] He re-

[1] *Philosophical Essays concerning Human Understanding*, p. 49. London Edition, 1750.

fused to acknowledge a Supreme Being, in the following words: "While we argue from the course of nature, and infer a particular intelligent cause, which at first bestowed and still preserves order in the universe, we embrace a principle which is both uncertain and useless, because the subject lies entirely beyond the reach of human experience."[1]

The miraculous evidences of Christianity were also opposed by Hume. His *Essay on Miracles* (1747), consists of two parts; the former of which is an attempt to prove that no evidence would be a sufficient ground for believing the truth and existence of miracles. Experience is our only guide in reasoning on matters of fact; but even this guide is far from infallible, and liable at any moment to lead us into errors. In judging how far a testimony is to be depended upon, we must balance the opposite circumstances, which may create any doubt or uncertainty. The evidence from testimony may be destroyed either by the contrariety and opposition of the testimony, or by the consideration of the nature of the facts themselves. When the facts partake of the marvelous there are two opposite experiences with regard to them, and that which is most credible is to be preferred. Now the uniform experience of men is against miracles. We should not, therefore, believe any testimony concerning a miracle, unless the falsehood of that testimony should be more miraculous than the miracle it is designed to establish. Besides, as we cannot know the attributes or actions of God otherwise than by our experience of them, we cannot be sure that he can effect miracles; for they are contrary to our own experience and the course of nature. Therefore, it is impossible to prove miracles by any evidence.

[1] *Philosophical Essays, &c.*, p. 224.

The second part of the *Essay on Miracles* is intended to show that, supposing a miracle capable of being proved by sufficient testimony, no miraculous event in history has ever been established on such evidence. The witnesses of a miracle should be of such unquestionable good sense, education, and learning, as to secure us against all delusion in themselves. They should also be of such undoubted integrity as to place them beyond all suspicion of design to deceive others. Then they should be of such credit and reputation in the eyes of mankind as to have a great deal to lose if detected in any falsehood. Last of all, the facts attested by the witnesses should be performed in such a public manner, and in so celebrated a part of the world, as to render detection unavoidable.[1]

Now, according to Hume, these requisitions are not met in the supposed witnesses of the miracles of Christ. Consequently, we are no more obliged to believe their accounts than the reports of miracles alleged to have been wrought at the tomb of the Abbé de Paris. All must be rejected together.

Hume's *History of England* met with a cold reception on its first appearance. But he lived to see the day when, as he egotistically said, "it became circulated like the newspapers." Yet he wrote that work not as an end, but as a means. Historical writing was then the medium in which it was common to couch theology or philosophy. Hume had a profound contempt for everything Puritanic on the one hand, and hierarchical and traditional on the other. He would make every trace disappear beneath his scathing pen. He ignored the development of religious life in England, and would subject all events which indicated a

[1] Leland, *View of Deistical Writers*, pp. 230-250.

deep Christian piety and purpose, to his cold system of philosophy.. Writing with an inflexible adherence to his theological opinions, he cast over historical events the drapery of his own interpretation. The question with him was not, "What is the history of England during the period of which I treat?" but "Does not the history of England sustain my philosophy?" And his own answer was, "Yes; I record facts, and draw my own conclusions. Is not that a good philosophy!"

Gibbon was even more of a Frenchman than Hume. Sundering his relation to Oxford in his seventeenth year, he embarked upon a course of living and thinking which, whatever advantage it might afford to his purse, was not likely to aid his faith. By a sudden caprice he became a Roman Catholic, and afterwards as unceremoniously denied his adopted creed. In due time he found himself in Paris publishing a book in the French language. He there fell in with the fashionable infidelity, and so far yielded to the flattery of Helvetius and all the frequenters of Holbach's house that he jested at Christianity and assailed its divine character.

While residing at Lausanne, Switzerland, he cultivated the florid French style of composition, and applied it in his *Decline and Fall of the Roman Empire.* That work has been severely censured, but despite its defects, it is one of the permanent master-pieces of English literature. In the fifteenth and sixteenth chapters the author gives his opinion of Christianity. He attributes the progress of the Christian religion to the zeal of the Jews, to the doctrine of the immortality of the soul as stated by philosophers, to the miraculous powers claimed by the primitive church, to the virtues of the first Christians, and to the activity of the Christians in the government of the church. He attributed to outward agencies what could have been effected only by inward forces. But he did not assume the philosopher's cap, for, not being metaphysical by nature, he never did violence to his own constitution. He has left much less on record against Christianity than Hume, but they must be ranked together as the last of the family of English Deists.

Gibbon made loud professions of independence and of an earnest desire for the enlargement of popular liberty. But he was less attached to principle than to expediency. At the very time the first volume of his history appeared, in which he pays lofty tributes to human freedom, he came into Parliament as an avowed abettor of the ministry of George III., in their attempts to subjugate the American colonies. He was doubtless well paid for his votes; for he was at the same time a member of the Board of Trade, a nominal office with a large salary.[1] A verse, attributed to Fox, expresses the popular sentiment concerning him;

"King George in a fright
Lest Gibbon should write
The story of England's disgrace,
Thought no way so sure,
His pen to secure,
As to give the historian a place."

In addition to these evidences of religious decay we may add the most unwelcome of all: the moral prostration of the English Church. Instead of being "a city set upon a hill," she was in the valley of humiliation; and few were the faithful watchmen upon her walls. The period commencing with the Restoration, and continuing down to the time of which we speak, was one

[1] Schlosser, *History of the Eighteenth Century*, vol. ii., p. 85-86.

of ministerial and laic degeneracy. Bishop Burnet, writing of his own generation, said, "I am now in the seventieth year of my age, and as I cannot speak long in the world, in any sort, I cannot hope for a more solemn occasion than this of speaking with all due freedom, both to the present and to the succeeding ages. Therefore I lay hold on it to give a free vent to those sad thoughts that lie on my mind both day and night, and are the subject of many secret mournings. I cannot look on without the deepest concern, when I see the imminent ruin hanging over this church, and, by consequence, over the whole Reformation. The outward state of things is black enough, God knows, but that which heightens my fears rises chiefly from the inward state into which we are unhappily fallen. . . . Our ember-weeks are the burden and grief of my life. The much greater part of those who come to be ordained are ignorant to a degree not to be apprehended by those who are not obliged to know it. The easiest part of knowledge is that to which they are the greatest strangers. Those who have read some few books, yet never seem to have read the Scriptures. Many cannot give even a tolerable account of the Catechism itself, how short and plain soever. This does often tear my heart. The case is not much better in many who, having got into orders, come for institution, and cannot make it appear that they have read the Scriptures, or any one good book since they were ordained; so that the small measure of knowledge upon which they get into holy orders, not being improved, is in a way to be quite lost; and they think it a great hardship if told they must know the Scriptures and the body of divinity better before they can be trusted with the care of souls." [1]

[1] *Pastoral Care.*

29

Archbishop Secker, who wrote at a later period, testifies to the same state of religious petrification: "In this we cannot be mistaken, that an open and professed disregard is become, through a variety of unhappy causes, the distinguishing character of the present age; that this evil is grown to a great height in the metropolis of the nation; is daily spreading through every part of it; and, bad in itself as any can be, must of necessity bring in others after it. Indeed it hath already brought in such dissoluteness and contempt of principle in the higher part of the world, and such profligate intemperance, and fearlessness of committing crimes, in the lower, as must, if this impiety stop not, become absolutely fatal. And God knows, far from stopping, it receives, through the ill designs of some persons, and the inconsiderateness of others, a continual increase. Christianity is now ridiculed and railed at, with very little reserve; and the teachers of it, without any at all."[1]

The Church had not the moral power or purity to assert her own authority. She had lost the respect of the world because she had no respect for herself. She was therefore enervated at a time when all her power was needed to resist the skeptical and immoral tendencies of the day. But a new religious power, from an unexpected source, began to influence the English mind. We refer to the movement inaugurated by the Wesleys and Whitefield, who were fellow-students in Oxford University. They were appalled at the dissoluteness of the students, the frigid preaching of the day, and the universal religious destitution of the nation. These themes burdened the hearts of the "Holy Club" at Oxford from day to day, and sent them from their cloisters to

[1] *Works*, vol. v., p. 306.

visit prisons, preach in surrounding towns, and impart religious truth wherever a willing recipient could be found. No sooner had John Wesley returned from his missionary voyage to Georgia than there were unmistakable evidences of the adaptation of the new preaching to the wants of the people. The masses, long affected by a deplorable indifference to religious truths and pious living, heard the earnest preaching of the Methodists with profound attention and in such large numbers that no impartial observer could doubt the peculiar fitness of Methodism to the existing state of society, morals, literature, and philosophy. As a result, the number of converts multiplied. The Established Church was aroused to activity. Dissenters began to hope for the return of the good days of Bunyan and Baxter and Howe.

Isaac Taylor says of the new influence, that "it preserved from extinction and reanimated the languishing nonconformity of the last century, which just at the time of the Methodist revival, was rapidly in course to be found nowhere but in books." But the Wesleyan movement made little impression on the literary circles to whom Bolingbroke, Hume, and Gibbon had communicated their gospel of nature. The poets continued to sing, the essayists to write, and the philosophers to speculate, in a world peculiarly their own. They shut themselves quite in from the itinerant "helpers" of Wesley. The large class of English minds which stood aloof from all ecclesiastical organizations, and failed to see any higher cause of the revival than mere enthusiasm, were the persons whom those writers still influenced. But it was plain to both the masters and their disciples that their principles were in process of transition. They were therefore ready for the reception of whatever plausible type of skepticism might present itself for their acceptance.

History is the illustration of cause and effect. The fountain springs up in one period, and generations often pass before it finds its natural outlet. The issue of the final efforts of English Deism, of the impure French taste, and of the works of the grosser class of literary men living in the last century, is now manifested in that spirit which welcomes the *Essays and Reviews*, and the criticism of Colenso. It is not true that these and similar publications have created a Rationalistic taste in Great Britain. The taste was already in existence, and has been struggling for satisfaction ever since the closing decades of the eighteenth century.

CHAPTER XX.

ENGLAND CONTINUED: PHILOSOPHICAL AND LITERARY RATIONALISM.—COLERIDGE AND CARLYLE.

ALL history betrays the operation of a compensating principle. The payment may be slow, but there is seldom total repudiation. An influence which departs from a country and sets in upon its neighbor, transforming thought, giving new shades to social life, and instilling foreign principles into politics, is sure, in course of time, to return from its wanderings, bearing with it other forces with which to react upon the land whence it originated. Thought, like the tidal wave, visits all latitudes with its ebb and flow.

The present condition of Anglican theology is an illustration of intellectual re-payment. Two centuries ago England gave Deism to Germany, and the latter country is now paying back the debt with compound interest. After the Revolution of 1789, and the brilliant ascendency of Napoleon Bonaparte, the French spirit rapidly lost its hold upon the English mind. But there immediately arose a disposition to consult German theology and philosophy. English students frequented the German universities, and the works of the leading thinkers of Berlin, Heidelberg, and Halle, were on sale in the book-stores of London. The intimate relations of the royal family of England to Germany, together with the alliance between the German States and Great Britain for the arrest of French arms, increased the tendency until it assumed importance and power. The fruit was first visible in the application of German Rationalism and philosophy to English theology. When Coleridge came from the Fatherland with a new system of opinions, he felt as proud of his good fortune as Columbus did on laying a continent at his sovereign's feet. Ever since that profound thinker assumed a fixed position, a reaction against orthodoxy has been progressing in the Established Church. There are reasons why the slow but effectual introduction of German Rationalism has been taking place imperceptibly.

The war which had agitated England, with the rest of Europe, came to a close in 1815. Immediately afterward domestic politics needed adjustment. "The disabilities were swept away," says a writer, "the House of Commons was reconstituted, the municipalities were reformed, slavery was abolished."[1] In due time the nation became adjusted to peace; the popular mind lost its nervousness; the universities returned to their sober thinking; and the Church took a careful survey to ascertain what had been lost in the recent conflict, what gained, and what new fields lay ready for her enterprise. But very soon fresh political combinations attracted the attention of all classes. The revolutionary changes and counter-changes in France were watched with eager attention lest Waterloo might be avenged in some unexpected manner. At home, church parties were reviving the old antagonisms described by the pen of Macaulay. The popular mind has thus been continually directed toward some exciting theme. England has not had a day of leisure during the whole of the last half-

[1] *National Review*, Oct., 1856.

century, when she could come to a judicious conclusion concerning that class of her thinkers who, though they make theology their profession, are so intensely independent as to attach themselves to no creed or ecclesiastical organization. But they have been thinking all the time, and the outgrowth of their thought is now visible.

English Rationalism consists of three departments: Philosophical, Literary, and Critical Rationalism. Whenever infidelity has arisen, whether within or without the Church, it has usually developed these forms. Philosophy has furnished undevout reason with a fund of speculative objections to revelation; literature has dazzled and bewildered the young and all lovers of romance; and criticism has seized the deductions of science, language, and ethnology, and by their combined aid aimed at the overthrow of the historical and inspired basis of faith. Each of these three agents is in constant danger of arrogance and error. The first, by a single false assumption, may lose its way; the second, by making too free use of the imagination, can easily forget when it is dealing with faith and facts; and the third, by one act of over-reaching, is liable to become puerile, fanciful, and unreliable. The philosopher, the *littérateur*, and the exegete need to be less observant of the surrounding world than of the purity of their own inner life and the teachings of the Holy Spirit.

Philosophical Rationalism in England commenced with Samuel Taylor Coleridge. A comprehensive view of that metaphysician produces a painful impression. Though gifted with capacity for any sphere of thought, he did not excel in either so far as to enable us to assign him a fixed place in literature. He is known as poet, theologian, and philosopher. But his own desire was that posterity might regard him as a theologian. In addition to this indeterminateness of position, which always seriously detracts from a great name, Coleridge presents the unfortunate example of a man who, instead of laboring with settled convictions, and achieving success by virtue of their operation, seems to have only striven after them. His indefinite status was the result of that theological difficulty which proved his greatest misfortune. His sentiments never partook of an evangelical character until the latter part of his life. His habits of thought had become confirmed, and it was quite too late to counteract the influence of many views previously expressed.

So far as we are able to collect the opinions of Coleridge by fragments from his writings, we discover two elements, which, coming from totally different sources, and originating in different ages, harmonized in his mind and constituted the mass of his speculations. One was Grecian, taking its rise in Plato and afterward becoming assimilated to Christianity at Alexandria. The other was German, derived directly from Kant, and undergoing no improvement by its processes of transformation at the hands of that philosopher's successors. "From the Greek," says Dr. Shedd, "he derived the doctrine of Ideas, and fully sympathized with his warmly-glowing and poetic utterance of philosophic truths. From the German he derived the more strictly scientific part of his system—the fundamental distinctions between the Understanding and the Reason (with the sub-distinction of the latter into Speculative and Practical), and between Nature and Spirit. With him also he sympathized in that deep conviction of the absolute nature and validity of the great ideas of God, Freedom, and Immortality—of the binding obligation of conscience—and generally of the supremacy of the Moral and Practical over the purely Speculative. Indeed, any one who goes to the study of Kant, after having made himself acquainted with the writings of Coleridge, will be impressed by the spontaneous and vital concurrence of the latter with the former—the heartiness and entireness with which the Englishman enters into the method and system of this, in many respects, greatest philosopher of the modern world." [1]

The Platonic element in the speculations of Coleridge is of earlier date than the German. It was his reliance until introduced to the captivating opinions of the philosopher of Königsberg. But it never wholly left him,—it was the enchantment of his life.

He had severe struggles. His conquest of the habit of opium-eating, contracted to soothe physical suffering, is an index of the persistent purpose of the man. At first an ardent Unitarian, he was once about to assume charge of a congregation at Shrewsbury. But he finally declined the offer, by saying that, "Active zeal for Unitarian Christianity, not indolence or indifference, has been the motive of my declining a local and solid settlement as preacher of it." [2]

The media through which he passed in search of light were numerous. He seems to have gone to Germany under the impression that he would there find what he had fruitlessly sought in England. No one will deny that the philosophy of Kant was better than the English empirical system of the eighteenth century, which was the best metaphysical pabulum he

[1] *Introductory Essay to Coleridge's Works.* Vol. i., pp. 21–22. Harper's edition.

[2] Letter dated Shrewsbury, Jan. 19th, 1798, to Mr. Isaac Wood, High St., Shrewsbury.

had received at home. He applied himself to the assiduous study of Kant's disciples, but the master satisfied him best. Nevertheless, Coleridge was not mentally adapted to the Kantian system. He had a psychical affinity for Schelling. He loved him as a brother. He was charmed with his vivid imagination, warm admiration of all natural forms, and ardent, impulsive temperament. Schelling's philosophy was Spinozism in poetry, and there can be no question of Coleridge's former adoption of some parts of the Hollander's naturalism. But his tenacity to them, as well as his subsequent affiliation with Schelling, was short-lived. When he awoke to the unmistakable stratum of Pantheism underlying Schelling's system, he hastily forsook it, and his diatribes indignantly hurled against one whom he had so enthusiastically admired are the more notable because of his former intense sympathy. From Schelling he returned once more to Kant as the thinker who had more closely approximated the truth. His mind must have undergone a total revolution when he could write such words as these : "Spite of all the superior airs of the *Natur-Philosophie*, I confess that in the perusal of Kant I breathe the air of good sense and logical understanding with the light of reason shining in it and through it; while in the Physics of Schelling I am amused with happy conjectures, and in his Theology I am bewildered by positions which, in their first sense, are transcendental (*überfliegend*), and in their literal sense scandalous."[1]

Coleridge became firmly settled in theistic faith. Occupying that as his final position, he is destined to wield a great salutary power over English thought. Dr. Shedd, in estimating the probable future influence

[1] *Biographia Literaria.* Appendix III., p. 709.

of his theistic system, says: "Now as the defender and interpreter of this decidedly and profoundly theistic system of philosophy, we regard the works of Coleridge as of great and growing worth, in the present state of the educated and thinking world. It is not to be disguised that Pantheism is the most formidable opponent which truth has to encounter in the cultivated and reflecting classes. We do not here allude to the formal reception and logical defense of the system, so much as to that pantheistic way of thinking, which is unconsciously stealing into the lighter and more imaginative species of modern literature, and from them is passing over into the principles and opinions of men at large. This popularized Naturalism—this Naturalism of polite literature and of literary society—is seen in the lack of that depth and strength of tone, and that heartiness and robustness of temper, which characterize a mind into which the personality of God, and the responsibility of man cut sharply, and which does not cowardly shrink from a severe and salutary moral consciousness. . . . The intensely theistic character of the philosophy of Coleridge is rooted and grounded in the Personal and the Spiritual, and not in the least in the Impersonal and the Natural. Drawing in the outset, as we have remarked above, a distinct and broad line between these two realms, it keeps them apart from each other, by affirming a difference in essence, and steadfastly resists any and every attempt to amalgamate them into one sole substance. The doctrine of creation, and not of emanation or of modification, is the doctrine by which it constructs its theory of the Universe, and the doctrine of responsible self-determination, and not of irresponsible natural development, is the doctrine by which it constructs its systems of Philosophy and Religion."[1]

[1] *Introductory Essay to Coleridge's Works*, vol. i., pp. 35-36.

The Platonic portion of the views of Coleridge is more apparent in his theology than in his philosophy. In his *Confession of Faith*, written November 3, 1816, he avows his adherence to some of the prime doctrines of revealed truth. He declares his free agency; defines God to be a Being in whom supreme reason and a most holy will are one with infinite power; acknowledges man's fallen nature, that he is "born a child of wrath;" and holds Christ Jesus to be the Word which was with God from all eternity, assumed human nature to redeem man, and by his merits secured for us the descent of the Holy Spirit and the impartation of his free grace. In the Preface to the *Aids to Reflection* he thus states his object in writing that work: "To exhibit a full and consistent scheme of the Christian Dispensation, and more largely of all the peculiar doctrines of the Christian faith; and to answer all the objections to the same, which do not originate in a corrupt will rather than an erring judgment; and to do this in a manner intelligible for all who, possessing the ordinary advantages of education, do in good earnest desire to form their religious creed in the light of their own convictions, and to have a reason for the faith which they profess. There are indeed mysteries, in evidence of which no reasons can be brought. But it has been my endeavor to show that the true solution of the problem is, that these mysteries are reason, reason in its highest form of self-affirmation."[1]

The distinctions and definitions of Coleridge occasion the most serious difficulty in the study of his opinions. His mode of statement more frequently than his conception subjects him to the charge of Rationalism. His life-long error of mistaking theology for meta-

[1] *Works*, vol. i., p. 115.

physics resulted in his application of philosophical terminology to theological questions; but making every reasonable allowance, we cannot doubt that he had defective views of some of the essential truths of Christianity. He clothes reason with authority to determine what is inspiration, by saying that there can be no revelation "*ab extra.*" Therefore, every man should decide for himself the character of the Scriptures. The power which Coleridge thus places in the hand of man is traceable to his distinction between reason and understanding. He makes the latter the logical, and the former the intuitive faculty. Even beasts possess understanding, but reason, the gift of God to no less creature than man, performs the functions of judgment on supersensual matters. "Reason," says he, "is the power of universal and necessary convictions, the source and substance of truths above sense, and having their evidence in themselves."[1] This admission to Rationalism has been eagerly seized by the Coleridgean school, and elaborated in some of their writings.

Sin, according to Coleridge, is not guilt in the orthodox sense. When Adam fell he merely turned his back upon the sun; dwelt in the shadow; had God's displeasure; was stripped of his supernatural endowments; and inherited the evils of a sickly body, and a passionate, ignorant, and uninstructed soul. His sin left him to his nature, his posterity is heir to his misfortunes, and what is every man's evil becomes all men's greater evil. Each one has evil enough, and it is hard for a man to live up to the rule of his own reason and conscience.[2] Redemption is not salvation from the curse of a broken law, and Christ did not pay a debt

[1] *Works*, p. 241. The full argument is contained on pp. 241–253.
[2] Ibid. vol. i., pp. 269–271.

for man, because the payer must have incurred the debt himself.[1] But the fruit of his death is the reconciliation of man to God. Man will have a future life, but it was not the specific object of the Christian dispensation to satisfy his understanding that he will live hereafter; neither is the belief of a future state or the rationality of its belief the exclusive attribute of the Christian religion, but a fundamental article of all religion.[2]

All attempts to determine the exact theological position of Coleridge from his own definitions are unsatisfactory. We must derive his real convictions from the spirit and not from the letter of his works. He was devout and reverent, never prosecuting his investigations from a mere love of speculation, but as a sincere inquirer after truth. But his statements have had their natural result in producing a large and vigorous school of thinkers. Never bracing himself to write a philosophical or theological system, but merely stating his views in aphoristic form—as in the *Aids to Reflection*—he scattered his thoughts as a careless sower, and left them to germinate in the public mind. But many of his opinions have been perverted, and speculations have been based upon them by numerous admirers who, proudly claiming him for authority, thrust upon the world those sentiments which bear less the impress of the master than the counterfeit of the weaker disciple.

A large cluster of important and familiar names appears in testimony of the deep and immediate impression produced by the opinions of Coleridge. Julius Charles Hare, not the least worthy of the number, has been one of the prominent agents in communicating to the English people the principles of that thinker, who

[1] *Works*, vol. i., p. 308.
[2] Ibid, p. 325.

was not superior to him in moral earnestness and profound reverence. When lecturing as Fellow of Trinity College, Cambridge, Hare was attentively heard by John Sterling, Maurice, and Trench. He drank deeply of the spirit of Coleridge, of whom he was ever proud to call himself a "pupil," and who, in connection with Wordsworth, was the instrumentality by which he and others "were preserved from the noxious taint of Byron."[1]

From whatever side we view Hare's life, it is full of interest. When very young he traveled on the Continent, and became delighted with the literature of Germany. He informs us that, "in 1811 he saw the mark of Luther's inkstand on the walls of the Castle of Wartburg, and there first learned to throw inkstands at the devil." His view of sacrifice was very superficial, and similar to that of Maurice. The Jewish offerings were typical "of the slaying and offering up of the carnal nature to God. . . . The lesson of the cross is to draw nigh to God, not by this work or that work, not by the sacrifice of this thing or that, but by the entire sacrifice and resignation of their whole being to the will of God."[2] Christ did not perform his important mission so much by his death as by his entire life, and his sufferings were only the completion of his task. "His great work was to be completed and made perfect, as every truly great work must be, by suffering. For no work can be really great unless it be against the course of the world. . . . It was by losing his own life in every possible way—by the agony in the garden; by the flight and denial of those whom he had chosen out of the world to be His companions and

[1] *Mission of the Comforter.* Note Sa.

[2] *Sermons on the Law of Self-Sacrifice, and the Unity of the Church.*

friends; by the mockery and cruelty of those whom his goodness and purity rendered more bitter against him; by the frantic and murderous cries of the people, whom he had loaded with every earthly benefit, and whom he desired to crown with eternal blessings; and by the closing sufferings on the cross—that Jesus was to gain his own life, and the everlasting life of all who will believe in Him. All this, then, the whole work of the redemption of mankind, does our Lord in the text declare to be finished.[1]

Hare declares the necessity of faith to Christian life, but he renders it more passive than active by saying that it is a receptive moral endowment capable of large development. Happy is the man who becomes inured to the exalted "habit of faith." Sin is more a matter of regret than of responsibility; inspiration is a doctrine we should not slight, but the language of the Scriptures must not be regarded too tenaciously; due allowance ought to be made for all verbal inaccuracies and discrepancies; miracles are an adjunct to Christian evidence, but their importance is greatly exaggerated, for they are a beautiful frieze, not one of the great pillars in the temple of our faith.

Notwithstanding these evidences of Hare's digression from orthodoxy, we cannot forget that consecration and purity of heart revealed in some of his sermons, and especially in the glowing pages of the *Mission of the Comforter*. His ministerial life was an example of untiring devotion, and we know not which to admire the more, his labor of love in the rustic parish of Herstmonceaux, or those searching rebukes of Romanism contained in the charges to his clergy. Independent as both his friends and enemies acknowledge him to have

[1] *Sermon on John* xix., 30.

been, his misfortune was an excessive reliance upon his own imagination and upon the opinions of those whom he admired. Nature made him capable of intimate friendships, both personal and intellectual. No one can examine his life without loving the man, nor read his fervent words without concluding that the Church has been honored by few men of his noble type. That self-sacrifice and sympathy of which he often spoke feelingly in connection with the humiliation of Christ, were the controlling principles of his heart. Let not the veil with which we would conceal his theological defects obscure, in the least, the brightness of his resplendent character and pure purposes.

No view of Hare's position can be complete without embracing that of his brother-in-law, Maurice; both of whom were ardently sympathetic with Coleridge. But while the former gave a more evangelical cast to his master's opinions than they originally possessed, the latter perverted them by unwarranted speculations. Maurice is now one of the most influential of the Rationalistic teachers of England. He has not employed himself, like Kingsley and others of the Broad Church, in publishing his theological sentiments in the form of religious novels, but has had the commendable frankness to state his opinions without circumlocution, and to furnish us with his creed in a single volume of essays.[1]

Maurice's notion of an ideal creation betrays the media through which he has received it,—from Coleridge to Neo-Platonism, and thence to Plato. The creation of herbs, flowers, beasts, birds, and fishes, as recorded in the first chapter of Genesis, was the bringing

[1] *Theological Essays.* Second Edition. London, 1853. Maurice has published thirty-four works. *Vid.* Low's *English Catalogue*, 1835–1862, pp. 509–510.

forth of kinds and orders, such as they were according to the mind of God, not of actual separate phenomenal existences, such as they present themselves to the senses of man.[1] The creation of man is disposed of in the same ideal way; so that we are inclined to ask the critic if man is not, after all, only a Platonic idea? "What I wish you particularly to notice," says he, "is that the part of the record which speaks of man ideally, according to his place with reference to God, is the part which expressly belongs to the history of CREATION; that the bringing forth of man in *this* sense, is the work of the sixth day. . . . Extend this thought, which seems to rise inevitably out of the story of the creation of *man*, as Moses delivers it, to the seat of that universe of which he regards man as the climax, and we are forced to the conclusion that in the one case, as in the other, it is not the visible, material thing of which the historian is speaking, but that which lies below the visible material thing, and constitutes the substance which it shows forth."[2]

Maurice assumes also, with Neo-Platonism, that Christ is the archetype of every human being, and that when a man becomes pure, he is only developing the Christ who was within him already. "The Son was really in Saul of Tarsus, and he only became Paul the converted when that Son was revealed in him. . . . Christ is in every man. . . . All may call upon God as a reconciled Father. Human beings are redeemed, not in consequence of any act they have done, of any faith they have exercised; their faith is to be grounded on a foregone conclusion; their acts are to be the fruits of a state they already possess."[3]

[1] *Lectures on the Old Testament*, p. 6.
[2] Ibid. pp. 3–6.
[3] *Unity of the New Testament.* *Introduction*, pp. xxi.–xxvi.

From this premise alone the theological system of Maurice may be accurately determined. Sin is an evil from which we should strive to effect an escape, but it is nothing more, neither guilt nor responsibility, only a condition of our life and not a consequence of actual disobedience of God's law, or the effect of his displeasure. Deep below it there is a righteousness capable of asserting its sovereignty. Job had a righteousness within him, which led him to say, "I know that my Redeemer liveth." Those persons who prate about our miserable condition as sinners, "have a secret reserve of belief that there is that in them which is not sin, which is the very opposite of sin. . . . Each man has got this sense of righteousness, whether he realizes it distinctly or indistinctly; whether he expresses it courageously, or keeps it to himself." [1]

The nature of the atonement, Maurice holds, is a subject of misconception, and the notions of it, as they now obtain in Christendom, darken and bewilder the mind. What Christ has really done for us through suffering was his matchless sympathy; he became our brother, and was not our mediatorial substitute but a natural representative. On this ground, a regeneration is communicated to all, not by virtue of any appropriating faith, but as a result of the sympathetic death of Christ. The justification of humanity has been secured by his incarnation, and the penalty resulting from sin is a mere scar of the healed wound. Natural death is not the separation of soul and body, though both are affected by it, for the body which seems to die is only the corruption resulting from our sins, and the real body does not die. Hence, there can never be any general resurrection or judgment.

[1] *Theological Essays*, p. 61.

It is astonishing that a man who unhesitatingly propagated these views, could hold any office within the pale of the Established Church ; but Maurice enjoyed high favor a number of years before his displacement. Though commencing life as a Unitarian and Universalist, he was rapidly promoted by the ecclesiastical authorities. He took no pains to conceal his theological opinions, and yet we find him advancing in King's College, London, from the Professorship of English Literature to that of Ecclesiastical History, and thence to the Chair of Divinity. Some time elapsed after the publication of the *Essays* before Dr. Jelf, Principal of the College, even read them, but having made himself acquainted with their contents, a correspondence took place between him and Maurice. The result was that the Council pronounced "the opinions expressed, and the doubts indicated in the *Essays*, and the correspondence respecting future punishments and the final issues of the day of judgment, to be of dangerous tendency, and likely to unsettle the minds of the theological students; and further decide that his continuance as Professor would be seriously detrimental to the interests of the College." [1] Maurice afterward held the office of Chaplain to Lincoln's Inn, but in 1860 he was appointed by the Queen to the district church of Vere St. Marylebone.

The relations of Maurice and Kingsley are most intimate, for besides their leadership of the Broad Church, they are the exponents of the so-called Christian Socialism.

Charles Kingsley has made a profound impression upon the present thought and life of England. He betrays his martial lineage in the vigor of his pen, and in that unswerving purpose to counteract what, in

[1] The date of this Sentence was Oct. 28th, 1853.

his opinion, are serious barriers to the progress of the age. That he should entertain sympathy with Coleridge might be expected from the very cast of his mind, but his adoption of such a large proportion of that thinker's sentiments may be due to his private education under the care of Derwent Coleridge, son of the philosopher. Though only forty-six years old, twenty of which have been passed in the rectorship of Eversley, an enumeration of his works shows him to have written theology, philosophy, poetry, and romance. But his publications betray unity of purpose. Instead of suffering Christianity to be a dead weight upon society, he would adapt it to the wants of the masses. He holds that when the adaptation becomes thorough, when, by any means, the people can be made to grasp Christianity, the reflexive influence will be so great as to elevate them to a point unthought of by the sluggish Church. But what is the Christianity which Kingsley would incorporate into the life of society? Upon the answer to this inquiry depends the difference between him and evangelical theologians.

The advocates of orthodoxy maintain that Christianity is a remedial dispensation, introduced to meet an evil which could not be counteracted by any other agency, human or divine; but with Kingsley it is only the outward exhibition of what had ever existed in a concealed state. Man has always been one with the Word, or Son of God, and, by virtue of the nature of each, they are in perfect union. Christ manifested the union first when he appeared on earth in the incarnate state, since he came to declare to men that they were not estranged from him, but had always been, and still were, in harmony with him. Men are not craven enemies of God, which error a harsh theology would make them believe. They are his friends, for Christ regarded them complacently as such; and the atonement must not be deemed the reconciliation of sinful humanity and angry Deity, but as the first manifestation of an ever-existing unity of the two parties. We need not pass through the long ordeal of repentance to be placed in the relation of sons; because we are all by nature "members of Christ, children of God, and inheritors of the Kingdom of Heaven." [1]

The Church, according to Kingsley, is the world in a certain aspect. "The world," says an English writer, in stating Kingsley's opinion, "is called the Church when it recognizes its relation to God in Christ, and acts accordingly. The Church is the world lifting itself up into the sunshine; the world is the Church falling into shadow and darkness. When and where the light and life that are in the world break out into bright, or noble, or holy word or deed, then and there the world shows that the nature and glory of the Church live within it. Every man of the world is not only potentially, but virtually a member of Christ's Church, whatever may, for the present, be his character or seeming. Like the colors in shot silk, or on a dove's neck, the difference of hue and denomination depends merely upon the degree of light, and the angle of vision. In conformity with this principle, Mr. Kingsley's theology altogether secularizes the Kingdom of Christ." [2]

Kingsley's views of the offices of the Holy Spirit indicate a decided approbation of the pantheistic theory. The third person of the Trinity operates not only upon

[1] *Sermons on National Subjects.* First Series. p. 14. London Edition.

[2] *Modern Anglican Theology.* By the Rev. J. H. Rigg. Second Edition. London, 1859. The student of contemporary theology will find this work the best summary of the opinions of Coleridge and his school.

man, but through him upon the secular and intellectual life of the world. Poetry, romance, and each act of induction, are the work of the Spirit, whose agency secures all the material and scientific growth of the world. Without that power, the car of progress, whether in letters, mechanics, or ethics, must stop.

Kingsley would elevate the degraded portion of the race until the lowest member be made to feel the transmuting agency of Christianity. He was first led into sympathy with the poor operatives in the English factories by reading Mayhew's *Sketches of London Labor and London Poor*, and, in connection with Maurice, organized coöperative laboring associations as a check to the crushing system of competitive labor. Their plans succeeded, and many abject working men have been brought into a higher social and moral condition than they had hitherto enjoyed. These humanitarian efforts have attracted large numbers to the reception of the tenets entertained by those putting them forth. "For," the unthinking say, "if the opinions of these men will lead them to labor on this wise for the social elevation of our fellow-beings, they must needs be correct, and if so, worthy of our reception." But if Neo-Platonism can make Maurices, Kingsleys, and a whole school of "Muscular Christians" and "Christian Socialists," nothing less than the pure religion of Christ can raise up Howards, Wilberforces, and Budgetts.

The philosopher has always exerted a great power upon those who do not philosophize. He is regarded by many as the inhabitant of a sphere which few can enter, and his dictates are heard as fiats of a rightful ruler. Those who cannot understand him fully often congratulate themselves that the few unmistakable grains they have gathered from his opinions are nuggets of pure gold, and entitled to the merit of becoming the world's currency. The philosopher is not his own interpreter. There has seldom been one who knew how to tell his thoughts to the masses. That is the province of the popular writers who have adopted his opinions, and know how to deal them out almost imperceptibly in the form of poetry and fiction. One great philosophical mind has sometimes dictated the literature of generations, and, in earlier periods, of entire centuries.

This influence of philosophy on literature is furnished with a new illustration at the present day; some of the most popular and attractive writers of Great Britain have extracted their opinions from one or more of the later philosophers of Germany, and incorporated them into current poetry, romance, and history. The effect has been to furnish the people with a literature which possesses all the weight of vital religious truth in the minds of those readers who prefer to derive their creed from some enchanter in letters to seeking it immediately from the Bible or its most reliable interpreters.

The department of literature in question inculcates as its cardinal principle that man is unconscious of his power, he can do what seems impossible, does not worship his fellows enough, is purer than his clerical leaders would have him imagine, and ought, like certain of his predecessors, to arouse to lofty efforts, assert his dignity and divinity, and strive to advance the world to its proper glory and perfection. The authors of these exciting and flattering appeals do not surround their theory with proper safeguards, nor do they tell the world that they have served up a delectable dish of Pantheism for popular deglutition.

The case is stated clearly by one who understands the danger of this tendency, and whose pen has already been powerful in exposing its absurdity. "In our general literature," says Bayne, "the principle we have enunciated undergoes modification, and, for the most part, is by no means expressed as pantheism. We refer to that spirit of self-assertion, which lies so deep in what may be called the religion of literature, to that wide-spread tendency to regard all reform of the individual man as being an evolution of some hidden nobleness, or an appeal to a perfect internal light or law, together with what may be called the worship of genius, the habit of nourishing all hope on the manifestation of the divine, by gifted individuals. We care not how this last remarkable characteristic of the time be defined; to us its connection with pantheism, and more or less close dependence on the teaching of that of Germany, seem plain, but it is enough that we discern in it an influence definably antagonistic to the spirit of Christianity."[1]

The parentage of literary Rationalism in England is attributable to Thomas Carlyle. Having "found his soul" in the philosophy of Germany, we hear him, in 1827, defending the criticism of Kant as "distinctly the greatest intellectual achievement of the century in which it came to light." But the opinions of Fichte and Richter have subsequently had more weight with Carlyle, and he has elaborated them in many forms. Fichte, in particular, has influenced him to adopt a theory which gives a practical denial to the Scriptural declarations of the fallen state of humanity. Effort being goodness, the exterior world is only tolerable because it furnishes an arena for the contest of work.

[1] *Christian Life*, p. 14. American Edition.

Man will never receive any prize unless he bestir himself to the exercise of his own omnipotence. Individual life is all the real life possessed by this world, and it is gifted with a spiritual wand capable of calling up wondrous forms of beauty and worth. It matters not so much what man works for, since his effort is the important matter. All ages have had a few true men. The assertion of self-hood constitutes greatness; and Zoroaster, Cromwell, Julius Cæsar, and Frederic the Great; heroes of any creed or no creed, Pagan or Jew, are the world's worthies, its great divinities. Men need not be conscious that they are doing great deeds while in the act, nor, when the work is accomplished, that they have performed anything worthy a school-boy's notice. On the other hand, worth is tested by actual unconsciousness, "which teaches that all self-knowledge is a curse, and introspection a disease; that the true health of a man is to have a soul without being aware of it,—to be disposed of by impulses which he never criticises,—to fling out the products of creative genius without looking at them."

Man is the centre of the universe, which is everywhere clothed with life. His is a spiritual power capable of effecting the great transformations needed by his fellows. Let him be earnest, then, and evolve the fruits of his wonderful strength. Since his mission is work, here is Carlyle's gospel which calls him to it: "Work is of a religious nature; all true work is sacred; in all true work, were it but true hand-labor, there is something of divineness. Labor, wide as the earth, has its summit in heaven. Sweat of the brow; and up from that to the sweat of the brain, sweat of the heart; which includes all Kepler calculations, Newton meditations, all sciences, all spoken epics, all acted heroisms, martyrdoms,—up to that 'Agony of bloody sweat,' which all men have called divine! O brother, if this is not 'worship,' then I say the more pity for worship; for this is the noblest thing yet discovered under God's sky." Work implies power, and power in the individual is what society needs to keep it within proper bounds. Social life requires the will of the single mind and hand; republicanism is therefore the dream of fanatics, and ought not to be tolerated anywhere. Popular rights are a fiction which the strong hand ought to dissipate at a thrust. The greatest men are the greatest despots, and the exercise of their unlimited authority is what entitles them to our worship. Napoleon III. preaches the pure gospel of politics in his *Life of Julius Cæsar*. Absolute subjection—call it slavery, if you please—is the proper state of large bodies of helpless humanity, who are absolutely dependent upon some master of iron will for guidance and development.

Such being Carlyle's view of human rights, it is not surprising that he has applauded the most gigantic effort in history to establish a government upon the system of human bondage. But all slavery will by and by vanish like the tobacco-smoke of "Teufelsdröckh." Part of the world's best work will be the unceasing effort for its universal and perpetual extermination; and posterity will honor those who labor for this consummation as greater benefactors and workers than all the divinities idolized by the author of *Sartor Resartus* and the *Life of Frederic the Great*.

While Carlyle's system does not appear to flatter humanity its effect is of that character. He would make his readers believe that they are pure, great, and capable beings like those deified by him. The adulation being too great for many who peruse his pages, large numbers of readers are led into dangerous vagaries. "The influence of Carlyle's writings," says an essayist, "and especially of his *Sartor Resartus*, has been primarily exerted on classes of men most exposed to temptations of egotism and petulance, and least subjected to anything above them,—academics, artists, *littérateurs*, strong-minded women, 'debating' youths, Scotchmen of the phrenological grade, and Irishmen of the young-Ireland school."[1] There are very many beside this grotesque group, who exclaim, with one of his warmest admirers, "Carlyle is my religion!" There are others again who say gratefully what John Sterling wrote him in his last brief letter, "Towards me it is still more true than towards England that no man has been and done like you."[2]

The time has not yet come when men can awake from the spell of a charmer like Carlyle. But the illusion will some day be dissipated, and many of his readers in Great Britain and America will feel deeply and almost despairingly that, in the original fountain of his teaching, there was "a poison-drop which killed the plants it was expected to nourish, and left a sterile waste where men looked for the bloom and the opulence of a garden of God." It behooves those who idolize him to examine the image before which they stand. He is a man of unquestioned boldness and some originality, and no one of the present generation has greater power to dazzle and bewilder the young. Happily, age brings with it the clearing up of much of the obscurity of youth, and on the additional light of increasing years we depend for the illumination of many a mind ob-

[1] *National Review*, Oct. 1856.
[2] *Life of Sterling*, p. 334.

scured by his sentiments. The late R. A. Vaughan, a careful observer of the tendencies of English thought, says: "It may not be flattering to Mr. Carlyle, but we believe it to be true that by far the larger portion of the best minds, whose early youth his writings have powerfully influenced, will look back upon the period of such subjection as the most miserably morbid period of their life. On awaking from such delirium to the sane and healthful realities of manful toil, they will discover the hollowness of that sneering, scowling, wailing, declamatory, egotistical, and bombastic misanthropy, which, in the eye of their unripe judgment, wore the air of a philosophy so profound."[1] The time will also come when Carlyle will be revealed to all in his true character: as the theologian preaching a pagan creed; as the philosopher emasculating the German philosophy which he scrupled not to borrow; as the stylist perverting the pure English of Milton and Shakspeare into inflated, oracular Richterisms; and as the arch demagogue who, despising the people at heart, assigned no bounds to his ambition to gain their hearing and cajole them into the reception of his unmixed Pantheism.

The periodical press has been a successful agency in the dissemination of literary Rationalism throughout the British Islands. Years before the recent discussions sprang up, the *Westminster Review* was the ablest and most avowed of all the advocates of the "liberal theology" of the Continent. It still rules without a rival. Emboldened by the late accession of sympathizers, it opposes orthodoxy and the Church with an arrogance equal to that of the *Universal German Library*, whose editor, Nicolai, is reported to have said: "My object is merely to hold up to the laughter and contempt of the

[1] *Essays and Remains*, vol. i., pp. 7–8.

public the orthodox and hypocritical clergy of the Protestant church, and to show that they make their own bad cause the cause of their office and of religion, or rather that of Almighty God himself,—to show that when they make an outcry about prevailing errors, infidelity, and blasphemy, they are only speaking of their own ignorance, hypocrisy, and love of persecution, of the wickedness of their own hearts concealed under the mantle of piety." [1]

From its character as a quarterly publication, the *Westminster Review* has the constant opportunity to reply to every new work of Christian apology, and to elaborate each new heresy of the Rationalistic thinkers. Assuming a thoroughly negative position, it repels every tendency toward a higher type of piety, and retards, as far as it can, the popular acceptance of the doctrines of Christianity. Its attacks on the sanctity of the Sabbath are bold, and carefully designed to affect popular sentiment. It gives its support to the fatal theories of Sociology, a system which holds "that so uniform are the operations of motives upon the actions of men that social regulations may be reduced to an exact science, and society be organized to a perfect model." It thus commits itself to the position that all history takes place by force of necessity.

The *Westminster Review* studiously opposes the orthodox view of inspiration, miracles, the atonement, and the Biblical age of the world and of man. It indorses the sentiments of the Tübingen school, and holds with Baur that if we would know the truth of the early Church, its entire apostolic history must be reconstructed. It is compelled to confess the recent advance of evangelical doctrines in the German mind, but sees

[1] *Sebaldus Nothanker.* Second Edition. 1774.

only evil in the fact, and utters this jeremiade: "This church sentiment, which has seized upon the whole of the *noblesse* in North Germany is becoming every year the sentiment of the clergy. The theological radicalism of the last period is now quite a thing of the past. The present is an epoch of restoration. Scientific criticism has no longer any interest; it is, who can be most orthodox, and reproduce more precisely the ideas of the sixteenth century. As the scientific and critical school is defunct, the mediation-theology, whose business was to compromise between the results of learning and the principles of orthodoxy, is necessarily in a state of decay. Its occupation is gone. This school of theologians, which numbers in its ranks some of the most respectable names in Germany, and which traces its origin to Schleiermacher, can scarcely be said now to make head against the sweeping current of Pharisaical orthodoxy. Some of its older representatives have been withdrawn from the scene either by age or death; others have followed the multitude, and conformed to the reigning 'churchmanship.' It is the old story enacted in the Catholic revival of the end of the sixteenth century, and at other times before and since. The reactionary clergy have succeeded in getting themselves regarded as the Swiss Guard of the throne. They stand between Royalty and Revolution. All the places in the gift of the crown—and all the places are in the gift of the crown—are filled on party considerations. Learning goes for nothing. Thus inferior men are elevated to a platform from which they deliver their dicta with authority, and ignorance can contradict knowledge at an advantage. The mutual understanding among the party enables them to puff each other's books, and run down their opponents. Only learning can get no hearing."[1]

A number of writers have been furnished with a creed by the literature of which we have spoken, and are now endeavoring to teach it to the people. Their system has many names, among which are, Positivism, Secularism, and Socialism. Consummate shrewdness is exhibited in its presentation to the people, "the children of this world" sustaining their old reputation for superior wisdom. The circulating libraries abound in its books, and the newspaper and six-penny pamphlet are used as instruments for its wider dissemination.

The Protestant church of Great Britain has no time for idleness, and cannot afford to waste any truth-power while so many enemies are assailing its walls. When the crisis shall have passed it will be seen that not a superfluous hand was lifted in the combat. What British and American Protestantism needs to-day is not a class of discoverers of new truth, but that the defenders of the old truth, availing themselves of every new step of science and criticism, be chivalric in opposing their adversaries, and watchful of the interests which God has placed in their keeping.

[1] October Number, 1863.

CHAPTER XXI.

ENGLAND CONTINUED: CRITICAL RATIONALISM—JOWETT, THE ESSAYS AND REVIEWS, AND COLENSO.

THE devout disciple of Christ regards the Scriptures with profound reverence, for they contain the doctrines which show him his path to the pure life of heaven. His theological opponents are not blind to this attachment, nor are they ignorant of the service of the Bible in supporting the entire Christian system. It could not therefore be expected that, while literature and philosophy were affected by Rationalism, the Scriptures should escape with impunity. There lies a deep destructive purpose beneath the brief utterance of Dr. Temple: "The immediate work of our day is the study of the Bible.[1]" The Critical Rationalism of England which is now attracting the attention of the civilized world is of recent growth, but the energy with which it has been cultivated is unsurpassed in the annals of skepticism.

Professor Jowett's commentary on the *Epistles to Thessalonians, Galatians, and Romans*, was published in 1855. Coming from a highly respectable source, and assailing the doctrines of revelation boldly, it was a clear indication of what might be expected from the Critical Rationalists as a class.

[1] *Essays and Reviews.* Edited, with an Introduction, by Rev. F. H. Hedge, D. D. Boston, 1862.

The doctrine of the atonement, according to this writer, is involved in perplexities whose growth is of more than a thousand years. Christ did not die to appease the divine wrath, and "sacrifice" and "atonement" were accommodated terms used by the apostles because they had been reared among the Jewish offerings and were familiar with them. The great advantage we derive from Christ is his life, in which we behold a perfect harmony of nature, absolute self-renunciation, pure love, and resignation. We know nothing of the objective act on God's part by which he reconciled the world to himself, the very description of it being a figure of speech. Conversion is not in accordance with the claims of orthodoxy, for while there were conversions in the early Church, there is no possibility of establishing a harmony between them and those which are now said to occur. The conversions of the first Christains were marked by ecstatic and unusual phenomena, whole multitudes were simultaneously affected, and the changes wrought were permanent; but the subjects were chiefly ignorant people, who no doubt did many things which would have been distasteful to us as men of education.[1]

The most noteworthy work of the Critical Rationalists is the *Essays and Reviews* (1861), a volume which consists of broad generalizations against the authority of the Bible as a standard of faith.

I. *The Education of the World.* By Frederic Temple, D. D. There is a radical difference between man and inanimate nature. The latter is passive, and subject to the workings of the vast physical machinery, but man is at no time stationary, for he develops from age to age, and concentrates in his history the results and

[1] *Commentary on St. Paul's Epistles.—Noyes' Essays*, pp. 222–276.

achievements of all previous history. There is no real difference between the capacity of men now and that of the antediluvian world; the ground of disparity lies in the time of development afforded the present generation. Thus a child of twelve stands at present where once stood the full-grown man.

There are three stages in the world's development: Childhood, Youth, Maturity. Childhood requires positive rules, and is made subject to them; youth is governed by the force of example; and manhood, being free from external restraints, must be its own instructor. We have first rules, then examples, and last principles:—the Law, the Son of Man, and the Gift of the Spirit. The world was once a child, under tutors and governors until the time appointed by the Father. Afterwards, when the fit season had arrived, the Example, to which all ages should turn, was sent to teach men what they ought to be; and the human race was left to itself to be guided by the instruction of the Spirit within.[1] The world, before the time of Christ, was in its childhood, when commands were given without explanation. The pre-Christian world, being in its state of discipline and childhood, was divided into four classes: the Roman, the Greek, the Asiatic, and the Hebrew, each of which contributed something toward the world's improvement and its preparation for the age of Example. The Hebrew did the most, though his work was of the same class and aimed at the same result. The Roman gave an iron will; the Greek, a cultivated reason and taste; the Asiatic, the idea of immortality, and spiritual imagination; and the Hebrew, the trained conscience.

The whole period from the close of the old Testament to the termination of the New was the time of the

[1] *Essays and Reviews*, pp. 5-6.

world's youth, the age of examples.[1] Christ came just at the right time; if he had waited until the present age his incarnation would have been misplaced, and we could not recognize his divinity; for the faculty of faith has turned inwards, and cannot now accept any outward manifestations of the truth of God.[2]

The present age is that of independent reflection and the supremacy of conscience—the world's manhood. Laws and examples are absolute, and should be forgotten, just as we look lightly upon the things of our childhood. The world has arrived at its present exalted state through a severe ordeal, but the grandeur of its position is sufficient to make it forget its trials. "The spirit or conscience [which are terms for reason] comes to full strength and assumes the throne intended for him in the soul. As an accredited judge, invested with full powers, he sits in the tribunal of our inner kingdom, decides upon the past, and legislates upon the future, without appeal except to himself. He decides not by what is beautiful or noble, or soul-inspiring, but by what is right. Gradually he frames his code of laws, revising, adding, abrogating, as a wiser and deeper experience gives him clearer light. He is the third great teacher and the last."[3]

In some aspects this essay is the least objectionable in the volume. Yet it contains radical errors which many a reader would accept without suspicion. The agency of the Holy Spirit in revelation is ignored, and the development through which the world has passed is confounded with civilization. This development is alleged to have occured in a purely natural way, the Hebrew type being no more a divine appointment than that of

[1] *Essays and Reviews*, p. 37.
[2] Ibid. p. 39. [3] Ibid. pp. 35-36.

the Grecian or Roman. The doctrines of Christianity were not clearly stated in the early Church, and the flight of eighteen centuries has been required to lift the curtain from them.[1] Conscience is placed above the Bible, and if the statements of the Scriptures be in conflict with it, allowance must be made for occasional inaccuracies, interpolations, and forgeries.[2]

II. Bunsen's Biblical Researches. By Rowland Williams, D. D. We here find the same deference paid to conscience as in the preceding essay. If it differ from revelation, man's own notions of right and wrong must prevail over Scripture. Dr. Williams is contented with arraying Bunsen's skeptical theories before the British public without formally indorsing them himself; yet, as their reviewer, he is evidently in complete harmony with the German author. For he carefully collects the chevalier's extravagant speculations; brings them into juxtaposition; admires the spirit, boldness, and learning which had given birth to them; and in no case refutes, but looks with complacence upon nearly every one. The impression of a candid reader of the essay must be, that the writer indorses almost all of Bunsen's opinions without having the courage to avow his assent. Of his hero he says, "Bunsen's enduring glory is neither to have faltered with his conscience, nor shrunk from the difficulties of the problem, but to have brought a vast erudition, in the light of a Christian conscience, to unroll tangled records; tracing frankly the Spirit of God elsewhere, but borrowing chiefly the traditions of his Hebrew Sanctuary." [3]

[1] For an able refutation of this point, *vid.* Houghton, *Rationalism in the Church of England*, pp. 127-136.

[2] *Essays and Reviews*, p. 54.

[3] Ibid. p. 60.

The absence of that reverence to be expected in all whose vocation enjoins the frequent reading of the sublime liturgy of the Church of England, produces a depressing influence upon any one not in sympathy with the doctrines of Rationalism. The Evangelical theologians are termed "The despairing school, who forbid us to trust in God or in our own conscience, unless we kill our souls with literalism."[1] The inquiries and successes of the German Rationalists are worthy of hearty admiration, for they are so great that the world has seldom, if ever, seen their equal. Bishops Pearson and Butler, and Mr. Mansel are seriously at fault in their notions of prophecy, and even Jerome is guilty of gross puerilities. There is no reason why Bunsen may not be right when he holds that the world must be twenty thousand years old; there is no chronological element in revelation; the avenger who slew the first-born, may have been the Bedouin host; in the passage of the Red Sea, the description may be interpreted with the latitude of poetry; it is right to reject the perversions which make the cursing Psalms evangelically inspired; perhaps one passage in Zechariah and one in Isaiah may be direct prophecies of the Messiah, and possibly a chapter in Deuteronomy may foreshadow the final fall of Jerusalem; the Messianic prophecies are mere contemporaneous history; and the fifty-third chapter of Isaiah is only a description of the sufferings of Jeremiah. Inspiration is too loftily conceived by "the well-meaning crowd," for whom we should manifest "grave compassion."

What is the Bible, continues the essayist, but the written voice of the congregation, and not the written voice of God? Why all this reverence for the sacred

[1] *Essays and Reviews*, p. 68.

writers, since they acknowledge themselves men of like passions with us? Justification by faith is merely peace of mind from trust in a righteous God, and not a fiction of merit by transfer. Regeneration is a correspondent giving of insight or an awakening of the forces of the soul; propitiation is the recovery of peace, and the atonement is our sharing the Saviour's Spirit, but not his purchase of us by his own blood. Throughout the Scriptures we should assume in ourselves a verifying faculty,—conscience, reason, or whatever else we choose to term it.

III. ON THE STUDY OF THE EVIDENCES OF CHRISTIANITY. By Baden Powell, M. A. The author of this essay having recently died, he has therefore incurred less censure than he would otherwise have received. The views here expressed, taken in connection with his more elaborate treatise on the *Order of Nature*, do not place him on the same theoretical ground with Hume and Spinoza; but the moral effect of the present attack upon miracles as an evidence of Christianity is not less antagonistic than the theories of either of those authors. Spinoza held that miracles are impossible, because it would be derogatory to God to depart from the established laws of the universe, and one of Hume's objections to them was their incapability of being proved from testimony.[1]

Professor Powell objects to them because they bear no analogy to the harmony of God's dealings in the material world; and insists that they are not to be credited, since they are a violation of the laws of matter or an interruption of the course of physical causes. The orthodox portion of the Church are laboring under the egregious error of making them an essential doctrine, when they are really a mere external accessory. Rea-

[1] *Replies to Essays and Reviews*, p. 135.

son, and not "our desires" must come to our aid in all examination of them. The key-note to Professor Powell's opposition is contained in the following statement: "From the nature of our antecedent convictions, the probability of *some* kind of mistake or deception somewhere, though we know not *where*, is greater than the probability of the event really happening in *the way* and from the *causes* assigned."[1] The inductive philosophy, for which great respect must be paid, is enlisted against miracles. If we once know all about those alleged and held as such, we would find them resolved into natural phenomena, just as "the angel at Milan was the aerial reflection of an image on a church; the balls of fire at Plausac were electrical; the sea-serpent was a basking shark on a stem of sea-weed. A committee of the French Academy of Sciences, with Lavoisier at its head, after a grave investigation, pronounced the alleged fall of aërolites to be a superstitious fable."[2]

The two theories against the reality of miracles in their received sense, are: *first*, that they are attributable to natural causes; and, *second*, that they may involve more or less of the parabolic or mythic character. These assumptions do away with any real admission of miracles even on religious grounds. The animus of the whole essay may be determined by the following treatment of testimony and reason: "Testimony, after all, is but a second-hand assurance; it is but a blind guide; testimony can avail nothing against reason. The essential question of miracles stands quite apart from any consideration of *testimony;* the question would remain the same, if we had the evidence of our own senses to an alleged miracle; that is, to an extra-

[1] *Essays and Reviews*, p. 120.
[2] Ibid. p. 155.

ordinary or inexplicable fact. It is not the *mere fact*, but the *cause* or *explanation* of it, which is the point at issue."[1] This means far more than Spinoza, Hume, or any other opponent of miracles, except the radical Rationalists of Germany, has claimed,—that we must not believe a miracle though actually witnessed.

IV. Seances Historiques de Geneve—The National Church. By Henry Bristow Wilson, B. D. The Multitudinist principle, or Broad Christianity, is advocated by the essayist with earnestness and an array of learning. The difficulty concerning the non-attendance of a large portion of the British population upon the ordinances of the Church is met by the proposition to abrogate subscription to all creeds and articles of faith, and thus convert the whole nation into a Broad Church. The youth of the land are educated into a false and idolatrous view of the Bible. But on the Census-Sunday of 1861, five millions and a quarter of persons, or forty-two per cent. of the whole population, were not present at service. Many of these people do not believe some of the doctrines preached; they have thought seriously, but cannot sympathize with what they are compelled to hear. If we break down all subscription and include them in the great National Church, we will approach the Scriptural ideal. Unless this be done they will fall into Dissenting hands, and die outside the Church of Christ. There are several proofs of the Scriptural indorsement of Nationalism; Christ's lament over Jerusalem declares that he had offered Multitudinism to the inhabitants nationally, while the three thousand souls converted on the day of Pentecost cannot be supposed to have been individual converts, but merely a mass of persons brought in as a body.

[1] *Essays and Reviews*, p. 159.

Some of the converts of the apostolic age did not believe in the resurrection, which fact implies that the early Churches took collective names from the localities where they were situated, and that doubt of the resurrection should now be no bar to communion in the National Church. Even heathenism in its best form proceeded on the Multitudinist principle, for all were included as believers in the faith of the times. The approval of reason and conscience, and not verbal adherence to human interpretation of Scripture, should be the great test of membership. Advice is administered by the essayist to the Church of which he is a clergyman, in this language: "A national church may also find itself in this position; which, perhaps, is our own. Its ministers may become isolated between two other parties,—between those, on the one hand, who draw fanatical inferences from formularies and principles which they themselves are not able or are unwilling to repudiate; and on the other, those who have been tempted, in impatience of old fetters, to follow free thought heedlessly wherever it may lead them. If our own churchmen expect to discourage and repress a fanatical Christianity without a frank appeal to reason, and a frank criticism of Scripture, they will find themselves without any effectual arms for that combat; or if they attempt to check inquiry by the repetition of old forms and denunciations, they will be equally powerless, and run the especial risk of turning into bitterness the sincerity of those who should be their best allies, as friends of truth. They should avail themselves of the aid of all reasonable persons for enlightening the fanatical religionist, making no reserve of any seemingly harmless or apparently serviceable superstitions of their own. They should also endeavor to supply to the negative theologian some positive elements in Christianity, on grounds more sure to him than the assumption of an objective "faith once delivered to the saints," which he cannot identify with the creed of any church as yet known to him."[1]

V. ON THE MOSAIC COSMOGONY. By C. W. Goodwin, M. A. The assumption is made that the Mosaic account of creation is irreconcilable with the real creation of the earth. We do wrong in elevating that narrative above its proper position, and orthodox geologists have grossly erred in attaching much importance to the language of the first chapter of Genesis. There is nothing poetical or figurative in the whole account; it contains no mystical or symbolical meaning, and is a plain statement of just so much as suited the Jewish mind. All attempts, however, to find any consistency between it and the present state of science are simply absurd. The theory of Chalmers and Buckland, and afterward that of Hugh Miller, are not tenable, for Moses was ignorant of what we now know, and his alleged description is contradicted by scientific inquiry. If then it is plain that God has not thought it needful to communicate to the writer of the Scriptural Cosmogony the knowledge revealed by modern researches, why do we not confess it? We would do so if it did not conflict with a human theory which presumes to point out how God ought to have instructed man.[2] The writer had no authority for what he asserts so solemnly and unhesitatingly, for he was an early speculator who stated as facts what he only conjectured as probabilities. Yet he seized one great truth, in which he anticipated the highest revelation of modern inquiry; namely, the unity

[1] *Essays and Reviews*, pp. 195-196.
[2] Ibid. p. 277.

of the design of the world, and its subordination to one sole Maker and Law-giver.[1] But no one contends that the Mosaic view can be used as a basis of astronomical or geological teaching; and we must therefore consider the Scriptural cosmogony not as "an authentic utterance of divine knowledge, but a human utterance, which it has pleased Providence to use in a special way for the education of mankind."[2]

VI. Tendencies of Religious Thought in England, 1688–1750. By Mark Pattison, B. D. We are surrounded with a Babel of religious creeds and theories, and it is all-important that we should know how we have inherited them. If we would understand our times, we must know the productive influences of the past; if we would thread the present mazes of religious pretension, we should not neglect those immediate agencies in their production that had their origin near the beginning of the eighteenth century. These agencies are three in number: 1. The formation and growth of that compromise between church and state which is called Toleration; 2. Methodism without the Church and the evangelical movement within it; 3. The growth and gradual diffusion, through all religious thinking, of the supremacy of reason. The theology of the Deistic age is identical with Rationalism. That Rationalistic period of England is divided into two parts: from 1688 to 1750, and from 1750 to 1830. The second age may be called that of evidences, when the clergy continued to manufacture evidence as an ingenious exercise,—a literature which was avowedly professional, a study which might seem theology without being it, and which could awaken none of the dormant skepticism beneath the

[1] *Essays and Reviews*, pp. 277-278.
[2] Ibid. p. 278.

surface of society.[1] The defense of the Deists was perhaps as good as the orthodox attack, but they were inquirers after truth, and being guided by reason, they deserve all commendation. Yet they only foreshadowed the glory of the present supremacy of reason. Deism strove eagerly for light; it saw the dawn; the present is the noonday. The human understanding wished to be satisfied, and did not care to believe that of which it could not see the substantial ground. The mind was coming slowly to see that it had duties which it could not devolve upon others, and that a man must think for himself, protect his own rights, and administer his own affairs.

Reason was never less extravagant than in this first essay of its strength; for its demands were modest, and it was easily satisfied,—far too easily, we must think, when we look at some of the reasonings which passed as valid.[2]

English Deism, a system which paralyzed the religious life and thought of the nation, has never had a more enthusiastic eulogist than the author of this historical plea for Rationalism. If the demands of the Deists were "modest," who shall be able to find a term sufficiently descriptive of the claims of their present successors?

VII. On the Interpretation of Scripture. By Benjamin Jowett, M. A. Professor Jowett, as commentator on St. Paul's epistles, had already so defined his position on the science of Scriptural exegesis, that we needed no new information to be convinced of his antagonism to evangelical interpretation. The present essay, which is the most formidable and destructive in

[1] *Essays and Reviews*, p. 287.
[2] Ibid. pp. 328-329.

the volume, commences with a lamentation over the prevailing differences in the exposition of the Bible. The Germans have been far more successful in this respect than the English people, the former having arrived at a tolerable degree of concurrence.

The word "inspiration" is a *crux theologorum*, the most of its explanations being widely divergent, and at variance with the original signification of the term. We make it embrace far too much, for there is no foundation for any high or supernatural views of inspiration in either the Gospels or Epistles. There is no appearance in those writings that their authors had any extraordinary gift, or that they were free from error or infirmity; St. Paul hesitated in difficult cases, and more than once corrected himself; one of the gospel historians does not profess to have been an eye-witness of the events described by him; the evangelists do not agree as to the dwelling-place of Christ's parents, nor concerning the circumstances of the crucifixion; they differ about the woman who anointed our Lord's feet; and the fulfillment of the Old Testament prophecy is not discernible in the New Testament history. To the question, What is inspiration? there are two answers: *first*, That idea of Scripture which we gather from the knowledge of it; and, *second*, that any true doctrine of inspiration must conform to all the ascertained facts of history or of science. The meaning of Scripture has nothing to do with the question of inspiration, for if the word "inspiration" were to become obsolete nothing vital would be lost, since it is but a term of yesterday. The solution of the various difficulties in the gospels is, that the tradition on which the first three are based was preserved orally, and, having been slowly put together, was written in three forms. The writers of the first three gospels were, therefore, not independent witnesses of the history itself. To interpret the Bible properly it must be treated as any other book, "in the same careful and impartial way that we ascertain the meaning of Sophocles or Plato. . . . Scripture, like other books, has one meaning, which is to be gathered from itself, without reference to the adaptations of fathers or divines, and without regard to *à priori* notions about its nature and origin. It is to be interpreted also with attention to the character of its authors, and the prevailing state of civilization and knowledge, with allowance for peculiarities of style and language, and modes of thought and figures of speech; yet not without a sense, that, as we read, there grows upon us the witness of God in the word, anticipating in a rude and primitive age the truth that was to be, shining more and more unto the perfect day in the life of Christ, which again is reflected from different points of view in the teachings of his apostles."[1]

The old methods of interpretation, Jowett concludes, must give place to this new and perfect system, for the growing state of science, the pressing wants of man, and his elevated reason demand it. If this liberal scheme be inaugurated we shall have a higher idea of truth than is supplied by the opinion of mankind in general, or by the voice of parties in a Church.

It is interesting to notice the opinions of the evangelical theologians of Germany, who have long been accustomed to attacks upon Christianity, concerning these English critics. "The authors of the essays," says Hengstenberg, "have been trained in a German school. It is only the echo of German infidelity which we hear from the midst of the English church. They appear to us as parrots, with only this distinction,

[1] *Essays and Reviews*, p. 446.

common among parrots, that they imitate more or less perfectly. The treatise of Temple is in its scientific value about equal to an essay written by the pupils of the middle classes of our colleges. . . . The essay of Goodwin on the Mosaic cosmogony displays the näive assurance of one who receives the modern critical science from the second or tenth hand. The editor [Hengstenberg] asked the now deceased Andreas Wagner, a distinguished professor of natural sciences at the University of Munich, to subject this treatise to an examination from the stand-point of natural science. The offer was accepted, and the book given to him. But after some time it was returned with the remark, that he must take back his promise, as the book was beneath all criticism. . . . All these essays tend toward Atheism. Their subordinate value is seen in the inability of their authors to recognize their goal clearly, and in their want of courage to declare this knowledge. Only Baden Powell forms in this respect an exception. He uses several expressions, in which the grinning spectre makes his appearance almost undisguisedly. He speaks not only sneeringly of the idea of a positive external revelation, which has hitherto formed the basis of all systems of the Christian faith; he even raises himself against the 'Architect of the world,' whom the old English Free Thinkers and Free Masons had not dared to attack."[1]

The *Essays and Reviews* were not long in print before the periodicals called attention to their extraordinary character. Had they not been the *Oxford Essays*, and written by well-known and influential men, they would probably have created but little interest, and passed away with the first or second edition. But

[1] *Evangelische Kirchenzeitung*, *Vorwort*, 1862.

their origin and associations gave them weight at the outset. The press soon began to teem with replies written from every possible stand-point. Volumes of all sizes, from small pamphlets to bulky octavos, were spread abroad as an antidote to the poison. From trustworthy statements we are assured that there have been called forth by the *Essays and Reviews* in England alone nearly four hundred publications. Hardly a newspaper, religious or secular, metropolitan or provincial, has stood aloof from the contest. Every seat of learning has been agitated, the social classes have been aroused, the entire nation has taken part in the strife. Meanwhile, the High Church and Low Church have united in the cordial condemnation of the work. Even some of the First Broad Churchmen have written heartily against its theology and influence.

A remarkable feature of the whole controversy is the judicial prosecution of the essayists. Petitions numerously signed were presented to the bishops, praying that some action might be taken against them. One protest contained the signatures of nine thousand clergymen of the Established church; and the bishops, without a single exception, took ground against the theological bearing of the *Essays and Reviews.* The Convocations of Canterbury and York, which possessed the full exercise of their legislative functions for the first time in one hundred and fifty years, declared against it, and pledged their influence to protect the church from the "pernicious doctrines and heretical tendencies of the book." After much deliberation and counsel, Dr. Williams and Mr. Wilson were summoned before the court of Arches, the chief ecclesiastical tribunal of England. Finally, June 21, 1864, decision was pronounced that they had departed from the teachings of the Thirty-Nine Articles on the inspiration of Holy Scripture, on the atonement, and on justification. They were therefore suspended for one year, with the further penalty of costs and deprivation of their salary. At the urgent solicitation of friends, in addition to their own strong desire to push their defense as far as possible, their case was brought before the Privy Council, a court of which the Queen is a member, and from which there can be no appeal. Contrary to the general expectation, the decision of the Court of Arches was reversed, and the essayists in question were restored to their functions. The reversal of the decision of the Court of Arches is couched in the following significant language: "On the general tendency of the book called 'Essays and Reviews,' and on the effort or aim of the whole essay of Dr. Williams, or the whole essay of Mr. Wilson, we neither can, nor do, pronounce any opinion. On the short extracts before us, our Judgment is that the charges are not proved. Their Lordships, therefore, will humbly recommend to Her Majesty that the sentences be reversed, and the reformed articles be rejected in like manner as the rest of the original articles; but inasmuch as the Appellants have been obliged to come to this Court, their Lordships think it right that they should have the costs of this Appeal."[1] This action was regarded by every skeptical sympathizer as a great triumph, and we may therefore expect the Rationalistic school to engage in

[1] *Ecclesiastical Judgments of the Privy Council*, p. 289. Edited by Hon. G. C. Brodrick, and the Rev. W. H. Freemantle. London, 1865. The members of the Queen's Privy Council are as follows: Earls Granville and Lonsdale; Duke of Buccleugh; Marquis of Salisbury; Lords Westbury, Brougham, Cranworth, Wensleydale, St. Leonards, Chelmsford, and Kindsdown; and Right Hons. Lushington, Bruce, Wigram, Ryan, Pollock, Romilly, Turner, Cockburn, Coleridge, Erle, and Wylde.

still more important enterprises than any to which they have addressed themselves.

The most outspoken and violent attacks of critical Rationalism in England are contained in the exegetical publications of Dr. John William Colenso, who, in 1853, was consecrated Bishop of Natal, South Eastern Africa. He had previously issued a series of mathematical works which obtained a wide circulation; but his first book of scriptural criticism was the *Epistle to the Romans, newly translated and explained from a Missionary Point of View.* Having completed the New Testament and several parts of the Old, he was laboring assiduously on a translation of the Bible into the Zulu tongue, when his former doubts concerning the unhistorical character of the Pentateuch revived with increased force. The intelligent native who was assisting him in his literary work asked, respecting the account of the flood, "Is all that true?" This, with other inquiries propounded to him by the Zulus, led him to a careful reëxamination of the Mosaic record.

The fruit of this additional study is the *Pentateuch and Book of Joshua critically examined, in Three Parts.* Appearing just at the time when the contest concerning the *Essays and Reviews* was at fever-heat, the Bishop's work added excitement to all the combatants.

Those who are intimately acquainted with the treatment of the Pentateuch and Book of Joshua by the most unsparing of the German Rationalists will at once see the resemblance between their views and those of Colenso. His aim is to overthrow the historical character of the early Scriptural history by exposing the contradictions and impossibilities contained therein; and also to fix the real origin, age and authorship of the so-called narratives of Moses and Joshua. "I have arrived at the conviction," says he, "that the Pentateuch, as a whole, cannot possibly have been written by Moses, or by any one acquainted personally with the facts which it professes to describe, and, further, that the so-called Mosaic narrative, by whomsoever written, and though imparting to us, as I fully believe it does, revelations of the Divine will and character, cannot be regarded as *historically true*. . . . My reason for no longer receiving the Pentateuch as historically true, is not that I find insuperable difficulties with regard to the *miracles* or supernatural *revelations* of Almighty God recorded in it, but solely that I cannot, as a true man, consent any longer to shut my eyes to the absolute, palpable self-contradictions of the narrative. The notion of miraculous or supernatural interferences does not present to my own mind the difficulties which it seems to present to some. I could believe and receive the miracles of Scripture heartily, if only they were authenticated by a veracious history; though, if that is not the case with the Pentateuch, any miracles, which rest on such an unstable support, must necessarily fall to the ground with it.[1]

In proof of this assumption the author selects a large number of inexplicable portions from the narratives in question, and uses all the resources of his talents and learning to prove them to be the fruit of "error, infirmity, passion, and ignorance." Hezron and Hanuel, he avers, were certainly born in the land of Canaan; the whole assembly of Israel could not have gathered about the door of the tabernacle; all Israel could not have been heard by Moses, for they numbered about two millions of people, according to the assumption of the Biblical narrative. The Israelites could not have

[1] *Pentateuch and Book of Joshua.* Part I., pp. 49, 51-52. Am. Edition.

dwelt in tents; they were not armed; the institution of the Passover, as described in the book of Exodus, was an impossibility, the Israelites could not take cattle through the barren country over which they passed; there is an incompatibility between the supposed number of Israel and the predominance of wild beasts in Palestine; the number of the first-born is irreconcilable with the number of male adults; and the number of the priests at the exodus cannot be harmonized with their duties, and with the provision made for them.[1] These, with other difficulties chiefly of a numerical nature, constitute the basis on which the Bishop builds his objections to the historical character of Exodus as an integral part of the Pentateuch.

In order to determine the true quality of the Book of Genesis, he brings out the old theory that the work had two writers, the *Elohist* and the *Jehovist*,—so called because of their separate use of a term for Deity. The Elohist was the older, and his narrative was the ground-work which the Jehovist used and upon which he constructed his own additions.[2] This Elohist account is defined to be "a series of parables, based, as we have said, on legendary facts, though not historically true." [3] The Pentateuch existed originally not as five books, but as one; and it is possible that its quintuple division was made in the time of Ezra. The writer of Chronicles was the same who wrote the books of Ezra and Nehemiah, probably a Levite living after the time of Nehemiah; the Chronicles were therefore written only four hundred years before Christ; but the Chronicler must not be relied on unless there is other

[1] *Pentateuch and Book of Joshua*, Part I., pp. 60, 78, 81, 94, 105, 118, 138, 141, 185.

[2] *Pentateuch and Book of Joshua.* Part II., p. 60.

[3] Ibid. p. 296.

evidence in support of his narrative. Exodus could not have been written by Moses or any one of his contemporaries. It is very probable that the Pentateuch generally was composed in a later age than that of Moses or Joshua.[1] Samuel was most likely the author of the Elohistic legends, which he left at his death in an unfinished state, and which naturally fell into the hands of some one of his disciples of the School of the Prophets, such, for instance, as Nathan or Gad.[2]

Yet the writer of the Pentateuch must not be reproached for his errors as much as those who would attribute to him infallible accuracy. He had no idea that he was writing truth. "But," says the Bishop, "there is not the slightest reason to suppose that the first writer of the story in the Pentateuch ever professed to be recording *infallible truth*, or even *actual, historical truth.* He wrote certainly a narrative. But what indications are there that he published it at large, even to the people of his own time, as a record of *matter-of-fact, veracious history?* Why may not Samuel, like any other Head of an Institution, have composed this narrative for the instruction and improvement of his pupils, from which it would gradually find its way, no doubt, more or less freely, among the people at large, without ever pretending that it was any other than an historical *experiment*,—an attempt to give them some account of the early annals of their tribes? In *later* days, it is true, this ancient work of Samuel's came to be regarded as infallibly Divine. But was it so regarded in the writer's days, or in the ages immediately following? On the contrary, we find no sign of the Mosaic Law being venerated, obeyed, or even known, in many of its most

[1] *Pentateuch and Book of Joshua*, Part II., pp. 83, 84, 115.

[2] Ibid. p. 160.

remarkable features, till a much later time in history."[1]

The excitement occasioned by the publication of these views of Colenso was second only to that produced by the *Essays and Reviews*. There was a decided disposition on the part of the ecclesiastical authorities to deal summarily with him, since he had been intrusted with the Episcopal office, and sent as a missionary to the heathen. Several of the Bishops early took ground against his destructive criticism, and refused to allow him to officiate within their dioceses. The Convocations of York and Canterbury united in condemnation of his work. There was a difference of opinion as to the best method of depriving him of his episcopal authority. In the dilemma it was resolved to appeal to him without any appearance of legal pressure; whereupon the Bishops of England and Ireland, with but three exceptions, Drs. Thirlwall, Fitzgerald, and Griffin, addressed him a letter, in which he was requested to resign his office, since he must see, as well as they, the inconsistency of holding his position as Bishop and believing and publishing such views as were contained in his exegetical works. His reply was a positive refusal, coupled with the statement that he would soon return to his See in Africa, there to continue the discharge of his duties. The Episcopal Bench of England failing to eject him, he was tried and condemned before an Episcopal Synod, which assembled in Cape Town, Southern Africa, on November 27th, 1863.

The charges against Colenso were:—his denial of the atonement; belief in man's justification without any knowledge of Christ; belief in natal regeneration; disbelief in the endlessness of future punishment; denial of

[1] *Pentateuch and Book of Joshua.* Part II., p. 292.

the inspiration of the Holy Scriptures, and of the truthfulness of what they profess to describe as facts; denial of the divinity of our blessed Lord; and depraving, impugning, and bringing into disrepute the Book of Common Prayer. Having been adjudged guilty, he was deposed from his office as Bishop of Natal, and thenceforth prohibited from the exercise of all ministerial functions within any part of the metropolitical province of Cape Town. Being absent in England at the time of the trial, Colenso was represented by Dr. Bleek, who protested against the legality of the proceedings and the validity of the judgment, at the same time giving notice of his intention to appeal. But the Metropolitan of Cape Town refused to recognize any appeal, except to the Archbishop of Canterbury, which must be made within fifteen days from sentence. Immediately after the deposition, the Dean of Natal, the Archdeacon, the parochial clergy, and the churchwardens of the diocese, signed a declaration, by which they pledged themselves not to recognize Colenso any longer as their Bishop.

Before Colenso was served with a copy of the decree against him, he issued a letter to his diocese, in which he denied the power claimed by the Metropolitan and the other bishops of Cape Town to depose him. He maintained that, of the nine charges brought against him, four had already been disposed of by the late judgment of the Privy Council in the case of the *Essays and Reviews*. In the meanwhile, his friends at home collected a fund of more than two thousand pounds to enable him to plead his cause before the English courts. The first proceeding in Great Britain commenced in 1863, before the judicial committee of the Privy Council. The case has finally been decided in Colenso's favor, the Lord

Chancellor declaring the sentence pronounced by the Bishop of Cape Town illegal, in the following words: "As the question can be decided only by the sovereign or head of the Established Church and depositary of appellate jurisdiction, their Lordships will humbly report to Her Majesty their judgment and opinion that the proceedings taken by the Bishop of Cape Town, and the judgment or sentence pronounced by him against the Bishop of Natal, are null and void."

But while this judgment of the Privy Council annulled the proceedings against Colenso, it also destroyed his Episcopal authority by pronouncing that the letters patent of the Queen, by which he was made Bishop, had neither been authorized by any Parliamentary statute nor confirmed by the legislative council of Natal. His continuance in authority, therefore, was made dependent on the voluntary recognition of the clergy within the diocese of Natal. But the latest intelligence reveals the important fact that the clergy unanimously refuse to recognize his Episcopal authority, and have asked the Bishop of Cape Town to administer the diocese until a new appointment can be made for the See of Natal. The trustees of the Colonial Bishops' fund have also declared that they will no longer pay the salary of Colenso. He has already set sail for Southern Africa, but on his arrival will find himself without a clergy or a people to recognize his jurisdiction. Dr. Pusey has written an interesting letter, in which he hails the decision of the Privy Council as an indication that the church of South Africa will soon be as free and prosperous as the Scotch Episcopal church and the church of the United States.

The remaining parts of the Bishop's *Commentary on the Pentateuch and Book of Joshua* have met with a tardy and cold reception. We accept this as a hopeful sign that no great portion of the people are willing to adopt his theological views. The first two parts, however, created an excitement which was not confined to Christian lands. Even a Mussulman addressed a letter from the Cape of Good Hope to a Turkish paper at Constantinople, in which he gives an account of the Christians in that colony, together with a description of their multiform dissensions. "Their priests," he writes, "all advocate different creeds; and as to their bishops, one Colenso actually writes books against his own religion." It may be more a gratification of the vanity than flattering to the piety of the late Missionary to the Zulus to be informed that already the Buddhists of India are making free use of his works as an invaluable aid in their controversies with the missionaries from Christian lands. Thus the herald of the cross of Christ in heathen nations must encounter not only the superstition and prejudices of paganism, but the infidelity exported from his own home, where for centuries the battles of the truth have been fought and won.

CHAPTER XXII.

ENGLAND CONTINUED: SURVEY OF CHURCH PARTIES.

THE Church of England has always been proud of the outward form of unity. Her rigid view of the sin of schism has induced her to submit to great elasticity of opinion and teaching rather than incur the traditional disgrace of open division. But on this very account she has never been free from internal strife. In everything but in name she has been for centuries not one church, but several. Her entire history discloses two tendencies balancing each other, and for the most part reacting to great advantage. The Sacramentalist party represents Romanizing tendencies, and is thoroughly devoted to "the sacramental services and the offices of the church, especially as performed according to the rubric." The Evangelical party is less formal, is in harmony with the Articles, aims to keep up with the accumulating religious wants of society, and lays stress upon the practical evidences of Christian life. Under these two standards may be ranked all those schools within the pale of the Church which have been growing into prominence since the closing years of the eighteenth century. We will only speak of the most influential parties, remembering, however, that each of them is again subdivided into various sections.

THE LOW CHURCH. Within a short time after the Church of England gave signs of religious awakening in consequence of the rise of the Wesleyan movement, the triumph of evangelical tendencies was complete. "In less than twenty years," says Conybeare, "the original battle-field was won, and the enemy may be said to have surrendered at discretion. Thenceforward, scarcely a clergyman was to be found in England who preached against the doctrines of the creed. The faith of the church was restored to the level of her formularies."[1] The revival was so thorough that it gave rise to a zealous class which was called by its friends the Evangelical Party, but by its enemies the Low Church.

The Low Church had its seat at Cambridge, and was conducted by vigorous theologians, who were encouraged and aided by highly-respected and leading laymen. Attaching new importance to the neglected doctrines, their principal themes were "the universal necessity of conversion," "justification by faith," and "the sole authority of Scripture as the rule of faith." They were worthy successors of the old Evangelical party, represented by Milner, Martyn, and Wilberforce. Through their agency there arose in the popular mind a dislike of ecclesiastical landmarks, the state church fell into disrepute, the broadest catholicity received hearty support, and personal piety was the acknowledged test of true religion. In 1828 Lord Russell, the leader of the Reform party, effected the abrogation of the Test Act,—a law which required all officers, civil and military, to receive the sacrament according to the usage of the Established church, and to take an oath against transubstantiation within six months after their entrance into office. The repeal

[1] *Essays Ecclesiastical and Social*, pp. 62-63.

immediately placed Dissenters and Catholics upon the same footing with members of the Established church, and was in itself sufficient to provoke opposition on the part of all who had not united in the evangelical movement. But the antagonism became still more decided when Parliament passed the Irish Church Property Act, in 1833, in spite of the determined remonstrances of the bishops. One half of the Irish bishoprics were thereby abrogated, Parliament assuming ecclesiastical authority. The people supported the Parliament, and in some instances public indignation was hurled at the bishops themselves.

The Low Church has always been on the side of popular reform. Not forgetful of its lineal descent from that evangelical spirit which animated Wilberforce, Stephen, Thornton, and Buxton, in their philanthropic labors, it has sought out the population of the factories and mines of England, and addressed itself to the relief of their cramped and stifled inmates. It has reorganized Ragged-Schools, and endeavored to reach all the suffering classes of the kingdom. Neither has it been found unmindful of the wants of the heathen world, for no sooner did the Low Church commence its public career than it founded the Church Missionary Society, which has established over one hundred and forty-eight missionary stations, sustains two hundred and sixty-six clergymen, and includes about twenty thousand members.[1] These labors have been abundantly successful, for besides the converted towns on the coast of Africa, "whole districts of Southern India have embraced the faith; and the native population of New Zealand (spread over a territory as large as England) has been reclaimed from cannibalism

[1] *Christian Work*, June, 1863.

and added to the church." The same party was chiefly instrumental in establishing the British and Foreign Bible Society, which has translated the Scriptures into one hundred and fifty languages, and distributes over two millions of copies annually.

The Low Church party was the first to tell England that her population had far outgrown her places of worship, and it accordingly devised means to remedy the evil. Archbishop Sumner founded the first Diocesan Church Building Society, in 1828; and after becoming Bishop of Chester consecrated more than two hundred new churches. Mr. Simeon of Cambridge had previously set the example of caring for the unchurched population by his personal labors and the outlay of his large private fortune. His name is now like "ointment poured forth" among the inhabitants of Bath, Clifton, Bradford, and other places. The Pastoral Aid Society was founded in 1836, and by its lay and clerical employees, is now ministering to the spiritual wants of over three millions of souls. The Low Churchmen have also established, in needy localities, Sunday Schools, Infant Schools, Lending Libraries, Benefit Societies, Clothing Clubs, and Circles of Scripture Readers. From the ranks of this party have arisen devout and zealous preachers, who, without any great natural endowments, have given their hearts to the work of saving souls. Hamilton Forsyth, Spencer Thornton, and Henry Fox, —the follower of Henry Martyn to Southern India,— are names which will ever adorn the history of the Church of England.[1]

At the present time the Low Church is leading the van within the Establishment, in all those movements which have the stamp of true piety. It is seeking

[1] Conybeare, *Essays Ecclesiastical and Social*, pp. 65–71.

out the abandoned and homeless wretches in the darkest sinks of London, reading the Bible to them, clothing, finding work, and training them to self-respect. Some of its clergy are among the most gifted and influential in Great Britain, whether at the editor's table, in the pulpit, or on the platform. The lofty position they have lately taken against the inroads of Rationalism entitles them to the thanks and admiration of Christendom.

Within the Low Church there are two subdivisions. The first is the Recordite party, so called from its organ. It intensifies the doctrines of the Low Church; on justification by faith it builds its view of the worthlessness of morality; on conversion by grace its predestinarian fatalism; and on the supremacy of Scripture its dogma of verbal inspiration. It holds strong Biblical views on the sanctity of the Sabbath, and both by the pulpit and the press, opposes the secularization of the Lord's day. The other party is sneeringly called the "Low and Slow," and corresponds with a similar faction within the High Church which enjoys the sobriquet of the "High and Dry."

After the evangelical movement had fully taken root there arose an antagonistic tendency; it was the old Sacramentalist party re-asserting itself. Oxford arrayed itself against Cambridge. The views of Laud had always found favor in the former seat of learning, and their adherents felt that the time had now come for their vigorous revival. They directed their opposition equally against Parliamentary usurpation and evangelical liberalism. The centre of the counter-movement was Oriel College, which, under Whately, Hampden, and Thomas Arnold, was already celebrated for its new spirit of free scientific inquiry. Keble, Pusey, Froude, and J. H. Newman, were here associated either as fellows or students. Froude recognized the truth of the saying of Vicentius: "*Quod semper, quod ubique, quod ab omnibus creditum est.*" He rose above his friends as leader of the whole movement.

The Conference which convened at Hadley, was the first organized demonstration against the evangelical portion of the Low Church. Its initiative act was the adoption of a catechism which contained the views of the High Churchmen, and was the first issue of the celebrated series of Tracts which gave to the new movement the name of Tractarianism. It was published in 1833, and the last of the series, the ninetieth, appeared seven years afterward. Newman and Pusey were the chief writers. Pusey preached a sermon in 1843 which avowed, with only slight modifications, the doctrine of transubstantiation; in consequence of which he was deposed from preaching to the university for the space of two years. The Romish church received flattering eulogy from all the High Churchmen or Tractarians. It was represented by them as the embodiment of all that was grand, imposing, and sound in art, poetry, or theology. When Newman went over to its fold, Pusey said of him: "He has been called to labor in another part of the Lord's vineyard." The High Church went so far in its opposition to the Low that many attached to the former felt more attracted to Roman Catholicism than to any form of Protestantism. Accordingly, at the close of 1846, one hundred and fifty clergymen and distinguished laymen had gone over to Popery.

The doctrines of the High Church may be divided into two classes: the material, or justification by sacraments; and the formal, or the authority of the church.

While it declares that we are justified by faith, it also holds that we are judged by works. Men are converted by grace, but Christians are regenerated by baptism. The Scriptures are supreme authority, but the "church hath authority in controversies of faith," by virtue of its apostolic descent. The watchwords of the High Church are, therefore, judgment by works; baptismal regeneration; church authority; and apostolical succession. Faith, it claims, does not justify us in and of itself, but simply brings us to God, who then justifies us by his free grace. Baptism is regeneration; in the New Testament the new birth is always connected with it; we are not born of faith, or of love, or of prayer, but by water and the Spirit. All Tractarians believe in the real presence of Christ, and only differ as to the mode in which he is present. The consecrated elements become really the body and blood of Christ by virtue of the consecrating word, though the change takes place in a spiritual and inexpressible way. Christ is a kind Saviour to those who partake of the sacrament of the Lord's Supper worthily, but a harsh judge to those who do it unworthily.

High Churchmen hold that the Church is a saving institution founded by Christ, and continued by apostolical succession. It is the only mediator of salvation in Christ in so far as it is the only dispenser of the means of grace, the only protectress and witness of the truth, and the highest authority in matters of faith and practice. There are three tests of the true Church: *first*, apostolicity, or the divine origin of the Church and its succession of apostles; *second*, catholicity, or the truth in matters of instruction and life communicated through the succession of the apostles, the truth in matters of faith and life as interpreted by Scripture and tradition; and, *third*, autonomy, or the absolute independence and supreme authority of the Church in faith and practice.

Apostolical succession was the first dogma in which all High Churchmen united. Connected with this opinion is the idea that the priesthood is the only mediatorial office between Christ and the congregation. The bishops are the spiritual sons of the apostles, and should be respected for their office' sake; Christ is the Mediator above, but his servant, the bishop, is his image on earth.[1] The Church has authority to forgive sins by the new birth, and to bring souls from hell to heaven.[2] Tradition must be respected not less than the Bible itself; the Old and New Testaments are the fountain of the doctrines, and the catholic fathers the channel through which they flow down to us.[3] The Bible must be explained, not by individual opinion, but by the church; for the Church is its rightful interpreter.

It must be said, in justice to the High Church, that while it attaches great weight to these views it does not discard those really important. It does not overlook the doctrines maintained by the majority of evangelical Christians. The moderate members of this party, especially, do not hold them as "the basis of their system, but only as secondary and ornamental details. Even against Dissenters they are not rigidly enforced. The hereditary non-conformist is not excluded from salvation. Foreign Protestants are even owned as brethren, though a mild regret is expressed that they lack the blessing of an authorized church government. Apostolical succession is not practically made essential to the being of a church, but rather cherished as a dignified and ancient pedigree, connecting our English episcopate with

[1] *Tract No.* 10. [2] Sewel.

[3] Pusey, *Preface to* 18th *vol. Library of Church Fathers.*

primitive antiquity, and binding the present to the past by a chain of filial piety. In the same hands, church authority is reduced to little more than a claim to that deference which is due from the ignorant to the learned, from the taught to the teacher."[1]

Of the general service rendered by the High Churchmen, the same writer says, "Their system gives freer scope to the feelings of reverence, awe, and beauty than that of their opponents. They endeavor, and often successfully, to enlist these feelings in the service of piety. Music, painting, and architecture, they consecrate as the handmaids of religion. Thus they attract an order of men chiefly found among the most cultivated classes, whose hearts must be reached through their imagination rather than their understanding. . . In the same spirit the writers of this party have contributed to the religious literature of the day many admirable works which under the guise of fiction teach the purest Christianity, and exemplify its bearing in every detail of common life. To the training of childhood especially they have rendered most valuable aid, by thus embodying the precepts of the Gospel. But we need not do more than allude to works so universally known and valued as those of Miss Sewell, Mr. Adams, and Bishop Wilberforce. Again the revival of the High Church party has effected an important improvement among the clergy. Many of these were prejudiced by hereditary dislike against the doctrines and the persons of the Evangelicals, and by this prejudice were repelled from religion. But under the name of orthodoxy and the banner of High Church, they have willingly received truth against which, had it come to them in another shape, they would have closed their ears and

[1] Conybeare, *Essays Ecclesiastical and Social*, p. 106.

hearts. A better spirit has thus been breathed into hundreds who but for this new movement would have remained as their fathers were before them, mere Nimrods, Ramrods, or Fishing-rods."[1]

Of all the men engaged in the Tractarian enterprise there was no one in whose religious and personal history a deeper public interest concentrated than in John Henry Newman. His ardent espousal of the High Church cause collected many friends about him at the same time that it organized numerous enemies. But he did not inquire concerning the number of his friends or foes, for he valued sincerity higher than favor or opposition. His previous history was not without incident. Thirteen years before the *Tracts for the Times* were published, he had been engaged in a controversy concerning baptismal regeneration, in which he defended the evangelical side.[2] Subject to various inner conflicts, and greatly influenced by the party-spirit which ran high, he finally entered the communion of the Roman Catholic Church. His view of the development of Christian doctrine is very favorable to his adopted faith. Development can be applied to anything which has real vital power; it is the key that unlocks the mystery of all growth; any philosophy or policy, Christianity included, requires time for its comprehension and perfection. The highest truths of inspiration needed only the longer time and deeper thought for their full elucidation, for perfection can be reached only by trials and sore conflicts. A philosophy or sect is purer and stronger when its channel has grown deep and broad by the flow of time. Its vital element needs disengagement from that which is foreign and temporary, and its

[1] *Essays Ecclesiastical and Social*, pp. 106-108.

[2] *National Review*, Oct., 1856.

beginning is no measure of its capabilities or scope. At first no one knows what it is or what it is worth, since it seems in suspense which way to go; but notwithstanding this, it strikes out and develops all its hidden world of force. Surrounding things change, but these changes only contribute to its development. Here below, to live is to change, and to be perfect is to have changed often. This is all true of Christianity; the lapse of years, instead of injuring it, has only brought out its power.[1]

These hints furnish a specimen of the ideal robe in which Father Newman clothes Romanism. But it will take a stronger intellect than his to show any harmony between his theory of development and the history of the papacy. He has once more assumed the pen of the controversialist. In the January number of *Macmillan's Magazine*, 1864, Kingsley, in a review of Froude's History of the reign of Queen Elizabeth, said, "Truth for its own sake has never been a virtue with the Roman clergy. Father Newman informs us that it need not be, and, on the whole, ought not to be; that cunning is the weapon which Heaven has given to the saints wherewith to withstand the brute man's force of the wicked world, which marries and is given in marriage." The venerable Father being thus assailed has given vent to his indignation by a defense of his life, under the title of *Apologia Pro Vita Sua*. It abounds in rare touches of satire; while Kingsley, in his reply, indicates excitement and bitterness.

The younger brother, Francis William Newman, has led a sad and changeful life. It has many features in common with Blanco White, both of whom betray the destructive absence of a positive evangelical faith. In

[1] *Development of Christian Doctrine.* Second Edition. London, 1846.

some skeptics there is a strength of will which gives a successful appearance to their cause in spite of all their doubts; but when the will is subjected to the domination of opinion; when religion, whether true or false, is not an appendage but the principle of life, the power of mere sentiment is fully manifested. The younger Newman is an illustration of the position in which one is left when he throws himself into the arms of a false creed.

He reveals his inner life in the *Phases of Faith*, one of the most touching pieces of biography in the realm of literature. While a student at Oxford, he became enamored with the "Oriel heresy about Sunday." One by one the views of the standard authorities of the Church lost their hold upon him, and he imbibed the opinion that the Old Testament is not really the rule of life, according to the Pauline idea; infant baptism is an excrescence of a post-apostolic age, and Wall's attempt to trace it to the Apostles a decided failure; Episcopacy has been so contemptibly represented by incumbents, some of whom opposed the Missionary and Bible Societies, that it is not entitled to respect; and the Church Fathers are greatly overrated, Clement alone being respectable.

Unable to find any theological resting-place, Newman went as a quasi-missionary to Bagdad. He returned to Oxford and gave himself up to his increasing doubts. Finally, becoming a Unitarian, the Scriptures present new difficulties; Christianity has been too highly praised and flattered; and has had the credit of doing a great deal which it has had no share in effecting. The Bible has not been found able to cope with fresh evils; and Romanism became corrupt and vicious with that book in the hands of the priesthood. But dissatisfied as

Newman is with the present, he takes a cheerful look upon the future. "The age is ripe," he says, "for something better, for a religion which shall combine the tenderness, humility, and disinterestedness which are the glory of the present Christianity, with that activity of intellect, untiring pursuit of truth, and strict adherence to impartial principle which the schools of modern science embody. When a spiritual church has its senses exercised to discern good and evil, judges of right and wrong by an inward power, proves all things, and holds fast that which is good, fears no truth, but rejoices in being corrected, intellectually as well as morally, it will not be liable to 'be carried to and fro' by shifting wind of doctrine. It will indeed have movement, namely, a steady *onward* one, as the schools of science have had since they left off to dogmatize, and approached God's world as learners; but it will lay aside disputes of words, eternal vacillations, mutual ill-will and dread of new light, and will be able, without hypocrisy, to proclaim 'peace on earth and good will toward men,' even toward those who reject its beliefs and sentiments concerning God and his glory." [1]

THE FIRST BROAD CHURCH. The division of the Broad Church into two parties has been produced by the recent discussion. The First Broad Church corresponds in the main with philosophical Rationalism. It commenced with Coleridge, was interpreted principally by Hare, was defended by the chaste and vigorous pen of Arnold, and is now represented by Maurice, Kingsley, and Stanley. It cannot be said to have a distinct creed. Its members being attached to the Established Church, they are distinguished peculiarly for their method of interpretation of the ar-

[1] *Phases of Faith*, pp. 233, 234. American Edition.

ticles of faith. "The Broad Church teachers give us readings of each dogma of the Atonement and Future Punishment." [1] They avow the main doctrines of the Gospel, but in such a modified sense that, they say, the same were held virtually by all Christians in every age; by Loyola and Xavier, not less than by Latimer and Ridley. They conceive the essence of Popery to consist, not in points of metaphysical theology, but in the ascription of magic virtue to outward acts. All who believe the Scriptures are, in their opinion, members of the household of faith. Salvation does not depend upon the ritual but upon the life; the fruits of the Spirit are the sole criteria of the Spirit's presence. They give prominence to the idea of the visible Church when they hold the Church to be a Society divinely instituted for the purpose of manifesting God's presence, and bearing witness to his attributes, by their reflection in its ordinances and in its members. If its ideal were fully embodied in its actual constitution "it would remind us daily of God, and work upon the habits of our life as insensibly as the air we breathe.[2] For this end, it would revive "daily services, frequent communions, memorials of our Christian calling, presented to our notice in crosses and wayside oratories; commemorations to holy men of all times and countries; religious orders, especially of women, of different kinds and under different rules, delivered only from the snare and sin of perpetual vows." [3]

The special defender of these views of the visible Church, the late Dr. Thomas Arnold, of Rugby, was a man of great industry, profound erudition, and extraor-

[1] Miss Cobbe, *Broken Lights*, p. 63. London Edition.

[2] Arnold, *Sermons*, vol. iv., p. 307.

[3] Ibid. *Introduction*, p. 56.

dinary power and tact in the management of youth. His sermons, delivered to his pupils at Rugby, were short, and usually written just before delivery in the school-chapel on Sabbath afternoons.[1] He interested himself in all questions of reform, education, politics, and literature. But he is best known as one of the leaders of the Broad Church, and in this light his theological opinions may be considered a fair sample of the theology adopted by that party in its earlier and purer days. With him, inspiration is not equivalent to a communication of the divine perfections. Paul expected the world would come to an end in the generation then existing. The Scripture narratives are not only about divine things, but are themselves divinely framed and superintended. Inspiration does not raise a man above his own time, nor make him, even in respect to that which he utters when inspired, perfect in goodness and wisdom; but it so overrules his language that it shall contain a meaning more than his own mind was conscious of, and thus give to it a character of divinity, and a power of perpetual application.[2]

According to Arnold, Christ was the sum of the Bible, and the centre of all truth. We cannot come to God directly; Christ is to us in place of God; and he is God, for to hold the contrary would be idolatry. Christ suffered for the Church, not only as a man may suffer for man by being involved in evils through the fault of another, and by his example awakening in others a spirit of like patience and self-devotion, but in a higher and more complete sense, as

[1] *Bibliotheca Sacra.* Jan. 1858. An excellent summary of the opinions of Dr. Arnold.

[2] Stanley, *Life and Correspondence of Arnold.* American Edition, p. 135.

suffering for them, the just for the unjust, that they, for his sake, should be regarded by God as innocent. In a deep sense of moral evil, more, perhaps, than in anything else, a saving knowledge of God abides. Sin must not be lightly considered. Christ's death shows it to be an exceeding evil; and the actions of whole days and weeks, passed as they are by too many in utter carelessness, are nothing but one mass of sin; and no one thing in them has been sanctified by the thought of God or of Christ.

The penalty of sin, according to Arnold, is one of the revelations of Scripture which men are least inclined to hear. It will be true of every one of us, that, unless we turn to Christ, it had been better that we were never born. If we fail of the grace of God there is reserved for us an indescribable misery. Conversion is the development of Christian life. It is growth. We must be changed during the three score and ten years of our life, not in the twinkling of an eye, but through a long period of prayer and watchfulness, laboring slowly and with difficulty to get rid of our evil nature.[1] By constant repentance and faith we ripen for heaven. Justification by faith is a reliance on what God has done for us; faith in Christ is not only faith in his having died for us, but in him as our present Saviour by his life. It is throwing ourselves upon him in all things, as our Redeemer, Saviour, Head, of whom we are members, and desire our life only for Him. Our dependence in Christ is not once only, but perpetual.

Arnold attached paramount importance to a proper understanding of the Church and its relations to the State. He held that the work of a Christian Church and State is absolutely one and the same, and that the

[1] *Interpretation of Scripture*, p. 493.

full development of the former in its perfect form as the Kingdom of God, will be an effectual means for the removal of all evil and the promotion of good. There can be no perfect Church or State without their blending into one.[1] The Church, during her imperfect state, is deficient in power; the State, in the like condition is deficient in knowledge; one judges amiss of man's highest happiness, the other discerns it truly, but has not the power on a large scale to attain it. But when blended into one, the power and knowledge become happily united; the Church has become sovereign, and the State has become Christian.[2] The Church has its living and redeemed members; it may have those who are craving to be admitted within its shelter, being convinced that God is in it of a truth; but beyond these, he who is not with it is against it.[3]

In intimate connection with Arnold stands the name of his friend and biographer, Arthur P. Stanley, Dean of Westminster, for some years a writer of celebrity in England. Two late volumes on the *Eastern* and *Jewish Churches* have given him a standing occupied by few theologians in the old or the new world. His style is gorgeous and enchanting, and his Rationalistic tendencies so subdued and covert that few would suspect him of sympathy with the Broad Church theology of the last ten years' growth. In his work on *Sinai and Palestine* he aimed to delineate the outward events of the Old and New Testament in such a way that they should come home with a new power to those who, by long familiarity, had almost ceased to regard them as historical truth; and so to bring out their inward

[1] Stanley, *Life and Correspondence*, pp. 341, 367.
[2] *Fragment on the Church*, p. 226.
[3] *Christian Life, its Course, &c.*, p. 358.

spirit that the more complete realization of their outward form should not degrade but exalt the faith of which they are the vehicle. But in subsequent works, Dean Stanley has clearly departed from an evangelical position, and we now find him in open sympathy with the Broad Church. This tendency was foreshadowed in his *History of the Jewish Church.* He describes miracles as one who prefers to omit, rather than state, his real objections to their reception. He seems to believe in Israel as an inspired people, more than in the Old Testament as a plenarily inspired book. He allows searching criticism into the Hebrew text, and does not seem disturbed by evidences of errors, contradictions, and phantasy. He does not know whether the Israelites were in Egypt two hundred and fifteen, four hundred and thirty, or one thousand years,—thus leaving an important question unsettled. Neither does he decide, with or against Colenso, whether the number of armed Israelites who left Egypt was six hundred or six hundred thousand men. He implies that monotheism was unknown before Abraham, and that the name Jehovah was not known to Abraham, Isaac, or Jacob. He cannot tell how the Israelites were supported in their journeyings; and ascribes the priesthood to an Egyptian origin. If we only admit the above arithmetical errors, and give up the Mosaic authorship of the Pentateuch, he thinks we should remove at one stroke some of the main difficulties of the Mosaic narrative.[1]

But Stanley has exposed his Broad Church sympathies more in a late review article than in any formal volume.[2] It is a discussion of the judicial proceedings

[1] *American Theological Review*, July, 1863.
[2] *Edinburgh Review*, July, 1864.

in connection with two authors of the *Essays and Reviews.* His theme permits a wide range, and he therefore dwells at length upon the whole question of ministerial teaching. He considers the final acquittal of the essayists one of the most gratifying events of the day. According to him, the questions raised by the work are, with few exceptions, of a kind altogether beside and beyond the range over which the formularies of the Church extend. No passage in any of the five clerical essayists contradicts any of the formularies of the Church in a degree at all comparable to the direct collision which exists between the High Church party and the Articles, or the Low Church party and the Prayer-Book; on the points debated in the *Essays and Reviews* the Articles and Prayer-Book are alike silent. Stanley rejoices that of the thirty-two charges presented against Mr. Wilson and Dr. Williams all were dismissed but five, and that for these "there was no heavier penalty than a year's suspension." He is in ecstacy that the judgment in the case of these two men has established the legal position of those who have always claimed the right of free inquiry and latitude of opinion equally for themselves and for both the other sections of the Church. By the issue of the litigation, he claims that great victories have been won, that henceforth ample freedom is left to all detailed criticism of the Sacred Text, so long as the canonicity of no canonical book is denied, and that the questions whether there be "one Isaiah or two, two Zechariahs or three, who wrote the Epistle to the Hebrews, and who wrote the Pentatouch, whether Job and Josiah be historical or parabolical, whether the Fifty-third Chapter of Isaiah or the Second Psalm be directly or indirectly prophetic, what are the precise limits of the natural and practical, what is the weight of internal and external evidence, whether the Apocalypse refers to the Emperor Nero or to the Pope of Rome; are to be settled according to the individual opinion of every clergyman of the Established Church." Stanley sneers at the Declaration of the Oxford Committee sent to every Clergyman of England and Ireland, "with an adjuration, for the love of God and out of duty to the souls of men, to sign it." That Declaration was a protest against the acquittal of the Essayists; and Stanley rejoices over the fact, that, though "every influence was used to get signatures to it, and was so concealed as to enlist the support of High and Low Church parties," the result was the signature of only one third of the London clergy, nine Professors at Oxford and one at Cambridge, eight out of the thirty English deans, two of the Head Masters of the Public Schools, and only six out of the fifty clerical contributors to Smith's *Dictionary of the Bible*; that more than one half of the rural clergy stood altogether aloof from the document; and that when it was presented at Lambeth only four of the twenty-eight Bishops loaned their countenance to its formal reception. Stanley looks into the future and sees permanent blessings bestowed upon the country by the "timely decision of the highest Court of Appeal" that it has "no jurisdiction or authority to settle matters of faith, or to determine what ought in any particular to be the doctrine of the Church of England, since its duty extends only to the consideration of that which is by law established to be the doctrine of the Church of England, upon the true and legal construction of her Articles and formularies." He is also pleased that the Supreme Court of Appeal has refused to pledge itself and the Church to any popular theory of the mode of justification or of the future punishment of the wicked; and that it now stands declared that it is no doctrine of the Church of England that "every part of the Bible is inspired, or is the word of God." The Dean also looks with complacency upon what he declares to be a fact, and which we are startled to hear; that "the belief in endless punishment is altogether fluctuating, or else expresses itself in forms wholly untenable . . . that the doctrine of endless torments, if held, is not practically taught by the vast majority of the Clergymen of England."

The First Broad Church will not accept entirely the theology contained in the *Essays and Reviews*, and complains of them that they are "almost entirely negative; hinting at faults in the prevalent religious opinions of the day, but not investigating them; indicating dislike to certain obligations which are imposed upon clergymen, but not stating or considering what those obligations are; leaving an impression upon devout Christians that something in their faith is untenable when they want to find in it what is tenable; suggesting that earnest infidels in this day have much to urge in behalf of their doubts and difficulties; never fairly asking what they have to urge, what are their doubts and difficulties." [1]

On the other hand, the First Broad Church will not unite in the organized opposition to that work, because the denunciations and appeals "took an almost entirely negative form; they contradicted and slandered objections; they were not assertions of a belief; they led Christians away from the Bible, from the creeds which they confess to certain notions about the creeds, from practice to disputation. They met no real

[1] Miss Cobbe, *Broken Lights*, p. 63. London Edition.

doubts in the minds of unbelievers; they only called for the suppression of all doubts. They confounded the opinions of the day with the faith once delivered to the saints. They tended to make anonymous journalists the law-givers of the Church. They tended to discourage clergymen from expressing manfully what is in their hearts, lest they should incur the charge of being unfaithful to their vows. They tended to hinder all serious and honest co-operation between men who are not bound together in a sectarian agreement, lest they should make themselves responsible for opinions different from their own."[1] Thus, while the First Broad Church occupies a neutral ground in the controversy now rending the whole structure of English theology, its moral force is all against Evangelical Christianity, and in favor of the usurpations of Rationalism.

But the theology maintained by the First Broad Church is little above that contained in the *Essays and Reviews* and similar Rationalistic publications. With them, the Scriptures are better than any other books of antiquity because they contain the most of God's will, not because they alone contain his will. "These books," says a writer, "have been filtered out, as it were, under his guidance, from many others which, in ages gone by, claimed a place beside them, and are now forgotten, while these have stood for thousands of years, and are not likely to be set aside now."[2] They are indifferent as to their date, authorship, or contents. "Men may satisfy themselves," the same writer continues, "perhaps if I have time to give to the study, they may satisfy me—that the Pentateuch was the work of twenty men; that Baruch wrote a part of

[1] *Tracts for Priests and People.* Preface, pp. 3–5. Am. Edition.

[2] Hughes, in *Tracts for Priests and People*, p. 28.

Isaiah; that David did not write the Psalms, or the evangelists the gospels; that there are interpolations here and there in the original; that there are numerous and serious errors in our translation. What is all this to me? What do I care who wrote them, what is the date of them, what this or that passage ought to be? They have told me what I wanted to know. Burn every copy in the world to-morrow, you don't and can't take that knowledge from me, or any man."[1]

The Mosaic cosmogony is not a matter of great consequence, but on a par with other cosmogonies, none of which are of any intrinsic value. "If all cosmogonies were to disappear to-morrow," says Thomas Hughes, "I should be none the poorer." The various difficulties of Scripture are not of sufficient moment to occupy much time or pains. Let the people be made to understand the liberal interpretations of what the cultivated teachers have to say, and that will be enough to meet the world's wants. Perhaps it is with secret admiration of Bunsen's *Bible-Work*, the greatest exegetical triumph of Rationalism, that Kingsley asks: "Who shall write us a people's commentary of the Bible?"

Redemption is accepted in the Coleridgean sense. It is a term which does not express a Scriptural fact, but is borrowed from earthly transactions. Christ's work in our behalf is of no special value in itself, its known effects being all that make it of moment to the human family.[2] We should look at the results and not at the cause. The sacrifice which Christ made was one of obedience to his Father's will; it does not free us and elevate us above the curse of a broken law, for, in a certain sense, the law has never been broken to the

[1] Hughes, in *Tracts for Priests and People*, p. 37.

[2] Garden, *Tracts for Priests and People*, p. 133.

extent that the evangelicals claim, nor does eternal punishment harmonize with enlightened and liberal notions of Divine mercy. Miracles are in danger of being worshiped by the friends of revelation. They have the misfortune of an improper term; wonders would be a far better word. Why not accept them in the domain of faith, since we meet with them in science?[1] Miracles of this kind, "wonders," are willingly conceded, for they are not suspensions or violations of the order of nature, but natural phenomena, whose laws we may not understand. The miracles of the New Testament are purely natural; but the people did not comprehend the laws which gave them birth, and hence they magnified them. "Where the people believed," says Mr. Davies, "rightly or wrongly, in evil spirits and sorcery, in malignant and disorderly influences proceeding from the spiritual world, there the powers of the true kingdom, the powers of order and freedom and beneficence, were put forth in acts which appealed directly to the minds of the ignorant and superstitious, and which proclaimed an authority stronger than that of demons. The common multitudes of Judea were of the class which thus required to be treated like spoiled and frightened children."[2]

THE SECOND BROAD CHURCH. This party maintains the avowed Rationalism of Jowett, the *Essays and Reviews*, and Colenso. Miss Cobbe, in defining the points of difference between it and the First Broad Church, says of the latter, "It holds that the doctrines of the Bible and the church can be perfectly harmonized with the results of modern thought by a new but legitimate exegesis of the Bible and interpretation of church

[1] Davies, *Tracts for Priests and People*, p. 167.
[2] Ibid. p. 167.

formulæ. The Second Broad Church seems prepared to admit that in many cases they can only be harmonized by the sacrifice of biblical infallibility. The First Broad Church has recourse, to harmonize them, to various logical processes, but principally to the one described in the last chapter, of diverting the student, at all difficult points, from criticism to edification. The Second Broad Church uses no ambiguity, but frankly avows that when the Bible contradicts science, the Bible must be in error. The First Broad Church maintains that the inspiration of the Bible differs in *kind* as well as in *degree* from that of other books. The Second Broad Church appears to hold that it differs in degree but not in kind. This last is the crucial point of the differences of the two parties, and of one of the most important controversies of modern times."[1] The First Broad Church has made antagonism to the doctrine of endless punishment one of its great specialties, while the Second Broad Church has made its most violent assaults upon the evangelical view of the inspiration of the Scriptures. The position of the latter is not fully defined. We may suppose, however, that in due time its apologists will assume an organized form, and perhaps produce their systematic theology.

We regret that the general opposition on the part of the clergy to the theology of the *Essays and Reviews*, on the first appearance of that work, has not been sustained. The Broad Church has therefore acquired many new adherents within the last two years. It is impossible to classify all the parties according to their exact numerical strength, and their approximate proportions, in round numbers, must answer our purpose. The clergy of the Church of England, exclusive of the

[1] *Broken Lights*, pp. 73–74.

Irish, amount at present to about twenty thousand, at home and abroad.[1] Making allowance for two thousand peasant clergy in the mountain districts, and missionaries in foreign lands, the remaining eighteen thousand may be classified as follows:

High Church.	Normal Type,—Anglican,	3,600
	Exaggerated Type,—Tractarian,	1,000
	Stagnant Type,—High and Dry,	2,500
Low Church.	Normal Type,—Evangelical,	3,500
	Exaggerated Type,—Recordite,	2,600
	Stagnant Type,—Low and Slow,	700
Broad Church.	Normal Type,—Theoretical and Anti-Theoretical,	3,100
	Exaggerated Type,—Extreme Rationalists,	300
	Stagnant Type,	700

Twelve years ago the twenty-eight Bishops and Archbishops of England stood thus: thirteen belonged to the High Church, ten to the Broad Church, and five to the Low Church. A distribution made at the present time would be much more favorable to the second party.[2]

It is a remakable feature of the activity of theological opinion in England that the same division of parties which exists in the Established Church also obtains

[1] Appleton's *American Cyclopædia*. Art. *Church of England*. Though the writer of this article says nothing of the Irish clergy, he has not included them, of course; having no doubt used the Clergy List of England and the colonies alone.

[2] We have based our division of the English clergy upon the calculation of the late W. J Conybeare, a Fellow in the University of Cambridge, and joint author with J. S. Howson, of *Life and Epistles of St. Paul*. (*Essays Ecclesiastical and Social*, pp. 157–158.) His figures applied to the year 1853, but we have included the subsequent increase of the clergy, and distributed the additional members according to the best information at command. If it be objected that we have classed too large a portion in the Broad Church, we reply, that if Dean Stanley's intimations concerning the absence of orthodox faith in the English clergy be well founded, we have fallen far short of attributing to that body a sufficient number of members. See his article in *Edinburgh Review*, July, 1864.

in other religious bodies. We do not speak of the Dissenting Churches, all of which have their shades of sentiment, but of the smaller and less influential organizations. The Jews, Roman Catholics, Quakers, and Unitarians have each their old and new schools,—the former adhering to the old and established standards, the latter striving to harmonize with modern science and free inquiry. The Jews have their Mosaic, Talmudic, and Phillipsohnic groups,—the last taking its name from its leader, and corresponding with the First Broad Church within the pale of Christianity.[1] The Rationalistic party in the Roman Catholic Church is now aiming to harmonize Popery and the philosophy of the nineteenth century. It has no distinctive name, but numbers many adherents. The Quakers, besides possessing a strongly conservative wing, have their advocates of the "Inner Light," who are pushing this destructive doctrine "to the full consequences developed by the Second Broad Church party in the National Church." The Unitarians are divided into the staid disciples of Priestley and Belsham, and the New School, who stand on the same ground with Theodore Parker in the United States. These are cordial admirers of the *Essays and Reviews*, and would rejoice to see the land overspread with radical Rationalism.

[1] Phillipsohn, Author of the *Religious Idea in Judaism, Islam, and Christianity*. Translated by Miss Ann Goldschmidt.

CHAPTER XXIII.

THE UNITED STATES: THE UNITARIAN CHURCH—THE UNIVERSALISTS.

The aspect of novelty in the religious and theological history of the United States, is unparalleled in the history of any European nation, and is traceable in part to the peculiarities of our political origin and career. The founders of our government were wise students of the philosophy of history, and it was their opinion that many of the misfortunes which had befallen the countries of the Old World, were produced by the improper association of temporal and spiritual authority. They therefore made provision for the permanent separation of Church and State. Their design, however, was accomplished only by degrees. Previous to the Revolution, but two States, Rhode Island and Pennsylvania, permitted religious toleration. It was declared in Maryland in 1776, and in 1786–89 was carried out in Virginia. The general government took the matter in hand in 1791; and, in that year, an amendment to the Constitution of the United States was adopted, which prohibited Congress in future from "passing any law establishing religion, or prohibiting its free exercise."[1]

It would seem that our forefathers were almost gifted with prophetic vision when they incorporated this statute with those other laws, which have contributed

[1] Smith, *History of the Church of Christ in Chronological Tables*, p. 74.

so much to our prosperity. It would not have been in harmony with their spirit, if, while constituting an independent government, they had made the Church dependent.

The principle of the union of church and state presupposes a greater degree of social purity than has existed in any nation. Moreover, the Church is thereby led to assume an authority to which she has no claim and which Christ never intended her to possess. Milton, whose clear and practical views of civil and ecclesiastical relations were only equaled by his lofty poetic conceptions of man's moral nature and history, says: "When the church, without temporal support, is able to do her great works upon the enforced obedience of man, it argues a divinity about her. But when she thinks to credit and better her spiritual efficacy, and to win herself respect and dread by strutting in the false vizard of worldly authority, it is evident that God is not there, but that her apostolic virtue is departed from her, and has left her key-cold; which she perceiving, as in a decayed nature, seeks to the outward fermentations and chafings of worldly help and external flourishes, to fetch, if it be possible, some motion into her extreme parts, or to hatch a counterfeit life with the crafty and artificial heat of jurisdiction. But it is observable that so long as the church, in true imitation of Christ, can be content to ride upon an ass, carrying herself and her government along in a mean and simple guise, she may be as she is a Lion of the tribe of Judah; and in her humility all men, with loud hosannas, will confess her greatness. But when, despising the mighty operation of the Spirit by the weak things of this world, she thinks to make herself bigger and more considerable, by using the way of civil force and jurisdiction, as she sits upon this Lion she changes into an ass, and instead of hosannas, every man pelts her with stones and dirt."[1]

The peculiarities which have characterized the history of the American church are well defined, and of the greatest value in all estimates of the theological status of the popular mind. They are grouped by Professor Smith in the following concise terms: "*First.* It is not the history of the conversion of a new people, but of the transplantation of old races, already Christianized, to a new theatre, comparatively untrameled by institutions and traditions. *Second.* Independence of the civil power. *Third.* The voluntary principle applied to the support of religious institutions. *Fourth.* Moral and ecclesiastical, but not civil power, the means of retaining the members of any communion. *Fifth.* Development of the Christian system in its practical and moral aspects, rather than in its theoretical and theological. *Sixth.* Stricter discipline in the churches than is practicable where church and state are one. *Seventh.* Increase of the churches, to a considerable extent, through *revivals* of religion, rather than by the natural growth of the children in an establishment. *Eighth.* Excessive multiplication of sects; and divisions on questions of moral reform."[2]

When we consider the intimate relations between France and this country during the first stage of our national existence, it becomes a matter of surprise that French infidelity did not acquire greater influence over our people. It was not wholly without power, and the first twenty-five years of our history witnessed greater religious disasters than have appeared at any subsequent time. Still it may be said with truth that skep-

[1] *The Reason of Church Government against Prelacy.* Ch. II.

[2] *History of the Church of Christ, &c.*, p. 74.

tical tendencies have never gained a permanent position in the United States, though our immunity from their sway has not been the result of indifference toward the great movements of Europe. The American has never been a cold observer of the hemisphere from which his forefathers came. We appropriate the treasures of the Old World, and love to call them our own. We are as proud of the martyrology and literature of England as if Latimer and Ridley had died for their faith on Boston Common, or Shakspeare and Milton had lived on the banks of the Hudson. The early legislation of our government having left the individual conscience to the exercise of its own convictions, each citizen has been more interested in whatever religious opinions might appear from European sources.

What then has been the reception in America of that system of skepticism which has produced ravages on the Continent, and now forbodes evil in our English mother-land? Is Rationalism likely to run its destructive cycle in the United States? Has the American church no antidote for the great theological errors of the present age?

The denomination most intimately associated with Rationalistic tendencies is the Unitarian Church. Boston is its centre, and New England the principal sphere of its existence.

The Venerable Stoddard, of Northampton, Massachusetts, became convinced that the custom of excluding unregenerate persons from the sacrament of the Lord's Supper was sinful; and in 1708 published a sermon declaring his views on that subject. He held that the participation of unregenerate people in the communion was highly beneficial to them; and that it was in fact a means by which they might become regenerated.

He defended his belief so zealously that he soon had the pleasure of seeing many followers gathering about him. The doctrine was termed the Half-Way Covenant System, and was adopted in the church at Northampton. Jonathan Edwards succeeded Stoddard, who was his grandfather; and, a few years after the great revival in which the former took an active part, he adopted the opinion that the Half-Way Covenant was injurious. Edwards refused to practise it, and in his *Treatise on the Qualifications for Full Communion*, he declared the necessity of regeneration. He was accordingly dismissed from his church.

This was the germ of American Unitarianism. Stoddard's adherents clung to their loose view of communion, while the friends of Edwards, being more spiritual, and many of them the fruits of the Whitefieldian revival, sustained the orthodox construction with energy. The Half-Way Covenant in due time called a party into existence, which "avoided all solicitude concerning their own spiritual condition or that of others; were repugnant to the revival spirit; must have a system of doctrines which could contain nothing to alarm the fears or disturb the repose of the members of the party. The doctrines of apostasy, dependence on grace for salvation, necessity of atonement, and special influence of the Holy Spirit, were all thought to be alarming doctrines. They were therefore laid aside silently and without controversy. Men were suffered to forget that the Son of God, and the Spirit, have anything to do with man's salvation."[1]

King's Chapel, Boston, was the first Episcopal church of New England. Its rector leaving with the British troops upon their evacuation of the town, Rev.

[1] Baird, *Religion in America*, pp. 547–562.

James Freeman was chosen in April, 1783, to occupy the vacant position. The services of the church were conducted after the Episcopal form, the Book of Common Prayer being still used. Mr. Freeman's views underwent a change, and he delivered a course of doctrinal sermons in which he indicated decided Unitarian proclivities. Accordingly he introduced a revised liturgy, corresponding with Dr. Samuel Clarke's *Revision of the Liturgy of the Church of England*, from which the doctrines of the Trinity and of the divinity of Christ were excluded. The congregation addressed a letter to Bishop Provost, of New York, in which inquiry was made, "whether ordination of Rev. Mr. Freeman can be obtained on terms agreeable to him and to the proprietors of this church." The bishop proposed to refer the question to the next general convention. But the congregation, disliking such hesitation, determined to ordain their rector themselves. Accordingly, on November 18th, 1787, the senior warden laid his hand on Mr. Freeman's head, and pronounced the declaration of ordination. The people responded "Amen;" and thus was effected the first ordination of a Unitarian minister in the United States.[1]

Wide circulation had already been given to Emlyn's *Inquiry into the Scripture Account of Jesus Christ*, which, in 1756, had been republished in Boston from the English edition. Before the close of the century the doctrines peculiar to Unitarianism became widely disseminated in that city and in other portions of the State. Belsham issued in London, 1812, his *Memoir of Lindsey*, which contained startling disclosures of the doings of the Unitarians in America. Belsham's informants

[1] *Unitarianism in its Actual Condition.* Edited by Rev. J. R. Beard, D.D. pp. 1–4. London, 1846.

were leading Unitarians of Boston, among whom was Dr. Freeman, whose letters covered a period of sixteen years, from 1796 to 1812. He communicated all the secret movements, growth, and dimensions of the party. Only a few copies of Belsham's work came to America, and they were hidden, lest any of the orthodox might see them. Finally, Dr. Morse obtained one, and soon published a pamphlet revealing its astounding contents. It now came to light, for the first time, that Unitarianism was a strong party; that every Congregational church in Boston, except the Park Street and Old South, had become Unitarian; and that there were seventy-five churches in other parts of New England which had adopted the same views. The Unitarians were now compelled to come out of their hiding-place, and the orthodox watched their movements with intense interest.

The zeal of the adherents of Unitarianism, however, did not diminish by exposure, and a very important event occurred, which indicated that their labors were successful. Dr. Ware, an avowed anti-Trinitarian, was chosen to the professorship of theology in Harvard College, in place of the deceased Dr. Tappan. The appointment created a profound excitement among the orthodox clergy, who were indignant at the procedure. But remonstrance was useless. Unitarianism was triumphantly domiciled at Cambridge, and many who designed preaching its tenets became attendants upon the lectures of Professors Ware and Andrews Norton. As a probable consequence of the great change in Harvard, the Andover Theological Seminary was established,[1]—an institution which, from its origin to the present time, has shed a beneficent lustre upon the

[1] Sprague, *Annals of the American Unitarian Pulpit. Historical Introduction*, p. xii.

entire country. Its students have never ceased to be ornaments to the American pulpit, while some of the number, proving themselves worthy successors of Carey, Marshman, Coke, and Ward, have labored in heathen lands with apostolic zeal.

The celebrated controversy between Drs. Channing and Worcester, occasioned by a pamphlet which appeared in Boston in 1815, under the title of *American Unitarianism*, led to the withdrawal of the Unitarians from the orthodox, and their formation into a distinct organization. Pursuing an aggressive policy, they organized congregations in various parts of New England, and in the cities of Philadelphia, Baltimore, Washington, and Charleston. This was the heroic age of the Unitarian church of America.

Channing became immediately the leader of the new sect. He represents the best type of Unitarianism. Pure in life, ardent in his attachments, and heroic in spirit, he was well adapted to advance the cause which he had espoused. He had no taste for controversy, but the circumstances connected with the prevalent theology made such a deep impression on his mind that he felt it his duty to aid in the revival of what he deemed a more liberal faith. Not indorsing the extreme Unitarianism of Priestley and Belsham, he took a middle ground between it and New England Calvinism. He was attentively heard in his church at Boston, and was listened to by large audiences wherever he preached or lectured.

His writings embrace a variety of topics, the chief of which, apart from religious themes proper, are slavery, temperance, education, and war. Within a few years his views have attracted increased attention in Europe. In France, MM. Laboulaye, de Rémusat, and

Renan have discussed them at length. Of his mental transitions, an admiring writer says: "From Kant's doctrine of the reason he derived deeper reverence for the essential powers of man; by Schelling's intimations of the Divine Life, everywhere manifested, he was made more devoutly conscious of the universal agency of God; and he was especially delighted with the heroic stoicism of Fichte and his assertion of the grandeur of the human will. But for his greatest pleasure and best discipline he was now indebted to Wordsworth, whom he esteemed next to Shakspeare, and whose '*Excursion*' came to him like a revelation. With Wordsworth's mingled piety and heroism, humanity and earnest aspiration, with his all-vivifying imagination, recognizing greatness under lowliest disguises, and spreading sweet sanctions around every charity of social life, and with his longings to see reverence, loyalty, courtesy, and contentment established on the earth, he most closely sympathized. From this time he began to engage more actively in political and philanthropic movements."[1]

Channing believed that orthodoxy was incalculably mischievous in its estimate of Deity and of human depravity. "God, we are told," says he, "must not be limited; nor are his rights to be restrained by any rights in his creatures. These are made to minister to their Maker's glory, not to glorify themselves. They wholly depend on him, and have no power which they can call their own. His sovereignty, awful and omnipotent, is not to be kept in check, or turned from its purposes, by any claims of his subjects. Man's place is the dust. The entire prostration of his faculties is the true homage he is to offer to God. He is not to exalt

[1] Appleton's *American Cyclopædia*. Art. *Wm. Ellery Channing*. W. L. Symonds, Esq., is the author of this biography.

his reason or his sense of right against the decrees of the Almighty. He has but one lesson to learn, that he is nothing, that God is All in All. Such is the common language of theology."[1]

Against these views he asserts man's free agency and moral dignity. His creed is the greatness of Human Nature; such greatness as is seen in the "intellectual energy which discerns absolute, universal truth in the idea of God, in freedom of will and moral power, in disinterestedness and self-sacrifice, in the boundlessness of love, in aspirations after perfection, in desires and affections which time and space cannot confine, and the world cannot fill. The soul, viewed in these lights, should fill us with awe. It is an immortal germ, which may be said to contain now within itself what endless ages are to unfold. It is truly an image of the infinity of God, and no words can do justice to its grandeur."[2] Instead of looking without for a basis of religion, we must commence at home, within ourselves. "We must start in religion from our own souls, for in them is the fountain of all divine truth. An outward revelation is only possible and intelligible on the ground of conceptions and principles previously furnished by the soul. Here is our primitive teacher and light. Let us not disparage it. There are, indeed, philosophical schools of the present day, which tell us that we are to start in all our speculations from the Absolute, the Infinite. But we rise to these conceptions from the contemplation of our own nature; and even if it were not so, of what avail would be the notion of an Absolute, Infinite existence, an Uncaused Unity, if stripped of all those intellectual and moral attributes which we learn only

[1] *Works, Introductory Remarks*, p. viii.
[2] Ibid. p. vi.

from our own souls? What but a vague shadow, a sounding name, is the metaphysical Deity, the substance without modes, the being without properties, the naked Unity which performs such a part in some of our philosophical systems. The only God whom our thoughts can rest on and our hearts can cling to, and our consciences can recognize is the God whose image dwells in our own souls. The grand ideas of Power, Reason, Wisdom, Love, Rectitude, Holiness, Blessedness, that is, of all God's attributes, come from within, from the action of our own spiritual nature. Many indeed think that they learn God from marks of design and skill in the outward world; but our ideas of design and skill, of a determining cause, of an end or purpose, are derived from consciousness, from our own souls. Thus the soul is the spring of our knowledge of God."[1]

The creed of the Unitarians must be studied as one would take soundings at sea. The measurement of one place is no guarantee of the depth in another. What was believed twenty years ago, may not be endorsed by the leaders of to-day. One writer of their fold says: "Unitarianism is loose, vague, general, indeterminate in its elements and formularies."[2] When George Putnam installed Mr. Fosdick over the Hollis Street Church, he said with commendable candor, "There is no other Christian body of which it is so impossible to tell where it begins and where it ends. We have no recognized principles by which any man who chooses to be a Christian disciple, and desires to be numbered with us, whatever he believes or denies, can be excluded."

But Unitarianism has ever remained true to a few points. One of them is antagonism to orthodoxy. It

[1] *Works, Introductory Remarks*, pp. xviii-xix.
[2] Ellis, *Half Century of Unitarianism*, p. 34.

was an old cry of the German skeptics, "Away with orthodoxy. It fetters us to forms and creeds, makes us blind devotees to system, converts us into bigots, and dwarfs reason into an invisible pigmy." Yet we frequently meet with language of similar import in the present day. If we did not know its authorship we could easily tell the ecclesiastical fountain whence it flows. "The implications of false and shallow reasoning," says an American Unitarian divine, "partial observation, intellectual grouping, moral obliquity, spiritual ignorance,—in short, of puerility and superstition involved in a large part of the appeals, the preaching, the cant terms, the popular dogmas, the current conversation of Christendom,—are discouraging evidences how backward is the religious thought of our day, as compared with its general thought; how little harmony there is between our schools and our churches, our thinkers and our religious guides, our political and national institutions and our popular theology. It is not Christianity—the rational, thorough, all-embracing Gospel of Christ,—which throws its blessed sanctities over and around our whole humanity,—which owns and consecrates our whole nature and our whole life—which is thus taught. It is a system which is narrower than Judaism, and compared with which Romanism is a princely and magnificent theology. I say advisedly, that if Protestantism endorses the vulgar notions of a God-cursed world,—a fallen race,—a commercial atonement,—a doomed and hell-devoted humanity,—a mysterious conversion,—a Church which is a sort of a life-boat hanging round a wreck that may carry off a few women and selfishly-affrighted men, leaving the bolder, braver, larger portion to go down with the ship; if this be the sum and substance of religion,—if these notions be the grounds of the late religious excitement and the doctrines which gave it power,[1]—then it is not so true to human nature, its wants and woes, its various and manifold tastes, talents, and faculties, as the old Catholic system,—and that, instead of trembling at the growth and prospects of Romanism in this country, we should more reasonably rejoice in its triumphs, as the worthier occupant of the confidence and affection of the people. But this narrow system, with all its arrogant claims to be the only Evangelical faith, is not Protestantism; or, rather, is not mere Protestantism." [2]

But the indeterminateness of Unitarian theology does not warrant us in passing over its tenets, as stated by writers held in good repute in that Church. It would be unfair, however, to claim that these are doctrines to which each must inflexibly adhere. The Unitarians neither exact nor desire conformity to authority; in fact they have no authority. Reason is left to place its own construction upon the truths of revelation. What, then, is the general Unitarian sentiment on those subjects whose essential importance is acknowledged by all Evangelical Churches?

Inspiration and the Scriptures. Channing and Dewey have held loftier views of the Bible and its divine origin than their less devout brethren. The latter has said that, "The matter is divine, the miracles real, the promises glorious, the threatenings fearful; enough that all is gloriously and fearfully true to the divine will, true to human nature, true to its wants, anxieties, sorrows, sins, salvation, and destinies; enough that the seal of a divine and miraculous communication is set upon that holy Book." [3] But reverence for the Scrip-

[1] These words refer to the great Revival in the winter of 1857-58.

[2] Bellows, *Restatements of Christian Doctrine*, p. 164-165.

[3] *Controversial Sermons*, No. 1.

tures is rapidly on the decline among the Unitarians,—the direct result of the influence of the German and English Rationalists. They call all believers in orthodox opinions, "Bibliolaters." They spurn the thought of an infallible Bible. "No wonder," they say, "that the Bibliolaters quail before the iconoclasm of Bishop Colenso, and, in their rage, call aloud for his excision from the Church; for, if a single one of the difficulties he accumulates can be proved a reality, the whole edifice of their faith topples to its fall. . . . . We believe that safety and sense can alone be found in our theory, which regards Scripture as credible though human, as inspired not in its form, but in its substance, of various and, in many cases, of unknown authorship, and representing different stages of culture. We cannot accept all its documents as of co-ordinate authority; nor in every one of its statements can we recognize a product of inspiration. We do not conceive ourselves bound, therefore, to defend the geology of Moses, or to admire the conduct of the Israelites in the extermination of the Canaanites; or to infuse a recondite spiritual meaning into the amatory descriptions and appeals of the Song of Solomon."[1]

God and Christ. God is the Universal Father. It must be forgotten that he is king; his paternal character alone must be borne in mind. He is a God of one person, not of three, and the doctrine of the Trinity is nowhere hinted at in the Bible, but is of Platonic origin. The Christian Fathers did not contend that it was contained therein. The view of three persons in one God is "self-contradictory, opposed to all right reason, positively absurd."[2] Christ is inferior and subordinate

[1] Orr, *Unitarianism in the Present Time*, pp. 54, 58, 59.

[2] Farley, *Unitarianism Defined*, p. 24.

to God. He is God in the same sense as the angels, Moses, Samuel, the Kings and Judges of Israel. They were gods in one respect,—the word of God was spoken to them. Christ is the chief one "to whom the word of God came." [1] In the New Testament, Christ is uniformly kept distinct from the Father, and the attributes which he possessed, wisdom, knowledge, and power, were endowments from God.

THE HOLY GHOST. The Holy Ghost is not a person, but is merely sent from the Father, or proceeds from him. The apparent presence of the Holy Ghost in Christ's farewell discourse is only a personification resulting from the peculiar nature of the Greek language, and the necessity of its syntax. Not being a person, the Holy Ghost cannot be God, and is, therefore, not self-existent, underived, and unoriginated. Wherever it is described as a person it is only the writer's striking form of speech; it is solely personification, just as we often find the case with the Law, Wisdom, Scripture, Sin, and Charity.[2]

HUMAN DEPRAVITY. The Unitarians have no place in their creed for man's natural sinfulness. It is, they say, a doctrinal innovation, having been propagated by Augustine in the fifth century. That God should create men who are naturally sinners is inconsistent with his parental character. "The doctrine is itself repulsive. The human mind revolts at it. If God our Creator has implanted within us a natural sense of right and wrong, that sense arraigns his character and conduct in creating us thus corrupt." [3] There is no such thing, the Unitarians contend, as the fall of man.

[1] Farley, *Unitarianism Defined*, p. 26.
[2] Ibid. pp. 122,123, 136.
[3] Ibid. pp. 156,157.

Adam was what we are. "Had he not sinned," one of their writers affirms, "our race would have continued perfect and happy without the necessity for progress, or the need of any of those educational and recuperative processes to which Providence has resorted. *Let those who can believe this!* Let those also who can, call the unfallen Adam and Eve satisfactory patterns and types of our complete humanity. Imagine a world of Adams and Eves, living in a garden, on spontaneous fruits, ignorant of the distinction between good and evil, and without any capacity of moral change or improvement! Can any amount of credulity enable an enlightened and candid mind of the present day to think this world originally made to be occupied by such a race; that unfallen Adams and Eves could ever have developed its resources, or their own powers, and capacities of moral and spiritual happiness? Can any subtlety perceive a true distinction between their condition and that of the innocent but feeble islanders of some few spots in the Pacific?[1] Can any degree of superstition regard a state of unfallen holiness, which allowed our first parents to succumb in the midst of perfect bliss, and under God's own direct care and instructions, before the first temptation, as superior to our present moral condition? If Adam fell, the race rose by his fall; he fell up, and nothing happier for our final fortunes ever occurred than when the innocents of the garden learned their shame, and fled into the hardships and experiences of a disciplinary and growing humanity. . . . The radical vice of the popular way of thinking about moral evil lies in the supposition that . . . . a state of spotless innocency is better than a

[1] Will the Reverend author be kind enough to inform the public of the name and exact locality of these innocent islanders?

state of moral exposure and moral struggle; and that all our humanity is not entitled to use development and play, in its grand career of being. On the other hand, the true theory of humanity presents us with a race brought into this world for its education, starting with moral and intellectual infancy, and liable to all the mistakes, weaknesses, and follies, which an ungrown and inexperienced nature begets."[1] There is far more virtue in the world than there is vice. We grossly mistake when we make notoriously vicious characters the type of humanity at large. "Man by nature, as born and brought into this world, is innocent, pure; guiltless because sinless; fitted for just that religion which Christ revealed to operate successfully and gloriously upon; not indeed holy, but capable of becoming so."

THE ATONEMENT. The orthodox view of the atonement is denied by the Unitarians. Sacrifices are of human origin, those of the Mosaic religion being solely ritual, and symbolical acts of faith and worship. Christ's death did not appease the wrath of God in any sense, nor is anything said in the Scriptures concerning Christ's sufferings as causing or exciting the grace or mercy of God. It is not stated that God is reconciled to us, but we to him. Christ suffered as an example. A writer already quoted says: "Especially were the anguish and patience of his final sufferings and his awful death upon the cross appointed and powerful means of affecting the mind of man."[2] Another author affirms: "Christ saves us, so far as his sufferings and death are concerned, through their moral influence and power upon man; the great appeal which they make being not to God, but to the sinner's conscience and

[1] Bellows, *Restatements of Christian Doctrine*, pp. 228-230.
[2] *Works of H. Ware, jr.*, vol. iv. p. 91.

heart; thus aiding in the great work of bringing him into reconciliation with or reconciling him to his Father in heaven. . . . Reconciliation is accomplished by Christ; by all that he was and is; all that he taught, did, and is doing; and by all that he suffered for our sake. Not by one but by all of these are we saved."[1] Christ's sacrifice was not made to God, for he did not need to be propitiated or rendered merciful, but simply with reference to man alone,—for his good; God's justice needed no pacification. "There can be no greater or more blinding heresy than that which would teach that Christ's sufferings, or any sufferings in behalf of virtue and human sins and sorrows, are strictly substitutional, or literally vicarious. The old theologies, perplexed and darkened with metaphysics and scholastic logic—the fruit of academic pride and the love of ecclesiastical dominion—labored to prove and to teach that Christ, in his short agony upon the cross, really suffered the pains of sin and bore the actual sum of all the anguish from remorse and guilt due to myriads of sinners, through the ages of eternity. . . . Our sense of justice and goodness so far as God himself is concerned, is vastly more shocked by the proper penalties of sin being placed upon the innocent than had they been left upon the guilty, where they belong. . . . The truth is, literal substitution of moral penalties is a thing absolutely impossible! Vicarious punishment, in its technical and theological sense, is forbidden by the very laws of our nature and moral constitution."[2]

Regeneration. This is a universal want, but it is entirely consistent with the purity of human nature. The natural birth gives no moral character; it is to be

[1] Farley, *Unitarianism Defined*, pp. 208-210.

[2] Bellows, *Restatements of Christian Doctrine*, pp. 306,307.

formed, and when formed, is called the "new birth." This is all that Christ meant when he said to Nicodemus, "Except a man be born again he cannot see the kingdom of God." Regeneration must not, therefore, be considered a consequence of human depravity, but a result of human purity. It is the development of that which is already good within us.

FUTURE PUNISHMENT. The Unitarians of America have, for the most part, adopted the Restitutional theories of Hartley and Priestley. Mr. Ballou claims "the whole body of Unitarians as Universalists." Punishment may be inflicted after death, but it will be temporary. "The punishments of hell are disciplinarian, and do not forbid the hope of remission and relief." [1]

The best method of determining the present spirit of Unitarianism is to observe the reception which it gives to the Rationalism that has grown up luxuriantly of late in England. The welcome has been most cordial. A Unitarian clergyman has become the American editor of the *Essays and Reviews*; [2] and hails the appearance of such a book as representing a new and better era in modern theology. He holds that the real "life of Anglican theology is now represented by such men as Powell and Williams and Maurice and Jowett and Stanley;" that the Broad Church is the only one which fully embodies true progress and conservatism; that Rationalism is the only alternative of Romanism; and that, as a matter of course, the former should be adopted. He expresses the hope that the spirit of Rationalistic criticism, "which is now leavening the Church of England, may find abundant entrance into all the churches of our land," and that the *Essays and Re-*

[1] Orr, *Unitarianism in the Present Time*, p. 8.

[2] F. H. Hedge, D.D.

views, "its genuine product, may contribute somewhat thereto."[1]

The quarterly organ of the Unitarians, *The Christian Examiner*, has passed an encomium on the same exponent of English Rationalism, in which it manifests no tempered gladness at skepticism within the pale of the church. It says, with undisguised satisfaction, that "either these seven essayists must have been in very close and intimate confidential relations as friends or fellow-students, and have held many precious conferences together in which they were mutually each other's confessors; or, there must be quite a large number of very able and very heretical sinners in the Church of England, within easy hail of each other, and so thick in some neighorhoods that it is the readiest thing in the world to pick out a set of them who, 'without concert or comparison,' will contribute all the parts of a *fresh and unhackneyed system of opinion*."

One of the most direct and outspoken of all the organized attacks of American Rationalism upon evangelical Christianity occurred at the first public anniversary of the Young Men's Christian Union, of New York. Its importance was due to the diversity of unevangelical bodies there represented, and to the celebrity of several of the speakers. Unitarianism, Swedenborgianism, and Universalism mingled in happy fraternity. The speakers were Drs. Osgood, Bellows, Sawyer, and Chapin; Rev. Messrs. Barrett, Peters, Mayo, Higginson, Miel, Blanchard, and Frothingham; and Richard Warren and Horace Greeley, Esquires.

The Union seems to have been designed as a counterpoise to the large and flourishing Young Men's Christian Association, which is comprised of earnest and active

[1] *Essays and Reviews, Introduction to Boston Edition.*

members of all orthodox denominations. The platform of the former may be determined from the following significant language: "The Anniversary of the Young Men's Christian Union was the first instance in which so many of the leading minds in the various branches of the liberal and progressive portion of the Christian church have met on one common platform, for the purpose of discussing the practical bearings of that higher type of Christianity which refuses to be limited by any dogma, or fettered by any creed."[1] One of the speakers, in explaining the relations of the Union to the church, said: "We maintain, then, that we are *in* the church, *are* the church—not a part of it, but the whole church, —having *in* us the heart and soul of orthodoxy itself, the essence of all that gave life to its creed, the utmost significance and vital force of what it taught and still teaches, in what we conceive to be a stuttering and stammering way, in a cumbrous and outworn language, with a circuitous and wearisome phraseology; but meaning really what we mean, and doing for men essentially what we are doing. All that we claim is a better statement of the old and changeless truth, a disembarrassed account of the ever true and identical story. . . . We have not separated ourselves from the brethren [orthodox]; we hold them in our enclosure; we are always ready to receive them, to welcome them. We are not expecting they will receive us, on account of their providential position. We have an intellectual perception of what the times demand and what the future is to be. We can see clearer than they. We can see why they are wrong; they cannot see why we are right—but they will presently. . . . The actual presence of God in the world, in all his love and mercy,

[1] *Religious Aspects of the Age.* Preface, p. 3.

supplying our deficiencies, helping our infirmities, consecrating and transforming matter, giving sanctity and beauty to life—this is what the *renewing* of the old faith offers to humanity.

"The indistinct perception of this faith and the divine craving to see it clearly, and bring it to the sight of others, has led to the existence and organization of the Liberal churches, and indirectly to the formation of the Young Men's Christian Union. Faith in man as the child of God, his word and residence, authorizing the freest use of thought, the profoundest respect for individual convictions, the firmest confidence in progress and in the triumph of truth; inspiring good will, humane affections, philanthropic activity, and personal holiness; faith in God as the Father of man—man's universal Saviour and inspirer—man's merit consists wholly in being his child and the pupil of his grace in nature, life, the church, and the unseen world—these are the permanent articles of Christian faith, which is not so much faith in Christ, as Christ's faith."[1]

It is difficult to conceive how the most of the speakers at the anniversary in question could have better served the interests of a bold and unmitigated system of Rationalism. The great evil of the day is declared to be dogmatism, against which every true friend of progress must deal his most destructive blows. Liberal minds must break loose from the fetters of authority, and give play to their own infallible reason. The Protestant evangelical church is placed upon the same footing with Romanism; both of which organizations unchurch all who do not conform to their creed. "The truth is," says a speaker, "this Protestant evangelical church is in the same chronic delusion as its enemy, the Roman Catholic church; it can propose no plan of

[1] Bellows, in *Religious Aspects of the Age*, pp. 109-111.

Christian union which will include the Christians of the country. Its only idea of union is the conspiracy of a few sects to take the kingdom of heaven by violence; monopolize its honors in this world and the world to come; and either compel the rest of mankind to come into its arrangement, or be turned into everlasting perdition—a proceeding which the American people, with due respect to the undeniable rights of this church, begs leave respectfully to decline,—and further to intimate, that it is not at all alarmed about the eternal consequences of a refusal to accede to the pretensions of an ecclesiasticism that assumes to be God's vicegerent to the United States of America."[1]

Great fault is found with the doctrines of the plenary inspiration of the Scriptures, and the efficacy of Christ's blood for man's salvation. God is in man; and man's moral instincts, intellectual mould, and spiritual senses are infinitely wiser than we conceive them to be. They are infallible in what they say of God, and are the best criteria of truth. How much the world has been given up to the worship of the Bible! "The Bibles will be left here to burn in the general conflagration with the other temporary representations of the Word of God, which is the eternal Reason, the foundation of our being." This Reason is the "elder Scripture of God,—the soul, the inspired child of the heavenly and eternal Father." The answer is given to the question, Why does orthodoxy believe in the efficacy of Christ's blood to save the souls of men? "It is because man distrusts his reason, and invents the infallible church, and then the infallible Scriptures, to supply his necessity of anchorage. He cannot think the God of the universe can be willing to save such a miserable sinner,

[1] Mayo, in *Religious Aspects of the Age*, pp. 68, 69.

and he invents a God of the church, who will. He does not believe anything men can do will entitle them to heaven, or that human lives can make them acceptable in the sight of God."[1]

From the preceding statements it will not be surprising to find some of the speakers apologizing for outright infidelity. "Mr. President," says one, "you, in the judgment of very many, are an infidel. The members of this Christian association occupy what is regarded an infidel position. And that very admirable constitution, which I have read to-day, if presented at a council of churches, commonly reputed orthodox, would be considered, doubtless, the platform of an infidel association. . . . Infidels, in all generations of the church, have been *progressive* in every direction; the believers in the present and the future; the people who had confidence in the improvability of man, and the perennial inspirations of God; the men and women who were persuaded that all the spheres of wisdom and excellence were opened to human powers, and that man was welcomed to all the treasure they contain. . . . They are a thoughtful, earnest, hopeful people, bent on finding the truth, and doing their duty."[2] Such infidels as these are claimed to have blessed the world. All liberal minds ought to catch their spirit and administer every possible blessing to struggling humanity. But there is a species of narrow-minded infidelity which must be shunned; and it is the only kind of which we need to forebode any evil. "The only infidelity to be feared," says Mr. Frothingham, "the only real infidelity which is a sin in the sight of God, is a disbelief in the primary faculties of the human soul; disbelief in the

[1] Bellows, in *Religious Aspects of the Age*, pp. 102,103.
[2] Frothingham, Ibid. pp, 121—126.

capability of man's reason to discriminate between truth and error in all departments of knowledge, sacred or profane; disbelief in the heart's instinctive power to distinguish good from evil; disallowance of the claims of conscience to pass a verdict upon matters of right and wrong, whenever and wherever brought up. They are the infidels who are untrue to the light they have; who deny the plenary inspiration of that elder Scripture written by the finger of God upon the human heart; who overlay their reason with heaps of antiquated traditions; who bid their conscience stand dumb before appalling iniquities in obedience to the ill-read letter of an ancient record; who, in the interest of power, wealth, worldliness, not seldom of unrighteousness and inhumanity, plead for a Tract society, a Bible, or a church; who compass sea and land to make a proselyte, and when he is made, are quite indifferent as to his being a practical Christian; who collect vast sums of money annually for the ostensible purpose of saving men's souls, practically to the effect of keeping their souls in subjection and blindness. As I read the New Testament, I find that Jesus charged infidelity upon none but such as these; the people who made religion a cloak for pride, selfishness, and cruelty; the conspicuously saintly people, who could spare an hour to pray at a street corner, but had not a minute for a dying fellow-man lying in his blood in a lonely pass. In the judgment of these, Jesus was the prince of unbelievers. Punctilious adherence to the letter, practical disbelief in the spirit—this is infidelity."[1]

The most important event in the history of the American Unitarian Church was the National Convention which met in New York, April 5th, 1865, and was pre-

[1] *Religious Aspects of the Age*, pp. 131-132.

sided over by Governer Andrew, of Massachusetts. Six hundred ministers and laymen, representatives of one hundred and ninety churches, were in attendance. The debates indicated wide diversity of sentiment, but there was no open rupture. The sessions were pervaded by a spirit of devoted loyalty to the civil government, liberality toward all Christian bodies, and zeal in organizing educational and missionary agencies throughout the country. An annual National Conference of Unitarian Churches was appointed for the future. The Convention was unable to arrive at a common system of belief. The following declaration of faith was presented by A. A. Low, Esq.:

" *Whereas*, Associate and efficient action can only be expected of those who agree in certain leading doctrinal statements or positions, *Resolved*, That without intending any intolerance of individual opinion, it is the right and duty of this convention to claim of all who take part in its proceedings, an assent to the fundamental doctrines hitherto held by the Unitarian body by reason of which it has acquired its standing in the Christian world, and asserts it lineage in the Christian Church; and, to this end, this convention declares as essentially belonging to the Unitarian faith: 1st. Belief in the Holy Scriptures as containing a revelation from God to man—and, as deduced therefrom, 2d. Belief in one God, the Father; 3d. Belief in one Lord Jesus Christ, our Saviour, the Son of God, and his specially appointed Messenger and Representative to our race, gifted with supernatural power, "approved of God by miracles and signs and wonders which God did by him," and thus, by divine authority, commanding the devout and reverential faith of all who claim the Christian name; 4th. Belief in the Holy Ghost, the Comforter;

5th. Belief in the forgiveness of sins, the resurrection of the dead, and life everlasting."

These resolutions were at first laid on the table, but afterward referred to a special commitee. The refusal of the Convention to adopt them indicates very clearly the unwillingness of a large portion of the Unitarian clergy of the United States to occupy an evangelical position.[1]

Closely allied to the Unitarians in spirit and in doctrine are the Universalists, who date the beginning of

[1] American Unitarianism is numerically decreasing. The most favorable estimate of its membership (Schem, *Ecclesiastical Year-Book*, p. 78), is thirty thousand. From Dr. Sprague's *Annals of the American Unitarian Pulpit*, pp. xx.–xxi., we derive the following statistical account of its present strength:

There are in the United States about 263 Societies, of which Massachusetts has 164, and the city of Boston 21; Maine has 16, New Hampshire 15, Vermont 3, Rhode Island 3, Connecticut 2, New York 13, New Jersey 1, Pennsylvania 5, Maryland 2, Ohio 5, Illinois 11, Wisconsin 2, and Missouri, Kentucky, Minnesota, South Carolina, Louisiana, California, and the District of Columbia, each one. There are about 345 ministers. There are two theological schools, one at Cambridge, founded 1816; the other at Meadville, Pa.; first opened in 1844, and incorporated in 1846. The Periodicals are, The Christian Examiner, tri-monthly, Boston; The Monthly Religious Magazine and Independent Journal, Boston; The Sunday School Gazette, semi-monthly, Boston; The Christian Register, weekly, Boston; and the Christian Inquirer, weekly, New York. The missionary and charitable societies are, the American Unitarian Association, founded in 1825, and incorporated in 1847; the Unitarian Association of the State of New York; Annual Conference of Western Unitarian Churches; the Sunday School Society, instituted in 1827, and reorganized in 1854; the Society for promoting Christian Knowledge, Piety, and Charity, incorporated in 1805; the Massachusetts Evangelical Missionary Society, instituted in 1807; the Society for Promoting Theological Education, organized in 1816, and incorporated in 1831; the Society for the Relief of Aged and Destitute Clergymen, formed in 1848, and incorporated in 1850; the Ministerial Conference; the Association of Ministers at large in New England, formed in 1850; the Benevolent Fraternity of Churches of Boston, organized in 1834, and incorporated in 1839; the Children's Mission to the Children of the Destitute, Boston, 1849; the Young Men's Christian Union, Boston, organized in 1851, and incorporated in 1852; the Boston Port Society, incorporated in 1829; and the Seamen's Aid Society of Boston, formed in 1832.

their strength in the United States from the arrival of the Rev. John Murray, in 1770. They unite with the Unitarians in rejecting the triune character of God, and hold that their view of the divine unity is as old as the giving of the law on Sinai. The doctrine of the Trinity is nowhere stated in the Scriptures, for God would then have given us a religion enveloped in mystery, which procedure he has studiously avoided. The Trinitarian view entertained by the orthodox is not only a self-contradiction, but would be a violation of the harmony and order everywhere perceptible in nature.[1]

Christ is next to God in excellence; he is "God manifest in the flesh;" that is, God has given him more of his glory than any other creature has enjoyed. Christ was simply sent by God to do a certain work, and served only as a delegate when he spoke and acted as one having authority.[2] The Holy Spirit exerts an influence upon the heart by purely natural methods. The new birth is therefore merely the result of ordinary means for human improvement.

The most important article of the Universalist creed is the final salvation of all men. The goodness of God is infinite, and therefore he will save all his rational creatures through Christ, his Son and Ambassador. Man suffers in this world the natural consequences of his wayward conduct; but when the penalty is once inflicted, there is no need of vengeance. The chief end of suffering in the present life is man's improvement and restoration to perfect happiness. Pain ordained for its own sake, and perpetuated to all eternity, would be a proof of infinite malignity. By virtue of God's benevolence, man's suffering has a beneficent element,

[1] Williamson, *Exposition and Defense of Universalism*, pp. 11-13.
[2] Skinner, *Universalism Illustrated and Defended*, pp. 51-56.

and must therefore be temporary and result in good.[1] When Christ comes to raise the dead, he will relieve from misery all the sons of men, give them a new life, and take them to himself.[2]

The adherents of Universalism insist upon philanthropy and the brotherhood of man. They hold that orthodox theology fosters harsh notions of God's character, fills the mind with superstition, and is the source of some of the most flagrant evils of the present age. "We regret," says one of their writers, "that the acknowledged faith and opinions have done no more to elevate the affections, and improve the condition of man. They have utterly failed to correct the heart or the life. They have disturbed his present peace, and darkened his prospects for the future. Thousands of the young and innocent have been induced to relinquish whatever is most beautiful in life—to give up all that renders religion attractive and divine, for a miserable superstition, which, like the Upas, fills the very atmosphere with death. I am reminded that this dark theology, like a great idol, has been rolling its ponderous car over the world for ages—I follow its desolating track, by the wreck of noble minds—by the fearful wail of the lost spirit, and the crushed hopes and affections of those I love! Oh! when I look at this picture, drawn with the pencil of reality, in all its deep shadows and startling colors, the brain is oppressed and the heart is sick; and while I would stifle the inquiry, it finds an utterance:—In the name of reason, of humanity and heaven, is there no hope for man?"[3]

[1] Appleton's *American Cyclopædia*, Art. *Universalists.*

[2] Williamson, *Exposition and Defense of Universalism*, pp. 140-155.

[3] Brittan, *Universalism as an Idea*, pp. 12,13. We get the following statistics concerning the present condition of the Universalists as a denomination from their Register of 1862: 23 State Conventions; 87 Local As-

This declamatory lament over the theology of the evangelical Christian church is a repetition of an old skeptical charge. It is the expression of a spirit similar to that which animated the German Rationalists, prompted the criticism of Colenso and of the *Essays and Reviews*, and is now ready to welcome any effort that may promise a revolution of the popular religious sentiment in Great Britain and the American Republic. Orthodoxy is unhesitatingly pronounced a public curse. In reply, we would request our skeptical opponents to remember the historical record of their principles, as seen in the social convulsions of Germany, in the immorality and revolutions of France, and in the religious indifference and prostration of England in the eighteenth century. We would remind them, further, that orthodox theology has here been in the ascendant, and that in no land are public morals purer, the laws more just, humanitarian enterprises better supported, material interests more progressive, or education better fostered than in the United States. The American Church laments that her faith has not been stronger and her zeal more fervent, but her history, with all its dark pages of hesitation and inefficiency, is the answer which she returns to the accusations of her Rationalistic opponents. Meanwhile, she proposes to continue her labor for human salvation, by the promulgation of her present system of theology, nor will she consider her mission accomplished until the gospel of Christ has been preached to every creature.

sociations; 1,279 Societies and 998 Churches; 724 Preachers; 8 Academies; 3 Colleges; 17 Periodicals. St. Lawrence University, N. Y. has a Library of 5,000 vols; and Tuft's College, Mass., which opened in 1854, one of 10,000 volumes. The Unitarians excel the Universalists in humanitarian efforts, but the latter surpass the former in periodical literature.

CHAPTER XXIV.

THE UNITED STATES CONTINUED: THEODORE PARKER AND HIS SCHOOL.

The early Unitarian Church of America was ardent in its attachment to the doctrine of miracles. An article which appeared in the *Christian Examiner* less than forty years ago, provoked great opposition because of its severe strictures on this branch of Christian evidence. The writer held that miracles, even if proved to have occurred, can establish nothing in favor of a religion which has not already stood the test of experience; and that the doctrines of Christianity must first be determined reasonable before we are compelled to believe that miracles were wrought in attestation of them. The elder school of Unitarians denounced his statements as open infidelity. A violent controversy ensued, but no schism took place. Theodore Parker stood at the head of the radical movement, and afterward labored unremittingly to disseminate his theological opinions. In him American Rationalism finds its complete personification. He represents the application of German infidelity to the Unitarianism of New England.

This celebrated advocate of temperance and freedom was prompted by a deep and unselfish love of his race. He was descended from a soldier of the Revolutionary army, and inherited that indomitable will, strong patriotic impulses, and native talents, which had characterized his ancestry for several generations. His mental qualities were of a lofty type. He was a linguist who, in correctness of speech and facility of acquisition, had few equals on this side of the Atlantic. His eloquence was stirring and popular, while his pen was facile and fruitful. Commencing to preach in West Roxbury, Massachusetts, the unusual character of his pulpit ministrations attracted public attention. On being invited to Boston, he assumed the pastoral relation over a newly-formed church, the Twenty-Eighth Congregational Society. In addition to his sermons, he lectured in all parts of the Northern States, and found time to write regularly for periodicals, compose original works, and make translations of German authors with whom his own theological opinions were in sympathy.

Though often in feeble health, he seldom allowed physical languor to intermit his work. When threatened with consumption he was induced to spend some time at Santa Cruz, whence he sailed for Italy. He died at Florence in the spring of 1860, not having completed his fiftieth year, and after a pastorate of only fourteen years at the Melodeon. He had often expressed a desire in earlier life that, like Goethe and Channing, he might not be deterred from labor by the prospect of immediate death. Shortly before his decease he addressed to his congregation in Boston a lengthy letter containing his experience as a minister. He now lies in the little cemetery outside the walls of Florence; his tombstone, at his own request, simply recording his name and the dates of his birth and death. He bequeathed his library, containing over thirteen thousand volumes, to the Free Library of Boston.

Our chief concern is with Mr. Parker as a theologian.

He was a stranger to moderation in every form. Having conceived certain skeptical views, he knew no terms strong enough to condemn the whole evangelical scheme. His chief defects of style are abruptness and occasional vulgarity, which no man more regretted than their author in his calmer hours. But there can be no apology for his dealing with serious subjects in that vein of sarcasm which reminds us of the grossness of the coarser brood of infidels. An English critic, noticing this defect, says: "His vigor of style was deformed by a power of sarcasm, which often invested the most sacred subjects with caricature and vulgarity; a boundless malignity against supposed errors. . . . He equals Paine in vulgarity and Voltaire in sarcasm."[1]

Parker felt that a bold course must be taken or orthodoxy could not be made to yield its position. His biographer informs us that when he was less than seven years of age "he fell out with the doctrines of eternal damnation and a wrathful God."[2] In later life, when striving to find the sources of what he considered the evils of the popular theology, he fixed upon two common idols: "the Bible, which is only a record of men's words and works; and Jesus of Nazareth, a man who only lived divinely some centuries ago. The popular religion is wrong in that it tells man he is an outcast, that he is but a spurious issue of the devil, must not pray in his own name, is only sure of one thing—and that is damnation. Man is declared to be immortal, but it is such immortality as proves a curse instead of a blessing. In fact this whole orthodox theology rests on a lie."[3]

His positive faith is comprehended in his own term,

[1] **Farrar**, *Critical History of Free Thought*, p. 324.
[2] **Weiss**, *Life and Correspondence of Theodore Parker*, vol. i., p. 30.
[3] *Discourse on Matters Pertaining to Religion*, pp. 5, 6.

"the Absolute Religion." God has created man with an intuitive religious element, the strongest and deepest in human nature, indestructible, and existing everywhere. Its legitimate action is to produce reverence, and ascends into trust, hope, and love, or descends into doubt, fear, and hate. Religion is not confined to one age, or people, or sect. It is the same thing in each man, "not a similar thing—but the same thing." Three forms of religion have existed, and each in turn has ruled the mind, —Fetichism, Polytheism, and Monotheism. The first can be distinctly traced in the mythical stories of Genesis, the second in pagan nations, and the third in these later times. Now, it is a very small matter in which one of these forms man has worshiped or may still worship. If he worship at all, he adores the true God, "the only God, whether he call on Brahma, Jehovah, Pan, or Lord, or by no name at all. . . . Many a swarthy Indian, who bowed to wood and stone; many a grim-faced Calmuck, who worships the great God of storms; many a Grecian peasant, who did homage to Phœbus-Apollo when the sun rose or went down; yes, many a savage, his hand smeared all over with human sacrifice, shall come from the east and the west, and sit down in the kingdom of God, with Moses and Zoroaster, with Socrates and Jesus,—while men who called daily on the only living God, who paid their tribute and bowed at the name of Christ, shall be cast out because they did no more."[1]

Christianity, with Parker, is not the absolute religion, because a better may be developed. The great difference between it and other religions is: *first*, in the point whence it sets out, other religions starting from something external and limited, but Christianity from

[1] *Discourse on Matters Pertaining to Religion*, p. 111.

the spirit of God in the soul of man speaking through reason, conscience, and the religious sentiment; *second*, it is not a system but a method of religion and life; and, *third*, its eminently practical nature. The Deity adored by many people is a pure fabrication, for superstition projects its own divinity, which of course will be after its own impure mould. Men call the phantom God, Moloch, or Jehovah, and then attempt to please the capricious being whom they have conjured up. The true idea of God is his infinite presence in each point of space; this immanence in matter is the basis of his influence; this imposition of a law is the measure of God's relation to matter; and the action of the law is therefore mechanical, not voluntary or self-conscious.

The Bible, according to the same method of argumentation, is as much a human book as the *Principia* of Newton. Some things in it are true, but no reasonable man can accept others. It is full of contradictions; "there are poems which men take as histories; prophecies which have not been and never will be fulfilled; stories of miracles that never happened; stories which make God a man of war, cruel, rapacious, revengeful, hateful, and not to be trusted. We find amatory songs, selfish proverbs, skeptical discourses, and the most awful imprecations human fancy ever clothed in speech." The minds of the writers of the Old Testament were not decided in favor of the exclusive existence of Jehovah, and all the early books betray more of a polytheistic belief than we find in the prophets. The legendary and mythical writings of the Hebrews prove unmistakably that man was first created in the lowest savage life; that his religion was the rudest worship of nature; and that his morality was that of the cannibal. All the civilized races have risen through various forms of developing faith before reaching refinement and true religion. We do not know who are the writers of most of the Scriptural books. Their records are at variance with science. The account of Jehovah's determination that the carcasses of Israel should fall in the wilderness because of disobedience, is a "savage story of some oriental who attributed a blood-thirsty character to his God, and made a deity in his own image, and it is a striking remnant of barbarism that has passed away, not destitute of dramatic interest; not without its melancholy moral." [1]

The prophets are claimed to have written nothing in general above the reach of human faculties. The whole of the Old Testament is only a phantom of superstition to scare us in our sleep.[2] The statements of the evangelists have a very low degree of historical credibility. Miracles are not impossible, because God is omnipotent; but our main difficulty is, that we cannot believe the accounts descriptive of them. The testimony and not the miracle is at fault. Inspiration is not at all peculiar to the Scriptures. All nations have had their inspiration; this is a natural result of the perfection of God, for he does not change; and the laws of mind are like himself, unchangeable. Inspiration, being similar to vision, must be everywhere the same thing in kind however much it differs in degree. The quantity of our inspiration depends upon the use we make of our faculties. He who has the most wisdom, goodness, religion, and truth is the most inspired. This inspiration reveals itself in various forms, modified by country, character, education, peculiarity. Minos and Moses were inspired to make laws; David, Pindar,

[1] *Discourse on Matters Pertaining to Religion*, pp. 333, 4.
[2] Ibid. p. 350.

Plato, John the Baptist, Gerson, Luther, Boehme, Fenelon, and Fox were all inspired men. The sacraments of the Church were never designed to be permanent. In illustration of them, Parker sacrilegiously quotes,

> "Behold the child, by nature's kindly law,
> Pleased with a rattle, tickled with a straw;
> Some livelier plaything gives his youth delight,
> A little louder, but as empty quite."

The Christian Church is held to be a purely human mechanism, and the great defect of Protestantism is its limit of the power of private inspiration. God still inspires men as much as ever, and is immanent in spirit as in space. This doctrine, which is Spiritualism, "relies on no church, tradition, or Scripture, as the last grand and infallible rule; it counts these things teachers, if they teach, not masters; helps, if they help us, not authorities. It relies on the Divine presence in the soul of man; the eternal word of God, which is truth, as it speaks through the faculties he has given. It believes God is near the soul as matter to the sense; thinks the canon of revelation not yet closed, nor God exhausted. It sees him in Nature's perfect work; hears him in all true Scripture, Jewish or Phœnician; stoops at the same fountain with Moses and Jesus, and is filled with living water. It calls God, Father, not King; Christ, brother, not Redeemer; Religion, nature. It loves and trusts, but does not fear. It sees in Jesus a man living manlike, highly gifted, and living with blameless and beautiful fidelity to God, stepping thousands of years before the race of man; the profoundest religious genius God has raised up; whose words and works help us to form and develop the native idea of a complete religious man. But he lived for himself; died for himself;

worked out his own salvation, and we must do the same, for one man cannot live for another more than he can eat or sleep for him. It is not the personal Christ but the spirit of Wisdom, Holiness, Love that creates the well-being of man; a life at one with God. The divine incarnation is in all mankind."[1]

Such is the faith avowed and enforced by Theodore Parker. It goes but little beyond a belief in God's existence and general participation in human life. It is sometimes difficult to distinguish his views of Deity from Pantheism; but on more than one occasion be expressed his total dissent from the peculiarity of the Hegelian system. He holds that all we see about us and feel within us testifies of God. Neither speculative nor practical atheism can produce good in the world; we must believe in God's existence, else we have no power whatever to explain the harmony in nature, providence in individual and national life, existence and immortality of the soul, and the suffering to which we fall heir.[2] But Theism clears up every difficulty, and sheds its light upon all departments of human life. This alone can overthrow the popular orthodox theology and enthrone the religion of the Absolute, or true Spiritualism in its stead.

It is a question of grave importance how far the skepticism of Unitarianism, Universalism, and Pantheism has been influential upon the American Church, and how great is the number of those who have become more or less tinctured with the Rationalism of the last five years' importation. Parker claimed that the liberal or Rationalistic thinkers were largely on the increase; but he also informs us that the translation by himself of *De Wette's*

[1] *Discourse on Matters Pertaining to Religion*, pp. 477, 478.

[2] *Sermons of Theism, Atheism, and Popular Theology*, pp. 51–55.

Introduction to the Old Testament, not only proved a financial failure, but that it has had "no recognition nor welcome in America; that it has never had a friendly word said for it in any American journal."[1] Skepticism has been proclaimed principally by public lectures, and, in this form, has made little pretension to logical, exegetical, or metaphysical power. Youths have manifested a decided taste for the works of Carlyle, Emerson, and Parker, while the *Phases of Faith* is one of the most thumb-worn of all the volumes of our circulating libraries. Yet American Rationalism still lacks consistency and system.

The history of Rationalism proves that the evil is of slow and insidious growth. The young are most susceptible of its influence. The Sunday Schools of the various evangelical Churches are usually supplied with large libraries of religious books. But many works of pernicious tendency have been known to find a place upon shelves designed for better service.

A recent juvenile publication of skeptical character has probably been read by many children whose parents had taught them that all Scripture is given by inspiration of God.[2] This neat and attractive little volume is worthy of the disciples of Paulus and Semler. It is an advocate, under the most fascinating garb, of the very Rationalism which now threatens the American Church. The author claims that the patriarchal history is made up of little scraps of poetry; the fall of our first parents was their seeing a dark veil one day in their wandering, and they, in consequence thereof, went out of the pleasant place where they had been dwelling; the deluge was simply a metaphorical de-

[1] Weiss, *Life and Correspondence of Theodore Parker*, vol. i., p. 402.

[2] *Stories of the Patriarchs*, by Rev. O. B. Frothingham. Boston, 1864.

scription of the increase of evil among men; the ark was only a mystical vessel typifying faith, truth, and other correctives of sorrow and sin; "there never was a single man Noah, who put all those creatures into a boat and saved himself;" no sacrifice appeared to Abraham when about to offer Isaac, but "his lifted arm seems to be seized as by the hand of an angel;" the crossing of the Red Sea by Israel, and the destruction of Pharoah and his host, were the natural results of tide and storm; the bitter waters were sweetened by a friendly weed that grew close at hand; the speaking of Balaam's ass was only the twirling of his long ears and loud braying; and the walls of Jericho fell merely by the natural force of loud, fearless, and honest speaking, —just as West India Slavery tumbled down by the agency of the noble voices that thundered, trumpet-like, in righteous indignation against it.

While speaking of Mr. Frothingham's juvenile work, we do not forget that he has lately sounded the alarm of "Liberal Christianity" for those who have passed the age of childhood. Many of his Unitarian brethren will hardly agree with his radical Rationalism. Belonging to the extreme Left Wing, he holds that it is the province of liberal Christians to slough off the absurd doctrines now prevalent,—"not to remould the age,—to recast it, to regenerate it, to cross it or struggle with it, but to penetrate its meaning, enter into its temper, sympathize with its hopes, blend with its endeavors. The life of the time appoints the creed of the time, and modifies the establishment of the time. The great mark of our generation is a deep faith in the soul's power to take care of itself, and a desire that it may exercise that power to the utmost. Away with fears! Away with despairs! Away with devils! Away with perdition!

Away with doom! Protestantism has the poison in its heart. From our own liberal theology, the elements of unnaturalism, preternaturalism, supernaturalism, have disappeared almost as completely as they have from the systems of science. The grand achievement of Christianity was the emancipation of human nature from its terrible Jewish thraldom. Its revelation seems to have been, that men could judge for themselves what is right,—could please God by being true to themselves,—could find the blessed life by returning to the simplicity of little children,—and could bring in the kingdom of heaven by yielding to the solicitations of kindness. Man greater than the Sabbath; man greater than the temple; man greater than the priesthood or the law. The religion was a consecration of Nature; the abolishment of the old oppressive hierarchies, and a cordial invitation to the heart to make a religion for itself. Just so far as it was in the deepest and purest sense 'natural' religion,—just so far as it emancipated the moral forces of humanity,—was it quick and quickening. . . . Human nature, under liberty, will vindicate itself as a divine creation. The freer it is, the more harmonious, orderly, balanced, and beautiful it is. . . . Nature's seers, running their eye along the line of the moral law, catch vistas in the future brighter than those that now are fading from the Old Testament page; and Nature's prophets, putting their ear to the ground, hear the murmur of nobler revelations than were ever given to the old oracles now moving their stiffened lips in death. Humanity's heresiarchs are lordlier than inhumanity's priests. The soul's image-breaking is diviner than the prelate's worship. Knowledge distances faith. Human solidity more than makes good the Catholic's Communion. The revelation of universal law makes the belief in miracle seem atheistical; and the irresistible grace of the spirit that lives, and moves, and discloses its being in humanity, sweeps past the dispensations of Catholic and Protestant Christendom, as the eagle distances the dove."[1]

We would not utter a syllable of needless alarm; but is it not time that the American Church take note of the efforts by which the Rationalists of every grade are striving to take away the cardinal truths of the Christian revelation? Their predecessors in Europe sought to make children ashamed of the old truths by casting sarcasm on the strong faith and evangelical piety of the forefathers. They then aimed to show that the Church and theology are altogether behind the age, and that science and art are advancing with a rapidity which must leave all dogmatism and authority far behind. They afterward examined the Scriptures by the light of Reason alone, and, by this idea, deluded multitudes of the young and inexperienced into the darkness and doubt which were never removed.

This last effort may be the next one to which American Rationalism will address itself. The Church in this country has partaken of the pride awakened by our unexampled national prosperity; and many of her noblest sons had well-nigh come to the conclusion, before the outbreak of the late civil war, that she must inevitably prosper, simply because of the remarkable temporal blessings which God had lavishly given. But without faith nothing can be accomplished, and three decades may be sufficient to so change the whole

Sermon on the *New Religion of Nature*, before the Alumni of the Cambridge Divinity School. Published in the *Friend of Progress*, November, 1864.

aspect of our religious life that the Church may become thoroughly Rationalistic; her sanctuaries frequented, and her posts of honor occupied, by the worshipers of Reason. The fidelity of the past will not be able to meet the emergency of the present. The Church in the wilderness was not permitted to lay up manna in advance.

Our civilization is undergoing a complete revolution. The field is newly ploughed by the events of the last few years, and it becomes the Church to scatter the seeds of truth with an unsparing hand. If this land is to be blessed with pure faith, as in past years, a faith strong enough to repel every blow of Skepticism, to the Church, as an instrument, and not to our natural growth, shall be attributed this popular prosperity. If we would secure for future years an uncorrupted faith, the enaction of pure laws, the introduction of the Gospel into every social class, an increased enthusiasm in missionary labors, the intense union of all parts of our country, and the united progress of piety and theological science, the duty of the present hour must be discharged.

CHAPTER XXV.

INDIRECT SERVICE OF SKEPTICISM—PRESENT OUTLOOK.

The most important successes of man are born of his severest trials and most persistent struggles. Sometimes principles have required the combats of centuries before they become the possession of a heroic people. The value of the prize may in most cases be accurately estimated by the length of time and the outlay of effort expended for its attainment. "Men of easy faith," says a wise observer of human deeds, "and sanguine hope, have sometimes, after one great commotion and change, joyously assured themselves that this would suffice. The grand evil is removed; we shall now happily and fast advance with a clear scene before us. But after a while, to their surprise and dismay, another commotion and dismay has perhaps carried the whole affair back, apparently, to the same state as before. Recollect the history of the Reformation in this land; begun by Henry VIII., established, it was gladly assumed, by his son. But that youth dies, and then we have the instant return of Popery, in all its triumph, fury, and revenge. After a while Queen Mary departs, and all pious souls exult in liberation and Protestantism. But then again, in Elizabeth's time, there comes a half-papist, severe spiritual tyranny. Later down, after the overthrow of the tyrant Charles, there arose for the first time, a prospect of real religious liberty. But his son resumes the throne, and all such liberty was abolished, and so continued long; and another revolution was required that religious faith and worship might be free."[1]

But when the English Reformation did come it was worth all its cost. The Church would not barter it to-day for the commercial value of continents,—no, not if she were told that the refusal would cost her whole centuries of poverty and sorrow, many more martyrdoms, and a second home in the catacombs.

The various conflicts with infidelity have been scarcely less terrible than the determined efforts made for the preservation of the faith of the Gospel against the persecutions of the Roman Emperors and the popes of the inquisitorial period. For there are two kinds of suffering in defense of truth; that manifested by endurance of the body when physical pain is inflicted, and that which the mind undergoes when plausible error makes its fascinating appeal. And he who can resist the pretenses of infidelity and remain pure amid the general waste of faith, has moral power enough to attest his love of truth by dying in its behalf. God takes note of all offerings which we bring, whether it be a lacerated body in an age of persecution, or a sorely-tried but yet purely-kept conscience in a period of devastating irreligion. The same benignant Father who welcomed the sacrifice of the unblemished heifer was ready to receive the humbler offering of a pair of turtle doves.

One of the general principles on which we based the present historical inquiry, was the undesigned, but real service rendered the cause of truth and the Church by skepticism. It is yet too soon to prove the validity of this position in reference to the present manifestations

[1] John Foster, *Broadmead Lectures*, vol. i., p. 309.

of Rationalism in England and the United States. They are yet incomplete, and not until a system of doubt has completed its cycle, are we enabled to determine the evil which it has inflicted and the general benefit which it has indirectly accomplished. When we look, therefore, at the developed types of error which have arisen and made their impress on the public mind, we are forced to the conclusion that, as God holds truth in his hand and makes it minister to the good of his cause, so does he possess complete control of error, and sometimes causes its wildest vagaries to contribute to the advancement of those interests which they were designed to subvert. The promoters of the evil are none the less responsible, though their works terminated in an unexpected issue. "It must needs be that offenses come; but woe to that man by whom the offense cometh."

This principle of God's moral government has long been denied a recognition. The purely literary historian has here been in advance of the student of religious events, for he has conceded and defended the principle when tracing the career of military chieftains, who aimed solely at the conquest of nations and the increase of temporal power. He has shown how the devastations of an Alexander, a Hannibal, and a Napoleon have been the unexpected instruments of great popular blessings. Ecclesiastical historians have frequently regarded all skeptical tendencies as evil in all their consequences; but it is a far more exalted view of God's ceaseless care of the interests of his Church, to consider him as the All-powerful and All-loving, causing even "the wrath of man to praise him."

A glance at the various departments of theology which have received most attention within the last half century, will prove that Rationalism has been the undesigned means of contributing to their advancement. The faith of the public teacher determines the faith and practice of the masses; and those who are the commissioned expounders of truth for the people have to-day a more substantial basis of theological literature, than their predecessors possessed before Rationalism appeared in Germany. As some of the grandest cathedrals of Europe, originally built by the Roman Catholics, and designed by them for the perpetual dissemination of the doctrines of Popery, are now the shrines of Protestant worship, so have those weapons which were shaped for fierce assaults upon inspiration been wielded in its defense. "Rationalism was not to be simply ignored," says Schaff, "but in the hand of that Providence which allows nothing to take place in vain, must serve the purpose of bringing to a new form the old, which, in its contracted sphere—that of mere understanding—it had profanely demolished. By this means a freer activity and fuller development were secured, and that want which lies at the root of all Rationalism, was supplied; namely, that religious truth shall not be confronted with the subjective spirit in the form of mere outward authority, but, in an inward way, become fully reconciled to it in the form of conviction and certainty."[1]

The Rationalists at one time deemed the criticism of the Scriptures their strongest fortress. This is evident from their numerous works on the authenticity of the Biblical books, and on the text itself. They perused the Church Fathers for corroborative opinions, applied themselves to the oriental languages with a zeal worthy of a better purpose, traveled through countries mentioned in the Bible in order to study local customs and popular traditions, and searched the testimony of both

[1] *What is Church History?* p. 15.

ancient and modern writers with an enthusiasm seldom surpassed. Their purpose was, to maintain the human character of the Bible. Now what do we behold? Those researches have been employed by evangelical critics for a higher end, and are powerful auxiliaries in the defense of the divine authority of the Scriptures. The Hebrew learning of Gesenius, for example, is the most available instrument in the hands of the orthodox theologian in his study of the Old Testament. The most critical and accurate of the Rationalists have, in almost every case, told us some truth which the professed friends of revelation had not possessed, and which the Church might have been compelled to seek for centuries without success.

Church history was crude and ill-written before the Rationalists expended their toil and learning upon it. They investigated the fountains; made the storm-beaten monuments, old coins, and medals disclose their long-kept secrets; and threaded the labyrinths of secular history, written in almost every European language, in order that nothing serviceable to their cause might be lost. As an illustration of the impetus imparted to this sphere of theological science, we may state that between the years 1839 and 1841, there were published in Germany over five hundred works on church history alone.[1] "Almost every theologian of any name," says Schaff, "has devoted a portion at least of his strength to some department of church history. Besides this, however, it is found to receive the homage of all other departments,—Exegesis, Introduction, Ethics, Practical Theology, etc., in this respect: that for any work to be complete it is felt necessary that it should, in the way of introduction, present a history of the subject with which it is em-

[1] Winer, *Handbuch der Theologischen Wissenschaft*, 1838–1842.

ployed, and have also due regard to views different from its own. Let any one look into any of the later commentaries by Bleek, Harless, Tholuck, Steiger, Hengstenberg, Fritzsche, and Rückert; or into the dogmatic works of Twesten, Nitzsch, Hase, and the monograph of Julius Müller on sin, and he will soon learn how entirely the whole present theology is pervaded with historical material from beginning to end."[1]

In the conception of church history as a science, the Rationalists also displayed a wisdom which had ever been wanting. "Rationalism," says Schaff again, "has been of undeniable service to church history. In the first place, it exercised the boldest criticism, placing many things in a new light, and opening the way for a more free and unprejudiced judgment. Then again it assisted in bringing out the true conception of history itself, though rather in a mere negative way. Almost all previous historians, Protestant as well as Catholic, had looked upon the history of *heresies* as essentially motion and change, while they had regarded the church doctrine as something once for all settled and unchangeable; a view which cannot possibly stand the test of impartial inquiry. For though Christianity itself, the saving truth of God, is always the same, and needs no change, yet this can by no means be affirmed of the apprehension of this truth by the human mind in the different ages of the Church, as is at once sufficiently evident from the great difference between Catholicism and Protestantism; and within the latter, from the distinctions of Lutheranism, Zwinglianism, and Calvinism. But Rationalism now discovered fluctuation, motion, change, in the Church, as well as in the sects; thus taking the first step towards the idea of organic

[1] *What is Church History?* p. 17.

development, on which the latest German historiography is founded."[1] We deem this testimony in favor of our position as of no ordinary value, coming as it does from one so intimately acquainted with the issues involved, and yet in no sympathy with the skepticism of any age.

The Rationalistic divines have also been the indirect means of a better estimate of the life of Christ. The replies to the work of Strauss present, as we have before intimated, the most complete portrait of the career of the Messiah ever drawn by uninspired authority. The symmetry, scope, power, and sympathy which revealed themselves through his entire ministry are so described by Neander, and those in harmony with him, that their representation of the Messiah must ever perform an invaluable service in theological literature. Had the attack never been made we would not now enjoy the benefit resulting from the counter-blow. "These replies," says Schwarz, "constitute an important literature of themselves, in which scarcely any theological name of importance is absent, and in which many obscure pastors from all parts of Germany have brought the fire-bucket of their knowledge in order to extinguish the flame that threatened to consume them and their village-churches together with the historical basis of Christianity. . . . Concerning the theological discussion originated by Strauss, our attention is turned toward those works which undertake to answer specifically the critical questions under consideration. His celebrated work was the signal for a totally new gospel criticism. A succession of works appeared at but brief intervals that discussed in a far more thorough method than Strauss had done those important

[1] *History of the Apostolic Church*, p. 80.

questions concerning the relations of the gospels to each other, their signification, age, and authenticity."[1]

So, too, has the criticism of the apostolic age by the Tübingen school aroused the friends of evangelical Christianity to inquire into the same period, and see whether their own ground was really defensible. It was a fortunate day for them when their attention was directed thither. For the church enjoys thereby a much clearer conception of all those great movements that had their origin in the time of the apostles, of the relations in which those men stood to the Divine Founder, of the gradual dissemination of the gospel, of the general condition of the infant church, and of its interpretation of the doctrines promulgated by Christ, than could have been acquired by all the ordinary methods of investigation.

Taking the past as a present instructor, we fear no permanent evil results from the recent popular Lives of Jesus by Renan and Strauss. These men have written for the masses, and their appeal is to the plain mind. They would portray Christ in such a light that even the least intelligent mind might be brought into living sympathy with his humanity. Now, when their view of him shall have been faithfully answered by presenting his divine character to the common understanding, who will say that the present generation of Christ's skeptical biographers have written in vain? Those authors, having seen the necessity of a popular understanding of Christ, describe him as a man like ourselves. They have written from a wrong standpoint, but if their labors can suggest to evangelical theologians the immediate necessity of a popular view of Christ as our Redeemer, we will not believe that

[1] *Geschichte der Neuesten Theologie.* Second Edition, pp. 105, 152.

their labors, though exerted for a different purpose, are without good fruits. The people need to perceive clearly the character of Christ—not to look upon him as far off, but near at hand, not to regard him as the cold, indifferent observer of our conduct, but as that Friend who, being our Elder Brother, enters into sympathy with the humblest of his followers, and suffers not a sparrow to fall without his notice.

We are confirmed in our opinion of the ultimate advantages from Renan's representation of Christ by the testimony of M. de Pressensé. This distinguished theologian was recently returning from the Holy Land, whither he had gone "to seek to lay hold of the holy likeness of Christ that he might present it to his countrymen," when he stopped at Altenburg to attend the session of the Evangelical Church Diet of Germany. Speaking of the indirect service of Renan, he used the following earnest language: "I too wish to expose to you the advantages of the recent attacks against our faith, for, in my eyes, they by far outweigh the inconveniences and the perils. Without doubt, this falsification of the holy type which we adore may well deceive the public mind, for it fell into a community of religious ignorance, into a country in which modern Catholicism —I mean to say Italian, or rather Roman Catholicism, which has but too much prevailed over that of our Pascals and our Bossuets—had more and more reduced religion to a servile submission towards the Papacy and superstitious worship of the deified creature, thus preventing the direct intercourse of the soul with the gospel and with him who fills the gospel. And then, M. Renan's book at bottom flattered all the bad contemporaneous instincts; it made the apotheosis of that melancholy and voluptuous skepticism which covers up with a certain distinction and a certain charm the most positive materialism; it flattered our languid wills, substituted the worship of the beautiful for the worship of the holy, and authorized, by the false ideal which it presents to us, a factitious religious sentiment, which demands no sacrifice, no manly act, covers up the cross under flowers, and at last only gives back to humanity its old idol, newly carved and painted. This idol is no other than humanity itself. This mixture of atheism and sensibility was particularly dangerous, because it met preëxistent tendencies, and colored them with a fallacious poesy. The art of the historian, or rather of the romance-writer [Renan], consisted in his hiding the entire absence of all belief under graceful metaphors and an unctuous style, just as the brilliant snow of the Alps covers up the abyss and deprives the traveler of the salutary horror which would save him. You see, my friends, I do not diminish the perils of a book which has had in its two editions a sale of two hundred thousand copies. And yet, I persist in believing that the advantages are greater than its disadvantages."

Neither do we apprehend any ultimate disaster from the Skeptical Scientific School. Darwin, Buckle, and others have striven diligently to impress upon the public mind the opinion that there is an antagonism between science and revelation, and that it is of such character as to render Christianity a useless appendage to human society.

Now, in order to counteract the influence of their sentiments, the evangelical theologian should take no partial or prejudicial views of science, or of its necessity for the defense of Scriptural truth. The course adopted by the Roman Catholic Church in reference to the discoveries of some of the noblest of her sons was suicidal.

When Galileo was forced to recant his theory of the earth's revolution, the advance of papacy was arrested. To all outward appearance there is an incompatibility between the claims of geology and the Mosaic cosmogony. Shall we say that geology is false, and the six days of the Mosaic narrative must be understood in their literal sense? This presents the dilemma either to reject geology as a spurious science, or to discard revelation. We will not accept such an alternative, and rather say, "Geology is a noble science, but it is yet an infant. When it reaches its majority we shall see a harmony,—inexpressibly beautiful and proportionate,—between its discoveries and the inspired word of God."

We must not charge the errors of scientific skeptics to the department of inquiry in which they labor. The perversions and errors of science, and not science itself, are at enmity with revelation. Mr. Darwin's theory of development seems to be in outright opposition to the Scriptural account of the animal creation. But there is no occasion of alarm at what he has said, for neither he nor all who think with him can invalidate the truths of Scripture. We should despise no theory that aims at our better comprehension of great truths; for the day will come when science, in its mature glory and strength, shall cast its human lustre on all the pages of divine truth.

The true way to meet the writings of skeptics in the Church is by calm replies to their charges, and by immediate ecclesiastical discipline. Every word or act that savors of tyranny or undue exaction creates friends for them, and when for them, for their opinions also. Mere general remarks in reply to their attacks will accomplish nothing. Little advantage would be gained if every preacher in Great Britain and America were only to say, "Bishop Colenso is in error." But it will be a public benefit if he be treated with personal kindness of expression as a brother-man, his arguments examined, and their obnoxious fallacy proved. The Church should deal toward the foes of her own household with the greatest possible caution, else the reaction will be of lasting evil. Neander taught a lesson for all coming time when a royal edict was about to appear forbidding the entrance of Strauss' *Life of Jesus* within the Prussian dominion. He violently opposed it, and gave it as his opinion, that "the work of Strauss, though not profound, was written with much talent, and that throughout, science predominated over and extinguished sentiment. That, in truth, the writer appeared to be guided by singular good faith, but that his mythical system did nevertheless undermine Christianity; and that if it spread, it might be feared that it might destroy Christian faith; but, yet, that it would be a great mistake to interdict the work; since, when once interdicted, it could not be refuted, and by such a measure it would acquire an undue importance."

But whatever precautions are taken in dealing with skepticism, it is essential that the spirit of unity pervade all evangelical denominations. During the Peninsular War, the Duke of Wellington, observing that one of his officers of artillery was serving a gun with remarkable precision against a body of men posted in a wood to the left, rode up to the subaltern, and said: "Well aimed, captain; but no more,—they are our own 99th!" A similar mistake has sometimes been committed by ecclesiastical organizations, which, instead of aiming at the common enemy, have expended too much valuable time and energy in efforts to defend their individual creeds. A more intense harmony of all the friends of orthodoxy is a condition of permanent success. The theological crisis of to-day may be followed by others more severe. But the Faith of the Church teaches the invaluable lesson that God designs, by the ordeal of the earthly crucible, to prepare her for higher honor and perfect service. She does not desire a premature termination of the season of proof.

"From darkness here, and weariness,
We ask not full repose,
Only be Thou at hand.—

* * * * * * *

The wanderer seeks his native bower,
And we will look and long for Thee,
And thank Thee for each trying hour,
Wishing, not struggling, to be free."[1]

[1] Keble, *Christian Year*.

APPENDIX.

LITERATURE OF RATIONALISM.

I.—GERMANY—HOLLAND—SWITZERLAND.

AUBERLEN, C. A.—Die Göttliche Offenbarung, 2 Bände, Basel, 1861–64.

ÄUSERUNGEN üb. Renan, Strauss u. ähnliche Bücher. Anon. Tüb., 1864.

BALMES, J.—Briefe an einem Zweifler, Aus d. Span. übersetzt, von F Loruiser, Regensburg, 1864.

BAUR, F. C.—Die Tübinger Schule und ihre Stellung zur Gegenwart. Tübingen, 1859.

BEYSCHLAG, W.—Uber das "Leben Jesu" v. Renan. Halle a. S. 1864.

BOCKSHAMMER, G. F.—Offenbarung und Theologie. Stuttg. 1822.

BÖHME, C. F.—Christliches Henotikon. Halle, 1827.

——— Die Sache des rationalen Supranaturalismus, geprüft und erklärt. Neust. 1823.

BRETSCHNEIDER, K. G.—Ueber die Grundprincipien der Evang. Theologie. Altenburg, 1832.

——— Zwei Sendschreiben an einem Staatsmann. Leipzig, 1830.

BRONSVELD, A. W.—Oorzaken der verbreiding van het rationalisme in ous land, sinds de laaste jaren der vorigen eeuw. Rotterdam, 1862.

BRUNNER, S.—Der Atheist Renan u. Sein Evangelium. Regensburg, 1864.

BUCHER, J.—Das Leben Jesu v. Dr. Fr. Strauss nach der neuen "f. das Deutsche Volk," beab. Augsburg, 1864.

CASSEL, P.—Über Renan's Leben Jesu. Berlin, 1864.

CHANTEPIE DE LA SAUSSAYE.—La Crise Religieuse en Hollande. Leyde, 1860.

CLAUSEN, PROF.—Katholicismus u. Protestantismus, 3 Bände. Translated by Fries. Latest Edition, 1828.

The author, a moderate Rationalist, attempts in vain to identify Protestantism and Rationalism.

CLEMEN, C. F. W—Die Rationalisten sind doch Christen. Altenbg. 1829.

CÖLLN, D. G. K. VON, UND SCHULTZ, DAV.—Über Theologische Lehrfreiheit auf den Evangelischen Universitäten. Breslau, 1830.

CORNIL, A.—Ludwig Feuerbach u. Seine Stellung zur Religion u. Philosophie d. Gegenwart. Frankfurt a. Main, 1851.

DA COSTA.—The Four Witnesses. Holland.

This work relates to the Four Evangelists, and is a reply to Strauss.

DEUTINGER, M.—Renan u. das Wunder. München, 1864.

DE WETTE.—Über der Verfall der Protestantischen Kirche in Deutschland, und die Mittel, ihr wieder aufzuhelfen. Reformationsalm.—1817, S. 296 ff.

——— Religion und Theologie. Berlin, 1817.

——— Theodor oder des Zweifler's Weihe. 2 Bde. Berlin, 1822.

DIESTELMANN, TH.—Beleuchtung d. Lebens Jesu f. das Deutsche Volk, v. D. F. Strauss. Hannover, 1864.

ENGELHARDT, M.—Schenkel und Strauss. Erlangen, 1864.

FELDMANN, T. C.—Der Wahre Christus u. sein rechtes Symbol. Altona, 1865.

FEUERBACH, F. L.—Das Wesen d. Glaubens im Sinne Luther's. Leip., 1844.

FREI-RELIGIÖSEN (die) in ihrer Blösse. Brandenburg, 1862.

FREPPEL, PROF.—Kritische Beleuchtung d. Ernst Renan'schen Schrift: Das Leben Jesu. Wien, 1864.

FRICKE, G.—Ueber Renan's Leben Jesu. Heidelberg, 1864.

FRITZSCHE, CH. F.—De Rationalismo commentatt. II; in den opuscul. academ. Tur.—1846.

FROST, W.—Das Leben d. Anti-Christus nach Ernst Renan. Wien, 1864.

GEBHARD, F. H.—Die letzten Gründe des Rationalismus in einer Widerlegung der Briefe Zöllichs. Arnst., 1822.

GERBER, J. H.—Supranominalismus, ein neues System der Theologie, oder die endliche Versöhnung zwischen Rationalismus und Supranaturalismus in wissenschaftliche Nothwendigkiet. Leipzig, 1843—44.

GERLACH, H.—Gegen Renan, Leben Jesu. Berlin, 1864.

GESS UND RIGGENBACH.—Apologetische Beiträge. Basel, 1864.

GROEN VAN PRINSTERER, G.—Le parti anti-revolutionaire et confessionel dans l'église réformée des Pays-Bas. Amsterdam, 1860.

GURLITT, J. GFR.—Rede zur Empfehlung des Vernunftsgebrauch's bei dem Studium der Theologie. Hamburg, 1822.

HAAR, B. TER,—Pictures from the History of the Reformation. 1855.

A prize work, written to strengthen the faith of Protestants.

——— Vorlesungen über Renan's "Leben Jesu." 1864.

HAFFNER.—Die Deutsche Aufklärung. Mainz, 1864.

HAGENBACH, K. R.—Kirchengeschichte d. 18 und 19 Jahrhunderts. 3 Aufl. Leipzig, 1856.

——— Die sogenannte Vermittelungstheologie. Zürich, 1858.

——— History of Doctrines. Revised Edinb. ed., with large additions. By Prof. H. B. Smith. New York, 1862.

HAHN, A.—De Rationalismi, qui dicitur, vera indole et qua cum naturalismo contineatur ratione. Lips. 1827.

——— Ueber die Lage des Christenthums unserer Zeit, und das Verhältniss der Christlichen Theologie zur Wissenschaft überhaupt. Leipz. 1832.

HANEBERG, D. B.—E. Renan's Leben Jesu beleuchtet. Regensbg. 1864.

HANNE, J. W.—Rationalismus und spec. Theologie in Braunschweig. Braunschweig, 1838.

HARMS, C.—Thesen Luther's mit andern 95 Sätzen. Kiel, 1817.

——— "Dass es mit der Vernunftreligion nichts ist." Kiel, 1819.

HAVET, E.—Kritik üb. "Das Leben Jesu" v. E. Renan. Mannheim, 1863.

HEINRICH, J. B.—Christus: Kritik des Rationalismus, des Straussischen Mythicismus u. d. Lebens Jesu v. Renan. Mainz, 1864.

HELD, C. F. W.—Jesus der Christ, mit Rücksicht auf d. Rationalismus u. Skepticismus d. Gegenwart. Zürich, 1865.

HENHOFER, A.—Der Kampf d. Unglaubens m. Aberglauben u. Glauben. Heidelberg, 1861.

HENKE, C. L. TH.—Rationalismus u. Traditionalismus im 19. Jahrhundert. 1864.

HERING.—Die Akephaler unsrer Zeit. Leipzig, 1825.

HERINGA, J. E.—Het gebruiken Misbruik der Kritik. Holland, 1793.

HOFSTEDE DE GROOT, P.—Die Gröninger Theologen. Gotha, 1863.

HÜFFELL, L.—Friedensvorschläge zur Beendigung des Streits zwischen bibl. Christlichen Theologen und Rationalisten; Zeitschrift für Predigerwissenschaften. Bd. 2. St. 1.

HUNDESHAGEN, K. B.—Der Deutsche Protestantismus. 3 Aufl. Frankfort a. Main, 1850.

HURTER, H.—Ueber die Rechte der Vernunft und des Glaubens. Innsbruck, 1863.

KÄHLER, L. A.—Supranaturalismus und Rationalismus in ihrem gemeinschaft. Ursprunge, ihrer Zwietracht u. höhern Einheit. Leipzig, 1818.

KAHNIS, K. F. A.—Der innere Gang des deutschen Protestantismus seit Mitte des vorigen Jahrhunderts. Leipzig, 1854.

KAMPE, F.—Geschichte der religiösen Bewegung d. neuern Zeit. 2 Bde. Leipzig, 1852—53.

KEIM, I.—Der Geschichtliche Christus. Zürich, 1864.

KLEUKER, J. F.—Ueber das Ja und Nein der Bibl. Christl. u. der reinen Vernunfttheologie. Hamburg, 1819.

Compare, Ueber die Altonaer Bibel. 1818.

——— Ueber den alten und neuen Protestantismus. Bremen, 1823.

KÖHLER, A.—Die niederländisch-reform. Kirche. Erlangen, 1856.

KUENEN, A.—The Pentateuch and Book of Joshua critically examined. Translated from the Dutch by Rt. Rev. J. W. Colenso. London, 1865.

LANG, H.—Dogmatik. Berlin, 1858.

——— Ein Gang durch die Christliche Welt. Berlin, 1859.

——— Religiöse Charactere. Winterthur, 1862.

LORGION, E. J.—The Pastor of Vliethinzen; or, Conversations about the Groninger School. Capetown, 1865.

A novel, translated from the Dutch, for the use of Colonists in Southern Africa.

LUTHARDT, C. E.—Die modernen Darstellungen des Lebens Jesu. Eine Besprechung der Schriften von Strauss, Renan, etc. Leipzig, 1864.

MEYER, J.—Das Leben Jesu v. Dav. Frdr. Strauss. Leipzig, 1865.

MICHELIS, F.—Renan's Roman vom Leben Jesu. Münster, 1864.

NEUESTER NACHTRAG zu Renan's Leben Jesu. Berlin, 1864.

NICOLAS, A.—Die Gottheit Jesu. Regensburg, 1864.

NITZSCH, C. L.—Ueber das Heil der Theologie durch Unterscheidung der Offenbarung und Religion als Mittel und Zweck. 1830.

NOACK, L.—Die Freidenker in der Religion. Berne, 1853.

OOSTERZEE, J. J. VAN.,—Geschichte oder Roman? Das Leben Jesu v. E. Renan beleuchtet. 1863.

OPZOOMER, C. W.—De waarheid en hare kenbronnen. Amsterdam, 1862.

PAULUS, H. E. G.—Zeitgemässe Beleuchtung des Streites zwischen dem Eingebungsglauben und der Urchristlichen Denkglaubigkeit. Wiesbaden, 1830.

PETRENZ, K. A.—Wie hast du Renan's Leben Jesu aufgenommen? Neu-Ruppin, 1864.

RAUMER, F.—Schwarz, Strauss, Renan. Leipzig, 1864.

RIGGENBACH, C. J.—Der Heutige Rationalismus besonders in der Deutschen Schweiz. Basel, 1862.

RITTER, H.—Ernst Renan üb. die Naturwissenschaften u. die Geschichte. Gotha, 1865.

RÖHR, J. F.—Briefe über den Rationalismus. Aachen, 1813.

——— Grund-und-Glaubenssätze der Evang.-protest. Kirche. 1832-1834.

ROMANG, J. P.—Ueber Unglauben, Pietismus u. Wissenschaft. Zürich, 1859.

ROSENKRANZ, K.—Kritik d. Principien d. Strauss'schen Glaubenslehre. Leipzig, 1844.

ROYAARDS, H. J.—Geschiedenis van het Christendom. Nederland, 1853.

RÜCKERT, L. J.—Der Rationalismus. Leipzig, 1859.

RUMPF.—Kirchenglaube und Erfahrung, 1854.

——— Bibel und Christus, 1858.

RUTHENUS, K.—Der formale Supernaturalismus oder d. einzig mögliche Weg zur einer Ausgleichung der stritenden theolog. Partheien. Leipzig, 1834.

SARTORIUS, C.—Die Religion ausserhalb der Grenzen der blossen Vernunft. Marburg, 1822.

——— Ueber die Unwissenschaftlichkeit und innere Verwandschaft des Rationalismus uud Romanismus. Auch u. d. Tit: Beiträge zur Evang. Rechtglaubigkeit. 1 Hft. Heidelberg, 1825.

SCHENKEL, D.—Die Religösen Zeitkämpfe. Hamburg, 1847.

——— Das Characterbild Jesu. Wiesbaden, 1864.

——— Die Protestantische Freiheit in ihrem gegenwartigen Kampfe in der Kirchlichen Reaktion. Wiesbaden, 1865.

SCHLOSSER, F. C.—Geschichte d. 18 und 19 Jahrhunderts. (First two vols.) Heidelberg, 1843.

SCHOLTEN, J. H.—Oratio de pugna theologiam inter atque philosophiam recte utriusque studio tollenda. Leipzig, 1847.

——— Dogmatices Christianæ Initia. Editio II. Leyden, 1858.

SCHOTT, H. A.—Briefe über Religion und Christlichen Offenbarungsglauben. Jena, 1826.

SCHRÖTER, W.—Christianismus, Humanismus und Rationalismus in ihrer Identität. Leipzig, 1830.

SCHUBERT, F. W.—Die Freien Gemeinde unserer Zeit. Berlin, 1850.

SCHUDEROFF, J.—Briefe über den Rationalismus und Supernaturalismus, in Journal für Veredlung des Prediger- und Schullehrerstandes. Jahrg. 1811. Bd. 2. St. 3.

SCHULTHESS, J. UND ORELLI, J. K.—Rationalismus und Supernaturalismus, Kanon, Tradition und Scription. Zürich, 1822.

SCHULTZE, L.—Die Wunder Jesu Christi mit Beziehung a. d. Leben Jesu v. Renan. Königsberg, 1864.

SCHWARTZ, C.—Zur Geschichte d. neuesten Theologie. 3 sehr verm. Auf. Leipzig, 1864.

SEPP, DR.—Thaten u. Lehren Jesu; auf die jungsten Werke v. Renan und Strauss. Schaffhausen, 1864.

STÄUDLIN, C. F.—Geschichte des Rationalismus und Supranaturalismus. Göttingen, 1826.

STEFFENS, H.—Von der falschen Theologie und dem Wahren Glauben. Breslau, 1831.

STEIGER, W.—Kritik des Rationalismus in Wegscheider's Dogmatik. Berlin, 1830.

STRAUSS, D. F.—Das Leben Jesu. Berlin, 1835.

——— Das Leben Jesu f. das Deutsche Volk bearb. Leipzig, 1864.

TAFEL, F. I.—Das Leben Jesu,—gegen die Angriffe d. Dr. Strauss u. d. Unglaubens überhaupt. Basel, 1863.

THEILER, C. G. W.—Christus und die Vernunft. Leipzig, 1830.

——— Aphorismen zur Verständigung über den sogenannten alten und neuen Glauben. Leipzig, 1839.

THOLUCK, A.—Vermischte Schriften II., "Geschichte der Umwälzung der Theologie seit 1750." Hamburg, 1839.

——— Die Lehre v. der Sünde und vom Versöhnen. 7 Auf. Hamb. 1851.

——— Vorgeschichte des Rationalismus. Zwei Theile. Berlin, 1859–'62.

——— Geschichte d. Rationalismus. Erste Abth. Berlin, 1865.

TITTMANN, J. A. H.—Über Supranaturalismus, Rationalismus, u. Atheismus. Leipzig, 1816.

ULLMANN, K.—Theologisches Bedenken auf Veranlassung des Angriffs der evangel. Kirchenzeit, auf den Hallischen Rationalismus. Halle, 1830.

Together with many other articles of similar character in "Studien und Kritiken."

VERANTWORTUNG (zur) des Christlichen Glauben. 10 Vorträge von Riggenbach, Auberlen, Gess, und andere. Basel, 1862.

VOIGHTLÄNDER, J. A.—Der Rationalismus nach seinen philosophischen Hauptformen und in seiner historischen Gestalt. Leipzig, 1830.

WEGSCHEIDER, J. A. L.—Institutiones Theologiæ Christianæ Dogmaticæ. Halle, 1815. 8th Ed. 1844.

WEIDEMANN, K. A.—Die Neuesten Darstellungen d. Lebens Jesu von Renan, Schenkel, Strauss. Gotha, 1864.

WIESINGER, A.—Aphorismen gegen Renan's Leben Jesu. Wien, 1864.

WIGGERS, J.—Kirchlicher oder reinbiblischer Supranaturalismus? Leipzig, 1842.

WISLICENUS, G. A.—Die Bibel, für denkende Leser betrachtet. Leipzig, 1864.

WÖLLWARTH, F.—Gedanken üb. das characterbild Christi, von Schenkel. Stuttgart, 1865.

ZEITFRAGEN RELIGIÖSE, Unparteiisch beurtheilt v. e. Laien. Tüb., 1864.

ZÖCKLER, O.—Die Evangelien kritik u. das Lebensbild Christi nach d. Schrift. Darmstadt, 1864.

ZÖLLICH, C. F.—Briefe über den Supranaturalismus; eine Gegenschrift zu den Briefen über den Rationalismus. Sondershausen, 1821.

RATIONALISTIC PERIODICALS.

ALLGEMEINE KIRCHLICHE ZEITSCHRIFT.—Published by D. Schenkel, Elberfeld, 1860–'65.

ANNALEN.—Published by Schulthess, 1826–30.

DEUTSCHKATHOLISCHES SONNTAGSBLATT.—Wiesb., 1851–'65.

FREIES (FÜR) RELIGIÖSES LEBEN.—Breslau, 1848.

The Journal of the "Friends of Light."

KIRCHE DER GEGENWART.—Biedermann und Fries. Zürich, 1845–'50.

KIRCHEN-UND-SCHULBLATT.—Weimar, 1852–'65.

PREDIGERBIBLIOTHEK.—Published by Röhr, 1820–'48. Continued by H. Lang, to 1816.

PROTESTANTISCHE BLÄTTER, Für das evang. Oesterreich.—Wien, 1863–'65.

PROTESTANTISCHE KIRCHENZEITUNG.—H. Eltester und Carl Schwartz. Berlin, 1854–'65.

This quarterly is the leading organ of the German Rationalists.

SONNTAGSBLATT.—Uhlich. Gotha, 1850. Quarterly.

SOPHRONIZEN.—Published by Paulus, 1819–'30.

THEOLOGISCHE JAHRBÜCHER.—F. Chr. Baur und E. Zeller. Tübingen, 1842–'56. Not continued.

ZEITSCHRIFT FÜR WISSENSCHAFT. THEOLOGIE.—A. Hilgenfeld. Halle, 1858–'65.

ZEITSTIMMEN AUS D. REFORMIRTEN KIRCHE DER SCHWEIZ.—H. Lang. Winterthur, 1859–'66.

II.—FRANCE.

ARNAUD, A.—Les Orthodoxes et le Parti libéral protestant. Paris, 1864.

ASTIE, J. F.—Les deux Théologies nouvelles dans le sein du Protestantisme Français. Paris, 1862.

BIERMANN, C.—Foi et Raison. Paris, 1860.

BOISSONAIS, L.—Doctrine de la nouvelle école d'apres MM. Réville, A. Coquerel fils, et Colani. Paris, 1864.

BUISSON, F.—L'orthodoxie et l'Evangile dans l'Eglise reformée. Paris, 1864.

CASSAN-FLOYRAC, L'ABBÉ.—Le Rationalisme devant la Raison. Paris, 1858.

COLANI, T.—Ma Position dans l'Eglise de la Confession d'Augsbourg. Paris, 1860.

——— Jesus Christ et les Croyances messianiques de son Temps. Paris, 1864.

COQUEREL, A.—Christologie. Paris, 1859.

COQUEREL, E.—M. Guizot et l'Orthodoxie protestante. Paris, 1864.

——— Libéreaux et orthodoxes. Paris, 1864.

DUNAIME, L'ABBÉ J.—De la Raison dans ses Rapports avec la Foi. Paris, 1858.

FAYET, A.—Lettres à un rationaliste sur la philosophie et la religion. Paris, 1864.

FRANCHI, A.—Le Rationalisme. Bruxelles, 1858.

FROSSARD, C. L.—L'orthodoxie de l'Eglise réformée de France. Paris, 1864.

GUIZOT, F.—Méditations sur l'Essence de la Religion Chrétienne. Paris, 1864.

LARROQUE, P.—Renovation réligieuse. Paris, 1859.

——— Examen Critique des doctrines de la religion Chrétienne. Paris, 1859.

LUPS, L'ABBÉ J.—Le Traditionalisme et le Rationalisme. Liege, 1859.

NICOLAS, M.—Études Critiques sur la Bible. Paris, 1861.

PRESSENSÉ, E. DE.—Le Pays de l'Evangile; Notes d'un voyage en Orient. Paris, 1865.

REMUSAT, C. DE.—Philosophie Religieuse. Paris, 1864.

RENAN, E.—Études d'histoire Réligieuse. 3d Edition. Paris, 1858.

——— Vie de Jésus. Paris, 1863.

LITERATURE ARISING OUT OF THE PUBLICATION OF RENAN'S "LIFE OF JESUS."

AUGÉ, L.—Neuf pages décisives sur la Vie de Jésus de M. E. Renan. Paris, 1863.

BAUDON, P. L.—M. Ernest Renan, le prophete et le vrai fils de Dieu. Paris, 1863.

BLOCH, S.—M. Renan et le Judaïsme. Paris, 1863.

BONALD, M. de.—Mandement portant condamnation du livre intitulé: la Vie de Jésus, par E. Renan. Paris, 1863.

BONNETAIN, J.—Le Christ-Dieu devant les Siècles. M. Renan et son roman du jour. Paris, 1863.

BOURQUENOUD, A.—Les Distractions de M. Renan. Paris, 1863.

BOYLESVE, M. de.—M. Renan, défenseur de la foi d'apres un procédé nouveau. Paris, 1863.

CARLE, H.—Crises des croyances. M. Renan, et l'esprit de système. Paris, 1863.

CASTAING, A.—Jésus, M. E. Renan et la science. Paris, 1863.

CHAUVELOT, B.—M. Renan. Paris, 1863.

CHERET, L'ABBÉ.—Lettres d'un curé de campagne à M. Renan. Paris, 1863.

CLABAUT, L'ABBÉ.—E. Renan et l'Evangile. Paris, 1863.

COCHIN, A.—Quelques mots sur le Vie de Jésus de M. E. Renan. Paris, 1863.

COLANI, T.—Examen de la Vie de Jésus de M. Renan. Strasbourg, 1864.

CONSTANT, B.—Les contradictions de M. Renan. Paris, 1863.

CORRESPONDANCE APOCRYPHE entre M. E. Renan et sa sœur Ursule. Paris, 1863.

DELAPORTE, A.—La Critique et la Tactique, à propos de M. Renan. Paris, 1863.

DES GRANGES, F.—Une Échappé sur la Vie de Jésus d'Ernest Renan. Paris, 1863.

DESHAIRES, G.—La Vie de Jésus, les Évangiles, et M. Renan. Paris, 1863.

Evangile (le cinquième) de M. Renan,—par M. H. D. Paris, 1863.

Felix, R. P.—M. Renan et sa Vie de Jésus.

——— Quelques mots sur le livre de la Vie de Jésus. Paris, 1863.

Foisset.—Ernest Renan : Vie de Jésus. Paris, 1863.

Fregier, J. C.—Jésus devant le droit, ou Critique judiciare de la Vie de Jésus de M. E. Renan. Paris, 1863.

Freppel, L'Abbé.—Examen Critique de la Vie de Jésus de M. Renan. Paris, 1863.

Ginouliac.—Lettre à l'un de ses vicaires généraux sur la Vie de Jésus par M. E. Renan. Paris, 1863.

Guettée, L'Abbé.—Refutation de la prétendue Vie de Jésus de M. Renan. Paris, 1863.

Havet, E.—Jésus dans l'histoire. Examen de la Vie de Jésus par Renan. Paris, 1863.

Hello, E.—M. Renan et la Vie de Jésus. Paris, 1863.

Hervé.—Divinité de Jésus. Réponse à M. Renan. Paris, 1863.

Jourdain, A.—Réfutation rationnelle de la Vie de Jésus. Paris, 1863.

Lacordaire, R.—Aux Lecteurs de M. Renan. Paris, 1863.

Larroque, P.—Opinion des Déistes rationalistes sur la Vie de Jésus, selon M. Renan. Paris, 1863.

Lasserre, H.—L'Evangile selon Renan. Paris, 1863.

Latour.—Une réponse à M. Volusien Pagès. Réfutation d'une Réfutation, de M. Renan. Paris, 1863.

Laurentie.—Le Livre de M. E. Renan, sur la Vie de Jésus. Paris, 1863.

Le Peltier, E.—Vie de E. Renan. Paris, 1863.

Leroy, E.—Réponse d'un poëte à M. E. Renan. Paris, 1863.

Levy, Le Rabbin.—La Synagogue et M. Renan. Paris, 1863.

Loyson, J. T.—Une prétendue Vie de Jesus, ou M. E. Renan. Paris, 1863.

Macrakis, A.—Le Vrai Jésus Christ opposé au Jésus faux imaginé par M. E. Renan, et son Ecole sceptique. Paris, 1863.

Magué, C.—Jésus Christ, ou la Vérité vraie dans la question du moment. Paris, 1863.

Marrot, M.—La Vie de M. Renan et le Maudit. Paris, 1863.

Maubert, H.—Nicodème, étude sur M. Renan. Paris, 1863.

Maurette, O.—Jésus et la vraie Philosophie. Paris, 1863.

Meignan.—M. Renan réfuté par les Rationalistes Allemandes. Paris, 1864.

Michon, J. H.—Deux Leçons à M. Renan. Paris, 1863.

Milsand, Ph.—Bibliographie des Publications relatives au livre de M. Renan, Vie de Jésus. Paris, 1864.

Mirville, J. E.—Le Vrai Secret de M. Renan. Paris, 1863.

Monot, E.—À propos du livre de M. Renan, la Vie de Jésus. Paris, 1863.

Monsieur Renan en face du miracle ; par un Croyant. Paris, 1863.

Olgo, S.—Reflexions d'un orthodoxe de l'Église grecque sur la Vie de Jésus, de M. Renan. Paris, 1863.

Orsini, L'Abbé.—Réfutation du livre de M. Renan. Paris, 1863.

Orth, N. J.—La Vie de Jésus, selon M. Renan. Paris, 1863.

Pagès, V.—M. Renan et son siècle. Paris, 1863.

Parisis.—Jésus Christ est Dieu : démonstration. Paris, 1863.

Passaglia, P. C.—Étude sur la Vie de Jésus de E. Renan. Paris, 1863.

Pavy.—Observations sur le roman intitulé Vie de Jésus par E. Renan. Paris, 1863.

——— Conference contre le livre de M. Renan. Paris, 1863.

Pé De Arros, J.—Coup d'œil sur la Vie de Jesus de M. Renan. Paris, 1863.

Philips, J. P.—Dieu, les miracles, et la science. Paris, 1863.

Pinard, L'Abbé.—Notes à l'usage des lecteurs du Jésus de M. Renan. Paris, 1863.

Pioger, L. M.—Divinité de Jésus prouvée par les faits. Réponse à M. Renan. Paris, 1863.

Plantier.—Un panégyriste de M. Renan. Paris, 1863.

——— Instruction pastorale contre la Vie de Jésus par Renan. Paris, 1863.

Potrel, E.—Vie de N. S. Jésus Christ, réponse au livre de M. Renan. Paris, 1863.

Poujoulat.—Examen de la Vie de Jésus de M. Renan. Paris, 1863.

Pressensé, E. de.—L'École critique et Jésus Christ, à propos de la Vie de Jésus de M. Renan. Paris, 1863.

Réville, A.—La Vie de Jésus de M. Renan devant les orthodoxies et devant la critique. Paris, 1863.

Roussel, N.—Le Jésus de M. Renan. Paris, 1863. [1863.

Saas, A.—Épitre à M. E. Renan contre la "Vie de Jésus." Paris,

Saint-Semmera.—Ecce homo, critique impartiale de la Vie de Jésus de M. Renan. Paris, 1863.

Troghoff-Kerbiquet.—La Défense de l'Evangile. Épitre en vers à M. Renan. Paris, 1863.

Vie (la) et la Mort de Jésus, selon Renan. Havet, et Remusat. Paris, 1864.

Réville, A.—De la Redemption. Paris, 1859.

——— Essais de critique religieuse. Paris, 1860. [1841.

Saintes, Amand.—Histoire Critique du Rationalisme en Allemagne. Paris,

Scherer, E.—Mélanges des critiques religieuses. Paris, 1860.

Secrétan, C.—La Raison et le Bonheur. Paris, 1863.

RATIONALISTIC PERIODICALS.

Disciple (le) de Jésus Christ, (Monthly.) Redacteur: M. E. Haag. Paris, 1840-65.

Le Lien; Journal des Eglises réformées de France, (Weekly.) Redacteurs: A. Coquerel, fils; et Étienne Coquerel. Paris, 1862-65.

Nouvelle Révue de Théologie, (Quarterly.) Redacteur: T. Colani. Strasburg, 1858-65.

Revue Germanique, (Monthly.) Paris, 1858-65.

III.—GREAT BRITAIN—UNITED STATES.

BANNERMANN, J.—Inspiration, the Infallible Truth and Divine Authority of the Holy Scriptures. Edinburgh, 1865.

BARKER, T.—Strictures on Maurice's Doctrine of Sacrifice. London, 1858.

BAYNE, P.—Testimony of Christ to Christianity. London, 1862.

BEARD, T. R.—Voices of the Church in reply to Dr. Strauss. London, 1845.

——— Christ the Interpreter of Scripture. London, 1865.

BELLOWS, H. W.—Re-statements of Christian Doctrine. New York, 1860.

BIRKS, T. R.—Lectures on Modern Rationalism and Inspiration. London, 1853.

——— The Bible and Modern Thought. With Appendix. London, 1863.

BLAKE, B.—Infidelity Inexcusable. London, 1855.

BÖHM, C. J. T.—Lights and Shadows in the Present Condition of the Church. London, 1860.

BRODERICK AND FREEMANTLE.—Judgments of the Judicial Committee of the Privy Council. London, 1865.

CANDLISH, R. S.—Examination of Maurice's "Theological Essays." London, 1854.

——— Reason and Revelation. London, 1859.

CHRISTIAN SECTS in the Nineteenth Century. London, 1850.

CHRISTIE, T. W.—Rationalism the Last Scourge to the Church. London, 1861.

CLOSE, F.—The Footsteps of Error traced through a Period of Twenty-Five Years. London, 1863.

COBBE, FRANCES POWER.—Religious Demands of the Age. Boston, 1863.

Reprint of the Preface to London Ed. of Theo. Parker's Works, which are edited by this Authoress.

——— An Essay on Intuitive Morals. London, 1864.

——— Broken Lights. London, 1864.

A survey of the present condition of Church Parties in England.

——— Religious Duty. London, 1864.

COLENSO, BP.—Village Sermons. London, 1853.

——— St. Paul's Epistle to Romans. Newly Translated. London, 1861.

——— Pentateuch and Book of Joshua critically examined. London, 1862-64.

WORKS CALLED FORTH BY THE ABOVE COMMENTARY.

ALPHA.—Bishop Colenso and the Pentateuch. Vindication of the Historical Character of the Old Testament. London, 1863.

ANTI-COLENSO.—By Johannes Laicus. London, 1863.

ASHPITEL, F.—Increase of the Israelites in Egypt shown to be probable from the Statistics of Modern Population; with an Examination of Bishop Colenso's Calculations on the Subject. London, 1863.

BARRISTER (A).—History against Colenso. Dublin, 1863.

BARTHOLOMEW, J.—All Scripture given by Inspiration of God. London, 1863.

Beke, C. T.—A Few Words with Bishop Colenso. London, 1862.

Benisch, A.—Bishop Colenso's Objections to the Pentateuch and Book of Joshua critically examined. London, 1863.

Biber, G. E.—The Integrity of the Holy Scriptures and their Divine Inspiration and Authority vindicated. London, 1863.

Bible in the Workshop.—By two Working Men. London, 1863.

Bible (the) in the Gospels.—By Alpha. London, 1863.

Biden, J.—Religious Reformation imperatively demanded. Bishop Colenso's Enquiries answered. London, 1864.

Birks, T. R.—The Exodus of Israel; a Reply to Recent Objections. London, 1863.

Briggs, F. W.—The Two Testimonies. Last objections to Rationalism. Being a Reply to Bishop Colenso's Pentateuch and Book of Joshua. London, 1863.

Browne, G. H.—The Pentateuch and the Elohistic Psalms, in reply to Bishop Colenso. London, 1863.

Bullock, C.—Bible Inspiration. London, 1863.

Candlish, R. S.—Lectures on the Book of Genesis. 3 vols. London, 1862.

Carey, C. S.—The Bible or the Bishop? London, 1863.

Carylon, C.—A few more words addressed to the Bishops, &c. London, 1863.

Chamberlin, W.—A Plain Reply to Bishop Colenso. London, 1863.

Colenso, Bishop.—Letter to the Laity of the Diocese of Natal. London, 1864.

Written on the subject of the Bishop's prosecution.

——— Trial of the Bishop of Natal for erroneous Teaching. Cape Town, 1864.

——— Foreign Missions and Mosaic Traditions. A Lecture. London, 1865.

Cumming, J.—Moses Right and Bishop Colenso Wrong. Popular Lectures in Weekly Numbers. London, 1863.

Davidson, P.—The Pentateuch vindicated from the Objections and Misrepresentations of Bishop Colenso. London, 1863.

Drew, G. S.—Bishop Colenso's Examination of the Pentateuch Examined. London, 1863.

Family of Judah: a Refutation of Colenso's First Objection to the Pentateuch. By a Layman. London, 1863.

Fowle, W. H.—A Few Remarks on Bishop Colenso on the Pentateuch. London, 1863.

Fowler, F. W.—Vindex Pentateuchi. An Answer to Bishop Colenso on the Pentateuch. London, 1863.

Garland, G. V.—Plain possible Solutions of the Objections to Bishop Colenso on the Pentateuch. London, 1863.

Gaussen, L.—The Canon of Holy Scripture. London, 1863.

Gibson, J.—Present Truths in Theology. 2 vols. Glasgow, 1863.

Green, W. H.—The Pentateuch vindicated from the Aspersions of Bishop Colenso. New York, 1863.

Gresswell, E.—Objections of Bishop Colenso. Part I. considered. London, 1863.

GRIFFIN, J. N.—Dr. Colenso and the Pentateuch. Dublin, 1863.

HARE, W. H.—Letter to Bishop Colenso. London, 1863.

HAYCROFT, N.—Moses and Colenso; or, the Divine Authority of the Books of Moses and the Objections of Dr. Colenso. London, 1863.

HIGGINSON, E.—The Spirit of the Bible. 2 vols. London, 1863.

HILL, M.—Christ, or Colenso: a full Reply to Bishop Colenso's Objections. London, 1863.

HIRSCHFELDER, J. M.—The Scriptures Defended. Reply to Colenso. Toronto, 1864.

HISTORIC (The) Character of the Pentateuch Vindicated; Reply to Part I. of Bishop Colenso's "Critical Examination." Lond., 1863.

HOARE, W. H.—Letter to Bishop Colenso. London, 1863.

HOUGHTON, W.—Some of Bp. Colenso's objections examined. London, 1863.

INGRAM, G. S.—Bishop Colenso answered. London, 1863.

JEWISH (A) Reply to Dr. Colenso's Criticism on the Pentateuch. London, 1865.

JONES, E. R.—Christ's Testimony to Moses. London, 1863.

JONES, Sir W.—Christianity and Common Sense. London, 1863.

JUKES, A.—The Types of Genesis considered. London, 1863.

KIRKUS, W.—Orthodoxy, Scripture, and Reason. London, 1864.

LAYMAN (A) of the Ch. of England. Historical Character of the Pentateuch. Reply to Colenso's "Critical Examination." London, 1863.

LAYMAN (A).—New Testament and the Pentateuch. London, 1863.

McCAUL, A.—An Examination of Bishop Colenso's Difficulties with regard to the Pentateuch. London, 1864.

McCAUL, J. B.—Bishop Colenso's Criticism criticised. London, 1863.

McNEILE, H.—Historical Veracity of the Pentateuch. London, 1863.

MAHAN, M.—Spiritual Point of View; an Answer to Bishop Colenso. New York, 1863.

MANN, J. H.—Moses defended against the Attacks of Dr. Colenso. London, 1863.

MARSH, J. B.—Is the Pentateuch Historically True? Lond., 1863.

MARSHALL, JUDGE.—Full Review and Exposure of Bishop Colenso's Errors and Miscalculations in his work. London, 1864.

MAURICE, F. D.—Claims of the Bible and of Science. Lond., 1864.

MOON, R.—The Pentateuch and Book of Joshua considered with Reference to the Objections of the Bishop of Natal. Lond., 1863.

MOORE, D.—Divine Authority of the Pentateuch Vindicated. London, 1864.

MOREAU, E. B.—Examination of some of Bishop Colenso's Objections. London, 1863.

MOSAIC ORIGIN OF THE PENTATEUCH, in connection with Parts 2 and 3 of Bishop Colenso's Critical Examination. London, 1864.

MOZLEY, J. B.—Subscription to the Articles. London, 1863.

OLLIVANT, A.—A Second Letter to the Clergy of Llandaff. London, 1863.

PAGE, J. R.—The Pretensions of Bishop Colenso considered. London, 1863.

PALMER, G.—Scripture Facts and Scientific Doubts. London, 1863.

PENTATEUCH (THE) AND ITS OPPONENTS. London, 1863.

PHILLPOT, H.—The Textual Witness to the Truth and Divine Authority of the Pentateuch. London, 1863.

POSSIBILITIES OF CREATION. London, 1862.

POST, J.—The Bible for All. London, 1862.

PRESBYTER ANGLICANUS.—Critical Analysis of the Pentateuch. London, 1863.

PRITCHARD, C.—Vindiciæ Mosaicæ. London, 1863.

RASK, R.—A Short Tractate on the Longevity ascribed to the Patriarchs. London, 1863.

RATIONALISM UNPHILOSOPHICAL, AND FAITH THE GIFT OF GOD. London, 1863.

REMARKS ON BISHOP COLENSO'S WORK; OR, RATIONALISM SHOWN TO BE IRRATIONAL. London, 1863.

ROGERS, B. B.—Free Inquiry into Colenso's Difficulties. Lond., 1863.

ROGERS, H.—A Vindication of Bishop Colenso. Edinburgh, 1863.

SAVILE, B. W.—Man; or, the Old and New Philosophy. Lond., 1863.

The author controverts the views of Darwin, Owen, Huxley, Bunsen, Colenso, and others.

SCOTT, W. A.—Moses and the Pentateuch: a Reply to Bishop Colenso. London, 1863.

SILVER, A.—The Holy Word in its own Defense: addressed to Bishop Colenso. New York, 1863.

SINCLAIR, J.—On Free Thought. London, 1865.

SPRY, W. J.—Bishop Colenso and the Descent of Jacob into Egypt. Pt. I. London, 1863.

STANLEY, A. P.—A letter to the Lord Bishop of London on the State of Subscription in the Church of England and in the University of Oxford. London, 1863.

SWETE, H. B.—What is the Right Method of conducting the Defense of the Old Testament in the Rationalistic Controversy which has come upon the Church? London, 1863.

TAYLOR, I.—Considerations on the Pentateuch. London, 1863.

THORNTON, T.—Life of Moses. London, 1863.

TURNER, J. B.—An Answer to the Difficulties in Bishop Colenso's Book on the Pentateuch. London, 1863.

TYLER, T.—Christ the Lord; with a Reply to Bishop Colenso. London, 1863.

WHAT IS TRUTH? A Letter to Bishop Colenso. London, 1864.

WICKES, W.—Moses or the Zulu? London, 1863.

WORDSWORTH, C.—Inspiration of the Bible. London, 1863.

DAVIDSON, Dr. S—Treatise on Biblical Criticism. London, 1855.

DEWAR, E. H.—Brief History of German Theology. London, 1844.

DONALDSON, T. W.—Essay on Christian Orthodoxy. London, 1857.

DRAPER, J. W.—Intellectual Development of Europe. New York, 1863.

ELLIOTT, W.—Old Theology the True Theology. London, 1861.

ESSAYS AND REVIEWS. London, 1861.

WORKS ARISING FROM THE ABOVE OXFORD ESSAYS.

AIDS TO FAITH, Replies to Essays and Reviews. London, 1863.

BAYLAY, C. F. R.—"Essays and Reviews" compared with Reason. London, 1861.

BUCHANAN, J.—"Essays and Reviews" Examined. London, 1861.

CLOSE, F.—Critical Examination of "Essays and Reviews." London, 1861.

DENISON, G. A.—Analysis of "Essays and Reviews." London, 1861.

DIALOGUES ON ESSAYS AND REVIEWS. London, 1862.

GIRDLESTONE, E.—Remarks on Essays and Reviews. Lond., 1861.

JELF, R. W.—Evidence of Unsoundness in Essays and Reviews. London, 1861.

KENNARD, R. B.—Essays and Reviews. Protest addressed to the Bishop of Salisbury. London, 1861.

—— The Essays and Reviews: their Origin, History, General Character and Significance, Persecution, Prosecution, the Judgment of the Arches Court, Review of Judgment. London, 1863.

LUSHINGTON, S.—Judgment delivered on Essays and Reviews. London, 1862.

MILTON, J.—Prophecy of Essays and Reviews and his Judgment. London, 1861.

MOBERLY, G.—Remarks on Essays and Reviews. London, 1861.

REPLIES TO ESSAYS AND REVIEWS, by Goulburn, Rose, and others. London, 1862.

WORN-OUT NEOLOGY.—Strictures upon Essays and Reviews. London, 1861.

FARRAR, A. S.—A Critical History of Free Thought in Reference to the Christian Religion. London, 1863.

FISHER, G. P.—Essays on the supernatural Origin of Christianity. With special reference to the Works of Renan, Strauss, and the Tübingen School. New York, 1865.

FRANKLAND, B.—Intuitionalism; or, Insufficiency of Pure Reason. London, 1861.

FROTHINGHAM, O. B.—Tales from the Patriarchs. Boston, 1864.

FURNESS, W. H.—Jesus and his Biographers. Boston, 1838.

GAGE, J. A.—The Life of Jesus a Fact, not a Fiction. A Response to M. Renan's Vie de Jésus. London, 1863.

GARBETT, E.—Bible and its Critics. Boyle Lectures for 1861. Lond. 1861.

GOULBURN, E. M.—Inspiration of the Holy Scriptures. London, 1857.

GREG, W. R.—The Creed of Christendom. London, 1863.

HAMILTON, W. T.—Defense of the Pentateuch against Scepticism. London, 1852.

HEBERT, C.—Neology not True and Truth not New. 2d Ed. London, 1861.

HEDGE, F. H.—Reason in Religion. Boston, 1865.

HEURTLY, C. A.—Inspiration of Holy Scriptures. London, 1861.

HOOKER, W.—Philosophy of Unbelief. New York.

HUGHES, T.—Religio Laici. London, 1861.

IRRATIONALISM OF INFIDELITY, a Reply to Newman's "Phases." London, 1853.

JAMES, H.—The Old and New Theology. London, 1861.

JELF, W. E.—Supremacy of Scripture, a Letter to Dr. Temple. London, 1861.

KINGSLEY, C.—Sermons for the Times. London, 1858.

——— Sermons; Good News of God. London, 1859.

LANGFORD, J. A.—Religious Skepticism and Infidelity. London, 1850.

LECKY, W. E. H.—History of the Rise and Influence of the Spirit of Rationalism in Europe. 2 vols. London, 1865.

LEE, W.—Recent Forms of Unbelief; Some Account of Renan's Vie de Jésus. London, 1864.

MCCAUL, A.—Rationalism and Deistic Infidelity. Three Letters. London, 1861.

MCCOMBIE, W.—Modern Civilization in Relation to Christianity. London, 1863.

MACKAY, R. W.—The Tübingen School and its Antecedents: a Review of the History and Present Condition of Modern Theology London.

——— Rise and Progress of Christianity. London, 1854.

MALAN, S. C.—Philosophy or Truth? London, 1865.

MANSEL, H. L.—Limits of Religious Thought; Bampton Lectures. London, 1859.

——— Examination of Maurice's Stricture on Bampton Lecture. London, 1859.

MAURICE, F. D.—Claims of the Bible and of Science. London, 1862.

——— Theological Essays. 2d Ed. London, 1853.

——— What is Revelation? London, 1859.

MIALL, E.—Basis of Belief: Examination of Christianity. London 1861.

NELSON, D.—Infidelity; its Cause and Cure. London, 1853.

NEWMAN, F. W.—Phases of Faith. London, 1860.

——— Essays towards a Church of the Future. London, 1854.

——— Theism, Doctrinal and Practical. London, 1858.

——— The Soul: its Sorrows and Aspirations. London, 1861.

——— Sermons on Theory of Religious Belief. London, 1844.

——— Development of Christian Doctrine. London, 1846.

NOYES, G. N.—Theological Essays. 3d Ed. Boston, 1860.

This work contains essays by Rowland Williams, Jowett, Powell, Stanley, and others. It advocates the Broad Church theories.

O'CONNOR, W. A.—Miracles not Antecedently Incredible. London, 1861.

PALMER, G.—Scripture Facts and Scientific Doubts. Edinburgh, 1863.

A Defense of Scripture from the objections of Geologists, Statisticians, and others.

PARKER, THEO.—Discourses on Religion. Boston, 1842.

——— Sermons on Theism, Atheism, and Popular Theology. Boston, 1853.

——— Ten Sermons on Religion. Boston, 1853.

——— World of Matter and Mind. Boston, 1865.

Extracts from unpublished sermons.

PARKINSON, R.—Rationalism and Revelation. London, 1838.

PATON, J. B.—A Review of the "Vie de Jésus" of M. Renan. London, 1864.

PEABODY, A. P.—Christianity the Religion of Nature. Boston, 1863

PEARSON, T.—Infidelity. Republished from London Ed. in N. Y., 1853.

PORTER, J. L.—The Pentateuch and the Gospel. London, 1864.

PROGRESS OF RELIGIOUS THOUGHT, as illustrated in the Protestant Church of France. Ed. by J. R. Beard. London, 1861.

This work contains essays by Messrs. Colani, Scholten, Reville, Scherer, and Renan.

PUSEY, E. B.—Historical Inquiry into German Rationalism. London, 1828.

——— Daniel the Prophet. London, 1865.

RATIONALISM AND REVELATION.—(Anon.) London, 1865.

RELIGIOUS ASPECTS OF THE AGE. New York. 1858.

RIGG, J. H.—Modern Anglican Theology. London, 1859.

RIPLEY.—Latest Forms of Infidelity. Boston, 1840.

ROBINS, S.—Defense of the Faith: Forms of Unbelief. London, 1861.

ROSE, H. J.—State of Protestantism in Germany. 2d Ed. London, 1829.

RYDER, A. G.—Scriptural Doctrine of Acceptance with God, considered in reference to Neologian Hermeneutics. London, 1865.

SAWYER, L. A.—Daniel with its Apocryphal Additions. Boston, 1863.

SCHAFF, P.—Germany; its Theology, &c. Philada., 1857.

——— The Person of Christ; The Miracle of History, with a Reply to Strauss and Renan. Boston, 1865.

One of the best of the recent replies to the Rationalists.

SCHAFF AND ROUSSELL.—The Christ of the Gospels, and the Romance of M. Renan. London, 1864.

SCHMUCKER, S. M.—Errors of Modern Infidelity Refuted. Phila., 1848.

SEAMAN, M.—Christian Armed against Infidelity. London, 1837.

SEWELL, W.—On the Inspiration of the Holy Scripture. London, 1861.

SMITH, C.—Prize Essays on Infidelity. London, 1861.

SMITH, G.—Rational Religion and Objections of Bampton Lectures for '58. London, 1861.

SQUIER, M. P.—Reason and the Bible. New York, 1860.

STANLEY, A. P.—The Bible: Its Form and Substance. London, 1865.

TAYLOR, J. J.—Retrospect of Religious Life in England. 1845.

TESTIMONY of Skeptics to the Truth of Christianity. London, 1861.

THOMPSON, R. A.—Christian Theism. London, 1863.

TRACTS FOR PRIESTS AND PEOPLE, by various writers, 1st and 2d series. London, 1862.

TUCKER, L.—Lectures on Infidelity. New York, 1837.

TULLIDGE, H.—Triumphs of the Bible. New York, 1863.

A defense of Scripture against the objections of the Skeptical Scientific School.

WALKER, J. B.—Philosophy of Skepticism and Ultraism. New York, 1857.

WALTHER, D.—Reply to Newman's Phases of Faith. London, 1851.

WHATELY, ABP.—Essays on Dangers to Christian Faith. London, 1857.

WESTFIELD, T. C.—Seven Essays on Universal Science, embracing Investigations of the Mosaic Cosmogony, and the Interpretation of the Scriptures. London, 1863.

A Defense of the Harmony of Science and Revelation.

WILLIAMS, R.—Rational Godliness after the Mind of Christ. Lond., 1855.

WOODMAN, W.—Is the Bible a Divine Revelation? London, 1862.

WOODSWORTH, C.—Inspiration of the Bible. Five Lectures. London, 1862.

YOUNG, J.—Christ of History: an Argument. 3d Ed. London, 1861.

——— Province of Reason; a Criticism on Mansel. London, 1860.

YOUNG, J. R.—Modern Skepticism, viewed in Relation to Modern Science. London, 1865.

This work is an excellent answer to the doctrines of Colenso, Huxley, Lyell, and Darwin, respecting the Noachian Deluge, the Antiquity of Man, and the Origin of Species.

LITERATURE OF UNITARIANISM AND UNIVERSALISM.

For the bibliography of the Trinitarian Controversy in England, extending through the former half of the eighteenth century, consult Watts' Bibliotheca Britannica, 4 vols. Edinburgh, 1824; and Biographia Britannica, 7 vols. folio, 1747. Concerning the discussion on 1 John, v. 7, consult Darling, Cyclopædia Bibliographia; London, 1854. For other Unitarian publications, in addition to those mentioned below, see Beard, *Unitarianism in its Actual Condition*, pp. 327-29.

The following table of Unitarian and Universalist Literature has reference to only two doctrines: the Trinity and Future Punishment.

BAKER, A.—Our God a Consuming Fire. London, 1864.

BARCLAY, J.—Socinianism and Irvingism Refuted. London, 1845.

BARLING, J.—Review of Trinitarianism. London, 1847.

BARLOW, J. W.—Eternal Punishment and Eternal Death. London, 1864.

BARRET, B. F.—Letters on the Divine Trinity. New York, 1860.

——— Christ the Interpreter of Scripture. London, 1865.

BEARD, J. R.—Historic and Artistic Illustrations of the Trinity. London, 1864.

——— Unitarianism in its Actual Condition. London, 1849.

——— Reasons why I am a Unitarian. London, 1860.

BELLOWS, H. W.—Phi Beta Kappa Oration. 1853.

Until the middle of the year 1850, this author was the principal writer for the *Christian Inquirer*, New York.

BELSHAM, T.—Calm Inquiry into Script. Doctrine concerning the Person of Christ.

BROOKS, E. G.—Universalism a Practical Power. New York, 1863..

BROTHERS' CONTROVERSY ON UNITARIAN OPINIONS. London, 1835.

BURNAP, G. W.—Unitarianism. Boston, 1855.

——— Trinity. Boston, 1845.

——— Evidences. Boston, 1855.

CARPENTER, L.—Examination of the Charges against Unitarians. Bristol, 1820.

Channing, W. E.—Complete Works. 6 vols. Boston, 1841-46.

Channing, W. H.—Memoir of W. E. Channing. 3 vols, 1843.

Clark, D. W.—Man all Immortal. Cincinnati, 1864.

Coute, J.—Essays on Socinianism. London, 1850.

Denison, H. M.—Review of Unitarian Views. Louisville, Ky., 1855.

Dewey, O.—Discourses; Controv. Theol., etc. 6 vols. 1846–47–63.

Dexter, H. M.—Verdict of Reason on the question of the Impenitent Dead. Boston, 1865.

Disney, J.—Remarks on Tomline's Charge. London, 1812.

——— Sermons. 4 vols. London, 1793-1818.

Ellis, G. E.—Half Century of the Unitarian Controversy. Boston, 1857.

Farley, F. A.—Unitarianism Defined. Boston, 1860.

Furness, W. H.—Jesus and his Biographers. Boston, 1838.

——— History of Jesus. Boston, 1850.

———Veil Partly Lifted. 1864.

The author repudiates the atonement. "The doctrine of the Atonement," says he, "which is especially cherished as the distinguishing idea of Christianity, is only a form of the radical error from which false religion has sprung ever since the world began; the error, namely, of supposing that human guilt is to be expiated, not by change of character, but by offerings and sacrifices." The sacrifice of Christ "is the world-old error, thinly disguised, culminating in its most monstrous form. Even if it were new, it has no place among the teachings of Jesus. He never taught this nor any of its associated dogmas. Not a word of his gives them the slightest color of authority." Pp. 4, 5. Such language comes with an ill grace from one who attacks M. Renan. See Chapter on Christ's "childlikeness." Wherein, we ask, is the Frenchman worse than the Philadelphian?

Gage, W. L.—Trinitarian Sermons to a Unitarian Congregation. Boston, 1860.

Hare, E.—Principal Doctrines of Christianity Defended against the Errors of Socinianism. New York.

Hovey, A.—State of Impenitent Dead. Boston, 1859.

Hudson, C. F.—Debt and Grace. Boston, 1857.

——— Human Destiny; a Critique of Universalism. Boston, 1861.

Job the Abbot.—Reasons for Abandoning Trinitarian Doctrines. London, 1841.

Jones, T.—Immanuel; or, Scriptural views of Jesus Christ. Lond., 1856.

Kenrick, T.—Unitarian Exposition of the New Testament. New York.

Ker, W.—The Popular Views of Immortality, Everlasting Punishment, and the State of Separate Souls, brought to the Test of Scripture. London, 1865.

Kidd, W. J.—Reflections on Unitarianism. London, 1835.

Kohlman, A.—Complete Refutation of Unitarianism. Washington, 1821.

Lake, C. W.—The Inspiration of Scripture and Eternal Punishment. London, 1864.

Landis, R. W.—Immortality of the Soul, and Final Condition of the Wicked. New York, 1859.

One of the best arguments in favor of Eternal Punishment.

Lardner, N.—Complete Works. 17 vols. London, 1727–57.

Letters on Nature and Duration of Future Punishment. London, 1835.

Lindsey, T.—Apology. London, 1774.

——— Sequel. London, 1776.

LINDSEY, T.—Historical View of Unitarian Doctrine from Reformation. London, 1783.

——— Vindiciæ Priestlianæ. London, 1788.

MARTINEAU, J.—Rationale of Religious Inquiry. London, 1839.

——— Endeavors after the Christian Life, 2 vols. London, 1843.

——— Studies of Christianity. London, 1858.

MATTISON, H.—Immortality of the Soul. Philadelphia, 1865.

MELLIS, J.—Lectures on Points of the Unitarian Controversy. London, 1846.

MINTON, S.—Lectures on Unitarianism. London, 1847.

MITCHELL, E.—The Christian Universalist. New Haven, 1833.

MONSELL, C. A.—Sermons: Temporal Punishment of Sin. London, 1845.

MOORE, D.—The Age and the Gospel: to which is added a Discourse on Final Retribution. London, 1865.

MORSE, J.—True Reasons. Boston, 1805.

——— Appeal to the Public. Boston, 1814.

MORTLOCK, E.—Sermons on Doctrine of the Trinity. London, 1844.

NEMESIS SACRA.—Inquiries into Scriptural Doctrine of Retribution. London, 1856.

NEWTON, SIR I.—Views on Points of Unitarian Doctrine. Republished. London, 1856.

NOEL, B. W.—Christianity compared with Unitarianism. London, 1851.

NORTON, A.—True and False Religion; in *Christian Disciple.* 1820–'22.

——— Genuineness of the Gospels, 3 vols. Boston, 1851–'44.

——— Tracts concerning Christianity. Cambridge, 1852.

——— Internal Evidences. Boston, 1855.

——— Statement of Reasons. Boston, 1856.

ORR.—Unitarianism in the Present Time. Boston, 1863.

OSGOOD, S.—Christian Biography. New York, 1851.

——— The Coming Church and its Clergy. 1858.

PALFREY, J. G.—Evidences of Christianity. Boston, 1843.

PEABODY, A. P.—Christian Doctrine. Boston, 1844.

——— Christianity the Religion of Nature. Boston, 1863.

POWER, J. H.—Exposition of Universalism. New York.

PRICE, R.—Dissertations on Provid. Christianity. London, 1772.

——— Sermons on Christian Doctrine. London, 1787.

PRIESTLEY, J.—Defenses of Unitarianism, 2 vols. London, 1787–89.

For full account of this writer's many works, consult Darling, Cyclopædia Bibliographica, pp. 2454–58.

SALMON, G.—The Eternity of Future Punishment. London, 1865.

SHERLOCK, W.—An Essay on Future Punishment. London, 1865.

SHORT REASONS FOR BELIEF IN THE DIVINITY OF CHRIST. London, 1843.

SOPER, E.—Doctrine of the Trinity proved from Scripture. London, 1853.

SPRAGUE, W. B.—Annals of the American Unit. Pulpit. New York, 1865.

STUART, M.—Exegetical Essays on Future Punishment. London, 1848.

THAYER.—Theology of Universalism. Boston, 1862.

THOMPSON, J. P.—Love and Penalty. New York, 1865.

THOMPSON, S.—Scripture Refutation of Unitarianism. London, 1838.

TURNER, W.—Lives of eminent Unitarians. London, 1840-3.

UNITARIAN, How I BECAME A.—By a Clergyman of the Protestant E. Church. Boston, 1852.

UNIVERSALISM AGAINST ITSELF.—Cincinnati, O.

UNIVERSALISMUS, DER.—Gott alles in Allen. Stuttgart, 1862.

WARE, H.—Complete Works. Boston, 1847.

WARE, W.—Lettters to Trinitarians and Calvinists. Boston, 1820.

——— American Unitarian Biography. Boston, 1850.

WHATELY, A.—Scriptural Revelation respecting Future State. Lond., 1858.

WHITMAN, B.—Friendly Letters to a Universalist. Boston, 1850.

WHITTEMORE, T.—History of Universalism. New Ed. Vol. I. Boston, 1860.

WILLIAMSON, H.—Exposition and Defense of Universalism. New York, 1840.

WILSON, J.—Scripture Proofs of Unitarianism. Boston.

WOODS, L.—Letters to Unitarians, and Reply to Dr. Ware. New York.

WORCESTER, N.—Review of Testimonies, etc., in *Bible News*. Boston, 1810.

——— Address to Trinitarian Clergy. Boston, 1814.

YATES.—Vindication of Unitarianism, 4th Ed. London, 1850.

UNITARIAN PERIODICALS.

CHRISTIAN EXAMINER, Boston.

CHRISTIAN INQUIRER, New York.

CHRISTIAN REGISTER, Boston.

JOURNAL OF AMERICAN UNIT. ASSOC. Boston.

MONTHLY CHRISTIAN REGISTER, Boston.

MONTHLY RELIGIOUS MAGAZINE, Boston.

RELIGIOUS EDUCATOR, Boston.

UNIVERSALIST PERIODICALS.

BROAD CHURCH PULPIT, New York.

CHRISTIAN AMBASSADOR, New York.

CHRISTIAN FREEMAN, Boston.

CHRISTIAN REPOSITORY, Montpelier, Vt.

GOSPEL BANNER, Augusta, Me.

HERALD AND ERA, Indianapolis, Ind.

MANFORD'S MAGAZINE, St. Louis, Mo.

MYRTLE, Boston.

LADIES' REPOSITORY, Boston.

STAR IN THE WEST, Cincinnati, O.

STAR OF THE PACIFIC, Petaluma, Cal.

TRUMPET, Boston.
UNIVERSALIST HERALD, Montgomery, Ala.
UNIVERSALIST QUARTERLY, Boston.
YOUNG CHRISTIAN, Cincinnati, O.
YOUTHS' FRIEND, Cincinnati, O.

For full bibliographical accounts of the controversy between the orthodox theologians of New England and the Unitarians, during the present century; and of the discussion on the Person of Christ provoked by the speculations of Horace Bushnell, consult Hagenbach, *History of Doctrines*, Smith's Ed. New York, 1862.

INDEX.

www.ingramcontent.com/pod-product-compliance
Lightning Source LLC
LaVergne TN
LVHW021057110826
845150LV00001B/93

* 9 7 8 1 4 2 5 5 6 6 7 5 3 *